CONGRESS VOLUME

EDINBURGH 1974

SUPPLEMENTS

TO

VETUS TESTAMENTUM

EDITED BY

THE BOARD OF THE QUARTERLY

G. W. ANDERSON - P. A. H. DE BOER - HENRY CAZELLES
J. A. EMERTON - W. L. HOLLADAY - R. E. MURPHY
E. NIELSEN - R. SMEND - J. A. SOGGIN

VOLUME XXVIII

LEIDEN
E. J. BRILL
1975

G. W. Anderson

CONGRESS VOLUME

EDINBURGH

1974

LEIDEN
E. J. BRILL
1975

ISBN   90 04 04321 7

CONTENTS

CONTENTS

PREFACE

The Eighth Congress of the International Organization for the Study of the Old Testament was held from 18 to 23 August 1974 under the Presidency of the Rev. G. W. ANDERSON, D.D., Theol. D., F.B.A., Professor of Hebrew and Old Testament Studies at the University of Edinburgh. The Secretary of the Congress was the Rev. Dr J. P. Ross, also of Edinburgh University, and the efficiency with which it was organized won the admiration of all who were present. The University made us welcome both by entertaining us at a reception in the Old College and by making available accommodation in the Pollock Halls of Residence near Holyrood Park. The fact that it was possible to eat and sleep in the Hostels close to the building where most of the meetings were held made much easier the informal contacts and discussions that are among the most valuable parts of any successful conference. The Pollock Halls were also able to serve an excellent banquet on the final evening, when the President added to the interest of the occasion by arranging for bagpipes to be played. No one at the Congress was left in any doubt that it was being held in Scotland, and not in England.

The present volume includes all the papers that were read by invitation except Professor E. G. CLARKE's on 'Jacob's dream at Bethel as interpreted in the Targums and the New Testament', which, it had already been arranged, was to appear in *Studies in Religion*, IV.4 (1974-5). The volume cannot give a complete account of all that happened at the Congress, but it is worthy of mention that several informal meetings were held to discuss particular subjects. Thus, scholars interested in the Targums met and agreed to hold similar meetings during future Congresses; and the hope was expressed that the I.O.S.O.T. would continue to include papers on Targumic studies in the programme.

It is usual at Old Testament Congresses for one afternoon to be devoted to an outing, and the place of interest that was visited in 1974 was St Andrews, where we were welcomed and given tea by its ancient University. Despite the changes that have taken place since Dr JOHNSON's visit in the eighteenth century, it was still possible for us to say that we had been 'entertained with all the elegance of lettered hospitality', and that we left St Andrews 'with good wishes, having reason to be highly pleased with the attention that was paid us'.[1] Those words could justly also be used of the University of Edinburgh and of everyone there who helped to make the Eighth Congress such a success.

J. A. EMERTON

---

[1] Samuel JOHNSON, *Journey to the Western Islands of Scotland,* cited from the edition by R. W. CHAPMAN published in Oxford, 1924, pp. 5, 8.

TWO SCOTTISH SEMITISTS

BY

GEORGE W. ANDERSON
Edinburgh

If in your tour of Edinburgh you look from Princes Street up the Mound, you will see a building the entrance of which is flanked by twin towers: New College, a theological college, originally of the Free Church of Scotland and now of the Church of Scotland, the seat of Edinburgh University's Faculty of Divinity. If you pass through the archway between the towers, cross the quadrangle, go up the imposing flight of steps and enter the building which now faces you, the Assembly Hall of the Church of Scotland, you may see the spot where WILLIAM ROBERTSON SMITH stood to defend himself against the charges of heresy brought against him in the protracted legal proceedings (1876-81) which ended with his deposition from his chair in the Free Church College in Aberdeen. Among all those who have learned or taught Hebrew in Edinburgh, ROBERTSON SMITH and his great teacher ANDREW BRUCE DAVIDSON stand supreme; and if, when our Congress meets in this place, it is fitting to say something about Hebrew and Old Testament Studies in Edinburgh, it is their work and influence above all that should be remembered. There is also a double chronological appropriateness in recalling them at this time. It is just a hundred years since ROBERT RAINY, who exercised a decisive influence in the ROBERTSON SMITH case, was appointed Principal of New College. In the same year the first edition of DAVIDSON's famous *Hebrew Grammar* was published here in Edinburgh. Moreover, in this international gathering it is worthy of note that both DAVIDSON and ROBERTSON SMITH were, in very different ways, mediators of the influence of German critical scholarship to this country.

An adequate appraisal of the achievement of either of these men would call for far more time than I have at my disposal; an adequate comparison of their respective contributions to Semitic and Old Testament studies is quite out of the question. I must content myself with a much more modest undertaking: to sketch briefly the salient biographical and bibliographical data, to indicate as best I

may what manner of man each of them was, and to offer some comments on the perplexing fact, that throughout the proceedings against
ROBERTSON SMITH, DAVIDSON his teacher remained silent.

The two men were strikingly different in personality, yet similar
in being outstanding examples of a type which was common in
Scotland, and particularly in the north-east of Scotland, at that time:
the gifted young man who came from a humble or even a poor home,
and who, by a combination of ability, love of learning, and hard work,
acquired a sound education and ultimately an honoured place in one
of the professions.

ROBERTSON SMITH was born in 1846 in the village of Keig in
Aberdeenshire, where his father was Free Church minister. Before
he was six he had learned the Hebrew alphabet, an item of knowledge which he lost and had to acquire again in later life. Before he
was twelve he had undergone what his father described as 'a work
of grace', something which he did not lose or unlearn for as long as
he lived. His education began in his home and was continued at the
University of Aberdeen, at New College, Edinburgh, and at the Universities of Bonn and Göttingen. While in Edinburgh he also served
for two years as assistant to the Professor of Physics. In 1870, on the
completion of his theological course, he was elected to the Chair of
Hebrew and Old Testament Exegesis in the Free Church College at
Aberdeen. It is not surprising that there were those who doubted
the wisdom of the appointment, for he was young and had had no
pastoral experience. It was neither his youthfulness nor his inexperience that stirred up the storm which broke out some five or six
years later, but rather a combination of learning, lucidity of thought
and expression, single-minded devotion to truth, and an unshakable
conviction of his own orthodoxy as a Reformed churchman.
ROBERTSON SMITH was no self-proclaimed rebel, challenging the
Church to discard its heritage or to modify its standards. To the end
of his life he maintained that his methods and views were fully compatible with the faith to which, as a minister of his Church, he was
expressly commited.

The immediate occasion of the charges brought against him was
the appearance, in December 1875, of the article "Bible" in volume
III of the *Encyclopaedia Britannica*. ROBERTSON SMITH's critical views,
and in particular his acceptance of the composite authorship and
centuries-long compilation of the Pentateuch, his contention that
Israelite prophecy was not primarily predictive, and his rejection of

the Davidic authorship of the great majority of the Psalms, led to a crescendo of protest and a long drawn out conflict in the courts of the Free Church. Into the intricacies of this case I cannot now enter. They are presented in detail and with ample documentation in *The Life of William Robertson Smith*, by J. S. BLACK and G. W. CHRYSTAL, London 1912.[1]

On 27th May 1880, it seemed that a victory had been won for critical liberty. By a small majority the General Assembly cleared ROBERTSON SMITH of the charge of heresy and reinstated him in his professorship, from which he had been temporarily suspended, but found him guilty of having made "unguarded and incomplete statements" and admonished him to exercise greater discretion in the future. The verdict was publicly accepted by ROBERTSON SMITH with a modesty which did not conceal his satisfaction that a moral victory had been won. His supporters in the General Assembly were jubilant. WELLHAUSEN, LAGARDE, NÖLDEKE, KUENEN, and other scholars sent their congratulations. But the triumph was short-lived. On 8th June volume XI of the *Encyclopaedia Britannica* appeared, containing SMITH's article, "Hebrew Language and Literature". Though the article had been completed months before, it seemed to many to be a challenge to SMITH's critics and out of keeping with his recent acceptance of the Assembly's admonition; to his most determined adversaries it gave an opportunity of returning to the attack. New proceedings were instituted; and as the tortuous and often embittered debate continued, it became increasingly clear that if the verdict went against SMITH it would not be because his views had been shown to be false but because, whether they were true or false, his presentation of them was disturbing the peace of the Church. The foremost advocate of this line was Dr. ROBERT RAINY, Principal of New College and Professor of Church History. In the early stages of the case he had appeared to adopt a mediating position between SMITH and his critics and even to defend critical liberty; but he had held from the beginning that a minister who could not be convicted of heresy might nevertheless, as a teacher, forfeit the Church's confidence. He became convinced that this was true of ROBERTSON SMITH. The verdict of the Assembly of 1880 appeared to have undermined RAINY's posi-

---

[1] The case, and the personalities involved in it, are described from another point of view by P. CARNEGIE SIMPSON in Chapter XII of his superb *Life of Principal Rainy*, 2 vols., London 1909. A briefer account is given in Chapter XII of *The Life of Alexander Whyte D. D.*, by G. F. BARBOUR, London 1923.

tion. In the final phase of the conflict his influence again became dominant, and it was in effect his arguments that carried the day. On 26th May 1881 the Assembly finally deposed SMITH from his Chair.

By a striking coincidence, the person appointed to undertake SMITH's work until a permanent appointment could be made was GEORGE ADAM SMITH, then only twenty-four years old, who was himself charged with heresy in 1902 but acquitted on the motion of Principal RAINY. It is related [2] that when the *locum tenens* called on the deposed professor seeking advice, ROBERTSON SMITH asked him fiercely, "What would you do, if I should refuse to obtemper the decision of the Assembly and insist on taking the class myself?" Then, was the reply, "I would be proud to go and sit among your students."

From Aberdeen ROBERTSON SMITH moved to Edinburgh, where he could more effectively carry out his work as joint-editor of the *Encyclopaedia Britannica*, to which he had been appointed within days of the Assembly's final decision. Two years later the opportunity of returning to academic life came when he was offered and accepted the post of Lord Almoner's Professor of Arabic at Cambridge. For the remainder of his life Cambridge was his home. In 1885 he was elected a Fellow of Christ's College; the following year he became University Librarian; and in 1889 he succeeded his friend WILLIAM WRIGHT as Sir Thomas Adams Professor of Arabic. In 1894, while still at the height of his intellectual powers, he died.

Short and stormy as his career had been, his literary output was impressive in quality, quantity and range. His *Encyclopaedia Britannica* articles alone are a substantial and distinguished literary production. But on the present occasion I must restrict myself to brief references to four books which represent two periods in his career and two aspects of his intellectual development.

In the opening months of 1881, when the final phase of the long conflict had not yet reached its climax, SMITH responded to the invitation of some six hundred leading members of the Free Church and delivered in Edinburgh and Glasgow a course of public lectures, explaining his views and the evidence and arguments on which they were based. That a sustained exposition of Old Testament criticism could attract and hold large audiences is eloquent testimony to the level of intelligent interest which the ROBERTSON SMITH case had aroused in Scotland and also to the skill of the lecturer. It is even

---

[2] LILIAN ADAM SMITH, *George Adam Smith: A Personal Memoir and Family Chronicle*, London 1943, p. 19.

more remarkable that, during a particularly bitter phase of a controversy which had dragged on for five years, SMITH could expound his subject with exemplary objectivity and lucidity and with an uncanny absence of polemic. The lectures were published as *The Old Testament in the Jewish Church*, London 1881, [2]1892, a volume which, nearly a century later, retains its place as one of the classic introductions to the Old Testament and still brings vividly before us the energy and penetration of that marvellously clear mind.

During the winter following the Assembly's decision SMITH delivered a second course of lectures in Edinburgh and Glasgow under similar auspices. These were subsequently published as *The Prophets of Israel and Their Place in History to the Eighth Century B. C.*, London 1882.[3] Like its predecessor, this volume is as free from petulant self-defence as it is from unseemly abuse of SMITH's critics. Written to meet a contemporary need, it is still a work of fundamental importance for the study of the earlier prophets. It brought out, even more clearly than its predecessor, the implications of a critical study of the Old Testament for the understanding of the history of Israel's religion. As SMITH himself was to point out in a later work, a sound critical foundation was also indispensable for "an effective comparison of Hebrew religion as a whole, with the religion of the other Semites".[4] It was to the wider study of Semitic religion and society that he devoted particular attention in the latter part of his career.

On the final day of the General Assembly of 1880, which had acquitted but admonished SMITH, there appeared in the *Journal of Philology*, No. 17, an article from his pen entitled "Animal Worship and Animal Tribes among the Arabs and in the Old Testament".[5] The stimulus for this new stage in SMITH's researches came from the totemistic hypothesis of the Scottish anthropologist J. F. McLENNAN; its further development is seen in SMITH's later work, *Kinship and Marriage in Early Arabia*, Cambridge 1885, [2]London 1903, which, together with his article "Sacrifice" in the *Encyclopaedia Britannica*, vol. XXI, prepared the way for his greatest work, *Lectures on the Religion of the Semites: The Fundamental Institutions*, London 1889, [2]1894, [3]1927. This is not the place to comment on the criticisms which have

---

[3] The second edition, London 1907, contains an introduction and additional notes by T. K. CHEYNE.

[4] *The Religion of the Semites*[3], London 1927, p. xv.

[5] Reprinted in J. S. BLACK and G. CHRYSTAL (eds.) *Lectures and Essays of W. Robertson Smith*, London 1912, pp. 455-483.

been made of the totemistic hypothesis, of SMITH's undue concentration on the evidence from Arabia, and of his excessive emphasis on communion as the fundamental concept in sacrifice. The relation of his theories to subsequent research was indicated by STANLEY ARTHUR COOK[6] in the introduction (pp. xxvii-lxiv) and notes (pp. 495-692) which he contributed to the third edition of *The Religion of the Semites* and by JAMES MUILENBURG in the prolegomenon (pp. 1-27) to the 1969 reprint. Whatever in these works may have been superseded or corrected by more recent study, the greatness of SMITH's achievement is incontestable. In his earlier writings he had been a mediator of new methods; in these he was a pioneer.

I have already noted that SMITH did not see in his critical views any contradiction of the Reformed orthodoxy which he professed. Indeed, he stoutly maintained that they were the logical outcome of the theological heritage of the Reformation. It has sometimes been questioned whether, had he lived longer and had opportunity to carry further his researches in anthropology and comparative religion, he might not have modified his theological position. What is clear is that to the end of his life he remained convinced of the supernatural character of the religion of Israel. He ended the last of his third series of Burnett Lectures with this comment on the contrast which he had drawn between Israelite religion and other Semitic religions: "The burden of explaining this contrast does not lie with me. It falls on those who are compelled by a false Philosophy of Revelation to see in the Old Testament nothing more than the highest point of the general tendencies of Semitic religion. This is not the view which that study commends to me. It is a view which is not commended, but condemned by the many parallelisms in detail between Hebrew and heathen story and ritual; for all these material points of resemblance only make the contrast in spirit the more remarkable."[7]

---

[6] COOK was among the last of those who studied under SMITH at Cambridge. As one who belonged to the last generation of COOK's own students at Cambridge, I recall vividly the enthusiastic veneration with which he often spoke of his great master.

[7] J. S. BLACK and G. W. CHRYSTAL, *The Life of William Robertson Smith*, pp. 536f. (The third series of Burnett lectures was never published.) It is interesting to compare the words of Nathan Söderblom when, on the last day of his life, he decided that the title of the published form of the Gifford Lectures which he had delivered in Edinburgh should be *The Living God*: "Det finns en levande Gud, jag kan bevisa det genom religionshistorien" ("There is a living God. I can prove it by the History of Religions"). See N. KARLSTRÖM (ed.), *Nathan Söderblom in Memoriam*, Stockholm 1931, p. 23; B. SUNDKLER, *Nathan Söderblom: His Life and Work*, London 1968, p. 426.

After commenting on the widespread interest aroused by the ROBERTSON SMITH case both in Scotland and far beyond it, P. CARNEGIE SIMPSON makes the following comment: "All this makes the more noticeable, the reticence of one who, before almost any one else, might have been expected to declare himself for and aid the liberal interest. Certainly, one of the strange things in the story is that in such a momentous struggle for critical liberty within the Free Church of Scotland, the illustrious critical scholar of that Church, to whom the Church had the right to look for guidance on such a question and to whom all the land would have listened as the master (and who had been ROBERTSON SMITH's master), took no lead and—except for one non-committal review of contemporary works on Old Testament literature—uttered, in public, no voice. He always, of course gave his vote for Professor Smith, but it was always a silent vote. I shall not attempt to account for this here except to say that the suggestion that A. B. Davidson was a coward is one I decline even to discuss. But whatever its cause—whether simply the sensitive scholar's shrinking from the ecclesiastical arena, or a Hamlet-like irresolution, or an Ecclesiastes-like feeling (to use one of his own startling phrases) of 'the resultlessness of all struggle for knowledge', or a temperamental self-distrust and diffidence, or whatever else—it could not but be observed by many spectators. One can see him still—there, on that back bench, sitting through the long debates, his fine head now sunk deep on his breast as though he were uncertain about duty or opinion, and now thrown up and poised a little to one side to hear, while the wistful smile—sharpening at times to the ironic—plays gently on lips so firmly sealed."[8]

ANDREW BRUCE DAVIDSON was born in 1831 near Ellon, Aberdeenshire, where his father, a former quarryman, had leased the small farm of Kirkhill. After graduating at Marischal College, Aberdeen, he studied theology at New College, Edinburgh. Since the foundation of the College in 1843 the Chair of Hebrew had been held by "Rabbi" JOHN DUNCAN, a man of vast linguistic erudition (it was said that he could "talk his way to the Wall of China"), conservative orthodoxy, and memorable eccentricity. What he imparted to his students was by way of discursive conversation rather than systematic teaching, and by a hermeneutic which owed nothing to critical method. He undoubtedly influenced DAVIDSON deeply; but a more striking contrast to the

---

[8] *The Life of Principal Rainy*, vol. 1, pp. 354 f.

method and spirit of DAVIDSON's later work as teacher and scholar could hardly be imagined. For a time DAVIDSON studied in Göttingen under EWALD, from whom he received intellectual stimulus of a very different order.

In 1858 he became tutor in Hebrew at New College; and five years later he was appointed colleague and successor to DUNCAN, after whose death in 1870 he became sole Professor. In these days when student influence in academic affairs is still regarded as an innovation, it is interesting to note that his nomination for the Chair was suppported by a memorial presented by eighty-six of his students. Seven years later the entire student body of New College supported ROBERTSON SMITH's nomination for the Aberdeen Chair.

During his long tenure of the Chair, which ended with his death in 1902, DAVIDSON, by his writing, and above all by his teaching, carried through a silent revolution: the adoption of a sound critical method in the study of the Old Testament and the presentation of biblical theology in a framework not of traditional dogmatics but of historical development. This revolution was adumbrated in his first major work, *A Commentary, Grammatical and Exegetical, on the Book of Job, with a Translation*, Vol. I, Edinburgh 1862, written while he was still Hebrew tutor. It has been described as "the first really scientific commentary on the Old Testament in the English language". Unfortunately, it was never completed; but in 1884 DAVIDSON published in the Cambridge Bible series a complete commentary on Job which is an outstanding example of his critical discernment and his quality as an exegete and theologian.[9] His commentary on Ezekiel in the same series [10] is of similar excellence. It was precisely DAVIDSON's caution as a critic and his power as a theological expositor that gave to his commentaries an enduring quality which makes them still worth consulting when other more daringly original works by some of his contemporaries belong to the academic lumber which is best forgotten. Venturing into the New Testament field, DAVIDSON produced a commentary on the Epistle to the Hebrews (Edinburgh n.d.? 1882) in a series of Handbooks for Bible Classes. The treatment is so detailed and the exegetical analysis so subtle that the reader cannot but wonder how Bible Classes were conducted in those days.

---

[9] A new edition, revised by H. C. O. LANCHESTER, appeared in 1918.
[10] First edition 1892; revised edition by A. W. STREANE, 1916.

Of the remainder of DAVIDSON's published work the best is contained in dictionary articles, notably those on "God (in OT) "and "Prophecy and Prophets" in J. HASTINGS' *Dictionary of the Bible*. The magisterial quality of these makes one sadly aware of what he might have given us. Of all his generation in this country he was supremely endowed to write an Old Testament theology. At his death he left substantial materials for such a work; but when *The Theology of the Old Testament*, 1904, was published, it was all too evident from the repetitions and unevennesses, that the editor, S. D. F. SALMOND, had been unable to present the materials at his disposal as the author himself would have done. In passage after passage the authentic DAVIDSON appears; but the volume resembles the impressive fragment of an unfinished building surrounded by heaps of material which might have been used to complete the symmetry of the structure. *Old Testament Prophecy*, Edinburgh 1904, is at best an editorial disaster, at worst an editorial crime, for which DAVIDSON's successor, J. A. PATERSON was responsible. Materials composed in the early part of DAVIDSON's career, containing views which he subsequently discarded, are lumped together with his more mature writing. A similar lack of discrimination characterizes PATERSON's editing of *Biblical and Literary Essays*, Edinburgh 1902.

No work of DAVIDSON's has been more widely used than his *Introductory Hebrew Grammar*, Edinburgh 1874; and here, at least, he has been competently served by two successive editors. The 19th-24th editions were produced, with considerable revisions, by Professor J. A. McFADYEN. More radical revision has been made in the 25th (1962) and 26th (1966) editions by Professor J. MAUCHLINE. Probably no elementary Hebrew grammar has had so long a life and so wide an influence. The companion *Hebrew Syntax*, Edinburgh 1894, ³1912, is of comparable excellence.

DAVIDSON was a reluctant but impressive preacher. A. J. GOSSIP once wrote of him, "To run second to that master is honour enough for anyone".[11] After his death two volumes of his sermons were issued: *The Called of God*, Edinburgh 1902, and *Waiting upon God*, Edinburgh 1903. The former of these contains a short Biographical Introduction by A. T. INNES.[12]

It was above all as a teacher that DAVIDSON excelled. In spite of

---

[11] In W. M. MACGREGOR, *The Making of a Preacher*, London 1945, p. 10.
[12] For a fuller account of DAVIDSON's career see J. STRAHAN, *Andrew Bruce Davidson, D.D., LL.D., D.Litt.*, London 1917.

his shyness and diffidence, his personality made an even deeper impression than his learning and his gifts as a teacher. Of that there is
abundant evidence in the reminiscences of his professoriate which
have been preserved. His effectiveness in the lecture room was enhanced by a pungent wit which in a lesser man might have been a
handicap. In returning a student's essay he remarked, "Your essay is
too long Mr A----; perhaps you could leave out half of it—*either
half.*"[13] He treated Scripture with reverence, but not with the exaggerated solemnity which inhibits common sense, as is shown by
a footnote in his commentary on Ezekiel in which he does not
spare even the great JOHN CALVIN: "In regard to ch. iv. 1-3 Calvin
remarks, Hoc fuit puerile spectaculum, nisi a Deo jussus fuisset
propheta sic agere. But that which would be puerile unless commanded by God remains puerile in itself, and the sound sense of men will
conclude that God did not command it." [14]

The extent and power of DAVIDSON's influence are seen in part
in the number of Old Testament scholars and teachers who had been
his students, of whom WILLIAM ROBERTSON SMITH, GEORGE ADAM
SMITH, and JOHN SKINNER were the most distinguished. But they
are seen there only in part, for there went out into the ministry of the
Free Church, year after year for more than a generation, men who in
DAVIDSON's lecture room had learned to use the methods of criticism
without uncritically accepting the latest conclusions of the critics,
and to see the Old Testament in historical perspective without losing
a sense of its abiding truth. Without striving or crying aloud, DAVID-
SON thus fought on another front the campaign which ROBERTSON
SMITH waged in the courts of the Church and on the public platform.

What, then are we to make of DAVIDSON's enigmatic silence during
the ROBERTSON SMITH case? Rejecting all of the tentative explanations offered by CARNEGIE SIMPSON in the passage quoted above,
DAVIDSON's biographer has suggested that one important reason may
have been that, while he agreed with ROBERTSON SMITH's general
position, he disapproved of his aggressiveness and pugnacity, holding
that they were likely to harm the life of the Church.[15] If so, he had
something in common with RAINY, though he always voted for
SMITH, whereas RAINY not only voted against him but actively sought

---

[13] P. CARNEGIE SIMPSON, *Recollections, Mainly Ecclesiastical but Sometimes Human*,
London 1943, p. 32.

[14] *The Book of the Prophet Ezekiel*, Cambridge 1893, p. xxix, n. 1.

[15] J. STRAHAN, *op. cit.*, Chapter XV.

to bring about his deposition. This may indeed be a partial explanation. No doubt the profound difference in temperament between the
two men also provides part of the solution. SMITH was in many ways
the antithesis of the shy, diffident DAVIDSON. He was ever eager to
meet his enemies' attacks and at times seemed to invite them. He
was ready of speech and delighted in argument. The elder DELITZSCH
aptly said of him, "Der Verstand prädominiert". Yet, with all the
differences between the two men, I suggest that there may fitly be
applied to both of them a phrase from Isaiah which SMITH often
quoted and which he painted with his own hand in the corner of Sir
George Reid's portrait of him: *hamma'ᵃmîn lō' yāḥîš*—"he that be-
lieveth shall not make haste". This sums up SMITH's attitude during
the long and bitter conflict, and not only then. It also sums up DA-
VIDSON's attitude during the long years of quiet teaching in which he
brought about the silent revolution of which I have spoken. DA-
VIDSON did not have the dash of a cavalry leader, and his strategy
was not revolutionary but Fabian. As we look back on the struggle
for critical freedom and for a sounder understanding of the Old
Testament, we may fitly apply to him the words of ENNIUS: *unus homo
nobis cunctando restituit rem.*

HERMENEUTICAL PROBLEMS OF A LITERARY STUDY OF THE BIBLE

BY

A. ALONSO-SCHÖKEL
Rome

A Situation

I think that the observation of Emil STAIGER on literary science is still valid: "Strange lot that of literary science: he who pursues it ends up either without science or without literature".[1]

And I would add that this statement is no less valid when applied to the literature of the Old Testament. That many narratives of Genesis, Judges, Samuel, and Kings, that many oracles of the prophets, the Song of Songs and Job are literature, is denied by no one; that they should be studied as literature, is accepted by few. Why?

In his *Introduction to the Old Testament*, G. FOHRER is afraid of a "sterile aestheticism"; Kl. KOCH is concerned with the history of forms and understands by form almost exclusively the form of literary genre.[2] It is very difficult to find other motives because authors ordinarily prescind without giving explanations. Admittedly, omissions are not usually justified.

But let us return to STAIGER's statement. On the one hand, one would tend to say that the authentically valid in literary matters is elusive, not capable of being controlled systematically, not an object of scientific study; it pertains rather to feeling, to impressionistic observation, to unaccountable taste; it is the danger denounced by W. RICHTER on one occasion. On the other hand, if one insists in analyzing forms rigorously, the object of study becomes formal, irrelevant for the meaning. The rigorous study of form leads to a sterile formalism.

Whoever dares to step into the arena will perish on the horns of the dilemma. I am willing to admit to such fears and misgivings. If literary form is pure form, irrelevant and extrinsic to the meaning, then it does not interest us for the study of the Bible. When one

---

[1] Emil STAIGER, *Die Kunst der Interpretation*, Zürich 1955, p. 12.
[2] Kl. KOCH, *Was ist Formgeschichte?*, Neukirchen 1967².

rejects studies in form, there arises a hermeneutical problem, which has scarcely yet been posed.

State of the Question

Is form meaningful? Are there meaningful formal elements? If the answer is yes, then we will have to cut our way through the form to arrive at the fullness of meaning; if the answer is no, then the study of form is a worthless pastime.

I. VIDETUR QUOD NON

1. Distinction of two autonomous worlds

One must clearly distinguish the poetical and literary world from the didactic and utilitarian world. The work of art is autonomous, meant for aesthetic delight, for disinterested contemplation. The aesthetic is a specific and autonomous category.

The theory of the separation of the two worlds reached its high-point in the last century, under the influence of an idealist philosophy; it extended beyond philosophy, and even today has not completely died. Art for the sake of art proclaimed the supremacy of the aesthetic and declared exterritorial the zones occupied by the work of art (one of the functions of the museum).

The poet neither affirms nor denies. Consequently, he neither informs, nor teaches, nor preaches. Poetry and literature are meant for aesthetic delight or for entertainment; has it not been said that poetry is a higher form of entertainment?

To these elements could be reduced the psychological investigation regarding the "attitude or aesthetic emotion" as an autonomous and radically different experience.

The critic of plastic arts, Clive BELL, once wrote in *Art* (London 1914):

> There must be some one quality without which a work of art cannot exist ... What quality is common to Santa Sophia and Windows of Chartres ...? Only one answer is possible—significant form. In each, lines and colours combined in a particular way, certain forms and relations of forms stir our aesthetic emotions.

If the art object simply produces aesthetic emotion and if the poet neither affirms nor informs, then this could lead us to the affirmations of Max EASTMAN against the poets: "they are fighting for the right of literary men to talk loosely and yet be taken seriously in a scientific age."[3]

I do not think that this is the position of exegetes today. Clearly, not of all; if of some, it is not fully acknowledged. But it was, nevertheless, useful to present the negation of the meaningfulnes in its most radical way, because when one reads certain commentaries, the suspicion arises that they are founded on similar non-formulated, much less criticized, presuppositions.

2. *Distinction of two separable components*

Leaving behind the distinction of two completely different worlds, we turn our attention to a more moderate negation based on the distinction of two separable components. In a literary work one can perfectly separate two aspects: the what and the how. If we get tired of calling them content and form, we can call them *Gehalt und Gestalt* (O. WALZEL), idea and expression (G. FLAUBERT), message and style; or we can invent other equivalent pairs.

Once the distinction is made, we assign each element to a field of study. Exegesis is concerned with defining rigorously the meaning or content or message of a biblical text. If anyone has time and inclination, he may give himself to biblical rhetoric without being disturbed; his work is innocuous as long as it is ignored.

This theory may be expressed in two formulations: one more extreme, the other more moderate.

a) The literary works which we may find, for example, in the Old Testament have a meaning in spite of the form; to fix our attention on the form distracts from the meaning. This is just what happened to the listeners of Ezekiel (xxxiii 31-33):

> "You are no more to them than a singer of love songs with a lovely voice, or a clever harpist";

they went to hear the rhymer, they celebrated his couplets and his voice; until one day, much to their sorrow, they discovered "that a prophet had been living in their midst". (In parenthesis: if the form was a hindrance, why did Ezekiel compose and recite his oracles in artistic fashion?)

More than one exegete implicitly assumes this attitude. To study the form of the OT is to diminish its importance; at best, it distracts

---

[3] Max EASTMAN, *The Literary Mind*. Quoted by Laurence LERNER, *The Truest Poetry*, New York 1964, p. 15.

from that which is really important. It cannot be denied that the conclusion is respectable; it can be discussed, however, whether the premise is correct.

But is this not defended by JAKOBSON when he distinguishes in language the poetical function from the referential or denotative? "This function, by promoting the palpability of signs, deepens the fundamental dichotomy of signs and objects." I do not think so, because his distinction is analytical and is counterbalanced all through his article.[4]

b) In less radical terms the objection may be so formulated: the literary work has a meaning apart from the form, prescinding from it. In the genetic order, the author is supposed to have the meaning already realized and perfect in his mind before clothing it with the form. It is the old metaphor of the dress, or of the "miscuit utile dulci," which Qohelet already knew (xii 10): "He chose his words to give pleasure, but what he wrote was the honest truth." Let us remember that Plato placed rhetoric beside the cosmetic and culinary arts.

I think this is the most widely extended hermeneutical presupposition among exegetes. If the meaning precedes the form, then we must undo what has been done, prescinding from the form, in order to arrive at the meaning; if the form is extrinsic and neutral to the meaning, then we must separate it or root it out in order to retain the meaning. In either case, the study of the form is either useless or serves only to reject the form, just as the beautifully-colored skin of a fruit is thrown away.

This attitude acknowledges that there are literary works in the OT which could be studied as such. At the same time, it affirms that exegesis studies them as religious or historical works. It is an attitude which purports to be critical because it discerns, but which has not criticized its presupposition, namely, that the form does not carry meaning.

3. *Witness of modern studies*

The third negation comes from some undertakings in the science of language and literature which for different reasons seem to deny meaning to the form.

---

[4] R. JABOBSON, "Linguistics and Poetics," in *Style in Language*, ed. by Thomas E. SEBEOK, Cambridge 1964[2], pp. 350ff.

a) Let us begin with Russian or Slavic formalism, which though becoming old in its formulation, is still actual in its influence. The classics of this school, PROPP, SHKLOVSKY, MUKAROVSKY, etc. are being translated and read with renewed interest. Now, according to the description of René WELLEK,[5] the Russian formalists gorged themselves with the study of literary procedures:

> Device (priyom) became for them the only legitimate subject matter of literary study with the result that form was replaced by a mechanistic concept of the sum of techniques or procedures which could be studied separately or in diverse interlocking combinations . . . They were positivists with a scientific, almost technological ideal of literary scholarship . . . Though their tools were immeasurably finer, they returned to the old rhetorical formalism.

This undertaking was denounced as sterile formalism by orthodox ideology; today it seems to come to life again together with similar denunciations proposed and accepted in other latitudes. It is understandable that exegesis be not interested in such a study of form.

b) There is a more subtle difficulty which could also be placed in the first part of STAIGER's dilemma regarding that which defies analysis in literature. It is admitted that forms are meaningful, but not so in the articulated systems studied by modern linguistics. In more technical terms, the stylistic factors would be "suprasegmental."

Let us explain this: an ascending intonation which is contraposed to a descending one in order to distinguish the question from the answer is strictly an object of linguistics, since it functions as diacritical opposition, no less than the distinction between p and t on the level of phonemes. Chinese tones also have phoneme-value and are thus objects of structural linguistics. However, an expressive intonation due to continuous variations which express and modulate emotion, would not be a linguistic factor; it does not proceed by discontinued oppositions, does not articulate meaning structurally. Now, stylistic factors would belong in this realm; they would be suprasegmental or paralinguistic.

In fact, despite the progress attained by modern linguistics in recent years, it has contributed almost nothing to the question of style. If it has thus far advanced so little in the field of semantics, we cannot demand ripe fruits in the field of style. As thought-pro-

---

[5] René WELLEK, *Concepts of Criticism*, Yale 1969[5], pp. 65ff.

voking contributions we may quote the Symposium edited by Thomas A. Sebeok entitled *Style in Language* (MIT Press, Cambridge 1966) and *Essais de stylistique structurale* of Michael Riffaterre (Flammarion, Paris 1971).

We can add another aspect, namely, that formal analysis confronts concrete literary works at the level of discourse, not of language; whereas structural analysis pays attention above all to language. Only recently has it begun to operate on discourse.

When this idea is applied to exegesis the following results: Those formal and meaningful values will pass by unperceived by the exegete lacking sensitivity, like counterpoint by an ear only accustomed to melody. The sensitive exegete will perceive them, but will not make them objects of his personal research and writings; the sensitive reader will perceive them without the explanation of the commentator. At most, he will utter an adjective or interjection without thematizing them in a metalanguage.

c) In recent years, in the field of narration, a structural analysis has been developed which abstracts forms and functions to compile a kind of universal grammar of narrations; if not universal, at least a general grammar of the various narrative fields. Here belong, above all, the French group around *Communications* Cl. Brémond, R. Barthes, and naturally the venerable Vladimir Propp. Experiments of this structural technique in exegesis are being realized with variable success. The Colloquy of Chantilly seems to me to be the current most interesting exposition.[6]

Now, does not this analysis prescind from the meaning? Is it not a kind of pure narrative syntax, a system of functions independent of semantics? This question was posed in the discussions of Chantilly (pp. 252ff.).

But if the structural analysis of narrations prescinds from the meaning, then it is understandable that exegetes want to have nothing to do with such formalism; they are interested in meaning. If structural analysis excludes semantics, then two parallel fields of work will arise.

We have come to the end of the first part *videtur quod non* with a reasonable collection of arguments: the distinction of an autonomous aesthetic world; the distinction of the constitutive elements of the literary work, that is, form and content as perfectly separable elements (in its extreme and moderate form); the more or less sweeping

---

[6] *Exégèse et herméneutique*, ed. by Xavier Léon-Dufour, Paris 1971.

affirmations of the formalist school, of structural linguistics, of a structural analysis of narrations. All of these arguments are good enough to justify the exegete who excludes the study of forms from his scholarly work—or at least to soothe his conscience. When a monumental introduction to the Old Testament, like EISSFELDT's, has scarcely anything to say about formal values, then it seems to be justified by hermeneutical principles. And the introduction of EISSFELDT is not the only one!

II. SED DICENDUM

I am going to propose one statement with variations, rather than a series of statements:

In literature the form is meaningful.

In science the form is subservient to the meaning; in literature the form creates meaning.

There is no realized and perfect meaning before it takes verbal form.

The perfect separation between form and content is, in fact, impossible.

In literature the meaning exists in and through the form.

The concrete literary work is a sign constituted by the correspondence of the signifier with the signified.

When we begin to nuance statements, we could say that there are forms which are purely formal, rhetorical recourses which are purely rhetorical. We may recall verbiage in poetry, Assianism, the conventions and mannerisms denoting affiliation to a certain school . .. In general we can say that the amount of purely formal elements abounds more in third-class writers and in decadent schools. From this it does not follow that every form is "pure form".

III. RESPONDEO

1. The separation of these two worlds, the aesthetic and the non-aesthetic, is recent and artificial. Irwin EDMAND [7] shows in the light of history that many philosophers wrote artistically: HUME, BERKELEY and HOBBES, DESCARTES and PASCAL, SCHOPENHAUER and NIETZSCHE, BERGSON and SANTAYANA, and the patriarch of all, PLATO:

---

[7] Irwin EDMAN, "Philosophy and the Literary Artist," in *Spiritual Problems in Contemporary Literature*, New York 1957².

It is an ironic coincidence that Santayana writes so well, that for nearly a generation the philosophers hardly knew he was a philosopher at all. They have learned better now. For a long time they were extremely suspicious of anybody who wrote so beautifully.

H. G. GADAMER,[8] in particular, devotes the first section of his book to describing the historical process by which the aestheticist conception is surpassed:

> Die Transzendierung der ästhetischen Dimension. 3. Wiedergewinnung der Frage nach der Wahrheit der Kunst: a) Die Fragwürdigkeit der ästhetischen Bildung; b) Kritik der Abstraktion des ästhetischen Bewusstseins.

But, do not these two authorities prove exactly the opposite? That philosophers and artists should be studied for what they say and not for the way in which they say it; that the philosophers mentioned here belong to the history of philosophy and not to the history of literature. And is this applicable to Plato or Lucretius?

This objection brings us to the next part of the paper. It will suffice for the moment to recall GADAMER's conclusion applied to the Bible: the OT does not cease to be literature by being a collection of religious texts, and viceversa.

2. Separation of two components: form and content.

a) GADAMER shows how the distinction between the what and the how of a literary work or of plastic arts is the result of "aesthetic abstraction"—a secondary, not a primary phenomenon. Originally the representation and what is represented coincide; what is represented, that is to say, not in terms of referent, but in terms of meaning.

I would admit that the distinction is no mere invention of romantic philosophy. When classical rhetoric taught in the *progymnasmata* to change figures of speech and images in a literary work *salvo modo sensu poetae*, it was presupposing that figures of speech and images were something extrinsic to, and perfectly separable from, the meaning.[9] Or it is using the word *sensus* with singular narrowness. These are laboratory separations, exercises in isolating, as someone learning the piano, who with four fingers stuck to the keys, over and over again lifts one at a time.

---

[8] H. G. GADAMER, *Wahrheit und Methode*.
[9] H. LAUSBERG, *Handbuch der literarischen Rhetorik*, München 1960, II, p. 223.

With regard to JAKOBSON, whom we mentioned above, it is enough to read his article to see that his interest for the form brings him to discoveries of meaning; naturally, understanding by meaning the total communication of language and not just the denotative or referential function.

b) The separation of the study of the OT as a collection of literary works and as a collection of religious texts, that is to say, the distinction between the study of form and of content, although it has theoretical value, is not fully realizable in practice. This is attested by the failure of authors in attempting to classify what pertains to the form and what pertains to the content of a concrete work. There are, of course, details which can be easily catalogued as form; and there are works in which the formal element is more easily separable from the content, for instance, the didactic poems. They are exceptions even within Wisdom literature.

"A door turns on its hinges, a sluggard on his bed" (Prov. xxvi 14). Who is able to say what is form and what is content in this proverb? Who will be able to separate the two?

Let us take the case of poetic imagery: is it a simple formal recourse which does not change the meaning of the statement or concept? The meaning of an image is not a concept which may be substituted for it, nor is it the referent or objective reality about which one speaks. In Ps. xix 5-7, the image of the warrior satisfied after a night of love and refreshed to commence the gigantic journey from horizon to horizon is the meaning of the poem: it is not the astronomic body which astronomers describe as the sun of our system, one among many . . . The poetic image is not copy of an original or archetype (*Abbild eines Urbildes*); it is presentation (*Darstellung*) in which the sun and its function are manifested figuratively; the sun acquires a meaningful quality by entering into a new universe of representations. Sun at once humanized and super-human, powerful and obedient, loving and strong, punctual and efficacious. A primordial analogy of beings is discovered in the poem—the astronomic and the human— which a conceptual statement is not capable of manifesting. The image has been a cognoscitive instrument, figurative manifestation of being.

The meaning of the image cannot be reduced to what it refers to—here astronomic body—not even to a presupposed concept in the mind of the author. When the commentator explains these verses in conceptual terms, his explanation is not the meaning extracted from the pericope, but rather an orienting of the reader to enable him to read and see the image correctly. Exegesis does not give the meaning according to the formula "Work minus form equals meaning" (W-f = M), so that the text could be suppressed as unnecessary; exegesis is an introduction to reading or giving an account of what has been apprehended in the reading. And this apprehension precisely occurs in the total and unitary perception, previous to any presumed aesthetic abstraction. The reason is that the literary work is a revealing of meaning, and not a concealing of meaning through the artifice of form.

Images, whatever their character may be: metaphors or comparisons or symbols, refute the theory of a perfect separation of form and content in poetry. Since I cannot develop this important theme here, I would like to refer to a recent study, which opens a path in this field of biblical research: Rémy LACK, *La symbolique du livre d'Isaïe* (Rome 1973).

3. a) and c)

To answer the objection coming from Russian formalism it may suffice to take into account the suggestions of R. WELLEK himself in the work cited above and in others to which he makes reference:

> A concept of stratification, developed also in my and Austin Warren's *Theory of Literature* (1949), allows us to return to concrete analytical work without having to surrender the basic insights into the wholeness, totality and unity of content and form (p. 68).

Regarding the structural analysis of narrations, I think that P. RICOEUR has given the most convincing answer in the already quoted Symposium of Chantilly and in some of his other articles.

b) Structural linguistics and style.

If one day M. Joos excluded from the science of language the emotive factors, which he considered to be "non-linguistic," that attitude has already been surpassed.[10] The profession of JAKOBSON has more authority: "Linguista sum; linguistici nihil a me alienum puto".[11] The factors of style are facts of language, and cannot, therefore, be banished from the science of language. It would be both an intolerant and dangerous attitude.

---

[10] M. Joos, "Description of Language Design," *Journal of the Acoustical Society of America*, XXII (A50), pp. 701ff.

[11] SEBEOK, l.c., p. 377.

The study of style in language must operate at the two levels of language and discourse. In the similar way in which phonemes, morphemes, words within their range of meaning are described, a structural ordering of "stylemes" could be tried. It would be an analogical transposition, like the one being realized in the field of narration. Operating with the system of substitutions and other inductive methods, we could establish oppositions and groupings, which would lead to various paradigms. Perhaps others may prefer a transformational method, on the way to a "generative stylistic."[12] In any case, the concept of function is essential, if we do not want to fall again into a merely rhetorical and formalistic classification. There can be "universals of style" and there can be stylistic elements proper to culture or language. What has already been done in the biblical field, could perhaps be formalized with recent methods.

Of no less importance is the analysis at the level of discourse, that is, of individual works; in them the universal and generic adopts an individual configuration which can be described in a sufficiently rigorous meta-language. A serious analysis of a poem cannot be satisfied with grammar, which in itself could be sub-stylistic, nor with a generic classification. And this under pain of not perceiving the meaning in its concreteness and richness, of mutilating what had to be unfolded.

Let us look at some examples. The first is well-known and recognized by all. We have talked of two opposite melodic forms with diacritical value to distinguish question from answer. It is a grammatical, syntactical fact. Many centuries ago, on the level of style, rhetoric recognized the question having the value of emphatic affirmation or negation, the *"rhetorical question,"* and the statement with opposite value, or *"irony."* But irony can color a whole literary work or a main section of a work; for instance, Judith's irony regarding Holofernes and the author's irony regarding some of his characters is a constitutive element for the meaning of the work. He who does not perceive it, will falsify the meaning in some cases, and miss half of it in others. One of the principal tasks of the exegete should be to analyze and expound this formal quality and its function in the work; this is not usually done. In the book of Jonah irony has been commonly detected and at least recorded; its analysis could be developed more through the various scenes until its culmination

---

[12] Cfr. the endeavor of H. GÜTTGEMANNS to produce a 'generative poetic', in the periodical *Linguistica Biblica*.

in the sarcasm of the author and the condescending humor of God.

Another example at the level of language: the capacity to differentiate meaning. Language has its marks to distinguish meaning: phonemes in lower levels of expression, semantic fields as closed structures. Literary language triumphs with its inexhaustible capacity to nuance, underline, refer, suggest, relate. Only that the correspondence between the device and its meaning is here much more fluid, so that it is necessary to judge carefully the function or functions of each device. A part of these formal devices have been organized by classical rhetoric and modern analysis. Others will be analyzed.

At the level of discourse: the correspondence signifying - signified, which forms the sign in language, also operates in the literary work, though with greater complexity.

For instance, in onomatopoeia the sound materializes the meaning in a sonorous justification of the *lexeme*; it is a stylization of the sound referred to effected by the instruments of language itself. The onomatopoeia may extend to a whole verse, fashioning its dominant sonority. And it can even be a dominant structure in a short poem.

Often in *syntagmata* position decides or discerns the meaning: subject and object, attribute and predicate; position is a formal pointer of the signifying (which could very well be opposed to the chronological or causal order of the signified). The *syntagmatic* scheme establishes relations of meaning among its members by the use or non-use of particles and by their position in the statement. The same occurs in a more complex way in a literary work considered as macro-syntagma: the position of an element can modify its meaning, the relations between the members constitute or modify or enrich the total meaning. In principle this can happen both in a primary and in a secondary composition.

Let us consider in Ezekiel xxxi, the exaltation and fall of the imperial tree. Beginning with *v.* 15 the image of the tree fades away; when it is mentioned, it does not succeed in creating a coherent image, but rather causes the opposite effect. (And this in spite of the double-meaning of the word *shadow* and despite the fact that the adjective "*uncircumcised*" may be applied to fruit trees.) However, *vv.* 10-14 develop the image of the tree with perfect coherence: the semantic field—going up and coming down, ascending and falling, height and depth—unifies in a powerful way *vv.* 2-14, drawing the curve of physical elevation, spiritual conceit, and ultimate fall; and within this range the two extremes are perfectly joined, the 'garden of the gods' and 'the pit of the earth'. This is valid even if it is shown that these verses were not composed at one sitting.

IV. New objection and return to praxis

1. *Insto*

If the content is not perfectly separable from the form, if the two constitute a unitary whole, the researcher who discovers and expounds the content will have also arrived at the form. Not to notice it or analyze it explicitly does not mean that he has not perceived it or communicated it. It makes no difference whether one begins with one or the other.

It is not so; because form is expression of content and not vice-versa. In other words, the signified is expressed in the signifying.

But there are deep structures which by transformation produce diverse surface structures, and simple elements of meaning (semes) which by combination produce sememes or words. It would happen, in a similar way, with the profound structure of the signified which comes through in the signifying. I say that this is true on the level of realization; on the level of perception, however, we begin with the signifying (well-known are the problems connected with a componential analysis when the language in question lacks words to express certain components). The reader and interpreter of a text have only the text before themselves, not a pre - existent or underlying meaning. It is the task of the reader and the interpreter to perceive and explain all the significant marks of the text as well as its configuration.

2. But let us return to the *present situation*, which we may now consider under the perspective of what we have said.

We find at times the formal observation thrown in to the commentary in passing, without really taking advantage of its significative function: "here there is a chiasm, an alliteration, an anaphora, etc.". There is also the reference and even formal exposition of significative forms, which are ordinarily restricted to generic forms or literary genres. Gunkel's leadership is only half-operative today since his stylistic analysis of individual works has not formed a school. If the reason for this is that his method was not sufficiently refined, nowadays we can achieve such refinement.

Moreover, it is an incoherent situation. First, because authors who in theory seem to reject formal analysis, in practice do not abstain from making incidental observations. This incoherence in

theory and practice shows the existence of presuppositions which
are neither conscious, nor analyzed, much less criticized. Another
incoherence is the incidental character of such observations, even
found in a series like the *Biblischer Kommentar*, which professes to
devote a section to form.

Finally, the present situation is scarcely reflexive and coherent.
There is no systematic program of action nor a solid front of resistance; what reigns is an atmosphere of lack of interest and trust,
which is only occasionally broken by already established habits.
We find, moreover, limited geographical zones where literary interest
is kept alive (for instance, the leadership of MUILENBURG in California; studies of structuralism in France).

I would like to offer a few suggestions for this situation:

a) To clarify the non-reflective presuppositions of our activity,
precisely in this field, and in collaboration with related disciplines.

b) When teaching and learning Hebrew, not to be content with
grammar, but to include also stylistics and poetics; as it used to
be done in the study of the classical Greek and Latin authors as
well as in other literatures.

c) To pay more attention to individual forms in commentaries;
although by doing this we may have to abandon genetic speculations
and the growing number of hypotheses which can neither be verified
nor falsified.

Epilogue on translation

To translate is to interpret, to transpose from a linguistic structure
to another; in BETTI's terminology, it is an act of reproductive
interpretation. Just as the fact of translation poses multiple problems
to theoreticians of linguistics (see G. MOUNIN, *Les problems théoretiques
de la traduction*), so also does it pose problems in the stylistic field.[13]

Among biblical commentaries we find on one extreme the translations of GUNKEL's team (SAT), the unfinished Job of HORST, and
on the other extreme the Isaiah of Ed. KÖNIG. The first think that
Hebrew poems must sound in the target language with the dignity,
the communicative force, and richness of the original; the second
thought that to understand poetry it had to be reduced to pedantic
prose. In reading chapters xl-lv of KÖNIG's translation of Isaiah, who
will think that that man had a vibrant, passionate, and moving message? Human communication is thus frustrated or seriously hampered.

---

[13] Cfr. *The Bible Translator*, XXII (1971), 38-44; XXIV (1973), 118-129.

In biblical translations for the use of the faithful the artistic instance usually prevails (Luther, King James, Martini, etc.); but this instance may at times fail to go the full way: by being excessively subjected to grammar, sacrificed to a mechanical literalism, or confined to privileged zones.

I would like to announce that in a few months a complete Spanish translation of the Bible will be published, which is based on reflected presuppositions of interpretation and on a systematic comparative analysis of stylistic or rhetorical devices of the original and target languages. This task has not been for us a luxury, but rather the effort to transpose the biblical text in its rich and complex concreteness; in other words, a hermeneutical task.

THE PURPOSE OF THE BOOK OF JONAH

BY

R. E. CLEMENTS
Cambridge

There has been considerable unanimity among scholars about the purpose of the book of Jonah, even where disagreements still continue about its literary form and character. Essentially this purpose is seen to be the presentation of an affirmation of the universal love and mercy of God, which Israel had come to know, in its reference to heathen peoples. Jonah the prophet, who represents Israel, is made to recognize that the divine mercy is not confined within the boundaries of Israel, but reaches out also to the heathen, as represented by the people of Nineveh. Thus the message of the book is summed up in God's speech to Jonah which brings the book to a close: "And should not I pity Nineveh, that great city, in which there are more than a hundred and twenty thousand persons who do not know their right hand from their left, and also much cattle?" (Jon. iv 11). The implied consequence of such a perception has been taken by some scholars to be a need for a mission to the heathen.[1] Throughout the book its theological presupposition is that Yahweh, the God of Israel, is universal creator and lord, and the implications of this which are regarded as elucidated by the narrative of Nineveh's repentance and Jonah's subsequent anger, are that this divine mercy must be extended to the gentiles. They are his people too, and so they must share the knowledge of his mercy and love. The message thus points to the need on Israel's part for a charitable attitude towards foreigners and charitable dealings with them, which, it is claimed, points towards a recognition of the need for missionary endeavour among them.

The background of the book, as thus interpreted, is usually found in the increasing sensitivity to the relationships between Jews and non-Jews in the Persian period, as portrayed in the administrative

---

[1] So for example H. H. ROWLEY, *The Missionary Message of the Old Testament*, London 1945, p. 69, "The author of the book of Jonah believed that God was the God of all men, and the faith of Israel to be shared by all".

measures introduced by Nehemiah and Ezra. At this time the Jerusalem community was beset with problems about retaining its religious identity which led to decisive measures to separate the Jewish community from aliens. The result was that a very noticeable separatist tendency entered into Judaism with consequences which appear very intolerant of non-Jews. The remarkable degree of freedom and benevolence accorded to subject peoples by the Persian administration would also readily support the belief that this period provided the historical background of the book of Jonah, with its implicit demand for an attitude of tolerance towards foreigners. In the story, the people of Nineveh, with their admitted ways of violence, do not threaten Israel's religion or its purity.

There have been some dissentients from this widespread agreement among scholars about this interpretation of Jonah, but they have been few, and even then the area of disagreement has been small. P. R. ACKROYD has raised afresh the possibility that the book is an allegory in which Jonah represents Israel.[2] The episode of his being swallowed by a fish is an interpretation of the nation's experience of exile in Babylon which threatened to destroy its consciousness of divine election to bring the knowledge of God to the nations. Yet this is to introduce an all-important interpretative factor which is nowhere evident in the book itself, and to focus attention on what is after all a very minor episode in the story. Thus there is in general a wide consensus of approval and acceptance of the universalist interpretation of the narrative of Jonah, with claims for its missionary implications, which is surprising in view of the uniqueness of such a conception in the Old Testament. The common linking of Jonah with the book of Ruth offers only a limited confirmation of such an interpretation since it is far from clear that such a universalist purpose is central to the story of Ruth. In line with this overall understanding of Jonah it has been suggested that in its general character and form it is a piece of didactic writing which has close affinities with wisdom where universalist tendencies are recognised.[3] Thus it may more properly be regarded as standing closer to the form of a didactic wisdom composition than to that of a prophetic book.

In spite of this agreement about the interpretation of the book of Jonah a number of difficulties arise in connection with it which

---

[2] P. R. ACKROYD, *Exile and Restoration*, London 1968, pp. 244f.

[3] So G. FOHRER, *Introduction to the Old Testament*, Eng. Tr. by D. GREEN, London 1970, p. 442.

invite further questions whether this is the correct understanding
of its purpose. In the first place the use of the term "missionary" in
connection with the book's message is more of a hindrance than a
help. Jonah is clearly in no way to be thought of as a missionary
to Nineveh, and his actions are very different from those of the
Jews of a later age who "traversed sea and land to make a single
proselyte" (Matt. xxiii 15). It is also not clear that the message of
the book can be properly said to imply a need for missionary action
of any kind. God's mercy which is extended to the people of Nineveh
after their repentance and fasting is nowhere related to their embracing
of the torah, their rejection of idolatry, their acceptance of circumcision, nor even to so basic a feature as a confession that Yahweh
the God of Israel is the only true God. It is true that Nineveh and
its inhabitants are shown to be within reach of the divine mercy, but
such a broad assumption about Yahweh's dealings with nations is
evident very much earlier in the literature of the Old Testament.
In itself it does not go as far as the promise that non-Israelite nations
will know that Yahweh is God, as asserted by Ezekiel and Deutero-
Isaiah (Isa. xlix 26; Ezek. xxxvi 36, 38; xxxvii 28). There is certainly
no hint anywhere in the book that, in the light of his experience,
Jonah was to do anything about bringing other peoples to a comparable act of penitence as that displayed by the people of Nineveh.
On the contrary, the interest is entirely taken up with Jonah's own
reactions to what has happened and its meaning for his work as a
prophet. The Ninevites and their king appear only as vague and
unreal figures participating in the story as little more than shadows.
Moreover in the all-important concluding remark by God, which
asserts the sovereign freedom of his mercy, the description of the
Ninevites can only be described as derogatory: "they do not know
their right hand from their left" (Jon. iv 11). It is surely not the way
to win love and respect for people by describing them as so con-
temptuously ignorant! The reference to "much cattle" adds further
to the attitude of disregard for the Ninevites as real people. Throughout the story the city of Nineveh and its people are not presented
in any way which can readily be directly related to their historical
role as arch-enemies and oppressors of Israel for more than two
centuries.

    To this lack of any clear missionary appeal in the story, and the
rather contemptuous way in which the Ninevites are described, we
must add further objections to the accepted view of the purpose of

the book. The entire story fails to raise any single example of those issues which we know deeply affected the relationships of Jews with non-Jews in the post-exilic period. The questions of mixed language, mixed marriages and of the complexities raised by considerations of cultic holiness and pagan uncleanness are not mentioned. Nor in fact is any of those factors dealt with which made Jewish life in the diaspora a difficult experience, and which increasingly brought conflict and required rulings of a separatist nature: dietary laws, heathen sexual licence, idolatry, blasphemy and so on. Political issues too remain unmentioned. If the intention of the book of Jonah is to encourage Jews to display to the heathen a charity and love comparable to that which God displays to the Ninevites, then it does nothing to show how this should be done, and what actions are required to express it. These considerations become all the stronger once we reflect upon the fact that the so-called separatism of Nehemiah and Ezra was not so much concerned with making a distinction between Jew and Gentile, a distinction which had existed in Israel in national terms for centuries, but with a division between Jews and those who laid claim to being Jews. The issues which reveal themselves in the Chronicler's history are primarily those of a growing separation between communities living in the territories of Judah and Samaria regarding the status and obligations of those who claimed to be heirs of the promises given to Israel. It is not clear that the book of Jonah has anything to say to such factions, except that the worst may be accepted by God if they repent. The problem of this era was not that of disbelief in the universality of the divine mercy, but the difficulty of understanding how this was to be related to a number of very complex religious, racial and political issues.

Not only does the universalist-missionary interpretation of Jonah leave a complete silence on those questions which were most prominent in connection with the relationships between Jews and non-Jews, but it also leaves unexplained a significant part of the story. After we have set aside the psalm of chapter ii as a later addition we are still left with a lengthy introductory narrative recounting Jonah's call, flight, and abandonment, and his being saved by a fish. This would appear to have little bearing on the subsequent act of divine mercy toward Nineveh, except as a preface, heavily weighted with irony. Never was a journey more painful, yet apparently more unnecessary than Jonah's!

In general therefore we can sum up this review of the accepted
critical understanding of the purpose of the book of Jonah by af-
firming that it fails to account for important aspects of the story,
and that it rests very heavily upon certain assumptions and identi-
fications which have to be supplied from outside the narrative
proper. What then are we to make of the story?

First of all, as a question of general method, we must accept that
the purpose of the book is straightforward, and that it lies evident
within the narrative which we have. We should rule out therefore
any hidden allegorical meaning which relies upon finding equivalents
for the actors in the narrative, especially since there is no hint anywhere that this is required. In fact the usual critical interpretation
appears to have arisen precisely as a result of following such a view
and regarding Jonah as a typical Jew and the Ninevites as typical
Gentiles. Rather we must see that this is a story which should be
viewed as a whole in which the action is of primary significance.
The attitude of Jonah is entirely determined by his response to what
happens, rather than by his feelings for, or against, the Ninevites.
This is well brought out in Jon. iv 2 where Jonah says: "Is not this
what I said when I was still in my own country? That is why I fled
in haste to Tarshish; I knew that you are a gracious God, merciful,
patient and full of love. You change your mind about bringing
evil." We must begin then by briefly summarising the action of the
book in order to understand its true nature. Only in this way can we
see why Jonah's response to what transpires calls forth Yahweh's
rebuke.

The first part of the story is an account of the prophet's call,
which is full of humour and irony, but which essentially retains the
basic form of the prophetic call-narrative. The main action follows
this with an account of the prophet's preaching to the inhabitants
of Nineveh. Their solemn act of contrition expressed by their fasting
and wearing sackcloth, is followed by Yahweh's decision not to
bring upon them the evil which he had threatened. The final scene
centres upon the dialogue between God and Jonah in which Jonah
expresses his anger that the evil which God had threatened through
the mouth of his prophet had not been performed. This appeared
to Jonah to render his journey to Nineveh needless. That this is
not the case, however, is demonstrated to the prophet by the growth
and sudden withering of a plant. He is made to learn the lesson that,
since he can feel pity for the plant, it is also right that God should

feel pity for the Ninevites and therefore spare them. It is a straight-forward example of the formulation of an argument on the analogy existing between a minor case and a major one.

We can discover in this the purpose of the story. It is first and foremost a tale which demonstrates the possibility of a change of heart both for man and for God. The story seeks to show that, since repentance is a possibility for man, who may, like the king of Nineveh, "remove his robe, cover himself with sackcloth and sit in ashes" (Jon. iii 6), it is also a possibility for God. In the light of man's actions God may "repent of the evil which he has said that he will do" (Jon. iii 10). What Jonah is so angry about is not that the people who benefit from this divine change of plan are Ninevites, for it is never so much as hinted that this is the reason for his dis-pleasure, but that the divine plan has been changed at all. Thus it is a story about God and his relationship with men, rather than about the relationships of Jews with Gentiles. Throughout the story Jonah is quite innocent of any feelings whatever about the Ninevites. His concern is entirely taken up with his prophetic message and the fact that, after all the trouble he has taken to proclaim it, it remains empty of its threatened fulfilment. This is why the events relating to the prophet's call and flight are an essential part of the story. They emphasise by the forcefulness of their dramatic irony that the prophet really had been called by God to proclaim his message. In spite of seeking to avoid carrying out his divine commission, Jonah was nonetheless compelled by God's providential actions to do so, and to go to Nineveh to proclaim its downfall. Yet even after this remarkable divine compulsion, the threatened disaster did not materialise and Nineveh was spared. The two parts of the action, the prophet's call and his preaching to Nineveh, belong together. The prophet had indeed been called by God to threaten Nineveh with doom; yet, in spite of this, doom had not befallen the city. The reason is made explicitly clear by the explanation that the people of Nineveh had repented in sackcloth and ashes, and so in con-sequence God had changed his mind about bringing disaster upon them. What Jonah finds difficult to accept is that this should be so, and that God should retain such sovereign freedom to act in this way. It is simply a feature belonging to the chosen setting of the story that the people threatened should be Ninevites, for it makes no difference to the point that is being made whatever race or religion they belong to. The purpose of the book is to demonstrate the

nature of God's dealings with men, particularly in regard to the
bearing this has upon prophecy. When God passes a sentence of
death upon a people, as he does upon the Ninevites, he leaves a
way of salvation open to them in the possibility of repentance. As
far as the intention of the author is concerned it seems primarily to
have been his purpose to show that such a way of salvation was a
possibility for Israel.

If this is the intention of the book then we must go on to consider
its religious background in order to see why it was important to make
such an assertion. Why was it necessary to demonstrate by such a
story that man is free to repent, and that this repentance will affect
the subsequent actions of God? It is because this point is assumed to be
obvious that scholars have failed previously to recognise it as the
primary aim of the book. Yet the point is not obvious, and the more
carefully we look at the form and character of prophecy in the Old
Testament, the more important it is that we should recognise the
way in which it only gradually acquired the character of a call to
repentance. From being on the fringe of the prophetic preaching
we find that a summons to repentance and a return to Yahweh was
brought more and more into its centre. This is well shown by the
revealing summary of what the prophetic preaching is about given
by the Deuteronomic Historian in 2 Kings xvii 13: "Yet Yahweh
warned Israel and Judah by every prophet and every seer, saying,
'Turn from your evil ways and keep my commandments and my
statutes, in accordance with all the law which I commanded your
ancestors, and which I sent to you by my servants the prophets'."
As a summary of the contents of the prophetic literature this is a
very striking and unexpected description, for nowhere in the collections of the sayings of the great pre-exilic prophets do they actually
address Israel or Judah in such terms. Basically the preaching of the
prophets consisted of an announcement of what God was about to
do, usually presented as a threat, backed up by the reason for God's
intention to act in this way. It was certainly possible to take this
as a fixed and unalterable decision, coming as it did from God.
Such a fatalistic understanding of the prophetic word, however,
is one that is opposed by the author of Jonah, although there is
evidence in the Old Testament that it was certainly held by some
in ancient Israel to be true, just as it has found many adherents since.
Admittedly most of the great prophets of the Old Testament do
appeal to their hearers to return to God, but they can only leave

open the question of what the future will be if this should happen. To sum up the prophetic message as a whole as a call to repentance is a very marked abbreviation of its great variety and its relationship to specific events. When, however, we look at the literature of the sixth century B.C. we find clearly that the theme of repentance has come more into the forefront of thought. In the book of Jeremiah, especially in its Deuteronomistic sections, the appeal for repentance becomes prominent,[4] and this is brought out still further in the overall structure and aim of the Deuteronomic History.[5] When we turn to the prophet Ezekiel we find similarly a new concern with the theme of repentance,[6] and more generally when we consider the way in which the collections of the preaching of the pre - exilic prophets have been edited, it becomes evident that such redaction saw in these words a continuing call for Israel to return to Yahweh.

The first piece of evidence in support of this view of the purpose of the book of Jonah is supplied by the reference to Jonah ben Amittai, the prophet who was from Gath-hepher, in 2 Kings. In 2 Kings xiv 25 this prophet is referred to as one who prophesied during the reign of Jeroboam the son of Joash, i.e. Jeroboam II (786-746 B.C.), and this is undoubtedly of significance for us since it is the only reference to the prophet Jonah outside the book about him. This Jonah is said to have prophesied that God would restore and expand the borders of Israel, which was fulfilled by the strong expansionist policy of Jeroboam II. Such an achievement posed questions against the impartiality of the divine justice since Jeroboam is said to have done "what was evil in the eyes of Yahweh", and it is reported that he "did not turn aside from all the sins of Jeroboam the son of Nebat" (2 Kings xiv 24). There are in consequence two appended comments to explain why God should have acted favourably towards Israel in his reign, in apparent contradiction to the demands of a just retribution of good and evil. The first of these comments concerns the wretched condition into which Israel had fallen, and which evoked the divine pity: "the affliction of Israel was very bitter, for there was none left, bond or free, and there was none to help Israel" (2 Kings xiv 26). The second of these comments is more cryptic and obscure, and may very well be an addition to the

---

[4] Cf. Jer. xviii 11; xxv 5; xxvi 3; xxix 10-14; xxxvi; xxxvii.

[5] Cf. H. W. WOLFF, "Das Kerygma des deuteronomistischen Geschichtswerks", *Ges. Stud. zum A.T.* (Th.B.22), 1973², pp. 315ff.

[6] So especially Ezek. xviii 1ff.

original Deuteronomic History: "But Yahweh had not said that
he would blot out the name of Israel from under heaven" (2 Kings
xiv 27). This verse has been the subject of an interesting study by
F. Crüsemann which has relevance for our conclusions.[7] To what
does this comment refer? Where might it have been thought that
Yahweh had said that he would blot out the name of Israel from
under heaven? Crüsemann concludes very convincingly that this
must be a reference to the preaching of Amos, who was active
during the period of Jeroboam's reign, and whose message was
that the end was about to befall Israel (Amos viii 2). Yet, as the
Deuteronomic Historian understood it, the end had not overtaken
Israel at this time. Amos's threats against the continued existence
of the Northern Kingdom seem clearly to have been taken to mean
that an end was about to befall all Israel; hence the need for the
inclusion of this comment in the narrative at this point. This is
precisely the problem that is taken up by the book of Jonah, although
it is dealt with in an entirely different way. When a prophet says that
a city or a people is about to be overthrown (cf. Jon. iii 4) it does
not necessarily mean that they will be destroyed, because there is
always the possibility that the people may repent. There would
then be a new situation of which God would take account. The
prophetic announcement of total disaster is not a forewarning of
an inflexibly determined fate, for history always lies open to the
sovereign freedom of God. This suggests that there is good reason
for thinking that the author of the book of Jonah was quite clearly
conscious of the setting of this prophet in history. Jonah belonged
to the age of Amos, when the message of doom had sounded forth
upon Israel in no uncertain terms. In the light of subsequent events
this message had been proved tragically close to the truth. First
with the overthrow of the Northern Kingdom and then with the
fall of Judah the people of Israel, as they had once been, had come
near to the point of death. For many this appeared to be God's
final word to his people, as Ezekiel had once hinted when he took
up the very words and message of Amos (Ezek. vii 5-13).

It is not surprising in consequence that the mood which overtook
those who survived this calamity was one of despair and resignation
to a hopeless fate. Twice in the prophetic literature of the exile we

---

[7] F. Crüsemann, "Kritik an Amos im deuteronomistischen Geschichtswerk",
Probleme biblische Theologie (G. von Rad Festschrift), ed. H. W. Wolff, München
1971, pp. 57-63.

find quoted a saying that was current at this time: "The fathers have eaten sour grapes and the children's teeth are blunted" (Ezek. xviii 2; Jer. xxxi 29). It is essentially a saying of despair, pointing to the people's sufferings as an inevitable fate from which they cannot escape. In Ezekiel xviii we have a long and discursive argument by the prophet aimed at showing that the reasoning behind such a saying was false, and that God had no desire that the wicked should die.[8] Rather it was his will that he should turn from his way and live (Ezek. xviii 23). By citing the example of particular cases in a methodically legal way Ezekiel demonstrates that "if a wicked man turns away from all his sins which he has committed and keeps all God's statutes and does what is lawful and right, he shall surely live; he shall not die" (Ezek. xviii 21). This is exactly the message of the book of Jonah, for this is precisely what happens to the Ninevites when they demonstrate their contrition by putting on sackcloth and ashes. They too can live.

We find the same theme developed in a comparable way in Jer. xxxi 29f., where the same despairing saying is cited: "In those days they shall no longer say: 'The fathers have eaten sour grapes, and the children's teeth are blunted.' Every one will die for his own sin; each person who eats sour grapes, his teeth shall be blunted." Here in this Deuteronomistic passage in Jeremiah the emphasis upon the freedom of the individual to repent and to save his life is less clearly brought out than in Ezekiel, but essentially it is the same message. God does not appoint a predetermined fate for men from which they cannot escape, but he deals with each individual for what he is and does.

Even more extensively and clearly the assertion of the freedom given to Israel to repent is brought out in the Deuteronomic History. Here, as M. NOTH points out,[9] there are surprisingly lacking the firm assurances of hope and restoration that one might have expected in a document coming from Judah after the catastrophe of 587 B.C. Yet it is difficult to see why the writer should have gone to such trouble to assert the justice of God's dealings with Israel if he had no hope at all for its future.[10] The answer to this problem must be that the aim of the authors of the history is to show that God has

---

[8] Cf. W. ZIMMERLI, *Ezechiel* (BKAT XIII/1), Neukirchen, 1969, pp. 413ff.

[9] M. NOTH, *Überlieferungsgeschichtliche Studien* I, Tübingen, rep. 1957, pp. 107f.

[10] Cf. G. VON RAD, *Old Testament Theology*, I, Eng. tr. by D. M. G. STALKER, London 1965, pp. 343ff.

given to his people room for repentance. The story of the nation's past is recounted in such a way as to show that when the people sinned they were justly punished. Yet this necessity for punishment did not rob God of his initiative nor frustrate his saving purpose, for whenever Israel's transgressions brought disaster upon them, when they repented Yahweh established a way of deliverance. For this divine power to save to become effective it was necessary that Israel should turn away from its sins and return to Yahweh. It is not difficult to find illustrations of this in the accounts of the judges and the kings. Overall the authors of the history see the Israel of their day plunged into a situation of defeat and oppression from which they can be freed only if they return to Yahweh. How he will deliver them is left open to an undetermined future, and the authors' concern is simply to demonstrate that Israel lives at a time when its one hope is to repent and to return to Yahweh. Israel can live, if first it is prepared to turn aside from its evil ways and return to God. God himself will then appoint his own way of salvation and will raise up his own chosen agents of deliverance.

We can cite a further area of Old Testament literature in support of the view that, in the aftermath of the exile, a deep and widespread concern grew up among those circles which looked for the restoration of Israel, to assert the necessity of repentance as the key to Israel's future. This lies in the editing of the prophetic literature generally, and especially in the books of Jeremiah and Ezekiel. The former book has passed through a most extensive process of editing and supplementation at the hands of Deuteronomic writers. Their concern is to bring out the message of hope which exists for Israel by showing the rightness of the punishment which has been inflicted upon Judah, and the assurance of restoration which Yahweh has given through his prophet Jeremiah. In this respect these writers carry the theology of the Deuteronomic movement a stage further than has been done in the History by spelling out much more clearly the message of hope of Israel's restoration. This hope is centred upon a return of the Babylonian exiles to their land and the rebirth of a united Israel under a Davidic king (Jer. xxxi 16-22; xxxii 42-44; xxxiii 14-26). Similarly in the book of Ezekiel the severe indictments of Israel for its sins, which serve to explain the threats which the prophet uttered against Jerusalem, have been supplemented by assurances of restoration, which give to them in their present form a very illogical conclusion (cf. Ezek. xvi 53-63; xx 33-38). These reassuring prophecies can have been added to the original indictments, only after the events of 587 B.C. were seen to have fulfilled their threatening contents. Why then did the prophet's hearers wish to retain the threats at all, if their forewarnings had been fulfilled? The answer must be that by preserving the threats and supplementing them with words of hope for Israel's restoration, they served together as an urgent appeal to the people to recognise the justice of God's ways and to return to him. Thereby they became an appeal for repentance. To have preserved the threats without the appended words of hope would have left the prophetic message open to the misunderstanding that it pronounced an irrevocably determined fate from which Israel could not escape. The addition of the words of hope shows that this is not so, and points to the credibility of repentance as a step towards salvation. It is precisely this theme that is the subject of the book of Jonah.

We can then bring together certain conclusions about this book. First of all it appears to have been written with a full awareness of the Jonah ben Amittai of 2 Kings xiv 25 before the author, who has fastened upon this prophet, not because he was an ardent nationalist, but because of the significant age in which he lived. Its purpose is to assert the possibility of repentance, involving a complete change of heart on man's part, of which God will then take full account in his dealings with him. This is related to the fact of prophecy which had acquired a unique and lasting importance for Israel as a result of the warnings given by the prophets of the downfall of both its kingdoms. To many the warnings must have appeared as God's last word to his people and to have constituted a death sentence from which there could be no reprieve. Yet all men may repent, even the most hardened sinner and the most ungodly of men. Thus the book of Jonah takes its setting from a historical situation in which Israel was heavily oppressed by the Assyrians. Nineveh and its inhabitants appear in the story because they are appropriate to this chosen historical setting. There is no attempt anywhere in the book to present the Ninevites as typical Gentiles, nor to explore in any fashion at all the complex questions relating to the relationships between Jews and non-Jews. Nor is any serious effort made to consider, or to pronounce upon, the issue of the ultimate fate of Gentile nations and peoples. In the story Jonah's dealings are almost exclusively with God, and the people of Nineveh are simply background figures, necessary for the story, but of no real interest to Jonah. That the book is included among the prophets is entirely appropriate, for although it is about prophecy, and is not a collection of explicit prophecies, the subject with which it deals is a truly prophetic one. This is in no way to deny that its narrative style and didactic techniques have affinities with wisdom. It would be surprising if it were not so in view of the wide connections of wisdom with instruction in general and the narrative arts in particular. As to the question of the date of the book we should perhaps look to a slightly earlier era than that usually ascribed to it. Thus we can consider the end of the sixth century B.C. as a period when its message would have been most particularly relevant, and as the age when the problem with which it deals is most extensively attested. That it could have arisen at a somewhat later time must also be admitted, since it cannot be held to belong to any one narrowly defined period. The theme of Jonah is the possibility of man's repentance, and its purpose is to show that where this occurs among men then it elicits a related change of purpose on the part of God.

MOSES VERSUS AMALEK

Aetiology and Legend in Exod. xvii 8-16

BY

G. W. COATS

Lexington

The narration in Exod. xvii 8-16 provokes interest, not only because it reports an ancient battle between the Amalekites and Israel, with Israel on the defensive, but also because it appears to be so completely isolated from its context. It has nothing to do with the complex of stories about Israel murmuring against Moses and Yahweh, just preceding it in Exod. xiv 1-xvii 7. It has no clear contacts with the traditions about Moses and his father-in-law, following in Exod. xviii.[1] Moreover, the allusion in xvii 8 to Rephidim stands in loose relationship to the narration itself and probably represents an accommodation of the pericope to the itinerary chain structuring the wilderness journey as a whole.[2] The narration thus functions as a part of the wilderness theme in the final redaction of the Pentateuch. But it fails to make use of basic motifs from the wilderness traditions. Moses makes no appeal to Yahweh for direction in the face of the Amalekite threat. Yahweh offers no instructions for meeting the crisis. There is no obvious divine protection from the enemy, no divine leadership, no divine initiative at all.[3] Indeed, neither the wilderness theme nor any of

---

[1] Exod. xviii is also isolated from its context. Brevard S. CHILDS, *The Book of Exodus; A Critical Theological Commentary* (*OTL*; Philadelphia: Westminster; and London: SCM Press, 1974), 326-329. CHILDS notes the shift by emphasizing that the writer slows the pace of his narrative, looking back at what has happened. "In ch. 18 the writer returns to Moses, the man."

[2] On the function of the itinerary as a structuring device for the wilderness theme, cf. George W. COATS, "The Wilderness Itinerary," *CBQ* XXXIV (1972), 135-152. On the isolation of this pericope, cf. Jakob H. GRØNBÆK, "Juda und Amalek. Überlieferungsgeschichtliche Erwägungen zu Exodus 17:8-16," *ST* XVIII (1964), 32. On the secondary character of the place name, cf. Martin NOTH, *A History of Pentateuchal Traditions*, trs. Bernhard W. ANDERSON (Englewood Cliffs; Prentice-Hall, 1972), 120, no. 340.

[3] The "rod of God," in *vs.* 9 carries the single reference to God in the narration of the event, apart from the aetiological elements in *vss.* 14-16. The aetiological elements do not point to this particular battle, however, but to coming perpetual

the other major structuring categories so commonly cited for analysis of the Pentateuch provide anything more than superficial
context for this account.

What, then, can account for the position of this pericope at just
this point in the Pentateuch? Indeed, what can most adequately
account for its presence in the Pentateuch at all? This question
proves more pressing when one considers the appearance of the same
tradition, although not in the same form, at other places in the
Old Testament (cf. particularly Deut. xxv 17-19 and 1 Sam. xv 2-3).
Thus, the governing question: Why does the tradition appear in
this particular form at just this particular place in the structure
of the Pentateuch?

I. FORM-CRITICAL ANALYSIS

J. Phillip HYATT suggests that "the narrative here is an aetiological
story, designed to explain the origin of the perpetual hostility between
Israel and Amalek, and also the origin of an altar, probably in the
vicinity of Kadesh, which had the name 'Yahweh is my banner' ".[4]
In so far as the final form of the story is concerned, HYATT's observation is accurate. Two aetiological elements appear at the end of
the unit, *vs.* 14 and *vss.* 15-16. And both relate to Israel's struggle
with the Amalekites. Their appearance here thus casts the unit as
an aetiology. Moreover, both elements point to a divine dimension
in the tradition. In *vs.* 14, the commitment to destroy the Amalekites
by blotting out their remembrance "from under the heavens" appears in a Yahweh speech to Moses. And in *vss.* 15-16 the altar
constructed by Moses carries a name which, though a bit obscure,
connects with an affirmation of Yahweh's perpetual war with the
Amalekites. With these elements, therefore, the impression of divine
absence in the unit is softened.

Yet, the aetiological elements are clearly secondary in the unit.

---

warfare with Amalek. It would be difficult to conclude that the event described
here derives from divine intervention simply on the basis of *vs.* 9. Cf. the discussion below.

[4] J. Phillip HYATT, *Exodus* (*New Century Bible*; London: Oliphants, 1917), 183.
For a similar position, cf. Martin NOTH, *Exodus, a Commentary*, trs. J. S. BOWDEN
(*OTL*; Philadelphia: Westminster, and SCM Press: London, 1962) 141. Kurt
MÖHLENBRINK, "Josua in Pentateuch," *ZAW* LIX (1942/43), 16-24. MÖHLEN-
BRINK agrees with this conclusion, suggesting moreover that the two aetiological
elements point to two recensions in the tradition, one with its center on Moses,
and the other and older with its center on Joshua. The Moses recension would
have converted the original form of the tradition from its Joshua center.

In both cases, the reference to Yahweh's relationship with the Amalekites develops a promise for what Yahweh is going to do, not what he has already done (cf. also Deut. xxv 17-19). In *vs.* 14 this point is clear by virtue of the verbal construction *kî māḥōh 'emḥeh.* And in *vs.* 16, the emphasis falls, not on this particular battle, but on a war of Yahweh against Amalek which will continue throughout the generations (*middōr dōr*). Brevard CHILDS highlights this problem by observing the rough connection between this perpetual enmity and the victory described in Exod. xvii.[5] Do the aetiological elements not tie more readily with that facet of this tradition that remembers a disastrous defeat inflicted by Amalek, such as is reflected in Deut. xxv 17-19? Thus, it would seem to me to be clear that the aetiological elements are not rooted intrinsically in the preceding verses but stand as an appendix.[6]

The one possible exception to this point lies in the argument that the stone in *vs.* 12 constitutes a parallel to the altar in *vss.* 15-16. The two would be a double explanation for an important stone at some particular locality. In that case, the second aetiological element would be rooted in an indispensable part of the story and suggest a primary function of the unit as aetiology.[7] Yet, the stone itself demands no particular emphasis in the movement of the narration. And no explicit tie to the stone can be seen in the aetiological elements. The aetiological character of the pericope thus appears to me to be secondary and unessential for the narration in *vss.* 8-13.[8] To limit discussion of the unit to its character as aetiology would thus misrepresent the basic movement of the whole.

The narration in *vss.* 8-13 reveals a structural design and intention

---

[5] CHILDS, p. 313.

[6] NOTH, *History*, p. 120, n. 343. This point seems justified to me. To define other elements of disunity in the narrative, leading to two distinct versions of the story, is not. Against MÖHLENBRINK, p. 18.

[7] NOTH, *Exodus*, p. 143. HYATT, p. 185, also notes some possibility for connecting the stone in *vs.* 12 with *kēs²yāh*, taking that phrase with the Vul., Sam. Pent., and Syr. as "throne of Yahweh." Cf. Rudolf SMEND, *Yahweh War and Tribal Confederation*, trs. Max ROGERS (Nashville: Abingdon, 1970), 79-80.

[8] The tradition in this unit may have been intended originally to explain the origin of the perpetual hostility between Israel and Amalek. Other appearances of the tradition concentrate on that facet. But if that is the case, the tradition history does not facilitate an exegesis of *this* narration very effectively. For even though the aetiological elements cast the final form of the unit as such an aetiology, the basic core in *vss.* 8-13 has no such interest. So, CHILDS, p. 315. Cf. Burke O. LONG, *The Problem of Etiological Narrative in the Old Testament* (*BZAW* CVIII; Berlin: Töpelmann, 1968), for principles in evaluating the question.

quite distinct from an aetiology. The account opens in *vs.* 8 with an announcement of the attack by the Amalekites. The body of the pericope, *vss.* 9-12, then focuses on *Moses'* response to the attack, not Joshua's, not even Yahweh's. That response breaks down into two major sections. The first, *vs.* 9, is a Moses speech, unveiling his plans for defense to Joshua. The speech details two particular facets: A) Under the commission of Moses, Joshua will select an army and head the fight with Amalek. B) Moses will go to the top of the hill with the "rod of God" in his hand. The second major section, *vss.* 10-12, reports how those plans were carried out. And the structure of the report follows the same twofold pattern of the speech: A) *Vs.* 10a picks up Joshua's work, while B) *vss.* 10b-12 describe Moses' work. The distinction in these descriptions between Joshua's work (A) and Moses' work (B) can be felt most obviously in length, and the distinction in length alone points to the structural emphasis on Moses. But that is not all. The description of Joshua's work carries the primary report that a battle was fought. But no details of the battle appear. The rise and fall of the battle come in the second part, the fruits of Moses' work. For when Moses holds his hands high the tide of the battle moves to Israel. But when he lets them fall, the tide turns to the Amalekites. Indeed, the outcome of the battle depends on Moses' ability to stay at his job. There is, then, no sound of clashing armies in this battle report. There is no blood and death. There is only the weariness of the central figure.

The narration concludes in *vs.* 13 with a report of the battle's outcome. The subject of the verb in this verse in Joshua. "Joshua mowed down Amalek and his people with the edge of the sword". But Joshua's position in this element does not elevate him in importance over Moses. To the contrary, his job is simple, a mopping-up action dependent on Moses' stamina and faithfulness at his post (cf. 1 Sam. xiv 6-15).

It would seem to be clear, then, that structure in this unit puts central weight on Moses, with his faithfulness and stamina the source of a major victory over an enemy. Several problems, at least, confront this conclusion.

First, if Moses is the central figure, with the focus of the unit on his crucial role, would not Aaron and Hur blur the focus? To hold one's hands high from morning to the setting sun is a virtue of outstanding quality, even for Moses. But when his arms grow weary, Aaron and Hur provide assistance. Would not that assistance detract from a central focus on Moses? Martin NOTH makes the point: "Yet here again some rivals, who are now insignificant, appear alongside of Moses, prompting one to conjecture that they have been pushed into their present subordinate position through a subsequent emergence of Moses in this particular narrative . . . Originally they were presumably the ones who carried out the action that was effective in granting victory. . . . It cannot at any rate be maintained that the figure of Moses is especially firmly anchored in Ex. 17:18ff."[9] The text itself, however, cannot support NOTH's conjecture. The tradition history behind the text may not have given Moses a role in this battle. But this narrative moves to the other extreme. Moreover, one cannot assume from the assistance Aaron and Hur give to Moses that Moses was never the central figure. A central figure in OT tradition, particularly a warrior in the field, commonly has a companion who serves him, an armorbearer (cf. 1 Sam. xiv 6-15; xxxi 1-7). But the armorbearer does not eclipse the role of his master.[10] The same point applies for Aaron and Hur. Their assistance emphasizes Moses' *weariness* to the very brink of his endurance. But their assistance also emphasizes his faithfulness to his task, his stamina in the face of limitations on his strength. He will do what he must do to win the battle even if it is beyond the normal limitations of his strength.

Second, Jakob H. GRØNBÆK, argues forcefully that this tradition must be taken as holy war tradition. "Moses führt den Israeliten eine Kraft zu, und diese Kraft kommt von Jahwe. So ist der Sieg über die Amalekiter der Sieg Jahwes, welches aber keineswegs ausschliesst, dass Josua es ist, der die Amalekiter mit dem Schwert schlägt. . . ."[11] And, one might add, this point would also not preclude the tradition's placing emphasis on the figure of Moses. But would the point not suggest that the primary focus falls, not so much on Moses, the servant of God, as on God, the source of the power for the victory? Particularly if the holy war element is understood explicitly as Yahweh war, the focus of the tradition must fall, not on Moses, but on Yahweh. *Vs.* 9b is crucial for this question:

---

[9] NOTH, *History*, p. 166. I see no evidence for reconstructing a Joshua form of the tradition as the Vorlage for the Moses tradition. The figure of Joshua is incidental in the text, always functioning as the servant of Moses, not as a primary figure in his own right. Against MÖHLENBRINK.

[10] On the role of the assistant in medieval legends, cf. Jan DE VRIES *Heroic Song and Heroic Legend*, trs. B. J. TIMMER (London: Oxford, 1963), 189-190.

[11] GRØNBÆK, p. 43. Cf. also SMEND, p. 103.

Moses announces that he will go to the top of the hill with the "rod of God" (*ûmaṭṭēh hā'ᵉlōhîm*) in his hand.[12] Would this designation not undergird GRØNBÆK's point, since the power Moses exerts is associated in some way with the rod and the rod derives finally from God (cf. Exod. iv 1-5)?

One way to resolve the problem is to consider this unique phrase as an insignificant and secondary facet of the narration since it has no function at all in the following verses.[13] Yet, the rod and the uplifted hand are parallel, as Hugo GRESSMANN suggested.[14] The parallel relationship can be substantiated by reference to the same parallel construction in Exod. xiv 16.[15] Is it possible, then, that only *hā'ᵉlōhîm* is secondary in this text, a pious gloss intended to give the unit a divine aura it does not otherwise have? Such an alternative can offer nothing more than speculation. The crucial point is that for both Exod. xiv and Exod. xvii the outstretched hand with its parallel in the outstretched rod is crucial for the emergence of the miraculous event. And certainly it is not possible to eliminate both elements as secondary. Moreover, the "rod of God" does nothing more in Exod. xvii than the rod without such a qualification in Exod.

---

[12] Hugo GRESSMANN, *Mose und seine Zeit, ein Kommentar zu den Mose-Sagen* (*FRLANT* XVIII; Göttingen: Vandenhoeck und Ruprecht, 1913), 157-160. In commenting on the connection between the rod and the aetiological elements, he observes: "Damit ist deutlich ausgesprochen, daß Jahwe mit dem Mose-Stabe identisch ist oder wenigstens aufs engste zusammengehört."

[13] NOTH, *Exodus*, p. 142. Part of the problem in this verse is the designation of the rod as the rod of God, a specification that occurs rarely in the exodus or wilderness traditions (cf. also Exod. iv 20). In fact, the rod is labelled at other points in the traditions quite explicitly as Moses' rod (cf. Exod. vii 19; viii 12; xiv 16).

[14] GRESSMANN, p. 158.

[15] Again, a textual problem arises. The parallel in Exod. xiv involves the rod without the designation "rod of God." But no question can be raised about whether the rod in Exod. xiv is traditio-historically the same phenomenon as the rod in Exod. xvii. Of more importance, the parallel in Exod. xiv involves the rod and the hand of Moses, cast as a singular noun. In Exod. xvii 8-11 the parallel is again between the rod and the *hand* of Moses, cast as a singular noun. But in *vs.* 12 the noun shifts to a plural form. HYATT, p. 184, asks: "Do we have here the conflation of two traditions, one emphasizing the rod in the hand of Moses, the other his lifting up of both hands alone?" MÖHLENBRINK, pp. 16-24, develops a similar position, casting the uplifted hands as an act of prayer (cf. particularly p. 19, and the commentaries he cites there). But that position is difficult to maintain (so, NOTH, *Exodus*, p. 142). Yet, the identity between the uplifted hand, with no rod at least explicitly in it, and the hands outstretched over the enemy seems strong to me. Evidence for two traditions is rather slim. Can we not more adequately explain the shift from singular to plural just in *vs.* 12 as an effort to accommodate the story to *two* assistants who supported Moses when he grew weary?

xiv or, for that matter, the hand in either tradition. Whether the designation of the rod as the rod of God is secondary, or the whole phrase is secondary does not alter the basic gesture. Moses stretches out the symbol of his power. And that act effects the event. The power derives from Yahweh. There is no doubt about that. But the only reference to God in the entire section of narrative in *vss.* 8-13 is hardly firm affirmation for contending that a major point of the unit is recognition of Yahweh's power. That element is simply not present.

How, then, is the rod/hand parallel to be understood? Does the parallel belong to plague tradition vocabulary and thus place the Moses-Amalek tradition back into the general organization of traditions around the exodus theme?[16] That alternative seems to me to be the weakest of any. There is no reference here to oppression by an unrelenting master. The enemy is not the Egyptian hoard. This tradition stands totally outside the framework of the theological organization that dominates the exodus theme. Yet, the rod in this pericope cannot be disassociated from the rod Moses employs in his dealings with the Pharaoh (cf. Exod. iv 20). It is possible to suggest that the rod appears in this text by virtue of its proximity with the Meribah story in Exod. xvii 1-7.[17] But that alternative does not seem to me to be viable. But even if one were able to show that the object enters this text as a part of the redaction bringing several stories together, he would still have the outstretched hand as a parallel that demands explanation. A more attractive alternative is to consider the rod, even the "rod of God", and its parallel in the hand of Moses as a motif that is peculiar to neither the exodus theme nor the wilderness theme, but to traditions centering in some manner on Moses. Albeit rooted in God's power, the rod is the instrument of the wonder-worker and characteristic of Moses traditions wherever they might appear.[18]

---

[16] Brevard S. CHILDS, "A Traditio-Historical Study of the Red Sea Tradition," *VT* XX (1970), 409, observes: "Whereas in the JE accounts the imagery associated with the plagues is entirely missing in the sea account, the reverse is true for P. Again the plague imagery returns: . . . 'Moses stretches out his hand.' (xiv 21)."

[17] GRØNBÆK, p. 33.

[18] CHILDS, *Exodus*, pp. 313-315, calls attention to the parallel in Balaam's curse. "In Ex. 17 the hands are the instruments of mediating power, as is common throughout the Ancient Near East. . . . This amoral element of the unleashing of power through an activity or a stance is still reflected in the story." To explore the "magical" element in this act contributes very little more in an evaluation of the narrative.

Still, must we not attach this tradition to the general collection of traditions about Yahweh war? Is this not a holy war, with the focus of attention thus by definition not on Moses, as it would seem on the surface, but on God?[19] First, it must be admitted that holy war motifs do appear here, and even more strongly in the Exod. xiv parallel. Thus, the instructions to select men (*beḥar-lānû*), implying a smaller band than was necessary, and the results of the battle cast as mowing down the enemy with the edge of the sword (*wayyaḥalōš yehôšuaʿ. . . . lepî-ḥāreb*) can stand in the context of holy war.[20] Second, the battle is for Israel clearly defensive. Moreover, the allusions to the tradition in Deut. xxv 17-19 and I Sam. xv 2, with no reference to Moses, as well as the aetiological elements would support the point. The traditio-historical background of the unit may well be rooted in holy war tradition from the tribe of Judah. Yet, this unit shifts the focus away from the battle. The structure of the unit places the center of gravity on the main strength of a single figure. Why would a holy war story pay so little attention to the details of the war? Why would its narration shift from the scene of the battle to a single vigil above the battle? And of even more importance, how can a holy war story fail to note that it was Yahweh, not Moses, who gave the enemy into the hands of the Israelites?[21]

It seems clear to me, then, that this pericope cannot be adequately described as an aetiology, although the final form of the unit has been transformed into aetiology by the appendix. Nor can it be adequately understood as a battle report with its roots in holy war tradition. Nor can one say that *this unit* was originally an Aaron story or a Hur story or a Joshua story. Indeed, one cannot even say with clarity that the unit is a story. Its structure maintains no consistent point of tension, but rather relies on relatively disjointed notations in order to emphasize, not the battle as an event in God's dealings with his people, but the stamina and faithfulness of Moses to his task. The point can be seen clearly in *vs.* 12, set in the contrast between the observation that "the hands of Moses were weary"

---

[19] So, GRØNBÆK, p. 44.

[20] The point can be supported by reference to Exod. xiv 13-14, 16, 25, 27, 30; Josh. vi 1-21.

[21] So, cf. SMEND, pp. 110-111. Num. xxi 21-31 also fails to note such an explicit attribution of success to Yahweh (but contrast Num. xxi 34). But there is a specific reason for its absence. The land of Transjordan is understood by the tradition as less than hallowed ground (cf. Josh. xxii 19) and thus not derived as an explicit gift from Yahweh's hand.

(*wîdê Môšeh kᵉbēdîm*) and the observation, "his hands were steady" (*wayᵉhî yādāyw ᵉᵃmûnāh*). The key term *ᵉᵃmûnāh*, connotes particularly faithfulness to an official task, not necessarily a military one (cf. 2 K. xii 16, xxii 7; 2 Chr. xxxiv 12. Cf. also 1 Chr. ix 22). And it is that faithfulness, depicted here in physical exertion, highlighted by the extended period of time and the struggle to maintain its standards, that carries the narration. As a narration designed to emphasize such virtue, the unit (particularly in *vss.* 8-13) can most adequately be understood as legend.[22] Moreover, its quality as legend is specifically *heroic*, even with the assistants and the field general.[23] The stamina of one man defines the quality and stature of *the* giant from Israel's past.

II. Structural and Theological Context

How, then, are we to understand the context for a heroic legend in the middle of the Pentateuch? The break between the murmuring stories (Exod. xiv 1-xvii 7) and the Sinai narrative (Exod. xix 1ff.) provides a seam in the redaction of the whole and thus a natural place to include distinct tradition elements. But is there any way to account for a heroic legend, with its focus on Moses, appearing in the middle of traditions classically understood as narrations of Yahweh's initiative in saving Israel? Does the heroic legend have any antecedents? Or is it totally isolated, not only from its immediate context, but also in the overall structure of the Pentateuch?

There are other Moses traditions with heroic motifs, also somewhat roughly integrated into the structural themes centering in the exodus and the wilderness.[24] The birth story, Exod. ii, contrasts with the introduction to the exodus theme in Exod. i, as Gressmann noted.[25] The one depicts the Pharaoh's desire to kill Hebrew male children in order to resolve the Hebrew problem and his anxiety over it. The other shows the Pharaoh attacking the Hebrew problem

---

[22] Ron M. Hals, "Legend: A Case Study in OT Form-Critical Terminology," *CBQ* XXXIV (1972), 166-176. I cannot see that the basic character of the narrative as *legend* has been altered by the aetiological elements. Rather, the aetiological elements appear as extrinsic additions. The latest form of the narrative is thus not simply aetiology, but legend plus aetiological appendices.

[23] For a definition of heroic, cf. de Vries, p. 180. For a slightly different approach, cf. H. Munro Chadwick and N. Hershaw Chadwick, *The Growth of Literature* (Cambridge: University Press, 1932), 1-18.

[24] The traditions derive almost entirely from J or JE. P seems to have conceived the Moses tradition in a different garb. Cf. Noth, *History*, pp. 262-276.

[25] Gressmann, pp. 1-4.

by heavy, oppressive labor. A combination of the two has the Pharaoh killing off his labor force, a problematic point of tension in final narration. The Moses-Jethro story, also in Exod. ii, stands over against the basic themes of the call narrative in Exod. iii, presenting Moses as a figure who by his show of strength wins his position in the household of Jethro, including one of his host's daughters as a wife.[26] Exod. xviii may perhaps appear also as a distinct tradition, structured into the Pentateuch at the redactional seam that offers position to the Moses-Amalek legend. And the narration presents Moses as the story-teller, with an impressive and successful account to tell. Finally, Deut. xxxiv incorporates heroic motifs into the Moses death report. And the report functions as a final pinpointing of Mosaic virtues.[27] To suggest that these traditions show rough integration with the structural themes of the exodus and the wilderness is not to say that they are antithetical to those themes. To the contrary, they complement in many respects the overall pattern. The birth of Moses sets the leader in Egypt, in a position of power, ready to observe the oppressed state of his people. The Jethro tradition provides a distinctive context for the call narrative. But they can also compete with the theological interests centering in Yahweh's initiatives, as I believe to be the case in the Moses-Amalek legend. I would suggest, then, that two complementing, at points competing, structural patterns must be recognized when one attempts to control the form-critical problem of the Pentateuch or Hexateuch. One is the general system of themes, centered around Yahweh's initiative on Israel's behalf. NOTH, ZIMMERLI, and VON RAD have defined the programmatic lines of these elements. The other is a system of heroic structure, centered around Moses' initiative on Israel's behalf. The two come together in the plague stories, even in the murmuring stories. Or the one can be elevated over the other (cf. Deut. xxxiv 6; Num. xxi 33-35). But in overall pattern they maintain a balance, an intricate interweaving of themes. This suggestion, incidentally, would shed some light on the Pentateuch-Hexateuch question. For the one scheme of structure would presuppose completion in Joshua, while the other would specifically prohibit continuation into Joshua.

---

[26] Cf. George W. COATS, "Moses in Midian," *JBL* XCII (1973), 3-10.

[27] Cf. George W. COATS, "Legendary Motifs in the Moses Death Reports," in *Proceedings of the Sixth World Congress of Jewish Studies* (Jerusalem: World Union of Jewish Studies, 1975).

In the final analysis, however, the most pressing difficulty regarding context for the heroic pattern in the Pentateuch is not structural but theological. God takes the initiative in promising his presence to his people. And he defends them, cares for their needs, and finally gives them the land, all in response to that promise. But where is the promise-fulfillment scheme in the heroic pattern? The description here centers in the trusted servant who by his own virtue can seize the initiative to act for his people. And that audacity receives the approval of God. It is important to note that the two spheres of theological interest are not antithetical. The promise-fulfillment scheme may not be present in the heroic pattern. But it does not deny the value of the heroic pattern. To the contrary, the Pentateuch holds the two in delicate balance.

It is at just this point that an important theological issue appears. To loose the balance between the two schemes is to distort the theology of the Pentateuch. If one should elevate the heroic beyond its limitations within the balance, the results would mythologize the tradition. The hero in effect becomes God.[28] But significantly the OT never succumbed to that temptation. Moses remained very much the flaw-filled hero, condemned to die before entry into the land. Indeed, one may wonder whether the remarkable paucity of references to Moses outside the Pentateuch reflects a reaction away from the temptation to elevate Moses farther than the tradition would allow. But to over-balance the tradition in the other way is more problematic, particularly for contemporary exegesis. Walter BRUEGGEMANN reflects on the problem: "Salvation revolves around deeds of intrusion which stress discontinuities between God and culture and bear witness to an invading God. This has been the God of Israel which the Church has celebrated, with special emphasis upon the Exodus traditions.... The Church has been so deeply committed to a theology of salvation that it could not affirm that man has potentiality for being able and responsible, trusted and effective in caring for the creation in which he finds himself."[29]

The tendency challenged by BRUEGGEMANN can be documented at several points. Karl BARTH once wrote, for example, that "as we can see already from the older historical records from Ex. 17:8f. on,

---

[28] DE VRIES, pp. 227-241. Cf. the discussion of this point in COATS, "Legendary Motifs in the Moses Death Reports."

[29] Walter BRUEGGEMANN, "The Triumphalist Tendency in Exegetical History," *JAAR* XXXVIII (1970), 374-375.

there is no contradiction in the fact that it is God who fights for the Israelites, and that the Israelite bravely grips and wields his sword in obedience to His command and implicit trust in Him."[30] To be sure, there is no contradiction in the balance. The heroic man can stand as an obedient servant of God. But Ex. xvii 8f. cannot really support the point. For there is no divine command here. BARTH uses the Moses story to illumine the role of David. But in the illumination the problem is even more pronounced. "These two things [God who fights and the Israelite who wields the sword] are so unified in the figure of David that in fact we can only see them together. Yet both are so related in the tradition that the whole light does not proceed from the sword of David, nor does it fall on him as the daring commander and royal general of Israel, but it proceeds from God and therefore shines on God. . . ."[31] In Exod. xviii, however, the light *does* fall on the daring commander. Gerhard VON RAD reflects the same tendency. "Not a single one of all these stories in which Moses is the central figure, was really written about Moses. Great as was the veneration of the writers for this man to whom God had been pleased to reveal Himself, in all these stories it is not Moses himself, Moses the man, but God who is the central figure."[32] But, such a conclusion does no justice to a *legend*. The *legend* is about Moses, and only through Moses is it about God.

The Pentateuch itself reveals evidence of a struggle with this balance. The oldest forms of the Sea tradition (Exod. xv) describe the event totally in terms of divine activity. But in the narrative (Exod. xiv) Moses enteres the description as an efficient agent. Moreover, in the plague narrative Moses and God interchange in the designations of principal agents (cf. Exod. vii 20-25). Yet despite the struggle, or perhaps precisely because of the struggle, the balance remains. And, in that balance, Moses appears as "a free adult who is given remarkable freedom. The theological foundation of the literature is the unspoken assumption that Yahweh stands by this man to whom he has committed himself, that the promise is now at the disposal of man, that man has been trusted with the promise."[33] BRUEGGEMANN's comments refer to David. But it seems

---

[30] Karl BARTH, *Church Dogmatics* (Edinburgh: T. & T. Clark, 1957), II 2, 375.
[31] BARTH, p. 375.
[32] Gerhard VON RAD, *Moses* (*World Christian Books* 32; London: Lutterworth, 1960), 8-9.
[33] BRUEGGEMANN, p. 372.

to me that the image applies also to heroic Moses, not apart from divine intervention, but balanced with it. If contemporary exegesis is to lay a solid foundation for a biblical theology, it cannot succumb to the tendency to tip that balance toward what BRUEGGEMANN labels a triumphalist position. His call to turn away from a triumphalist theology toward a more viable perception of the nature of man in wisdom tradition and its impact on Davidic formulation is justified. But the call should be expanded to include a more adequate perception of the image of man in the Pentateuch, particularly in the person of Moses. For Pentateuchal theology the balance is crucial. Moses is not simply the blind servant, dancing his minuet of obedience to the sound of an all-encompassing divine drumbeat. To the contrary, for Pentateuchal theology Moses is *both* servant of God *and* heroic giant.

BIBLICAL COLOPHONS: A SOURCE FOR THE "BIOGRAPHY" OF AUTHORS, TEXTS AND BOOKS

BY

H. M. I. GEVARYAHU

Jerusalem

We propose that the biographical elements of the headings of biblical texts and books were authored by scribes of the time of the exile and thereafter. I also suggest that most of the items in biblical superscriptions were originally written at the end of the text and in a later period transferred to the beginning.

In my address at the 7th Congress of this organization, I pointed out the existence of colophons in Masoretic texts of the Old Testament, similar to the Accadian colophons. However, when I delivered that lecture, I was not aware that superscriptions and titles also come under the classification of colophons. I am confident that by this approach we may widen our understanding of the "biography" of the biblical books.

Scholars who have dealt with this subject have concentrated their main effort on determining the periods to which various elements of the headings may be assigned. LINDBLOM,[1] for example, distinguishes between those who gathered literary works —"the collectors" during the era of the first Commonwealth, and the editors —"redactors" of the period of the Babylonian exile and the Second Commonwealth. In his opinion the original titles assigned by the former group (the collectors) were short:

"The Vision of Isaiah the Son of Amos".
"The Words of Jeremiah the Son of Hilkiah".
"The Word of the Lord that Came to Hosea the Son of Be-erie".

Only later, during the Babylonian exile and after the Return to Zion were the remaining chronological and historical details of the superscription added. Speaking of Amos, LINDBLOM states: The original superscription, "The words of Amos" derives from the "collectors" who was a disciple of Amos.

---

[1] J. LINDBLOM, *Prophecy in Ancient Israel*, 1965, p. 280.

Scott [2] assumes that the original heading was of wider scope and included the version: "The vision of Isaiah the son of Amoz, which he saw concerning Judah and Jerusalem." T. Lascow [3] thinks that the forms: "The word which Isaiah the son of Amos saw" or "The Vision of Isaiah" represent headings for certain chapters only "Titel fur Einzelstücke."

On the other hand the headings: "The words of Amos", "The Words of Jeremiah" represent according to Lascow the title for a collection of prophecies, i.e. relate to "Sammlung von verschiedenen Stücken."

Other scholars [4] believe that the elements of the superscriptions that were not derived from the contents of the books are original, while those that may be deduced from the contents of the books are considered to be of a later date. Thus the scholars try, each in line with his literary instinct, to form hypotheses about the way the various elements of the headings developed.

In this address I shall try to outline the history of superscriptions in the biblical literature, within the wider framework of the practices of the ancient scribes.

My first impulse to the study of this subject came from W. G. Lambert's [5] review of the corpus of Babylonian-Assyrian colophons by Hermann Hunger. [6]

Lambert describes the colophon as a scribal note containing information that the modern Western World puts on the title pages of books.

Accordingly, I decided to investigate if the Accadian colophon might serve as a starting point for a comparative study of the scriptural headings.

My investigation showed that the biblical colophon is something like an off-shoot of the Accadian colophon, except for some individual features of its own.

Thus, when Lambert compares the colophon to the title page of the modern book, he is right only in regard to some of the elements of the title pages of modern books. The basic element, however—the

---

[2] R. B. Y. Scott, *The Book of Isaiah*, The Interpreter's Bible, 1956, p. 165.

[3] Th. Leskow, "Redaktionsgeschichtliche Analyse von Micha 1-5," *ZAW* LXXXIV, (1972), pp. 61-64.

[4] For details see the article of Meyer Weiss, *Tarbiz*, XXXIV, (1965), pp. 308ff.

[5] W. G. Lambert, *Die Welt des Orients*, V (1970), pp. 290-291.

[6] Hermann Hunger, *Babylonische und Assyrische Kolophone*, 1968. Cf. E. Leichty, *The Colophon, studies presented to A. L. Oppenheim* (1964), pp. 147-154.

author's name—is absent in the Accadian colophon. That literature has generally been anonymous.

Another point of difference is that the Accadian colophon is always at the end of the Text ("Am Ende einer Tafel," as HUNGER correctly noted).

In comparison with the definitions and descriptions of the Accadian colophon offered by HUNGER and LAMBERT,[7] I shall point out the characteristics of the colophon in the biblical books:

Description of Colophons in the Bible

1. The scriptural colophon is a note of the copyist-scribe (who was not the author of the text) which furnishes, besides technical information on the origin, type and scope of the composition, biographical data of the author, his name, place, and period, and also information on persons having some connection with the given composition. Occasionally the "colophonist" evaluates the composition and indicates the use of it in line with the custom of his times.

2. The Superscriptions and Titles in the Bible were originally at the end of the text, but in time they were transferred to the beginning of the text.

3. The colophon in the Scriptures is only a remnant of larger colophonic material which like its Accadian counterpart, contained many technical details about the origin and nature of the text, and the names of the copyist-scribes. The editors of the Scriptures omitted most of this colophon material. Those remnants of the original colophons that were preserved were included in the body of the text and as part of it became canonical text.[8]

---

[7] HUNGER defines the Accadian colophon as follows:—
"The colophon is a notation of the scribe put at the end of the (Cimesform) tablet of literary content. The colophon contains data concerning the tablet and persons who have some connection with the given text."
LAMBERT describes the colophon as follows:—
"Cuneiform tablets ... often end with a scribal note containing the information that the modern Western world puts on the title pages of books: something that served as the title (often the first phrase of the work); appropriate designations for parts of a series ('First Tablet', 'Third Extract', etc.); information about the scribe and owner, and sometimes pious wishes for sundry ends. They vary from the briefest statement of the scribe's name, to a long paragraph of literary content ... A study of the titles and related matter would presume profound knowledge of all the relevant texts, to see how a given work was edited and presented in the scribal centers of particular periods."

[8] This definition holds true also for colophons in the apocryphal literature, the ancient Greek literature, and the early Christian writings. See my article "The colophon in Ben-Sira (Seirach) chap. 50; 27-29," which will appear in the Protocols of the World Congress for Jewish Studies.

In a monograph, *Prolegomena on the Corpus of Colophons in the Bible*, which I am currently preparing for publication, I listed nearly 18 types of colophons most of which resemble the Accadian, and some that already have features indicating a later Jewish development characteristic of the Second Commonwealth.

Our chief interest here is in the biographical colophon, which is the principal component of the superscriptions.

We found that the biographical colophon belongs to the latest stages of the literary activity of the copyist scribes. For example, the superscription to the book of Isaiah is of a later date than the several headings and colophons in the chapters of this book.

How did this come about? Which historical developments are responsible for the listing of these biographical headings? As already pointed out, we have to remember that the biographical element is omitted in the Accadian colophon. The reader of the Babylonian and Assyrian colophons will find in them plenty of technical data about the text that served as Vorlage for the copyist; the city or temple that the original came from, even the kind of material on which the original text was written; whether a clay or wooden tablet. Likewise, the name of the copyist and his ancestors and his social status were detailed. Sometimes even the name and status of the owner of the text [9] who commissioned the copying of it were listed, but we do not know of any Accadian colophon that mentions the name of the author.[10] Biographies were written of kings and rulers, but the man of the intellect, the creative Accadian author, was humble to a degree that astonishes the modern reader.

We may assume that both the biblical prophet or sage and the Greek poet Homer were, like their Babylonian colleagues, modest people who were reluctant to have their names recorded. (Moses, Joshua, the Judges and early prophets really belonged to the class of rulers: accordingly, we have their biographies and we know even where they were buried. Not so with regard to the "literary prophets.[11]") There can be no doubt that neither the prophets nor their disciples ever recorded in the headings of their writings the name of the

---

[9] On the distinction between the copyist-scribe and the owner of the text, see HUNGER, paragraph 9: "Schreiber und Eigentümer", pp. 8-11.

[10] HUNGER states that there is not one colophon that we can be sure of its containing the author's name; ibid., p. 9.

[11] On the subject of earliest biographies about philosophers and spiritual leaders (as distinguished from biographies) I wrote in my article "Baruch the Scribe" in the Jubilee volume in honour of President SHAZAR, 1973, pp. 198ff.

prophet during any period preceding the time of the destruction
of the first Temple.

TRANSITION FROM ANONYMITY TO NAMING THE AUTHORS

In my opinion, the change from anonymity to recording the
names took place during the era of the Babylonian exile. That was
the period when the status and prestige of the prophets rose: as
many became convinced that "a prophet was indeed in their midst,"[12]
that really a true word of the Lord had been spoken by Jeremiah of
Anathoth, as well as by the other prophetic preachers. People became
interested in prophetic books, and with it came the desire to know
the names and the times of the prophets. This revival of interest
may have begun at the end of the seventh or the beginning of the
sixth century.

From the knowledge we possess it appears that the writings of
Jeremiah were the earliest that carried headings, which included
the name of the prophet, over the several collections of his pro-
nouncements.[13]

In the sixth century, during the period of the exile and the subsequent Return to Zion, the practice of recording the names of the
prophets and sages in their books became general. In the fifth century,
in the days of Nehemiah, there was already in existence a collection
of canonized books that included the traditional versions of the
prophetic books.[14]

Where did the editors (redactors) of the Scriptures gather these
biographical data from? Obviously, from research in the text itself,
as well as from oral tradition. I imagine that the stories about the
clash between Amos and Amaziah the priest of Beth El-[15] those

---

[12] Ezekiel xxxiii 33.

[13] It appears that of the preaching prophets the prophecies of Jeremiah were
the first to be recognized as the world of the Lord, and held sacred by the whole
nation.

From evidence gathered in my article on "Baruch the Scribe" it can be seen
that the prophecies of Jeremiah were the first to be canonized in the book of
Prophets. In the Tractate Baba-Bathra, p. 14, Jeremiah is listed first in the book
of prophets.

[14] This is confirmed by the story in 2 Maccabees ii 13 about Nehemiah founding
and collecting a library that recorded the acts of the kings and (the books of)
prophets.

[15] The story about the sharp controversy between Amaziah the priest of
Beth-El and Amos, and the expulsion of the prophets from Beth-El (Amos
vii 12-17) interrupts the sequence of the uniform pattern of prophecies, all beginning with the phrase "Thus says the Lord", which extends from Chap. i to viii 3.

about the life of Isaiah son of Amoz,[16] the biographical notes on
Jeremiah (which incidentally represent the first biography in world
literature dealing with the life of a man of the spirit).[17] These stories,
I presume, were written close to the time when the superscriptions
were written. Such headings as: "אֲשֶׁר הָיָה" "that was", "who saw"
"אֲשֶׁר חָזָה", refer to events in the distant past; while such statements
as "אֵלַי" "The Word of the Lord Came to me" omitting the name are
the original message of the prophet.[18]

WERE THERE CATALOGUES OF AUTHÜRS IN ISRAEL?

There is a definite possibility that even prior to the destruction
of the Temple, i.e. before the time when titles of the texts came
into use, there were catalogues of a sort, which listed data that
eventually were included in the headings.

In this inquiry we may be aided by the catalogue of names of
books and authors published by W. G. LAMBERT, who gathered and
interpreted seven fragments of a catalogue found in the library of
Asshurlampal at Nineveh.[19]

According to LAMBERT, that is "the earliest document of any
civilization dealing with authorship." Lambert describes the working
method and accomplishments of the compilers of that catalogue.

I believe that the aforementioned story of that controversy originally was
spread orally and only at a later period it was recorded in its present place of the
text.

[16] The stories on the life of Isaiah in vi-ix 6, also known as "Denkschrift
Isaiah's", are different in their literary style from the style used in the "visions"
which precede and follow those biographical entries.

It seems that the "Visions" were committed to writing at a much earlier date,
with the biographical data added in a later period.

A distinction should also be made between the accounts in Chaps. xxxvi-xxxix
which were mainly drawn from the book of Kings and the "Denkschrift" in
vi 1-ix 6. The latter belonging to the circle of the prophet's disciples.

On the theme LIMMUDIM = disciples = scribes of the prophet see my
article in Beth-Mikra, 1971, pp. 451-456.

[17] The biographical material on Jeremiah precedes the similar writings on
the life of Pythagoras.

It seems that the biographical stories about Jeremiah were the first in world
literature to deal with the life of a man of the spirit.

Baruch the scribe who is credited with this biography, was the first to realize
the importance of recording for future generations the life history of Jeremiah
the prophet.

[18] For detailed discussion see my article "Baruch the Scribe".

[19] W. G. LAMBERT: "A Catalogue of Texts and Authors," Journal of Cuneiform
Studies, XVI (1962), 59ff.

"The importance of this catalogue lies in its manifestation of critical scholarship. The overwhelming majority of Babylonian texts circulated anonymously. Thus to draw up a list with authors' names was a task comparable with modern discussion on the origin of Homer or the Fourth Gospel. The big difference is that modern writers on problems of authorship expose every detail of their materials and reasoning, while the Babylonian author gives results only. Yet this feature is characteristic of Babylonian science generally. Basic materials and facts are normally put down without explanation. Whether it be omens, sign lists, or mathematical tables, matters of origin, purpose and significance were not written down. No doubt teachers supplied orally what needed to be known for such compilations to be meaningful."

In the biblical headings we can trace a typological similarity to the method used in compiling the material in the (Accadian) catalogues.

The compilers of the Accadian catalogue and the authors of the biblical superscriptions faced similar problems. for which they found similar solutions.

Let me list the informative data included in biblical headings, the long as well as the short ones:

1. Name of the composition, e.g.: "An oracle concerning Nineveh" (Nahum),[20] "The sayings of the wise" (Proverbs xxii 17; xxiv 23).[21]

2. Name of the composition, including the name of the prophet: "The words of Amos" (without naming his father).[22]

3. Name of the prophet as well as that of his father: "Isaiah the son of Amoz"; "Hosea the son of Be-eri".[23]

---

[20] The heading of the book of Nahum is composed of two elements: "The oracle concerning Nineveh" and "The book of the vision of Nahum of Elkosh". It is obvious that the first anonymous component, describing the nature of the prophecy, is the earlier of the two.

[21] Compare Proverbs xxii 17:

"Incline your ear, and hear the words of the wise," where the original verse most likely reads:

"The words of the wise: incline your ear and hear." Here the short title (the words of the wise) was incorporated in the body of the text.

To this class belongs also the title "These also are sayings of the wise" (Proverbs xxiv 23). Such titles mentioning "the wise" like those in the colophon of Ecclesiastes xii 9, 11, compare with their Accadian counterparts; where the corresponding term "UMMÂNU" is used. For further details see HUNGER, p. 180.

[22] As in the case of Amos, the name of the father is also omitted in the books of Micah, Obadiah, Nahum, Habakkuk, Haggai, Malachi, and the sages Job, and his friends: Eliphaz, Bildad, and Zophar.

[23] The books that list besides the prophet's name also the name of his father are: Isaiah, Hosea, Joel, Jonah, Zephaniah, and Zechariah.

Only Elihu of the Family Ram, the youngest of the sages in the book of Job is mentioned as the son of Barachel the Buzite.

4. The social or professional group to which the author belonged: "Amos who was among the shepherds"; [24] "Jeremiah of the priests who were at Anathoth".[25]

5. The title "prophet"! "The oracle which Habakkuk the prophet saw".

6. The town from which the prophet came to Jerusalem: "Micah of Moresheth", "Jeremiah of Anathoth", "Nahum of Elkosh".[26]

7. Concerning whom and to whom was the prophecy told: "Concerning Judah and Jerusalem", [27] to Moab.

8. The date of the prophecy: "In the days of Josiah . . . King of Judah in the 13th year of his reign". (Jeremiah)[28]

9. Chronology of the prophet's activity: "During the reign of the following Kings . . ." [29]

---

[24] It should be noted that from the grammatical viewpoint it does not necessarily follow that the "Noqdim" lived in Tekoa.

We may also interpret the verse: The words of Amos of Tekoa who belonged to Noqdim who lived in various places.

According to scriptures and other Near Eastern sources, the word NOQDIM clearly stands for "owner of sheep". But in time this name was applied to designate a type of priests: S. SEGERT, "Zur Bedeutung des Wortes NOQED," *W. Baumgartner Festschrift*, 1967, pp. 279-283.

In two Ugaritic colophons, a copyist-scribe states that he is a LIMMUD = disciple of one titled "Chief priest" and "Chief of the NOQDIM".

Perhaps the title NOQED eventually was used to designate also the writer of holy writ?

[25] The fact that Jeremiah was one of the priests of Anathoth is not mentioned in the text of the book. The author of the colophon could obtain this information from oral tradition only.

[26] The Talmud ruled that any prophet whose home town is not mentioned is presumed to have lived in Jerusalem (Megillah 15, p. 2).

[27] Scholars draw a distinction between the earlier form "Jerusalem and Judah" and the later "Judah and Jerusalem"; see H. WILDBERGER, *Jesaja*, BK, 1965.

In the book of Jeremiah you find also short titles, addressing themselves directly: "Concerning the prophets" (xxiii 9): "Concerning Moab"; "Concerning the Ammonites" (xlix 1), etc.

[28] It seems that originally the prophets used to date each one of their prophecies. The prophetic writing bore the character of documents = Urkunden.

In the course of time, most of the date-lines were omitted. See my article, "Baruch the Scribe".

On the dates in the heading of the book of Jeremiah, see Zalewski in his next article in *Beth-Mikra*.

[29] In a number of titles the time of the prophet is designated by naming the reigning kings of that period.

In: Isaiah, Jeremiah, Ezekiel, Hosea, Amos, Micah, Zephaniah, Haggai, and Zechariah.

Similarly in LAMBERT's Catalogue, and especially in catalogues found by VAN DIJK in Uruk, we find the designation of the time when a scholar created his work, by listing the period of some (apparently) famous sage or the king of that time.

10. Reference to historical events: "Two years before the earthquake". (Amos)[30]

11. The specific nature of a given psalm: "A prayer of one afflicted ... who pours out his complaint before the Lord". (Psalm cii)

Some of the data enumerated above are already to be found in the Mesopotamian catalogue; though not as frequently as in Scripture. According to LAMBERT, Mesopotamian authors "can be divided into those with given 'fathers' and those without any notice of ancestry. The latter are certainly the older group. All, however, are given a priestly title and are said to be scholars (ummânu) of particular towns." [31]

The same pattern can be seen in the superscription to the prophetic books of the Bible. In both literatures the name of the author's father is not always recorded, most probably because the compilers of the catalogues and superscriptions were unable to obtain this information.

We have reasonable ground to believe that catalogues similar to the type found in Assyria existed in Israel with regard to the biblical books.

In the opinion of W. ALBRIGHT, Psalm lxviii represents a list of 30 separate hymns which are cited by their opening words.[32] I am inclined to think that the verses in 2 Samuel xxiii 1-7 are a list of additional songs by David that are cited by their opening words.

I imagine that even the Baraitha of the tractate Talmud Baba-Bathra, p. 14, dealing with the names, the chronology and authorship of the books of the Bible is based on such a catalogue that details the names of authors and books.[33] My assumption is based

---

[30] Also compare Jeremiah xlvii 1: "Before Pharaoh smote Gaza". Perhaps it is intimated here that Jeremiah foretold this. See ELIZUR, *Studies in the book of Jeremiah*.

[31] In accordance with his opinion, LAMBERT classifies as follows:— The authors whose names are preserved fall into four classes: (i) gods, (ii) legendary and other humans of great antiquity, (iii) men without indication of family origin, and (iv) men described as "son" of an ancestral figure.

Based on this principle, I am inclined to draw the line between the older sages of the book of Job and the junior Elihu whose ancestors are listed. (Job xxxii)

On problems of ancestors, see W. G. LAMBERT, "Ancestors, Authors, and Canonicity," *JCS* XI, pp. 1ff.

[32] W. F. ALBRIGHT: "A Catalogue of early Hebrew Lyric Poems," *HUCA* XXIII (1950), pp. 1-39.

[33] I presume that the Talmudic passage in Baba-Bathra 14ff. indicates the existence of a compendium of lists and catalogues comprising the biblical books and persons connected with them. There we must distinguish between statements of the early Tanaim and the debates of Amoraim of a later period.

on the presence of typical characteristics, similar to those in the above-mentioned Assyrian catalogue.[34] All of which indicates the probable existence of catalogues of texts possible, also of authors in ancient Israel.

Should my hypothesis be correct, we may conclude that the "editors" of the headings in the Prophets, Wisdom books, and Psalms, made use of such catalogues. In spite of all this a basic difference still exists between the Babylonian and Israelite literary texts: The names of the authors of Accadian literature were never recorded in the texts themselves, as it later developed in biblical literature.

The Transfer of Colophonic Data from the End to the Beginning of the Text

Irrespective of the likelihood that an interim period when catalogues were used existed, it appears that there was a transition in biblical literature when the headings' data were transposed from the end of the texts to the beginning. The data now given in the Scripture headings were in most cases originally listed at the end of the text. Only by a slow process of transition were these data eventually transferred to the headings of the texts. Evidence for this supposition may be found in the following facts:

1. We have reason to believe that the Israelite scribes followed the method used by the Assyrian and Babylonian scribes (which was probably generally accepted) and listed colophonic notes at the end of the text.

The same method was in use in ancient Greek literature where the name of the author and the nature of his book were recorded at the end of the scrolls (in spite of the inconvenience to the reader). Wendell [35] thinks that this practice was taken up by the Greek scribes under the influence of the Accadian colophon which was introduced there by the Arameans.

---

[34] The Talmudic source deals with two problems:
A. The order of the Prophets and Scriptures (as to their time)?
B. Who were the authors?
To these two questions, especially to the latter, the Accadian Catalogue, provides the answer.

[35] C. Wendel, *Die Griechiösche-Rmische Buchbeschreibung verglichen mit der des Vorderen Orients*, 1949.
In time the Greeks also introduced the new method, namely to record the name of the book, that of the author, and other pertaining data at the opening of the book.
Still they continued at the same time the older method of listing this information also at the end of the books.

2. In the Bible we find indications of the transfer of these (colophon) notes:

A. "Halleluiah", which was mainly originally a colophon at the end of certain Psalms was transferred to the beginning. We find traces of this transfer in the Septuaginta. The Halleluiah in the Masoretic text in Psalms civ, cv, cxv is still at the end of the Psalms but the Septuaginta already moved the Halleluiah over to the beginning.

B. The Hebrew word למנצח (in English translation, "To the choir master"), which the Septuagint translates *Eis to telos* and the Vulgate *in finem*, was, in my opinion, originally at the end of the Psalms and was eventually transferred to the beginning.[36] This is evident from Habakkuk iii, written in the style of a prayer-hymn, which ends with: למנצח בנגינותי (usually translated "To the choirmaster with stringed instruments").

C. Biographical data of the kind found in the colophon appear at the end of the Septuaginta version of Job:[37] as well as in the original ending of Ben Sira, l 27-29. It shows that in these instances colophons of biographic content were left in their original place, i.e. at the end of the texts.

On this premise, namely the fact that data were at a certain period transferred from the end of the text to the beginning, we may solve some problems of exegesis. For example:

"The Thirtieth Year" of Ezekiel

A. Exegetes, both ancient and modern,[38] could not ascertain the exact meaning of the opening sentence of Ezekiel: "In the thirtieth year". Some understand it to mean the 30th year of the jubilee; others interpret it as the age reached by the prophet; in addition to many other suggested meanings. In my opinion, this note originally was a closing colophon: "In the 30th year [of our exile]".[39] This note along

---

[36] *Eis to telos* was interpreted by commentators of past generations to mean eternal life. I think that the original meaning of it was a closing musical note. But, since the meaning of the musical notes in Psalms was forgotten during the Babylonian Exile; especially after the term "to the Choirmaster" was transposed to the opening of the songs, the original meaning of the phrase was completely forgotten.

[37] I think that in this colophon we may detect the intention to gather biographical data about Job. This can be deducted also from "Testamentum Jobi", and the discussions on Job in the Talmud.

[38] See Commentary of W. ZIMMERLI, BK, 1969.

[39] A similar froze style appears in 4 Ezra iii, 1: "And it was in the thirtieth year after the destruction of the city", obviously following the text of Ezekiel. Perhaps 4 Ezra correctly interpreted the 30 years, to mean 30 years from the exile of Jehoiachin.

with additional biographical data was shifted to the opening of the book and became part of the anonymous opening: "The word of the Lord came to me" (i.e. Ezekiel).[40]

"I Love Thee" Psalm xviii 3

B. The Hebrew opening of Psalm xviii reads, "I love Thee O Lord my strength," ארחמך ה׳, חזקי, (a line omitted in the parallel text in 2 Samuel xxii), as illustrated:

Psalm xviii	and	*2 Samuel xxii*
To the Choirmaster. A Psalm of David		And David spoke to the Lord the words of this song on the day when the Lord delivered him
I love thee, O Lord my strength. The Lord is my rock and my fortress and my deliverer.		from the hand of his enemies and from the hand of Saul. He said, "the Lord is my rock and my fortress and my deliverer" . . . . .[41]

Literally translated, ארחמך means "I pity you," which sounds absurd in reference to God.[42] The modern translation is, "I love you," as the word is used in Aramaic, which was the dominant language during the Second Commonwealth.

In line with our previous suggestion we may conclude that ארחמך ה׳, חזקי, was originally a colophon that was like many others of the Psalms, transferred from the closing to the opening of Psalm xviii.[43]

Likewise the heading למנצח, "To the Choirmaster," is omitted in 2 Samuel xxii, which we can explain by recognizing this term as a colophon, that was at the end of Psalm xviii and was later transposed to the heading.

---

[40] In my paper "Prolegomena to Biblical Colophons" I attempt to trace the development of the present form of the heading of the book of Ezekiel. I presented some suggestions on the way the colophons that were originally at the end of the text were eventually merged with the text after their position was shifted from the end to the beginning of the text .

[41] See: Fr. M. CROSS and D. N. FREEDMAN, "A Royal Song of Thanksgiving," 2 Samuel xxii = Psalm xviii, *JBL* LXXII (1953), 15-34.

[42] For a detailed discussion see G. SCHMUTTERMAYER, RHM, *Biblica*, LI (1970), 499-532.

[43] The same principle may be applied to other literary compositions in the Bible. It may for instance be that the opening verse: "Then Moses and the people of Israel sang" (Exodus xv 1) originally came after verse 19 of this chapter: "When the horses of Pharaoh with his chariots went into the sea." That means when the song of the sea was still an independent composition. But after the "song" was incorporated in the book of Exodus, the verse "Then Moses, etc." was put at the beginning of the song.

Colophons Help Us to Understand the Evolution of Biblical Books

The examples just cited indicate that classifying some of the headings as colophons may prove to be an aid to the exegesis of the text.

We shall also find that the various colophons indicate the process how the individual prophecies grew to the proportion of the prophetical book.

Isaiah

Now let me illustrate my idea with regard to the book of Isaiah. In the first part of this book 15 colophonic items were preserved.[44] The earliest of them: Isaiah xxxviii 9 ... מכתב לחזקיהו מלך יהודה, "A writing [45] of Hezekiah King of Judah after he had been sick and recovered from his sickness". In the same class fall the short headings: "An oracle on Egypt" (xix 7); "On Tyre" (xxiii 1); etc.

We may venture the guess that the earliest heading that includes the prophet's name is: "The oracle concerning Babylon, which Isaiah the son of Amoz saw" (Isaiah xiii 1). Among the exiles in Babylon there was without a doubt a growing interest in prophecies from early Israel on the future of the Chaldean Kingdom. Accordingly, the "oracle concerning Babylon" circulated as a separate scroll. Eventually its title, "An oracle concerning Babylon" was enlarged to include also the words "which Isaiah son of Amoz saw".

The latest colophon in Isaiah is the heading of the book of Isaiah which was at one time the closing line of the book of Isaiah the son of Amoz.[46]

---

[44] The following headings include the prophet's name:
Isaiah i 1; ii 1; xiii 1; (xxxviii 8.-King's name). Headings titled as *visions* are in Isaiah: xvii 1; xix 1; xxi 1, 11, 15; xxii 1; xxiii 1.

In some instance exists some doubt if certain verses come under the classification of colophons. One of these: "There is no peace" says the Lord "for the wicked", Isaiah xlviii 22; also Isaiah lvii 20.

Without any definite commitment, I still am inclined to list these verses as colophons.

[45] This may be interpreted as a "Miktav", namely a stela that was erected (perhaps in temple court) to serve as a thanksgiving moment after the king recovered from his sickness.

See H. L. GINSBERG, "Psalms and Inscriptions," *L. Ginzberg Jubilee Volume*, 1945, pp. 159-171.

[46] Chapter i represents in the opinion of G. FOHRER, *ZAW* LXXIV (1962), 251-267, an anthology and summary of prophecies from different periods.

I believe that these summaries may be compared with the NISHU, often

We should bear in mind that as long as the present superscription of the book of Isaiah was in its original place, namely at the end of his prophecies, there was a distinct dividing line between the Isaiah the first and Isaiah the second. But when that closing colophon was transposed, to become the opening verse of the book, all the subsequent chapters authored by "Isaiah's school" [47] in later generations, came to be accepted as the authentic word of Isaiah the son of Amoz.

Hosea

We have in the beginnings and end of the Masoretic text of Hosea three colophons. The earliest of them is a didactic admonition at the end of the book (xiv 10): "Who is wise that he may understand these things, intelligent that he may know them? For the ways of the Lord are right, and the righteous shall walk in them, but the transgressors shall stumble in them".

The second colophon to be found in Hosea is a redactional note in i 2, which could be freely rendered: "This is the first section of Hosea's prophecy".

Finally, Hosea i 1, which is a superscription of the usual type at the beginning of the prophetic books. This appears to be the latest of the three colophons. (Additional colophonic remarks appear at Inscriptio and Subscriptio in the Septuagint manuscripts of Hosea and of other biblical books.)

Jeremiah

The book of Jeremiah contains more than 40 colophons,[48] starting with the lengthy superscription for the book, and extending to the headings for his numerous individual prophecies. This is, incidentally, an indication that these prophecies circulated as independent compositions before the editors assembled them.

In chapter xxxii dealing with Jeremiah's purchase of the field at Anathoth, the authentic beginning is verse 6: "Jeremiah said: The word of the Lord came to me . . . Your uncle will come and say to you: 'Buy my field'." But the five preceding sentences, in

referred to in colophons. Perhaps these summaries were made by the prophet or his disciple who learned them from his master.

On this assumption it might well be that Chapter i of Isaiah once was at the end of the book and eventually was shifted to the beginning.

See discussion of H. WILDBERGER, op. cit.

[47] For the meaning of LIMMUDIM (apprentice-scribes) in the book of Isaiah; see *Beth-Mikrah*, 1971, pp. 451-456.

[48] I discussed it in details in my article "Baruch the Scribe".

verses 1-5, have all the earmarks of a marginal colophonic note of Baruch the son of Neriah who supplemented various data to be preserved with the deed of the purchase.

The latest colophon in the book of Jeremiah is in lii 64: "Thus far are the words of Jeremiah."

Also the most comprehensive colophonic superscription in the Bible is that for the book of Jeremiah. Opinion among scholars is divided whether this detailed heading of the book of Jeremiah in its present form was authored by one person or is an aggregate of several components.

Midrash Sifrei states: "Jeremiah wrote two books," which is confirmed by other sources. In line with this, I assume that the first two verses of the heading of the book of Jeremiah represent the title to the book of prophecies during the reign of King Josiah.

And the third verse of that heading relates to Jeremiah's second book, which contains his prophecies in the time of Jehoiakim and Zedekiah, till the time of the exile.

Besides the two comprehensive collections of prophecies, there was an additional part, that included prophecies as well as historical data, all of the latter belong to the time after the destruction of the Temple.

Proverbs

In Proverbs we have a number of headings [49] which shed light on the history of the composition of the Wisdom literature scrolls. The most interesting colophon of this book is xxv 1, "These are also the proverbs of Solomon, which the men of Hezekiah, King of Judah copied out."[50]

It may be suggested that such anonymous headings as, "Words of the Wise" (xxiii 13); "These are also the sayings of the wise" (xxiv 23)—are earlier than those listing names of persons. Here, too, the latest title is that which appears at the beginning of the book: "The proverbs of Solomon, Son of David, King of Israel," with the added didactic admonition: "That men may know wisdom and instruction". . . . To understand a proverb and a figure, the words of the wise and their riddles. (Proverbs i 2-7).[51]

---

[49] The headings which include the names of persons in Chapters: iii 1; x 1; xxv 1; xxx 1, 15; xxxi 1.

[50] On this colophon, see my article in *Beth-Mikrah*, 1971, p. 368.

[51] The summarizing verse in Proverbs xxii 15:
"Folly is bound up in the heart of a child, but the rod
of discipline drives it far from him",
ties in with the didactic verses in Prov. i 2-6.
Compare similar didactic passages at the end of Hosea and Ben-Sira l 27-29.

I think that the heading as well as the didactic suggestions were originally at the end of this book, perhaps in xxii 17-18.

Psalms [52]

The number of colophons in the book of Psalms is greater than those in any of the other books in the Bible. In the Masoretic text and in the ancient translations of this book we may find a few hundred colophons.

Psalm lxxxviii—"A Song. A Psalm of the Sons of Korah.

To the Choirmaster: according to Mahaloth Leannoth. A Maskil of Heman the Ezrahite."

This superscription, more comprehensive than any other in the Psalms, consists of eight different elements, listing authors' names, possibly the owners' names besides musical notes.

It is apparent that the various data in this heading were successively added; the later elements being added with the preceding part left intact. The same thing happened in psalms where the superscription included seven, six or less elements.

Psalm xxx The Masoretic version runs: מזמור שיר חנכת הבית לדוד, "dedication of the house." Some interpret it to mean David's house of cedars; other are divided on whether it refers to the dedication of the first or second Temple. In the Talmudic tractate Sofrim we are told that the verse was sung at the rededication of the Temple by the Victorious Maccabeans.

However since the Septuagint heading of Psalm xcvii clearly indicates that Psalm xcvii was sung at the dedication of the second Temple, it is safe to assume that the title of Psalm xxx refers to an event during the reign of David.

The longest colophon at the end of individual Psalms is the one of Psalm lxxii: "Blessed be the Lord, the God of Israel . . . the prayers of David the son of Jesse are ended".

This colophon comprising five elements was also composed by more than one scribe at different periods which were eventually merged together. Parts of this colophon are quoted in a slightly altered version in 1 *Chronicles xvi* 36.

---

[52] See Summary of Studies on titles in the book of Psalms, by L. SABOURIN, *The Psalms*, 1969, pp. 9ff.

L. DELEKAT: "Probleme der Psalmenüberschriften," *ZAW* LXXVI (1964), pp. 280-291.

J. J. GLUECK, "Some Remarks on the Introductory Notes of the Psalms".

The Babylonian scribes used to mark texts designed for liturgical use with special marginal notes.[53] It is probable that such terms as "A Psalm," "Song" (of David) were originally marginal notes and were from there shifted to the headings.

At any rate, in the progress of time the colophonic notes fell into the following groupings:

Musical, ritual, liturgical notes and names of persons (David, Asaph, etc.) as well as historical events were included in super-scriptions. On the other hand, didactic admonitions,[54] prayers, wishes of a public or personal nature and technical remarks, such as "The prayers of David the son of Jesse are ended" remained at the close of the psalm.

Finally, I would like to draw attention to a colophon in Psalm cii which is unique: "A prayer of one afflicted, when he is faint and pours out his complaint before the Lord."

The colophonist implies that Psalm cii has the special quality of securing the divine succour for the poor and hungry.[55]

At the end Psalm cxlv in the qumran version, two words of a colophon remained: זאת לזכרון, "And this for a remembrance .."[56] It is possible that this note reflects a Talmudic tradition that reciting this song will assure for the reader life in "the world-to-come."[57]

It may well be that the two colophons which hint at the effectiveness of those psalms for certain purposes, prove that the numerous tales found in Jewish and non-Jewish folklore about the beneficial qualities of particular psalms have their roots in ancient tradition.

Studies on the Psalms: Papers read at the 6th meeting of Die O. T. Werkgemeenskap in Suid-Africa, p. 30.

O. Eissfeldt, "Die Psalmen als Geschichtsquelle," *N. E. Studies in honor of W. F. Albright*, 1971, pp. 97-101.

[53] W. G. Lambert, "The Converse Tablet: A Litany with Musical Instructions," in *N. E. Studies in honour of W. F. Albright*, 1971, pp. 337-339.

[54] Psalm i: "Blessed is the man" which is of the didactic category, probably was the closing chapter of one of the books of Psalms, possibly at the end of the 3rd book, i.e. Ps. lxxxix. Psalm ii (originally copied from an inscription) was added after this didactic psalm. Therefore it appears that after the canonization of the first three books of psalms the first two chapters were added. Eventually these two psalms were both transposed to the beginning of the book of psalms.

[55] In time, other beneficial qualities were credited to this song. In the book *SHIMUSH TILIM* dealing with the helpful qualities of the various psalms, it is stated that reading Ps. cii will be of help to the barren woman.

[56] J. A. Sanders, *The Psalms Scroll of Qumran Cave 11*, 1965, p. 38.

[57] "Whoever recites psalm cxlv, A Song of Praise, of David" is assured of life in the "world hereafter" (Tractate Berakhoth 4 p. 2).

Thus the value of the colophon is not limited to its application as exegesis of the Bible, but contains biographical data of the biblical books reflecting the life of the people of the Second Commonwealth.

In these colophons, especially in the book of Psalms, we sense the tie between the history of the people and the "history of the book".

Now I wish to re-emphasize some points: Judging by the internationally accepted methods used by the ancient scribes, we cannot accept the opinion of scholars that Amos himself wrote any part of the heading of his book. Neither can we agree with the view of LINDBLOM that a disciple of Amos wrote most of the heading of that book. Were this true, such a disciple would sure have mentioned the name of the prophet's father. This also applies to the father of Micah who remains anonymous. It is more likely that hundreds of years passed from the time of Amos to the date when the title of his book was generally known.

We admire the effort of the final editors of the Bible, who succeeded in gathering relatively many details about the occupation of Amos and the period of his activity, even though they failed to learn the name of his father.

I wish to stress again that the chronological data in the headings were mostly gathered from studying the text of the particular books. We may safely assume that when the title lines were fixed, such terms as חזון, "vision", דבר, "the word", משא, "an oracle", were already archaic, and no real distinction between their meaning was known. Only after the listing of the authors' names came into use, other additional elements of the superscription began to appear. Likewise, there is good reason to believe that the title headings of the books were the uniform work of one learned scribe or a circle of such scribes, who belonged to the same generation.

I listed here examples of the Old Testament Hebrew version, but many colophonic notes are also to be found in the Samaritan Pentateuch, the Greek, Syriac, Latin, Aramaic, Ethiopic and other Eastern and Western translations.

In conclusion, I think it would do credit to this congress if a group of experts in ancient languages and cultures would combine to compile a corpus of colophons in biblical literature that would include texts up to the time of the first printings. Such a corpus would provide a true picture of the evolution of this literature.

MYTH, LEGEND AND FOLK-LORE IN THE UGARITIC KERET AND AQHAT TEXTS [1]

BY

J. C. L. GIBSON
Edinburgh

Only stories about the gods can be myths. Where there is a myth we must also have a ritual. Even a nodding acquaintance with modern study in the theology of the Old Testament and the history of Israel's religion is enough to reveal the potent influence these two not entirely harmonious views have exercised, an influence that has unfortunately spilled over into the Ugaritic field. Thus the Baal texts have been called myths because they are exclusively concerned with the gods, and the Keret and Aqhat texts, legends or epics because their chief characters are human beings.[2] Yet at the same time scholars like T. H. GASTER or I. ENGNELL have busied themselves ferreting out a cultic *Sitz im Leben* for all three without being too troubled about which label to attach to them as long as they

---

[1] References throughout follow the enumeration in the official publication by Andrée HERDNER, *Corpus des tablettes en cunéiformes alphabétiques découvertes à Ras Shamra-Ugarit* (Paris, 1963), where the Keret tablets are nos. **14-16**, the Aqhat nos. **17-19**. The concordance table below should help those who use the rather more accessible handbooks by C. H. GORDON [*Ugaritic Textbook* (Rome, 1965)] or G. R. DRIVER [*Canaanite Myths and Legends* (Edinburgh, 1956)] or the translation by H. L. GINSBERG in the various editions of PRITCHARD's *ANET*; the VIROLLEAUD notations widely employed on the continent of Europe are given in the final column.

HERDNER	GORDON	DRIVER	GINSBERG	VIROLLEAUD
14	Krt	K I	Krt A	I K
15	128	K III	Krt B	III K
16	125, 126, 127	K II	Krt C	II K
17	2 Aqht	A II	Aqht A	II D
18	3 Aqht	A III	Aqht B	III D
19	1 Aqht	A I	Aqht C	I D

Occasional references to the Mesopotamian Gilgamesh myth are made simply by the page in *ANET*.

[2] In the well-known compendium edited by S. N. KRAMER, *Mythologies of the Ancient World* (Anchor Books, New York, 1961) neither the Keret nor the Aqhat text is treated in the section on Canaanite mythology (by C. H. GORDON); for a similar reason no doubt the Gilgamesh cycle is hardly mentioned in the Sumero-Akkadian section (by KRAMER himself).

were recognized to be primarily ritual texts.[3] There is a confusion here that needs to be cleared up, and if my recent reading on the subject of myth [4] is anything to go by, it will be best done by abandoning the first view as misleading if not indeed ingenuous, and by severely circumscribing the imperialistic pretensions of the second. Classical scholars, following the usage of the original Greek *muthos*, entertain no scruples about applying the name to heroic tales like those in the *Iliad* and *Odyssey*, so why should Ugaritic scholars, even if their Old Testament colleagues find it expedient to be different?[5] And because some myths can be proved to have ritual affinities—the Ugaritic Baal cycle may well be a case in point [6]—is obviously no reason for assuming that all have, and in particular that the Keret and Aqhat texts have.[7] Myth is so complex a word and is used in so

---

[3] T. H. GASTER, *Thespis: Ritual, Myth and Drama in the Ancient Near East* (New York, 1950), pp. 115ff. (on Baal), 257ff. (on Aqhat); I. ENGNELL, *Studies in Divine Kingship in the Ancient Near East* (Uppsala, 1943), pp. 110ff. (on Baal), 134ff. (on Aqhat), 143ff. (on Keret). There are differences between the positions of GASTER and ENGNELL, which I do not wish to minimize, but in their basic assumption of a ritual origin for the three texts they are at one.

[4] Particularly G. S. KIRK, *Myth: Its Meaning and Functions in Ancient and other Cultures* (CUP, 1971), and J. W. ROGERSON, *Myth in Old Testament Interpretation* (Berlin, 1974).

[5] The Greek section in KRAMER's compendium (by M. H. JAMESON) accords generous space to the heroic stories in Homer, and KIRK in his book refers frequently to the Gilgamesh cycle as a prime example of mythic thinking. The reason why Old Testament scholarship testily refuses to recognize this well-established precedent as valid is not difficult to find; myth must be rigorously kept apart from history, even legendary history, so that as effective a contrast as possible may be drawn between the historically based faith of Israel and the mythologically dominated culture of surrounding peoples [see, e.g., G. VON RAD, *Old Testament Theology*, I, Engl. transl. (Edinburgh, 1962), pp. 136ff.; G. E. WRIGHT, *The Old Testament against its Environment* (SCM Press, 1950), pp. 26ff.]. ROGERSON, *op. cit.*, pp. 85ff., 145ff., gives a penetrating critique of this position in its various ramifications, asking in effect whether Old Testament theologians might not be better advised to seek other language than that of a false myth-history antinomy to describe the unique nature of Israel's religion. He is surely right, but even as things stand at the moment, there is no need for other Semitic scholars to be influenced by a controversy that bears little on their subjects.

[6] See particularly J. C. DE MOOR, *The Seasonal Pattern in the Ugaritic Myth of Ba'lu* (Neukirchen-Vluyn, 1971); this is a controversial book, and I am not at present sure that I wish to assent to either its arrangement of the Baal tablets or its precise interpretation of the whole cycle, but the evidence it gathers linking the narrative on numerous occasions to cultic practice is so massive that it will not be easily countered.

[7] For a devastating attack on the ritual theory see KIRK, *op. cit.*, pp. 13ff. Even in the cases where myths and rituals are known to go together, the link is, it seems, often trivial and sometimes impossible to detect, which strongly suggests that it may be secondary.

many overlapping senses by philosophers, anthropologists, psy-
chologists and literary critics, not to mention theologians or for that
matter the man in the street, that it seems only commonsense to
eschew simplistic theories and if we have, as I have in this paper,
to reach some conclusions about whether such and such stories are
myths or not, to try to do so in terms of properties that are comprehensive rather than partisan and that therefore hold out some pros-
pect of wide acceptance.

  One such property is, I would argue, a capacity for the fantastic,
that power which so many of Homer's stories, for instance, possess
to transport the listener into a strange, larger than life, dream-like
world, in which in G. S. KIRK's happy phrase,[8] 'dislocations of
familiar and naturalistic connexions and associations' are constantly
occurring. Such an atmosphere is certainly present in full measure
in the two Ugaritic poems with which we are concerned, as when
in the Keret text the gods gather in assembly at the hero's palace
to bless his marriage and thereafter eight boys and eight girls are
born to his wife in the space of seven years (15 ii and iii), or the
supreme god El fashions a female demon who thereupon flies to
Keret's sickroom and dispels with her wand the disease that had
laid him low (16 v and vi), or as when in the Aqhat text not only the
divine craftsman Kothar-and-Khasis but Daniel's own daughter
Pughat bound over vast tracts of country to reach him (17 v 9ff.,
19 25ff.), or the goddess Anath turns her henchman Yatpan into
an eagle and looses him against the unfortunate Aqhat to peck him
to death (18 iv 16-37), or Daniel, hearing of his son's murder, has
professional mourners slashing their flesh for seven years (19 170ff.).
By itself, however, this property is not sufficient to distinguish
myth from non-myth; it is a bit *too* comprehensive, as a similar
aura of fantasy hangs over much of the world's folklore, for example
the Germanic fairy tales or the Greek fables or even some of the
Christian lives of the saints; it would be stretching the term to a quite
meaningless extent to call all of these myths.

  As I see it, at least one other general property has to be joined
with a capacity for the fantastic before we can meaningfully speak
of a myth, what in as careful language as I can muster I would call a
speculative or perhaps better, an ideological bias.[9] For a story to

---

  [8] *Op. cit.*, p. 268.
  [9] By this statement I intend to make room for several modern philosophically
or psychologically orientated theories that define myth in terms of primitive

be a myth it has not only to conjure up the traditional supernatural or bizarre imagery of a society, but it has in some way to reflect or confirm the outlook of that society—its world-view, if you like—by satisfying its most basic prejudices or palliating its most deep-seated anxieties. Where one or other of these properties is lacking, but only then, it would, I believe, make for clarification if we were to use other terms. Legend and folk-tale are probably the most apposite, though I would not wish against the plain evidence of the dictionary or indeed of everyday speech to restrict either of these to what is not myth. The distinction I am making is more diffuse and also more subtle. Thus a legend is a traditional story that has a basis, however flimsy, in history; it may be and often is tendentious, glorying in or justifying some tribal or national aspiration or custom, but only when a miraculous or incredible dimension is added does it become a myth as well as a legend. By the same token, a folk-tale is a traditional story that is fictitious and that usually treats of the macabre or the magical or the whimsical, its purpose being to entertain or titillate or possibly to edify or point a simple moral rather than to make propaganda; in this sense it may not be inappropriate to regard all myths as folk-tales or at least to recognize folk-lorist elements in them, but not all folk-tales are myths.

In the light of these broad definitions, broad not because broadness is a desirable feature of definitions but because with a word like myth it is an unavoidable one, let us now consider our two texts.

The story of Keret opens with a description of the king mourning the collapse of his hopes for the future, since death has deprived him of seven wives one after another before he could have children by them (**14** 1-25). The question immediately posed is, as G. R. DRIVER succinctly puts it,[10] how a king without wife and therefore heir can be truly king. Keret, in response to instructions from El received

---

mentality or proto-science or archetypal symbolism or the mediation of opposites, but I do not wish to be bound by any of them or to have to pronounce on their merits or demerits, which I am not in any case capable of doing. For discussion and evaluation see the books of KIRK and ROGERSON, in locis. The symposium by H. FRANKFORT and others, *Before Philosophy: The Intellectual Adventure of Ancient Man* (Penguin Books, 1949), is an example of one such approach that has been very influential in the biblical and oriental fields. For an interesting application of another (the so-called 'structuralist' approach) to Old Testament themes see E. LEACH, *Genesis as Myth and other Essays* (London, 1969); see also R. P. CARROLL, 'Some implications of Structuralism for Old Testament Studies,' *Transactions of the Glasgow University Oriental Society*, XXIV (1971-72), pp. 14ff.

[10] *Canaanite Myths and Legends*, p. 5.

in a dream, restores his position by invading the neighbouring kingdom of Udm and taking the daughter of its king in marriage and in due course begetting issue on her (**14** 26-**15** iii 25). As he is pictured rejoicing there is, however, an ominous hint (**15** iii 25-30) that a vow he had made to the goddess Athirat during the campaign (**14** 199ff.) has not been fulfilled; and soon afterwards Keret, for all that he is believed as a king to belong to the progeny of El, shows signs of failing strength and becomes so seriously ill that his life is despaired of (**15** v 10-22, **16** i/ii 1-23). He can no longer adequately administer justice (**16** vi 41-50) and his illness adversely affects the fertility of the crops (**16** iii 13-17). The question posed in this latter part of the story is how the fabric of a society can be maintained and its prosperity safeguarded by a king whose health is impaired. Following divine intervention the rains which had ceased return and Keret is miraculously cured and resumes his throne (**16** iii 1-vi 24). The story ends with an atttemp by one of the king's sons to usurp his place, which Keret, now recovered, is easily able to quash (**16** vi 25-58).

As so presented, the poem is a thematic unity and its main thrust is indisputably ideological. Keret is the typical sacral king of ancient Near Eastern belief, the channel of blessing to his community and the upholder of its order. As he suffers and prospers so do his land and people. Thus far I find myself in sympathy with A. L. MERRIL's discerning study.[11] I think, however, that MERRIL and some of the Scandinavian writers on whom he depends discount too hastily the possibility that behind the typical there lies some genuine historical reminiscence, at any rate in the account of Keret's expedition against Udm in the long first tablet of the text. This incident is elaborated much more than any other, and it is on the whole soberly and real-istically told with no sudden and disruptive incursions by deity. No-one now seriously espouses the interpretation of the early French commentators,[12] who found in this account allusions to Abraham's father Terah and a number of Israelite tribes and regarded it as depicting a Phoenician invasion of southern Palestine and Edom in the Patriarchal period. But that Keret and his rival Pabil, though neither their names nor those of their kingdoms occur in any historical

---

[11] 'The house of Keret: A study of the Keret legend', *Svensk Exegetisk Årsbok*, XXXIII (1968), pp. 5ff.

[12] E.g. R. DUSSAUD, *Les découvertes de Ras Shamra (Ugarit) et l'Ancien Testament*, 2nd edit. (Paris, 1941), pp. 160ff.

source, were actual figures of remote Syrian antiquity, the story of whose clash in war and subsequent alliance through intermarriage became in time the basis of a propaganda legend about the nature and value of kingship, I find it difficult to gainsay. Since the second part of the narrative, that concerning Keret's illness, is replete with the miraculous and the symbolic, it seems to me churlish to deny the label myth to the whole poem. If anyone wants to go further than this and invent a cultic slot for it, a royal wedding or an accession ceremony as suggested by J. GRAY [13] have in my opinion more to commend them than that grossly overemployed rite which we call the New Year festival.

The Aqhat text begins with an incubation scene in which Daniel, a patriarchal figure, prays for a son (**17** i 1-16); for otherwise there will be no-one to tend him in his old age and perform the necessary rites after his death (**17** ii 8-24). In response to his prayer and on the intercession of Baal, El grants him a son, who is called Aqhat (**17** i 16-ii 8). When he grows up his father orders a magnificent bow and arrows for him from Kothar-and-Khasis and warns him that the first fruits of the chase must be offered in a temple (**17** v). Aqhat may have failed to accord with this requirement, and this may have been a contributory cause of the disaster that subsequently befalls him. But in what survives of the narrative the chief cause is the envy of Anath the sister of Baal (**17** vi 10ff.); and when Aqhat, in words (**17** vi 33ff.) that for their daring recall Gilgamesh's rejection of Ishtar's advances (*ANET*, p. 84), refuses to give the weapons to her, she engineers his death with the cooperation of a thug called Yatpan (**18** iv). Aqhat is killed, but the weapons are accidentally destroyed and Anath is thwarted in her ultimate purpose (**19** 1-19). Following Aqhat's death Baal withholds the rain and the crops fail (**19** 38ff.). Daniel and his daughter, seeing eagles overhead and fearful that the land has been polluted by bloodshed and that the drought will therefore continue, carry out a fertility rite upon the few solitary shoots that remain in his fields (**19** 28-74). Meanwhile he is apprised that the victim of the suspected crime is his own son and, searching for Aqhat's remains, finds them in the gizzard of one of the eagles and duly buries them in the family vault (**19** 75-151). He then curses the towns nearest the scene of the crime and holds mourning ceremonies that last seven years (**19** 151-184). Thereafter Pughat with

---

[13] *The KRT Text in the Literature of Ras Shamra: A Social Myth of Ancient Canaan*, 2nd edit. (Leiden, 1964), p. 10.

her father's encouragement takes upon herself the duty of blood revenge, disguises herself as a serving girl and is received as such at Yatpan's tent (**19** 185ff.). Just as like Jael in the biblical story (Judges iv 17ff.) she is plying him with drink, the narrative tantalisingly breaks off.

Clearly at least one further tablet must have followed, and it is this lack that makes any overall interpretation of the Aqhat text so difficult; we simply do not know how the various strands in the narrative were resolved. But one point, already hinted at in my summary of the story, seems to me to be worth underlining even more strongly. The poem should not, in spite of some surface resemblances to the Keret text, be connected with a Canaanite royal ideology or ceremonial. The assumption of such as S. MOWINCKEL and G. R. DRIVER [14] that Aqhat is a wonder prince like the child of Isaiah vii 14 or ix 5 or the Messianic figure of Isaiah xi 1-9, because the provision of the rain essential for the growing crops depends upon his life, is quite invalid. The failure of fertility following Aqhat's death belongs along with the circling flock of birds of prey and the cursing of towns nearby to the symbolism attaching in ancient Semitic clan belief to unjust murder and blood revenge.[15] The words of David's lament over Saul and Jonathan in 2 Samuel i 21, so closely paralleled in Daniel's anxious prayer in **19** 38-46, derive eventually from the same thought background.[16] In fact, Daniel is only once called a king (**19** 151), and the picture of his house and activity that we are given has more in common with the touching portrayal of a village chief in the 29th chapter of the book of Job [17] or with the idyllic atmosphere of the Patriarchal narratives in Genesis than with the trappings of urban kingship—throne-room, court of nobles, large army, military caste system (**14** 90-91) and the rest—that meet us in the Keret text. Daniel wants a son not to succeed him on a prestigious throne, but to look after him when he is old, to lead him home when he has had too much to drink and to plaster the leaks in his

[14] S. MOWINCKEL, *He that Cometh*, Engl. transl. (Oxford, 1956), pp. 116ff.; G. R. DRIVER, *op. cit.*, p. 8.

[15] Cp. Hos. viii 1; Jerem. xlviii 40; Deut. xxi 1-9; 2 Sam. xxi 10ff. For an account of the institution of blood revenge and of the mentality that lay behind it see J. PEDERSEN, *Israel: Its Life and Culture*, I-II (London and Copenhagen, 1926), pp. 378ff.

[16] The old formula of cursing is poetically applied to Gilboa, where Saul and his sons met their death in battle.

[17] See PEDERSEN's fine paragraphs (*op. cit.*, pp. 363-4) linking this chapter to what he calls the 'old Israelite conception of life'.

roof in the wet season (**17** ii 19ff.); his daughter Pughat draws water at the well, works in the fields and is skilled in the spells associated with midwifery, and she lifts him on to an ass's back when he goes on a tour of inspection round his farm, accompanying him on foot (**19** 50ff.); and it is in the threshing floor by the village gate that he sits to judge the cause of the widow and the orphan (**17** v 6ff.). I prefer to think that in this homely picture of Daniel's manner of life we are in direct touch with the old Canaanite folk-hero of the same name who is mentioned along with Job and Noah in Ezekiel xiv 14, 20 and xxviii 3.[18]

What then of the patently fantastic and supernatural scenes, especially the exciting ones from an ideological or theological standpoint, in which Anath first tries to wheedle Aqhat's bow and arrows out of him by offering him immortality like Baal's (**17** vi 25ff.) and then, when he refuses, travels hotfoot to El's abode at the confluence of the rivers and having extorted his assent to her plan (**17** vi 46ff., **18** i 1-19), lures Aqhat to his death for what she clearly regards as his presumptuous behaviour (**17** vi 43ff.)? Though it is the son's name and not the father's that is attached to the tablets, my judgment is that these scenes are secondary, supplying for all their vigour only the backcloth against which Daniel's piety is put to the test. They play an identical role to those scenes in the prologue to the book of Job (i 6-12, ii 1-6) in which Satan accuses the patriarch before Yahweh in the heavenly court and gains his permission to persecute him. Just as Satan does not reappear in the epilogue, so I believe, with A. S. KAPELRUD, that Anath's part in the plot ceases with Aqhat's murder,[19] and I suspect that the marvellous bow [20] is

---

[18] See also Jubilees iv 20 (I owe this reference to Professor N. W. PORTEOUS of Edinburgh). The consonantal text of the Ezekiel passages has *dn'l*, the same as the Ugaritic form, suggesting that the name may be different from the Daniel of the biblical book. But no form *Dān'ilu* or *Dān'ēl* is otherwise attested, whereas a name *Da-ni-èl* (i.e. Daniel) is found as early as the time of the Mari letters (*ARM* VII iii 23; I owe this reference to Professor E. LIPIŃSKI of Louvain). Probably Ezekiel simply uses the traditional spelling of the name without the internal *mater lectionis* and the Massoretes are right in pointing *Dāni'ēl* (cp. Sept. Δανιηλ). The question of a possible connexion between the ancient sage and the wise man at the court of Nebuchadnezzar therefore remains open; see H.-P. MÜLLER, 'Magisch-Mantische Weisheit und die Gestalt Daniels', *Ugarit-Forschungen* I (1969), pp. 79ff., a study which has some points of contact with this paper, but is in my opinion too narrowly conceived.

[19] *The Violent Goddess: Anat in the Ras Shamra Texts* (Oslo, 1969), p. 81.

[20] T. H. GASTER in particular makes great play with this in his comparison of the Aqhat story with the Greek myth of Orion, the huntsman (*Thespis*, pp. 200ff.)

also incidental to the narrative. I would assume that the missing final tablet contained an account of the punishment of Yatpan, the human agent in the killing, and, the demands of blood revenge being thus satisfied, of Aqhat's resurrection by El in response again to Daniel's prayers and Baal's supplication, and of the return of fertility to the soil and of prosperity to Daniel's house. As thus reconstructed, the poem could well be the Canaanite original of the folk-tale alluded to by Ezekiel, which, as we now discover, concerns a village chief, the continuance of whose name is temporarily placed at risk through the death of his only son at the hands of a capricious deity, but who by his piety and faithfulness to clan custom ensures that things turn out alright in the end. We possess in the prose story into which the author of the book of Job inserted his poetic dialogue, fragments of a later Hebrew version of another of the ancient Canaanite tales mentioned by Ezekiel, which had, as far as we can see, a very similar moralizing purpose. If we make use of the terminology of Old Testament scholarship and add the adjective Wisdom to the label folk-tale, we have in my submission as accurate a designation of these two stories as we are likely to get.[21]

---

[21] Noah, the third of Ezekiel's exemplary wise men, was also noted for his 'righteousness' (Genesis vi 9) and this is doubtless why he is included with Daniel and Job. But the story of the Flood is a myth, not a folktale, since both in Genesis and in the primary Mesopotamian versions (see *ANET*, pp. 42ff., 93ff.) the speculative element quite overshadows any question of merit on the hero's part. Incidentally, it is probable that before the biblical writers made use of them, any older Hebrew-Canaanite versions of the Noah and Job stories circulated among the people as narrative poems not unlike that of Aqhat. For an arrangement of the Genesis FLOOD story that helps to bring out its poetic origin see U. CASSUTO, *A Commentary on the Book of Genesis*, Engl. transl. (Jerusalem, 1961ff.), Vol. II, Section One. It is a pity that CASSUTO rather spoils his case by refusing to distinguish between the J and P portions of this story, for as regards the former it is in my view a strong one; I hope to show this more clearly in a study I am preparing of the epic poetry sources of the J document in Genesis i-xi.

CHRISTIANITY, JUDAISM AND MODERN BIBLE STUDY

BY

M. H. GOSHEN-GOTTSTEIN
Jerusalem

To Chaim Rabin
On his sixtieth birthday
A token of friendship

The nature of my subject is such that I must ask your indulgence for a few preliminary remarks of a somewhat personal nature. Some of my listeners may be wondering—like myself—why I have finally made up my mind to tackle a topic which has little to do with Philology. After all, Professors are—in a way—also actors. Once an actor is cast in a certain role, his audience expects him to remain true to that character, with only minor variations.

For over a quarter of a century I have had the privilege to address congresses, and I have always stuck to philological subjects—in the realm of the Bible text and its versions, as well as in Semitic and Jewish studies in general. By the time I finish this paper, some members in this audience might wish I had remained faithful to that tradition, and rather reported on some new discovery or development in connection with one of the projects I have undertaken.

It is after much painful soul-searching that I have transgressed those self-imposed limitations. The reason is simple: there is ample opportunity to publicize discoveries, real or imaginary. But it is only once every few years that we have occasion to talk to each other at a gathering of our international organization. As the years pass by, I feel it is my duty to share some of my thoughts on this particular subject I have chosen with my confreres, beyond the boundaries of country and denomination. I do not expect a fruitful discussion to ensue right here and now. But I would feel gratified if the next few days would provide, in more intimate talks, some beginnings towards a deeper mutual understanding as regards the issues facing us.

My second remark: this paper trains the searchlight on one of the problems which I have encountered over the years in one of my fields of interest: the intertwined history of Biblical Studies and Semitic Philology since Renaissance times. Our paper tonight intends to single out one particular aspect; but ultimately it should be understood in the context of the entire inquiry.[1] If I were to define its character, I would perhaps say that it is a mixture of *Selbstbesinnung* and *status quaestionis* inquiry, based on a very personal interpretation of *Problemgeschichte*.

Yet it would be folly to ignore the dangers besetting our path. However historically-objective we wish to be, however much we strive to steer clear of the Scylla of apologetics and the Charybdis of deeply ingrained inter-denominational mistrust, the reading of history we shall suggest will be listened to by each member of this audience against the realities of the contemporary scene, as he reads it. In our world of ecumenical ideals, there are so many problematic levels of contact, interaction and conflict between Jews and Christians—nurtured by two millennia of theological feuds, abuse and persecution—that almost every expression is emotively charged, every turn of thought conjures up an unsavoury association. Our specific subject of inquiry borders on so many sensitive areas that it will be only the spirit of common scholarly endeavour that will permit all of us to listen to the reading of history to be proposed here, *sine ira et studio*.

Our next remark already leads up to the subject itself. Throughout our inquiry we shall have to remind ourselves of the terminological ambiguity inherent in the very expression "Bible Study". The study of the Bible is a multi-storeyed edifice. This is true diachronically—over two millennia of successive layers of exegetic endeavour, only partly obsolete—as well as synchronically. While academics may regard their form of penetrating into the world of the Bible as superior, academic study cannot be divorced from the

---

[1] I hope that the various projects I am engaged in will leave me some time to finish before long my book on this subject, scheduled for publication by Harvard University. I have not burdened this paper with footnotes of erudition since the points will be taken up there in detail. Two additional subjects to be taken up in that volume and connected somehow to the present paper are also about to be written up: "Ethiopic-Chaldean and the Beginnings of Comparative Semitics in Renaissance Times" (scheduled for JSS; abstract in *Acts of the Second International Hamito-Semitic Congress* (Florence 1974) and "Hebrew Vowels, Divine Inspiration and the Rise of Bible Criticism".

broad basis of "study" as an endeavour to comprehend the Divine word. Were it not for the conviction of hundreds of millions that the will and guidance of God can be ascertained through Bible study, there would be little room for academic study.

To be sure, there are theological and practical differences between Jew and Christian, Catholic and Protestant, about the implications of God's directing his word to man, and man's duties and rights in studying it. Studying the Bible provides faith and guidance to Christian and Jew alike, yet we shall have to realize that over and beyond such guidance, studying God's word is also a supreme divine command to be obeyed, as a day by day reality, by the practising Jew: והגית בו יומם ולילה—"Thou shalt meditate in it day and night". For over two thousand years it has been the ultimate aim of the exegete to reach back to the "true meaning", whatever the means employed. This was as true for the author of the Qumran Habakkuk scroll as it is today for the Professor in the Divinity School who starts his exegesis class by invoking the guidance of the Divine spirit.

No inquiry into the issues of Bible study can afford to ignore the ever-present impact of traditional study which provides the backdrop for the personal equation of each and everyone of us. Even in this generation of non-believing Bible scholars and atheistic theologians, he is a rare man whose roots do not reach into the soil of his own denominational tradition.

This accounts, *inter alia*, for the fact that up to this moment I could hide behind the term "Bible". But as we move on we must face the problem that this term means something different to me—and to a minority of those present—from what it means to the majority. We cannot evade the issue by saying "Old Testament". For, strictly speaking, that term is valid only within the frame of reference of a binary opposition.

There is yet another side to this problem: Jews and Christians alike are not always aware that the history of Old Testament studies has remained linked up for centuries—in matter, method and person—with New Testament studies, and that there exists down to our own times both interplay with and carry-over from New Testament problematics. One example out of many: at the starting point of post-medieval biblical studies looms the much belaboured *sola scriptura* slogan, leading up to the revival of exegesis from the *hebraica veritas*. Yet the whole issue of Old Testament exegesis was secondary.

It developed as of necessity on parallel lines to the positions taken towards the interpretation of the New Testament. When the Tridentine Council reaffirmed the traditional "scripture plus tradition" formulation, it was concerned basically with positions in New Testament theology: *ex ipsius Christi ore ab apostolis . . . ad nos pervenerunt*. The positions taken towards Old Testament exegesis were but a logical second step, which finally made Christian Hebraic studies into a powerful reality. This interconnection between Old and New Testament study, both in issues and persons, runs past the milestones of centuries: via MORINUS and SIMON, via SEMLER and WELLHAUSEN—down to the breakup into sub-branches in the present century.[2]

So much for the preliminary remarks—and our discussion may benefit if we are aware, how much of our own collective semiconscious past we are carrying with us, as we start our survey.

I have already indicated, up to which point in the past I intend to fling out the net in order to reach back to the beginnings of "Modern Bible Study". Let us not haggle over the exact year; for the deeper understanding of the specific issue at hand permit me to proceed on the basis of my thesis that in our times we are grappling with a development which has come round full circle after five centuries.

Leaving aside for the moment the precise interlacings of the triangle: Renaissance—Humanism—Reformation, we start with those decades around 1500 when the Church regained tools which enabled it to absorb the achievements of traditional Jewish Bible study. It was a unique set of partly interrelated circumstances. The spiritual crisis within the Church of the 15th century expressed itself in various ways, some of which led to a reawakening interest in Hebraic learning. Mystical leanings and the promise of alleged solutions contained in Kabbalistic writings made princes of the World and of the Church turn towards Hebrew.[3] At the other end of the scale, the Inquisition dealt with Jews and their books—and burning began to alternate

---

[2] The WELLHAUSEN period as the beginning of the breakup into sub-branches will be gone into in the volume mentioned above. Up to that period it was the rule rather than the exception that, in spite of preferred activities, most theologians regarded themselves as students of both the Old and the New Testaments.

[3] This motive was especially noticeable in the first generation of Christian Hebraists (PICO DELLA MIRANDOLA, EGIDIO DA VITERBO, REUCHLIN). In a way, REUCHLIN signifies the beginning interest in Hebrew beyond Kabbalistic and missionary motives.

with reading. Confiscated books ended up in monasteries, or else neophytes continued their previous activities as scribes under new auspices. To be sure, the newly achieved openness of Christian scholars towards the study of Greek had paved the way towards the quickly developing ideal of the *homo trilinguis*, who could study the Bible in its three languages.[4] Moreover, Hebrew printing had just been perfected at the right moment in history.[5] The stage for the revival of Hebraic learning was all set, when the Reformation began to sweep Central Europe and gave Hebraic studies their final impetus.

This is not intended as an exhaustive catalogue of circumstances. But it suffices to make us ponder the rather curious fact that the two focuses of medieval Jewish Bible interpretation—philological-rationalistic and mystical-kabbalistic—became under such changed conditions center points in the process of the revival of Christian Bible study.

I have already hinted at the fact that nothing is further from the truth than the oft-repeated partisan claim that it was the Reformation that was responsible for the Hebraic revival. But the Reformation very much—pardon the picture—jumped on the Hebraic band-wagon. It lay in the nature of things that the Reformers were in special need of that kind of learning. That need—together with the Humanist language ideal (not necessarily an ideal match)—got Hebraic studies to strike firm roots and to revolutionize the exegetical approach.

For our present purpose the steps can be outlined in bold strokes; the classical hermeneutical principle of Church-guided duplicity of *sensus literalis* versus *spiritualis* tended to give way to a stressing of the *literalis*.[6] Yet it took the particular twist of applying the *sola scriptura* principle with regard to the Old Testament in such a way, that the linguistic *Pshat* had to be searched for in "Rabbinic" commentaries, which more often than not were identified with the Ḳimḥi tradition.

To put it more bluntly: the first moment of truth came right there and then when Church tradition and Rabbinic exegesis clashed;

---

[4] Cf. John xix 20.

[5] The turn of the 15th century represents also a watershed in the history of Hebrew printing, since apparently no non-Jewish Hebrew printing antedates 1500.

[6] This approach is heralded by REUCHLIN's exercise *In septem psalmos poenitentiales hebraicos interpretatio de verbo ad verbum* (1512).

adopting what seemed to be the "true" *sensus literalis* amounted in fact to a substitution of the exegetical tradition of the "Rabbis"— a generic term in all such discussions—for the exegetical truth of the Catholic Church. In a world which had little love for living Jews, it was not only Catholic scholars that were quick to realize that paradox—and for instance, a man like LUTHER's rival Johann ECK, in his "Judenbuechlin" pointed out that theological absurdity.[7] Since positions of second and third generation protestant scholars— especially Calvinist—are often projected back into the first generation, it must be stressed that, for instance, LUTHER himself was fully aware that the spook of attempting to reach back to the *hebraica veritas* through the Jewish Bible and its commentaries could become dangerous. At the very moment when Christian Hebraists began to revolutionize their exegesis by following Jewish masters, he warned his followers not to learn from them anything but grammar alone because "die Jüden nicht wissen können virtutem omnium voca- bulorum ... viel weniger wissen sie vim phrasis, figurarum et idiotismorum".[8] Or, in a different formulation: "Das man die Sprache und Grammatica von jhnen lernet, das ist fein und wol gethan ... Aber unsern glauben und verstand der Schrift lernen sie nicht. Also sollen wir auch die Sprache von jhnen lernen. Aber jhren glauben und verstand, von Gott verdampt, meiden". Once the Christian Hebraist has learned the language, he is called upon to "clean the Bible" in the spirit of Christianity.[9]

Quotations could be multiplied; the position at the very outset— when the new conditions made the influx of Rabbinic exegesis for

---

[7] For instance in chapter 16 of his *Ains Judenbuechlins Verlegung* (Ingolstad 1541) he turns against the argument „Gott hab nit wöllen das der juden bücher ver- brent wurden der christenhait zu gut darmit durch Hebraische sprach die christen wider zum rechten verstand ihrs glaubens möchten kummen. Dann ich frag hie den zungen verkaufer ob er hie rede von der Hebraischen bibel oder von der Rabin glossen und vom Thalmud etc."

[8] Cf. L. GEIGER, *Das Studium der Hebräischen Sprache in Deutschland vom Ende des XV bis zur Mitte des XVI Jahrhunderts* (Breslau 1870), p. 6.

[9] "... Darumb hab ich gesagt das Mose und die Schrift bey den jtzigen Jüden nicht kendlich, noch der alte rechte Mose ist. So schendlich haben sie jn besüddelt mit jhrer Judas pisse." Hence the Christian Hebraists must "...reinigen uns die Ebreischen Biblia. Denn sol sie rein und wider gut Ebreisch werden, so müs- sens die christhen thun, die den verstand haben des Messias. ." My notes were made years ago from the large Weimar edition vol. LIII (1920), pp. 646f., which I cannot recheck at present. (The orthography is certainly mixed.) That whole paragraph will occupy us also in the context of the discussion on Hebrew vowels (cf. p.70, n. 1).

the first time possible—is clear. Needless to add that this "attraction plus rejection" attitude remains a theme with variations right down to our times.

Within the framework of our analysis we are in duty bound to look always at both sides. The ambivalence towards Jewish exegesis by Christian theologians was obvious. The traditional Jewish position was hardly less outspoken. As the midrash had put it long ago: the nations may learn the Thora. But the knowledge of the correct meaning was disclosed to Israel alone.[10] Only Israel knows the meaning of the words of the Thora—teaches the midrash; only Christians are able to comprehend the *vis* of the divine word— repeats LUTHER.

Small wonder that a few years later the second generation reformer Johann FORSTER—one of the most original Hebraists of his day— sums up: "*Dictionaria et Commentaria Judaeorum plus obscuritatis et erroris in ecclesiam Christi invexerunt quam lucis et veritatis*". Or—in a clinching punch line: "*in Rabbinis* οὐδὲν ὑγιές.[11] While some statements may appear to reflect a Christian-Jewish argument on Bible study—a continuation of a medieval dispute acted out against a Humanist-Reformation background—it was nothing of the sort. The historian is forced to conclude that the exegetical revolution, which lies at the basis of modern Bible study, did not reflect any Christian-Jewish dialogue. All discussion with regard to the merit of Hebrew exegetes was a purely internal Christian affair. Jewish teachers of Hebrew and Biblical exegesis in that generation were servants paid by their Christian disciples, unless they were recent converts.[12]

[10] "Since the Holy One, praised be He, foresaw that the nations are going to translate the Thora and read it in Greek, and they will say 'We are Israel'. . . He said unto them: 'You maintain that you are my children? . . . Only those who guard my 'mysteries' are my children' (מי שמסטורין שלי אצלו הם בניי). What is that? The Mishna." This ancient polemic (handed down with some variants) was discussed by URBACH, *Tarbiz* XVIII (1946), pp. 6f. See also his *The Sages* (Jerusalem 1969; in Hebrew), p. 271. See also M. KASHER, *Torah Shelemah* (Hebrew) vol. XXII (1967), § 201.

[11] See the introduction to his dictionary with its telltale title: *Dictionarium hebraicum novum, non ex Rabbinorum commentis, nec ex nostratium doctorum stulta imitatione descriptum, sed ex ipsis thesauris etc.*" (Basle 1557). FORSTER's work will be analysed in the volume mentioned above (p.70, n. 1).

[12] I do not think that from about the seventies of the 15th century down to the years after the Reformation there were many students of Hebrew who were not suspected of being of Jewish descent. Until modern times the credentials of men from Jacob PEREZ of Valencia and NIGRI down to BÖSCHENSTEIN continued to be discussed. Bearing in mind the events of Jewish history in those

Within half a century, between 1475 and 1525, the accumulated treasures of Jewish exegesis were made available to Christian Hebraists. Christian study entered a period of unprecedented expansion and deepening, quickly getting involved in critical appraisal by the sheer facts of juxtaposition.[13] Yet at that very point of history, external circumstances made Jewish study stagnate, and spiritual forces within Judaism concentrated once again on halachic and Kabbalistic writings.

Let me paint the picture in harsher colours: the events in the field of Bible study must be seen within the context of Jewish and European history around 1500. That very generation witnessed the flourishing of the last Jewish Bible scholars of the traditional kind— an ABRABANEL or a SFORNO—as well as the beginnings of a new type of Christian study, mainly in Switzerland and Germany, partly in Italy. God had once given the keys to his "mysteries" to Israel; those keys had now been handed over to the "nations", and Israel possessed no more treasures all its own. The nations added the new treasures to their old ones; Israel had no strength left for new creation.

It would lead us too far afield, were we to go into details, how the acquisition of traditional Hebraic knowledge became the starting point for both the study of Semitics and philological criticism—all within a few decades—culminating in such first fruits of critical study as MASIUS' *Josuae imperatoris historia*, published four centuries ago. As irony had it, while Jews not only had no part in that development—they were, in fact, at one of their many political and cultural low points—Christian theologians attacked each other with learned quotations from Rabbinic writings, to prove their exegesis and theology. To be sure, the dividing line between tendentious denominational querulence and creative inquiry always remained thin. Had HEINE been aware of all that, he might have enjoyed painting an (anachronistic) scenario in which Christian scholars outshine each other in quoting 'Tausves Jontef'—in BUXTORF's Basle, for example, rather than in Toledo.[14]

decades, many suspicions were well founded. Men like PICO, EGIDIO and REUCHLIN were the exception, not the rule.

[13] Within one century after the first stirrings of interest in Hebrew (1475-1575), Christian scholars not only knew all the "classical" Semitic languages, but also the Bible in all the versions (Greek, Aramaic, Syriac, Arabic, Ethiopic).

[14] "Er beruft sich auf die Mischna
  Kommentare und Traktate
  Bringt auch aus dem Tausves-Jontof
  Viel beweisende Citate etc."
I am using the Elster edition of HEINE's works, vol. I(²1893), p. 475.

The so-called "vowel dispute"—the fight over the authoritative character of Tiberian vocalization in the context of theopneustic fundamentalism, which reached its height in the 17th century BUXTORF-CAPELLUS controversy—is but a major example for an issue in Bible studies fought by Christian theologians outwitting each other in Rabbinics. For over three centuries the problem of Hebrew vowels loomes large as, perhaps, the outstanding single issue of philological Bible criticism, and its final consequences bedevil, unbeknown to most of us, our own philological practice. Every quotation from Talmud and Zohar was subjected to scrutiny. Yet ever since the first doubts were raised in the days of Elia LEVITA—who in a way represented the transitional generation of 1500—and down to 19th century LUZZATTO, this fierce battle of biblical erudition was often fought with Jewish pawns as a Christian theological exercise.

In the particular context of our inquiry it is decisive, that for centuries Jews do not reappear on the scene of Bible studies. To be sure, SPINOZA's *œuvre* cannot be divorced from his background; but it neither was nor became part of Jewish Bible study. The history of our discipline develops largely within Lutheran and Calvinist circles—with an occasional splash from the direction of the Paris *Oratoire*—down to the period of EICHHORN, DE WETTE, VATKE and EWALD, before Jewish scholars reenter the scene. The modern study of the Bible, both in its philological and theological implications, grew as an integral part of the development of modern European thought. Jews and Judaism as such had no place in it.

Were history governed by Hegelian aprioris, the reentry of Jewish scholars into the post-*Emanzipation* 19th century academic world should have led, in the field of Bible study, to a Judeo-Christian synthesis. For various reasons our *Wissenschaftsgeschichte* has never squarely faced the problem that hardly any Christian-Jewish confrontation occurred in our field throughout the 19th century. From the point of view of academic establishment, Biblical studies were pursued in the framework of "Theological Faculties" or their equivalent. This was not only a technical obstacle for the few Jewish youngsters who might have wished to enter the field. We have already alluded to the problem posed by the very definition of "Bible". No 19th century Jew could think of becoming a "Bible scholar" in the European sense, which almost of necessity entailed moving back and forth between the Testaments.

The founding fathers of the *Wissenschaft des Judentums*, a century and a half ago, did not omit the study of the Bible from their program by chance. They had set out to purchase the entrance ticket to enlightened academic circles by uncovering the hidden beauty of the spiritual treasures of Judaism. The Old Testament was no hidden treasure, and Christian scholars had decided by that time, anyway, that Judaism presented but an atrophy of the true biblical spirit.

ZUNZ and his high-minded companions lived in the academic atmosphere of post-EICHHORN criticism, which quite often entailed "academic"-theological judgments of Judaism. With all the upheaval created by formulations such as WELLHAUSEN's opening sentence "ob [das mosaische Gesetz] der Ausgangspunkt sei für die Geschichte des *alten Israel* oder für die Geschichte des *Judentums* d.h. der Sekte, welche das von Assyrern und Chaldäern vernichtete Volk überlebte"[15]—students of the history of Biblical studies have often tended to overhear earlier dissonances such as in DE WETTE's dictum: "das Judentum ist die verunglückte Wiederherstellung des Hebraismus".[16] That kind of teaching must be borne in mind if we wish to appreciate the various reasons why Jews stayed out of modern Bible study, practically thoughout the nineteenth century.

The 19th century enabled Jews to enter the modern academic world. They could become physicians and lawyers, mathematicians and philosophers. They could even indulge in "Judaic Studies". But Bible study—as it had grown organically in Christian schools of Divinity ever since the 1500 generation—remained, for all practical purposes, out of bounds.

Some features of future developments and configurations within our field of study were already visible during the past century—at least from the vantage point of hindsight. On the Christian side, Bible study tended to split apart into its sub-specializations, a split caused by more than just personal predelictions. Some scholars—starting with GESENIUS—were content to concentrate on strict philological exegesis. On the other hand, what is usually regarded as the major critical advance was achieved within the framework of isagogic monographical volumes, with considerable disdain for all-round exegesis. Lest we forget: biblical theology became a sub-discipline, keeping its traditional aloofness under changed circumstances. What ought to have developed into a constant give

---

[15] J. WELLHAUSEN, *Geschichte Israels* (1878). In later editions (*Prolegomena etc*) he substituted '*Religionsgemeinde*' for '*Sekte*'.

[16] Cf. L. PERLITT, *Vatke und Wellhausen* (BZAW XCIV) 1965, p. 92.

and take between the major sub-branches of Bible study, tended to break apart right at the time of the most impressive advances.

Against the background of those developments within the confines of Christian academic study we understand better what happened on the Jewish side. While Jews could not become Bible scholars in the full academic sense, they could exercise both their traditional know-how and their newly acquired Orientalist expertise in one particular field: philological exegesis. This was, perhaps, natural. By upbringing, by tradition, by interest—this was their field. Classical Jewish exegesis was largely philological-atomistic, not theological-synthetical.

It would be a fallacy to speak of 19th century modern Jewish Bible study as being parallel in any sense to Christian study. But precisely the split up within Christian academic Biblical studies enabled Jewish scholars to participate, and excel, in one branch. It is no coincidence that the erudition and critical acumen of men from GEIGER, FRANKEL, LUZZATTO etc. down to EHRLICH, BARTH, MARGOLIS did not turn into the direction of source criticism or theology, but towards some kind of sophisticated metamorphosis of traditional exegetical interest: biblical philology—comprising language, text and versions.

Just as a symptom: At the very time when the history of Israel was being "rewritten" by Christian theologians, the grand master of Jewish historical writing, Heinrich GRAETZ, erected his imposing edifice. To be sure, he took an active interest in the study of the Bible. Yet as a Bible scholar he steered clear of the game of rewriting biblical history and cutting up sources, but concentrated his ingenuity on exegetical conjectures, whatever they were worth.

The *Wissenschaftsgeschichtler* cannot afford to ignore the correlation between personal equation and academic professionalism. Throughout the 19th century there existed no academic framework for Jewish Professors whose field of specialization was the Old Testament. On the other hand, the "science of Judaism" was strongly tied to inner-denominational issues of the day, and perforce could hardly benefit from Christian participation. The only exception to this rule was, perhaps, Franz DELITZSCH—a man unique in more than one way.

Some members of this audience may be displeased, because of my apparent disregard of events on the extra-continental scene. I do not offer an apology. Were I to deal with the history of biblical criticism, I could have paid my respects to our Scottish hosts by mentioning a man like GEDDES (though I am not convinced they would have appreciated that reference). But for the purpose of the particular subject under consideration, it should be realized that the play is very much acted out against the cultural and political background of 19th century Central Europe. Hence we proceed to survey the Central European scene around the *fin de siècle*.

Pious outrage is not identical with professional scholarship—neither on the Jewish nor on the Christian side. David HOFFMAN, as a spokesman of Jewish neo-orthodoxy, exposed weaknesses in WELLHAUSEN's theory, just as did Christian scholars.[17] This did not make him a Bible scholar—although in some circles he is regarded as a Jewish St. George to WELLHAUSEN's dragon.

All in all, right into the early twentieth century, Jewish scholars tended to stay away from Biblical studies, in a comprehensive sense, just as they had stayed away throughout the preceding decades. Those who had meanwhile attained University positions as Semitists, like MUELLER or BARTH, were careful to stick to philological exegesis. And it was perhaps no coincidence that only the newly established center of the German-Jewish extreme reform-movement on American soil tried to compete with Protestant critics.[18]

Up to now we have been content to trace some developments and differences in attitudes to Bible study on both the Christian and the Jewish sides. But this is not quite identical with the problem of Christianity and Judaism in their attitudes towards Bible study—a much more delicate issue. Yet if we wish to understand at least some of the developments, we must not shy away from attempting to penetrate further.

The Jewish reader of DIESTEL's century-old *Geschichte des Alten Testaments in der Christlichen Kirche* (1869)[19] is struck by the recurrent theme of ambivalence within parts of the Church towards the Old Testament, down to some extreme attempts to discard it altogether. Precisely because all of us present here are united in our positive regard—whatever the precise shadings of theological evaluation—we may not always be aware of the manifold guises ambivalence has taken. What used to be disregarded as "Gnostic" heresy, reappeared

---

[17] *Die wichtigsten Instanzen gegen die Graf-Wellhausensche Hypothese* (Berlin 1902-16).

[18] The intriguing phenomenon of men like Moses BUTTENWIESER of Cincinnati (and his disciples) will be discussed elsewhere.

[19] A reworked edition of this classic has been announced for some time.

within Christianity time and again. GROTIUS's attempt to judge the Old Testament as profane literature is, of course, different from the opinions of MARCION and CELSUS, and HARNACK's position is not to be identified with a certain ideology of the vintage from the nineteen thirties.

While these are waves hitting the fringes, it cannot be ignored that any attitude towards the Old Testament built on the basis of Christianity—as opposed to attitudes by individuals who are Christians—is perforce built on certain dogmatic positions as regards Salvation History. Shadings of stress between men like PROCKSCH or KNIGHT, on the one hand, and EICHRODT and VON RAD on the other, do not obliterate the basic outlines of what a Christian theology of the Old Testament should be about. The gap dividing any such Christian attempt from a comparable Jewish theology may be something one should not mention in polite scholarly conversation; but its extent should not be minimized. Nor does it facilitate discussion across the borders that there exists a dilemma within Christian theology—as emphasized in recent discussions[20]—and within Jewish circles.[21]

It should be borne in mind that no system of biblical theology can exist *in vacuo*. Exegesis cannot be divorced from theology—and vice versa. It was, perhaps, no chance that it took a scholar like Franz DELITZSCH to spell out again the very truth which, as we have seen, LUTHER had expressed centuries earlier: if the exegete ceases even for one moment to disregard the presence of Christ in the Old Testament as an exegete, he ceases being Christian.[22] Philological exegesis is a sine qua non; but it is not everything.

Even the most sympathetic study of the Old Testament by Christians could never become more than an exercise in theological relevance, a matter of theory and faith. The drawing of consequences for everyday behaviour, in the very practical sense of "observing

---

[20] Cf. e.g. the introductory chapter of H. J. KRAUS, *Die biblische Theologie— ihre Geschichte und Problematik* (Neukirchen 1970).

[21] For the problem of "Jewish theology" see below. It is hardly a coincidence that Jewish scholars who can be called biblical theologians of sorts (such as HESCHEL, GORDIS and, perhaps, BERKOVITS) have functioned almost exclusively in the context of American theological seminaries. If we add the names of some non-American philosophers (like BUBER, NEHER) the list is almost exhaustive. If I am not mistaken, I am the first Professor of Bible at an Israeli University who insists on teaching a graduate course on "Biblical Theology".

[22] Note e.g. the *Vorbetrachtungen* in Franz DELITZSCH, *Messianische Weissagungen* (Leipzig 1890), esp. p. 5.

the Law", remained necessarily a Jewish preoccupation. Hence the reluctance of Jewish 19th century scholars to engage in critical games, which could ultimately bear on issues of daily life, must also be viewed from the angle of practical implications.

This gets us back to the fact that the problematics of Jewish 19th century Bible study got interwoven with the break-up of what had been more or less monolithic normative Judaism. No amount of terminological niceties can get us away from the simple requirement that halachic Judaism cannot but enforce certain positions vis-à-vis Bible study, positions which are categorically different from any kind of Christian literalism or fundamentalism. For certain aspects of the Holy, as crystallized in halachic Judaism, the rules of exegetical obsolescence do not hold good. Halachic Judaism cannot yield, even if there were an authority that could proclaim for it a new *Divino Afflante Spiritu*. The 19th century break-up within traditional Judaism was connected to something which was only partly similar to the differences between the orthodox and liberal factions of Christian theologians in their attitudes to criticism. As stated before, only on the very fringe of Reform Judaism there existed men able to combine their version of Judaism with literary criticism, as it had evolved in Protestant theological schools.

Our inquiry is getting near our own times—separated by hardly more than a generation. At this point matters become even more delicate. Not only because both Catholics and Jews start appearing on a scene which had been dominated almost exclusively by Protestant theologians, but also because we are about to lose the benefit of historical distance. Furthermore, up to now we could discuss the position or attitude of individuals who were either Christians or Jews. Only when Christian and Jewish scholars commence a free exchange of ideas, are we being faced squarely by what may be more than the individual encounter.

I am hardly exaggerating if I suggest that it is really only in the period after World War II that a new problem begins to emerge of which we are as yet only half-aware: Christianity and Judaism in their mutual relations vis-à-vis Modern Bible Study. It is precisely because this organization of ours has contributed so much in this period after World War II to provide for the free non-denominational meeting of scholars and uninhibited interchange of views that we should not shy away from efforts of self-analysis, even if it makes us feel somewhat uneasy. Only if we attempt to understand ourselves may we expect to be able to continue our path together.

One aspect of what has been happening in recent decades may be described as connected with the "objectivity syndrome". In all non-experimental fields of scholarship scholars have taken care to move into areas where their personal equation interfered as little as possible. This struggle for "objectivity" presents, of course, an almost unique problem in the field of Old Testament studies. Not only because of what I stressed in my preliminary remark about the ever-present multi-layer character of Bible study, but because practically all academic students of the Bible remain heavily indebted to their own tradition and upbringing.

Only during the past decades have we been thus facing a situation that on the one hand we are all toiling together in the same vineyard —apparently without differences—yet as regards the most fundamental issues we are very much either Christians or Jews. It is a fact that there are Christian and Jewish scholars of Islam, Buddhism and so on. There are no Muslim or Buddhist scholars of the Old Testament. Whoever is active in this field does not just happen to be Christian or Jewish. However we try to ignore it—practically all of us are in it because we are either Christians or Jews. There exists no control group of Muslim scholars by which to judge what is "objective"; there exists only the cumulative weight of scholarship developed in a Protestant academic world to which both Catholics and Jews are, relatively speaking, newcomers.

By its very nature, the study of the Old Testament becomes therefore the common meeting ground for the committed, where the dilemma between the scholarly strife for objectivity and the denominational (or even national-religious) committedness is being acted out. The inter-denominational aspect has emerged for the first time in the past generation; the "objectivity" aspect has been developing slowly ever since the beginnings of the branch of "Introductory Studies" almost two centuries ago, when old Johann David Michaelis summed up his work as *Einleitung in die göttlichen Schriften des Alten Bundes* (1787), while young Eichhorn started off, at the very same time (1780), by chosing an "objective" name, used ever since: *Einleitung in das Alte Testament*.

We have noted above that the nineteenth century witnessed the beginning of the break-up of Old Testament studies as an all-embracing field of inquiry. It may now be suggested that the trend towards real or imaginary objectivity, towards the minimizing of inbuilt denominational prejudices, joined up with the trend towards ever growing specialization. The two trends together have enhanced the tendency towards splitting apart of Old Testament studies, towards turning the empire of "theology" (in the old sense) to a confederation of semi-autonomous kingdoms.

If you permit me a personal point, I do not think it will be a coincidence that, if I shall be so lucky as to become a footnote in the textbooks of the future, it will be as a biblical philologist. I suspect there is more to this specialization of mine than just training and interest. It is here that the background differences between me and my most intimate friends and colleagues who adhere to other creeds can be almost worked down to nil. All in all, biblical philology in its present dimensions—as opposed to the days of MORINUS and CAPPELLUS—can be isolated pretty much from subjective attitudes.

By the same token, we have not given up hope of escaping complete specialization—if not in our publications, at least in our teaching. Yet more and more specialization lies ahead. Our students tend to become more "objective" and more specialized. Even the recent organizational splitting up of my own subbranch into organizations may foretell the story of a mixed future blessing.[23]

What is true for textual studies is true, *mutatis mutandis*, for archaeology, historiography, linguistics, etc. By their very nature the *ancillae* make for objectivity as well as for diminished denominational differences. Hence ancillary studies become our common ground in meetings and publications. It almost seems that the more impressive and general our international meetings become, the more we tend to pass over in silence those issues which should constitute the very core of our scholarly endeavour. Yet precisely because these are intertwined with issues of background and belief, the corollary of the newly established post World War II Protestant-Catholic-Jewish symbiosis in Old Testament studies seems to be-

---

[23] I am not sure how many of my colleagues still regard themselves as all-round "biblical philologists", let alone as students of both Bible and Semitics in the 19th century tradition. In any case, since this Congress I find myself belonging, in one capacity or another, to Boards or Committees dealing separately with the fields of Massora-, Targum-, Peshitta-, Septuagint-Studies. Despite the possible positive results of such organizational frameworks, I am not convinced it is all to the good. Having worked for two decades on the establishment of a comprehensive framework at the *Hebrew University Bible Project*, I can only hope that the next generation will not be too specialized to continue the work we have begun.

come that what really matters is better not discussed, that the mistress, which should rule from the center, vacates her position to ancillary studies, which may be carried out without giving offense.

Let me illustrate another aspect of this dilemma. Biblical *Religionswissenschaft*—history, phenomenology etc.—can well manage on "empathy"; theology thrives only on some kind of identification. This basic truth holds good not only for pre-Gablerian formulations, but even for the so-called 'critical theology of the Old Testament'. If you wish, the differentiation is already foreshadowed in Spinoza's hermeneutical paragraphs which teach us the difference between *veritas* and *verus sensus*.[24] How can we escape the corollary that this most central field of biblical scholarship is perforce partisan, denominational, subjective? Or—to apply a formulation used once by a former incumbent of the Chair in this University (N. W. Porteous): "For the Biblical Theology neutrality would be unscientific". Jew and Christian may meet on the common ground of *Religionswissenschaft*. It would be folly to expect them to agree within the framework of a "biblical theology". And if it is sometimes assumed tacitly that "theology" is by necessity an exclusively Christian branch of study, we had better realize that it is only the belated entry of Jews into 20th century Biblical scholarship that has prevented until now the development of a Jewish Biblical theology.

I trust I have made it clear that disregard of the history of the respective backgrounds of Christians and Jews—and for that matter of Catholics, Calvinists, Lutherans, etc.—may be all to the good for furthering practical ecumenical efforts. But such disregard neither assists our self-analysis nor leads to true and deeper mutual understanding and respect. Moreover, we must become aware of the danger that, precisely because of our deep commitment to non-denominational objectivity and unity, we might concentrate on certain fields and issues to the exclusion of others. Perhaps the fact that many senior Bible scholars shy away from tackling a full-scale exegetical enterprise and that it is almost exclusively scholars who continue the German Protestant tradition that are not afraid of carrying out this basic task, adds another dimension. In the spirit of these thoughts, permit me to use the last minutes of our inquiry for some more critical self-analysis of recent developments on the Jewish side.

---

[24] Cf. W. Stuerman's remarks on the *Tractatus* in *PAAJR* 1961, p. 133 f.

We have mentioned before the basic problem of committedness. Throughout our inquiry we have taken it for granted that such committedness is of a religious character. The most decisive change over the past decades that I perceive in this respect is that this basic premise of parallel committedness, by Christians and Jews, is slowly breaking down. Precisely because on the Christian side "religious" can be defined largely in terms of belief and faith, while on the Jewish side "religious" traditionally signified also "observant", the basis for committedness on the Jewish side has been changing rapidly.

The complexity of "cultural-national-religious" Jewish committedness cannot be gone into on this occasion. But facts must be faced: at the very point in history when Jewish Bible study became established as an academic subject—that is, in the decades before World War II—the basis of committedness began to change slowly. This can be almost traced by looking at the change of generations: from men like Benno JACOB, SEGAL, CASSUTO, TORCZYNER, KAUFMANN down to our own generation. Some of those present will appreciate my remark when I wonder aloud about the problematic aspect that many Jewish students achieve today identification towards commitment through an "objective" discipline, such as biblical archeology.

This development should not be divorced from its institutional background. I do not think that I am widely off the mark in assuming that the majority of my Christian colleagues present here are functioning within the framework of a School of Divinity, or its counterpart. Few Jewish scholars function in such a framework. The shift of the basis cannot be separated from the fact that there exist today large numbers of students who have to be prepared for a "secular" high school teaching career and who, in their turn, support a superstructure of University teachers who carry out the research work.[25]

On the Christian side we have concerned ourselves with the drifting apart into subbranches, with the prestige moving towards the ancillary, "objective", subjects. The Jewish side differs considerably. Here the drifting apart is almost exclusively acted out

---

[25] The establishment in Israel of Universities (and teachers' colleges) is, in sheer quantity, a factor which is bound to find its expression in the direction and type of work undertaken. The phenomenon of teaching Religion on American State campuses is only partly comparable.

between the different layers of study, traditional and academic. Academic study has moved largely towards critical and ancillary issues. Exegesis—the pride of traditional Jewish study—is hardly in evidence,[26] and it is no coincidence that the gap in "Jewish Biblical Theology "has so far been filled only by some attempts which hover between existentialist philosophy and neochassidic midrash (see above). Because of the ongoing process of secularization of traditional culture, academic study has not yet succeeded in forging new links with Rabbinic studies—which might eventually provide for Jewish biblical theology the diachronic counterpart to the teleology inherent in Christian Old Testament theology.

To apply self-criticism harshly, there are today Christian as well as Jewish Bible scholars. I can also perceive the attribute "Christian" being meaningful to some extent, when we speak of "Modern Christian Bible Study". I am not convinced that there exists as yet something fully comparable on the Jewish side—in spite of the immense activity of Jewish scholars during the past decades.[27]

Time has come for the final paragraphs. We have followed the growth and development of Bible Study, ever since the heritage of medieval Jewish exegesis started Christian scholars on their new path, five centuries ago. We have watched the eclipse of Jewish studies throughout the following dark centuries, while Catholic-Protestant rivalry and philosophical Enlightenment combined to prepare the ground for critical inquiry. We have witnessed Jews, gingerly re-entering the academic scene in the 19th century, calling for the emancipation of Judaic studies, steering clear of Bible study as it had developed in Theological Faculties—yet trying their hand at the critical study of Text and Versions. We have also noticed Jewish scholars practically turning their back on Contents Criticism, throughout the nineteenth century.

We have seen, how some representatives of a new generation of Jewish scholars—with the swinging back of the pendulum from

---

[26] I refer to the lack of full-scale academic commentaries, as opposed to papers dealing with specific points.

[27] As a personal aside: the strictly philological-exegetical work carried out at the *Hebrew University Bible Project* is now being supplemented by the studies carried out by the *Institute for the History of Jewish Bible Research* at Bar Ilan University, which I have recently helped to establish. This Institute should serve to further self-understanding of the Jewish contribution to Bible studies for over two millennia. One of its programs deals with the establishment of a central archive for Jewish Bible study since the early 19th century.

19th century extremes, since the beginning of our century—joined the ranks of "Higher" critics. We have traced the internal split within Christian study, the drifting apart, the specializations, the trend towards ancillary "objective" branches. We have, on the other side, taken notice of the one-sided developments of Jewish study, culminating in the rapid change of basis for commitment. We have tried to understand how all these various forces have worked together in establishing, especially after World War II, what appears to be a broad common Judeo-Christian basis for objective, non-denominational, study—a basis which all of us present share, of which we are justly proud, on which our very being here together is built.

But I have also tried to argue that this is not yet enough. It is our duty to realize that this apparent inter-denominational objective scholarly unity has been achieved at a price, that different forces combine to make us evade issues central to our existence and to our scholarship. As Bible scholars as well as Jews or Christians we cannot shirk the task of preparing ourselves for the next stage, in order to be able to face together our differences on those issues in Bible study which are being too often sidestepped.

Mr. CHAIRMAN, Ladies and Gentlemen: I have tried your patience sorely, not only by an overlong paper but by touching upon many issues which because of their very delicacy are much more conveniently avoided. While an inquiry such as I have suggested is, by necessity, subjective, I hope that this first large-scale attempt at understanding the growth of Modern Bible Study in its relationship with both Christianity and Judaism is worth the effort. The members of this organization have largely contributed—both in congresses and publications, during much of the decisive period since the end of World War II—towards the creation of a climate of common scholarly endeavour and mutual understanding in many fields of Biblical study. I trust you will all join me in expressing the hope that the same spirit will prevail when we attempt now to reach out towards further goals, towards an ever deepening understanding of our common, yet divided, heritage.

DOMAIN ASSUMPTIONS AND SOCIETAL MODELS IN THE STUDY OF PRE-MONARCHIC ISRAEL *

BY

NORMAN K. GOTTWALD

Berkeley, California

The American sociologist Alvin GOULDNER speaks of "domain assumptions," by which he means the key or master conceptual frames of reference which affect the kinds of models and hypotheses that are imaginable—and therefore possible—in an epoch or circle of scholarship. The commanding domain assumptions are characteristically unexpressed or half-expressed and unargued. Shifts in models and hypotheses occur when new domain assumptions arise under the pressure of accumulating evidence and, more especially, under the impact of new extra-scholarly intellectual and cultural climates.[1]

Precisely such a shift in domain assumptions is under way in the study of Israelite beginnings. In a volume shortly to be published, I attempt to articulate the old and the new domain assumptions and to offer a societal model for pre-monarchic Israel consonant with the new domain assumptions. I shall here summarize the main outlines of my argument, with particular attention to the links between the domain assumptions in ancient Near Eastern and biblical studies, on the one hand, and the models of Israelite society, on the other. By way of more detailed application, I shall have a few comments about the historical peculiarity of Israelite tribalism or "re-tribalization."

The history of the study of Israelite beginnings is a history of very slowly emerging self-consciousness about domain assumptions and societal models, chiefly I think because anthropology and sociology never have had the impact on biblical studies that the humanities have had. The traditional conquest/invasion model of Israelite origins scarcely raised a single sociological question because it

---

* The theses advanced in this lecture will appear in greatly expanded and documented form in the lecturer's forthcoming study, *A Sociology of the Religion of Liberated Israel, 1250-1000 B.C.*, Orbis Books: Maryknoll, New York, 1975.

[1] A. W. GOULDNER, *The Coming Crisis of Western Sociology*, 1970.

contained an implicit unexamined, albeit rudimentary, sociology of Israel. It assumed a twelve-tribe system composed of clans and families as sub-sets of tribes operating as an unquestioned counterpart to the miraculously formed religious community of Israel. The immigration model, especially in the form it assumed under NOTH's amphictyonic analogue,[2] pushed sociological considerations a bit farther into the foreground, but not so far after all—and perhaps for three main reasons:

1. NOTH's welcome systemic approach to Israel was really mainly focused on one societal segment, the cultic institutions, rather than on the entire social system.
2. NOTH's approach took for granted the semi-nomadic origins of Israel without argument.
3. NOTH failed to compare the structural locus of the amphictyony in Greece with the structural locus of the "amphictyony" in Israel. Had he done so, it would have been clear that the amphictyony in Greece was a secondary or tertiary formation within the wider society, whereas the presumed "amphictyony" in Israel was the encompassing framework of the entire society.

Within the last decade the revolt model of Israelite origins has exposed the social structural and developmental questions about early Israel in an emphatic and insistent manner. The fact that MENDENHALL prefaced and framed his model of "peasant revolt" or "withdrawal" with a discussion of pastoral nomadism and tribalism in relation to urban and rural modes of ancient Near Eastern life thrusts the problem of the modes of Israel's occupation of the land into a larger context, namely, the problem of the social organizational modes of the Israelite occupiers.[3]

Until very recent years the inquiry into Israel's early history was massively under the sway of at least three master ideas which I shall characterize as:

1. The Domain Assumption of Social Change by Population Displacement.
2. The Domain Assumption of the Creativity of the Desert in Initiating Social Change in Sedentary Regions.

---

[2] M. NOTH, *Das System der zwoelf Staemme Israels*, 1930, and, in brief compass, *The History of Israel*, 2nd ed., 1960 [Eng. trans. 1960], pp. 85-138.

[3] G. E. MENDENHALL, "The Hebrew Conquest of Palestine," *The Biblical Archaeologist Reader*, III (1970), 100-120 = *The Biblical Archaeologist* XXV (1962), 66-87; *The Tenth Generation. The Origins of the Biblical Tradition*, 1973.

3. The Domain Assumption of Arbitrary Social Change Produced by Idiosyncratic or Prominent Cultural Elements.

These domain assumptions may be briefly stated as follows:

1. It is assumed that a major socio-political shift or hiatus is most likely to have been the result of one demographic or ethnic group displacing another, either wholesale or as a ruling elite, whether by immigration or by military conquest.
2. It is assumed that the breeding ground and source of many such population displacements in the ancient Near East was the desert and that these displacements entailed an influx of military and cultural élan typical of the desert group, followed by an eventual transition of the immigrants or invaders from nomadic to sedentary life with resulting socio-political acculturation.
3. It is assumed that the most idiosyncratic, prominent or distinctive element of a new socio-political phase, especially as viewed in retrospect, must have been the nuclear factor which initiated other sorts of changes and constellated them into a new social system or culture. Since the religio-symbolic and cultic dimensions of Israelite society appear to be the most idiosyncratic elements, particularly as viewed from the perspective of later Judaism and Christianity, Yahwism is to be regarded as the isolate source and agent of change in the emergence of Israel.

The pressures and forces which have eroded these long-standing domain assumptions are numerous and I shall cite only a few of them in catalogue form: evidence from pre-history and ethnography that pastoral nomadism is a secondary outgrowth of plant and animal domestication in the sown land; indications from the study of zones of social organization and from cultural anthropology that seemingly sudden cultural and social change is as often the consequence of slow growth and sharpening social conflict within a population continuum as it is the result of fresh incursions of peoples, that conflict occurs as regularly within societies under single political regimes as between opposing states, and that technology and social organization shape ideas more profoundly by far than humanities-oriented scholars have understood; demonstrations from sociology of religion that the social functions of religion are intrinsic to the form religion takes even in its most distinctive higher features; signs from historical data on the ancient Near East and early Israel of the subsidiary role of pastoral nomadism within the village-based economy, of the desert as a zone of political resistance and asylum rather than the locus of alien political and military initiatives, and of Israel's fundamental cultural continuity with Canaan over a very wide repertory, including language and religious formations, simultaneously combined with Israel's sharp divergence from Canaan in the development both of tribalism in opposition to the state and of a distinctively elaborated religious system. Probably not the least as a general encompassing factor in the deterioration of the old domain asassumptions is the direct experience of social upheaval in the modern world which more often follows from technological change and from tension and conflict within populations over control of resources and their distribution than from actual population displacements.

New domain assumptions are implicit in sociological work on Israelite beginnings now going on in the United States, so far most fully published by George MENDENHALL, soon to be enlarged by this lecturer's publication, and shared in by a growing number of younger scholars. Among others, students of MENDENHALL at the University of Michigan and of Frank CROSS and Ernest WRIGHT at Harvard University have contributed measurably to this development, generally in the form of unpublished dissertations and brief articles. Similar trends toward the application of social scientific methods to ancient Israel are beginning to surface in Israel, in western Europe and in the third world. A parallel phenomenon is visible among students of the ancient Near East.

The emerging master concepts, in each case challenging and replacing its outmoded predecessor, may be characterized as:

1. The Domain Assumption of the Normalcy of Social Change by Inner Societal Pressure and Conflict.
2. The Domain Assumption of the Subordinate Role of the Desert in Precipitating Social Change.
3. The Domain Assumption of Lawful Social Change Produced by the interaction of Cultural Elements at Many Levels.

The substance of these new domain assumptions may be briefly stated as follows:

1. It is assumed that major socio-political shifts or hiatuses are to be expected within societies as the result of new technological forces, social conflicts and contending ideas in volatile interaction

and that social change due to population displacement or political conquest is to be posited only when specific evidence warrants.

2. It is assumed that semi-nomadism in the ancient Near East was economically and politically subordinate to and broadly integrated within the dominant agricultural zone and was never the source of massive population displacement or political conquest as commonly attributed to it.[4]

3. It is assumed that the initially or ultimately prominent or distinctive features of a society or culture must be viewed in the total matrix of generative elements and not over-weighted in advance as the all-powerful sources of inspiration or as the selective survival factors in the societal development. Thus, a critical generative role may well have been played by cultural elements which have been lost to view and must be recovered by careful research. In particular, ideational factors must be looked at not as disembodied prime movers but as the ideas of human beings in determinate technological and social settings in which the total mix of culture will tend to exhibit lawful or patterned configurations.[5]

Congruent with these domain assumptions, I propose a societal model for early Israel along the following lines: Early Israel was a slowly converging and constellating cluster of rebellious and dissenting Canaanite peoples distinguished by an anti-statist form of social organization with de-centralized leadership. This Israelite "devolution" or "winding down" from the city-state form of social organization took the shape of a "re-tribalization" movement among agriculturalists and pastoralists organized in economically self-sufficient extended families with egalitarian access to basic resources. Israel's religion, which had intellectual and cultic foundations in ancient Near Eastern-Canaanite religion, was idiosyncratic or mutational in a manner that its society was idiosyncratic and mutational, i.e., one integrated divine being existed for one integrating and egalitarianly structured people. Israel became that segment of Canaan which wrested sovereignty from another segment of Canaan in the

---

[4] For the evidence, see N. K. GOTTWALD, "Were the Early Israelites Pastoral Nomads?," *Proceedings of the Sixth World Congress of Jewish Studies* held in Jerusalem, 13-19 August, 1973.

[5] For a cogent, methodical, richly illustrated presentation of theories of lawful cultural change, see M. HARRIS, *The Rise of Anthropological Theory. A History of Theories of Culture*, 1968.

interests of village-based tribally-oriented "low politics" over against city-state hierarchic "high politics."

So far it can be seen that I am in broad agreement with MENDEN-HALL's basic design of Israelite origins. One of the points where we diverge, however, is the point at which he denies the sphere of politics to early Israel. MENDENHALL reads Israel's rejection of state power as tantamount to the rejection of socio-political power per se: "The starting point of politics is the concern for power, but the whole theme of early biblical history . . . is the rejection of power."[6] It is obvious, however, that without a central concern for marshalling and employing power Israel could never have come into existence. Prompted by his fascination with the suzerain-vassal treaty as the supposed model for Israel's early covenant, MENDENHALL has bracketed out the divine monopoly of power from socio-political analysis. Clearly, we face two interlocking sociological phenomena to be accounted for in their peculiar combination: 1) Israel challenged one form of power by means of another form of power, and 2) Israel consciously exercised power even as it consciously attributed the source of all power to its deity. In failing to deal with the Israelite power formation sociologically, it appears to me that MENDENHALL has not adequately assimilated the new domain assumption concerning lawful social change.

At this juncture I propose to follow up and extend somewhat the tribal model of early Israel, first in synchronic terms and then in diachronic terms.

A considerable body of social organizational work on the tribe suggests the following broad formal features or traits of tribal organization: [7]

1. The tribe represents a sharp increase in demographic size over the hunting and gathering or primitive agricultural band, normally a leap from fewer than one hundred people to several hundreds or thousands.
2. The population increase is closely connected with a more secure control over an enlarged food surplus.
3. The enlarged food surplus is secured not only by technological improvements but by more intricate social bonding by means of

---

[6] G. E. MENDENHALL, *The Tenth Generation*, p. 195.

[7] See, for example, M. SAHLINS, *Tribesmen*, 1968, and J. HELM (ed.), *Essays on the Problem of Tribe* (Proceedings of the 1967 Annual Spring Meeting of the American Ethnological Society), 1968.

many cross-cutting associations or sodalities which interconnect the residential units, notable among these associations being the exogamous clan.

4. The sub-divisions of the tribe are typically segmented, i.e., they are structurally and functionally equivalent and politically equal, so that in principle any one of them could be destroyed and the tribe would survive.

5. The tribe carries out its political functions by diffused or temporary role assignments in such a way that there is no political leadership network distinguishable from the network of social leadership, although the rudiments of specialized political leadership appear with the tribal chiefdom.

Viewed in the broad design of social forms, pre-monarchic Israel was clearly tribal in character. Israel's economy was a form of intensive rain agriculture with animal husbandry, an economy which capitalized on the recent introduction into the highlands of Canaan of iron implements for clearing and working the land, of slaked lime plaster for constructing water-tight cisterns to hold reserve water through the annual dry season, and of the art of rock terracing to retain and control the erratic rainfall. The members of Israelite society were arranged not only in large extended residence groups which were relatively self-contained socio-economic units and political equals but also in cross-cutting sodalities or sodality equivalents. Among these cross-cutting groupings were the protective associations of extended families (the *mishpāḥôth*, which were *not* exogamous clans in my view), the citizen army, the ritual congregation, the Levites (landless and distributed among the tribes), and probably also the Rechabites (understood as itinerant specialists in metal).[8]

On the other hand, Israel was not yet a state, which it became only fully under David. Tendencies toward the chiefdom and monarchy are clearly evidenced in Saul and even earlier in some of the diverse functionaries called obscurely "judges," notably Gideon and Abimelech, and perhaps also some of the so-called "minor judges" such as Ibzan. At its founding Israel had no specialized political offices rooted in a superordinate sovereignty and it resisted such institutions and offices strenuously even after reluctantly resorting to them in the face of the mounting Philistine military threat, which was itself a powerful and effective re-grouping of socio-political

---

[8] F. S. FRICK, "The Rechabites Reconsidered," *JBL* XC (1971), 279-287.

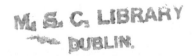

formations from the preceding era of Egyptian imperialism and Canaanite quasi-feudalism.

The defining feature of politics in old Israel was that political functions were diffused throughout the social structure or focused in temporary ad hoc role assignments. While the details of Israel's social structure (and especially of its "offices") are as yet unrecoverable in many respects, so that we do not possess the fully rounded cross-section we desire, all available information supports consistently the view that early Israel was tribal with fiercely resisted tendencies toward the chiefdom. And we are also able to establish beyond any shadow of doubt that this political feature of Israelite tribalism was not derived from pastoral nomadism but was securely rooted in a form of agricultural tribalism for which there are ample parallels in ethnography.

Of course the gross typological-evolutionary scale of band, tribe and state does not provide a finely calibrated historical understanding of specific societies. The historical locus of early Israel is thus of decisive importance for understanding the precise mix of factors and tendencies at work in its social organizational development.

The insights of Morton FRIED concerning tribal formations as "secondary phenomena" are pertinent for understanding Israel's peculiar tribalism, granting that FRIED's position is adjudged extreme by most anthropologists when applied to all tribal societies.[9] FRIED points out that many tribes are known to us in colonial situations where the external pressure of more highly organized and dominant civilizations leads to administrative synthesis and consolidation of the threatened society internally, so that it comes to present the form of a tribe to those who dominate the society. He cites the Makah of Washington State, the Tonga of northern Rhodesia and the Chiga of Uganda.

> Most tribes seem to be secondary phenomena in a very specific sense: They may well be the product of processes stimulated by the appearance of relatively highly organized societies amidst other societies which are organized much more simply. If this can be demonstrated, tribalism can be viewed as a reaction to the formation of complex political structure rather than a necessary preliminary stage in its evolution.[10]

---

[9] M. H. FRIED, *The Evolution of Political Society. An Essay in Political Anthropology*, 1967, pp. 154-174, and with some expansion in "On the Concepts of 'Tribe' and 'Tribal Society'", *Essays on the Problem of Tribe* (ed., J. HELM), 1968, pp. 3-20, accompanied by caveats and alternative views in several essays in the same volume, particularly those by G. E. DOLE, by H. S. LEWIS, and by R. COHEN and A. SCHLEGEL.

[10] M. H. FRIED, *The Evolution of Political Society*, p. 170.

FRIED notes that this is hardly a development peculiar to European colonialism since "the Roman, the Chinese, and other expanding state societies had grasped the essentials of divide and rule."[11]

If we modify his "most tribes" to "some tribes" or "many tribes", FRIED's insight may be taken seriously as an indication of the way a centralized state may intrude on simpler societies and harden them into certain social formations. But surely FRIED does not mean to imply that these simpler societies were entirely indisposed to the tribal direction in which the more organized societies pushed them. It would be stretching his argument ridiculously far to claim that segmentation and the exogamous clan were imposed by colonial powers. These integral elements of tribalism must be closely connected with economic production. FRIED himself admits the pertinence of Elman SERVICE's contention that the tribal organization extends the peace group and enhances military effectiveness in a world of competing bands and tribes, quite apart from and prior to the entrance of state societies on the tribal scene.[12]

Under the circumstances, FRIED's model must be altered considerably to apply to Israel. This can be done fruitfully if we allow not only that colonial centralized states can shape tribalism within a subject people, solidifying and skewing elements already present, but if we also posit that elements of the population within or adjacent to a centralized state may withdraw from it or rebel against it and develop less centralized social forms both as defensive mechanisms against the state and as constructive alternatives to the state. What these two versions of the social organizational effect of opposed centralized and uncentralized societies have in common is the abrasive or openly conflicting juxtaposition of societies at different organizational levels and the critical selective organizational impact of the "stronger" and more complex party upon the "weaker" and less complex party.

In my assessment we should view Israelite tribalism as a form chosen by people who consciously rejected Canaanite centralization of power and deliberately aimed to defend their own uncentralized system against the effort of Canaanite society to crush their movement. Israel's tribalism was an autonomous project which tried to roll back the zone of political centralization in Canaan, to claim territories and peoples for an egalitarian mode of agricultural and pastoral life. Unquestionably there were significant antecedent forms of struggle

---

[11] Ibid., p. 173.
[12] Ibid., pp. 164-165.

and modes of organization which fed into Israelite tribalism,[13] but in terms of demographic size, organizational novelty and political effectiveness there was a far greater qualitative leap from pre-Israelite to Israelite tribalism than there was from pre-colonial to post-colonial tribalism among the Makahs, Tongas or Chigas. The sum of these qualitative differences suggests that we should speak of Israel's adaptive tribalism as a "re-tribalization" movement.

All the evidence for early Israel points to its tribalism as a self-constructed instrument of resistance and of decentralized self-rule rather than tribalism as an administrative structure imposed by Canaanite rulers in order to govern their proto-Israelite or Israelite subjects. Seen from the perspective of Canaanite society, Israel was not a resistant colonial underling to be subdued but a foreign growth in its own body to be cut out. Seen from Israel's perspective, its tribalism was not a continuous ancient development to be preserved but a freshly constructed instrument for "cracking open" the centralized and stratified appropriation of natural and human resources of which the people forming Israel were an essential part prior to their act of revolt. Israel's tribalism was politically conscious social revolution and, more loosely, a civil war in that it divided and counterposed peoples who had previously been organized within Canaanite city states.

At this point, however, I would introduce another factor into the socio-political dynamics of Israelite origins, for it is the omission of this factor from MENDENHALL's model which contributes to the air of unreality which many critics have detected in his hypothesis. I refer to the fact that in virtually all such revolutions and civil wars the polarization of the populace is far from complete. There is evidence that a sizable part of the Canaanite populace was "caught in the middle," staying neutral as long as possible and only reluctantly moving toward one side or the other, thus constituting a socio-political segment whose loyalty or passive cooperation was actively sought by the contending parties.[14]

The implications of this concrete historical understanding of Israel's leap to tribalism are enormous. It means that our image of Israel's formation cannot be that of a continuous line of cultural evolution upwards from the band society to tribal forms of seg-

---

[13] For an explication of the immediate antecedents of Israelite tribalism, see N. K. GOTTWALD, *A Sociology of the Religion of Liberated Israel, 1250-1000 B.C.*, to be published in 1975, Chapters 8 and 9.

[14] Cf. ibid., Chapter 9, for a treatment of Canaanite enemies, converts, neutrals and allies vis-à-vis Israel.

mentation and sodality formation, nor can our image be that of a spill-over or eruption of pastoral nomadism from the desert into the settled land. Our image of Israel's formation must be that of a profound discontinuity in the hierarchic feudal social fabric of Canaan, a rupture from within centralized society. This rupture was accomplished by an alliance of peoples who withdrew directly from the Canaanite system with other peoples who, beyond the centralized system's immediate reach in the hinterland of Canaan, refused the customary path of being drawn into that system and accommodating themselves to it.

In terms of FRIED's typology, Canaan did not make an "appearance" in a long-developed or latent tribal society called Israel. To the contrary, Israel, with a mutant sophisticated tribal mode of organization, made an "appearance" within the social system and territorial domain of Canaan. The people who came to be Israelites countered what they experienced as the systematic aggression of centralized society by a concrete coordinated symbolically unified social revolutionary action of aggressive self-defense against that society. Appropriating the land and economic modes of production, this body of people organized its production, distribution and consumption along essentially egalitarian lines. The specific historic rise of old Israel was thus a conscious improvisational reversion to egalitarian social organization which displaced hierarchic social organization over a large area which had been either directly or indirectly dominated by Canaanite centralization and stratification for centuries.

The above model of Israelite re-tribalization as an inner Canaanite phenomenon raises whole chains of additional questions for further research and theoretical reflection. Is anything to be learned about the re-tribalizing confederacy of Israel from the history and typology of other inter-tribal confederacies such as the Iroquois Five Nations? Is there an analogy between post-Minoan and post-Mycenean Greek society and early Israel, as MENDENHALL has briefly suggested? Is anything further to be learned about the earliest Greek amphictyony of pre-Delphic times which centered at Pylae and which might after all be more cogently analogous with early Israel than the relatively late, perhaps already much decomposed, form of the amphictyony which NOTH treated? With what relevant social systems are we to compare early Israel? Certainly the Canaanite city-state and the Egyptian empire are prime units for comparison. But what of the 'apiru which appear in part as a special deviant form of passive resistance to Canaanite society and in part as a forerunner and contributory component of early Israel? How can our view of the previously over-inflated and misconstrued pastoral nomadic society be phrased so as to include it as a special ecological nuancing either of the city-state system or of the village-based agricultural system in conflict with the city-state? What allowance must be made for MENDENHALL's recent contention that there was a considerable movement of Luwians, Hittites, Hurrians and other northerly peoples into Palestine attendant on the incursion of the Sea Peoples?[15] Were these people carriers of a major new social system or, more likely, did they join the ranks of both sides of the inner-Canaanite struggle between low and high politics, or opt for uneasy neutrality? What are we to make of the Ammonites, Moabites and Edomites of whose beginnings we still know so appallingly little? Will the present slight improvement in our archaeological data on these trans-Jordanian peoples allow us to form any clearer picture of their social structure? This glaring blank in our knowledge of Israel's neighbors becomes all the more tantalizing in the light of the model advanced above for early Israel's social origins. Why were those Ammonites, Moabites and Edomites, whose origins are presumed to have been rather similar to Israel's origins, *not* a part of Israel? Why did the social revolutionary movement of early Israel extend only so far in the trans-Jordanian highlands and no farther? Were social elements among the Ammonites, Moabites and Edomites part of the general social uprising which failed to develop to a breakthrough point as it did with Israel? Finally, can a re-oriented Palestinian archaeology be of increasing assistance in checking social and cultural hypotheses, comparable for example with the function of "the new archaeology" in checking out hypotheses in new world ethnography?[16]

These are but a few of the proliferating questions which sharply pose the need for new research strategies and new forms of collaboration among specialists in order to seek additional evidence and to reassess old evidence within the framework of rapidly maturing sociological analyses of old Israel.

---

[15] MENDENHALL, *The Tenth Generation*, Chapter 6.

[16] A. E. GLOCK, director of excavations at Taanach, has proposed an ethnographic model for Palestinian archaeology in a paper on "Archaeological Systematics" which he presented to a seminar of resident fellows at the Albright Institute of Archaeological Research in Jerusalem on 3 May 1974. It is anticipated that a revised and enlarged form of this paper will be shortly published.

PRINCIPE CANONIQUE ET FORMATION DE L'ANCIEN TESTAMENT

PAR

E. JACOB
Strasbourg

Lorsqu'on traite du canon, on ne saurait entièrement négliger le témoignage de ceux qui ont été les premiers à en parler. Il y a au sujet de l'origine du canon deux sortes d'explications, les unes d'ordre mythique, les autres de nature plus historique. Parmi les premières il faut ranger celle de l'Apocalypse d'Esdras ainsi que la thèse de la Grande Synagogue qui par leur aspect global et leur affirmation d'une inspiration littérale ne peuvent être envisagées qu'avec une attitude extrêmement critique. Une prise au sérieux de l'histoire se trouve chez Ben Sira: par sa position-charnière entre le judaisme et l'hellénisme, par son souci de concilier tradition et culture, par son intuition d'une unité entre les trois parties constitutives du canon, il est le premier à nous introduire dans la problématique du canon. L'intuition de Ben Sira se trouve précisée et explicitée par Flavius Josèphe (Contre Apion I 37-42). Ce texte n'est pas seulement représentatif de la manière dont on concevait le processus historique — à ce titre il mériterait déjà notre intérêt — il contient aussi certains principes formels qui permettent de déceler les motifs profonds du devenir canonique de l'Ancien Testament. Les écrits réunis dans le canon sont des θεοῦ δόγματα, c'est à dire des expressions de la volonté de Dieu auxquelles en tant que telles on accorde foi τὰ δικαιῶς θεία πεπιστευμένα. Cette foi il s'agit d'y demeurer fidèle et d'être prêt, s'il le faut, à mourir pour elle. Les 22 livres du canon — ce chiffre a manifestement été choisi à cause du nombre correspondant des lettres de l'alphabet — ont entre eux une unité: contrairement aux μυριάδες βιβλίων des païens, ils ne sont pas ἀσυμφώνοι et μαχόμενοι; les écrivains sacrés ont écrit sous l'inspiration divine ἐπίπνοια fidèlement σαφῶς ce qu'ils avaient à communiquer; en cela ils ont agi comme des prophètes. Une succession prophétique ἡ τῶν προφητῶν ἀκριβὴς διαδοχή va de Moïse à Artaxerxès I (465-424), ce qui d'ailleurs est aussi l'opinion de l'Apocalypse d'Esdras. Ce principe de l'exacte

succession prophétique implique naturellement que le texte a toujours
été transmis fidèlement et qu'il ne supporte en conséquence ni
suppression ni adjonction. On peut retenir du texte de Josèphe les
enseignements suivants:

1. Le canon a son origine dans l'histoire et il a lui-même une
histoire. La notion d'un livre complet écrit par Dieu et descendu
du ciel, qu'on trouvera dans les apocalypses, ne représente pas la
ligne de force de l'Ancien Testament.

2. Le canon n'est pas d'emblée une réalité fermée. Sur ce point
Josèphe doit être lu à la lumière de Ben Sira pour qui l'existence du
canon est encore en pleine mouvance. Si au temps de Josèphe il
n'y a plus eu de contestation au sujet du contenu du canon, il y a
eu des opinions variées au sein des milieux juifs sur l'ordre des livres,
et sur leur valeur respective. Tous ceux qui se sont exprimés au
sujet du "canon" de Qumran, ont employé fort justement le mot de
"fluidité" qui s'applique autant au choix des livres qu'aux principes
de la canonicité.[1] Transmettre le canon traditionnel était sans doute
le souci essentiel de la communauté, mais en prenant la liberté de
privilégier certains livres par rapport à d'autres, et surtout en donnant
à l'interprétation une autorité aussi grande qu'à la tradition: ainsi
le pesher d'Habaquq affirme que la prophétie biblique ne deviendra
normative que lorsque le maître de justice, en l'occurrence le vrai
prophète, en révélera le sens véritable. De toutes façons il faut se
garder de considérer ce qui s'est passé à Qumran comme l'expression
de l'ensemble du judaisme.

3. D'après Josèphe les écrits canoniques forment une "symphonie".
Il nous place ici en face d'une question à laquelle l'herméneutique
et la théologie sont toujours à nouveau confrontées, celle de l'unité
de l'Ancien Testament. Mais on n'arrive pas à savoir si pour Josèphe
l'unité vient après le canon ou si, au contraire, elle est le motif qui,
en vertu d'une dynamique interne, pousse à la constitution d'un canon.
Nous pencherions pour notre part pour la deuxième hypothèse,
précisément à cause de la grande place qu'il accorde à l'élément
prophétique.

4. Les auteurs des écrits sacrés sont en effet des prophètes. Sur ce

---

[1] Il est certain que la situation à Qumran reflète une période antérieure au
pharisaïsme qui déniera toute inspiration aux écrits principalement d'ordre apocalyptique, en affirmant que le St. Esprit avait cessé d'être actif en Israel après la
mort des derniers prophètes Aggée, Zacharie et Malachie (cf. Yoma 9b, Sota 48b,
Sanhedrin 11a).

point Josèphe est en accord avec le témoignage du Talmud qui, en particulier dans le traité Baba Bathra 14b attribue la plupart des livres à des prophètes. Mais qu'est-ce qu'un prophète? Josèphe indique un point d'arrêt de la succession régulière des prophètes, mais le même Josèphe connait par ailleurs des manifestations prophétiques en milieu pharisien et essénien, et il y participe à l'occasion lui-même, encore que ces phénomènes prophétiques et l'attente du prophète eschatologique concernent davantage l'interprétation que la formation de la Bible.

Il n'est pas inutile de rappeler le témoignage de Josèphe au moment où nous sommes invités à faire de la critique du canon. Dans son petit livre *Torah and Canon*, James A. SANDERS [2] propose une nouvelle discipline ou sous-discipline des études bibliques qu'il intitule "canonical criticism". Il répond ainsi à la préoccupation de bien des spécialistes qui se résignaient difficilement à voir les problèmes du canon réduits à leur aspect extérieur et historique et relégués en appendice dans les manuels d'introduction, comme si la formation de la littérature de l'Ancien Testament n'avait rien à voir avec le canon. En insistant sur l'arbitraire et le hasard dans le processus de formation du canon, Johann Salomo SEMLER [3] avait rendu un immense service à la théologie, puisqu'il a permis de libérer la notion de parole de Dieu du carcan de l'orthodoxie traditionnelle et de son littéralisme. Il était sans doute nécessaire de se débarasser d'une notion globale et sacrale d'un canon, mais on peut se demander si en envisageant le canon sous l'angle de la limite et de la loi, on n'est pas passé à côté de l'intention du principe canonique, et si, sous prétexte de libérer le canon, on ne l'a pas fait éclater.[4] La tâche du "canonical criticism" consistera donc à ramasser les disjecta membra, non pas pour refaire ce que la critique issue du rationalisme a détruit et heureusement détruit, mais, en tenant compte de tout le travail critique portant sur la forme et la rédaction, de retrouver la vie qui

---

[2] *Torah and Canon*, Fortress Press, Philadelphia 1972, 124 p.

[3] *Abhandlungen von freier Untersuchung des Canon* (1771-1775). Au sujet des principes de SEMLER et de leur actualité v. H. DONNER, "Gesichtspunkte zur Auflösung des klassischen Kanonbegriffes bei Johann Salomo Semler", dans *Fides et Communicatio, Festschrift für Martin Dörne*, Göttingen 1970, p. 56-68.

[4] H. J. KRAUS (*Die biblische Theologie*, 1970, p. 345) après avoir souligné et approuvé la réaction contre la notion rigide du canon dans l'orthodoxie, ajoute cependant: "Die Frage ist nur, ob unter diesen mit der Kritik hochgespielten Voraussetzungen die Intention des Kanonprinzips und das Ereignis der Selbstdurchsetzung des kanonisch Umgrenzten in der Kirche überhaupt noch in den Blick gelangen kann."

est derrière le canon. SANDERS remarque fort justement que dans cette critique du canon l'accent doit être mis sur la fonction du canon plus que sur sa structure extérieure. Cela revient à poser la question fondamentale, celle de l'autorité d'une parole dans le contexte où elle est rapportée. Lorsque les prophètes annonçaient une parole de Dieu, ils le faisaient en vertu de critères dont ils étaient seuls juges et qui échappaient même à leurs contemporains les plus proches. Rechercher quelle était la forme première de cette parole est une entreprise qui n'est pas dénuée d'intérêt, mais de même que les sources qui alimentent un fleuve finissent par se confondre avec lui, la parole n'est saisissable que dans et à travers le courant de la tradition. Avant d'être un livre la Bible est une tradition. Qui dit tradition dit 'traditum', c'est à dire quelque chose qui a été reçu, qui a un jour été donné, qui a eu un commencement, mais dans l'Ancien Testament la tradition est liée à l'histoire d'un peuple chargé de la porter et de l'animer. C'est en tenant compte de l'*unité de la tradition* et de la *diversité de l'histoire* qu'on peut parler de l'unité de cet ensemble littéraire que nous appelons Ancien Testament. On a donné au cours des dernières décennies de multiples définitions de l'unité ou du centre (Mitte) de l'Ancien Testament. Nous donnerions volontiers notre préférence à celle de Rudolf SMEND [5] qui ne fait que reprendre une définition de WELLHAUSEN "Yahweh est le dieu d'Israel, Israel est le peuple de Yahweh"; on peut estimer que cette définition est trop vague pour mériter ce nom, elle a pourtant le grand avantage de lier l'Ancien Testament à la vie du peuple d'Israel et de mettre ainsi en lumière l'aspect dynamique et humain, qui devient souvent conflictuel, qui le caractérise. Nous compléterons cette définition par celle, très large aussi, de Georg FOHRER [6] qui voit les deux points focaux de l'ellipse de l'Ancien Testament dans la seigneurie de Dieu (Gottesherrschaft) et la communion avec Dieu (Gottesgemeinschaft), ce qui permet d'englober également ce qui appartient à la théologie de la création et qui ne sacrifie pas l'expérience individuelle à un idéal purement communautaire, reproche auquel la définition de SMEND-WELLHAUSEN ne saurait entièrement échapper. Permettre à Israel d'affirmer son identité au cours des variations de son histoire

---

[5] "Die Mitte des Alten Testaments", *Th. St.* CI, 1970, EVZ, 59 p.

[6] *Theologische Grundstrukturen des Alten Testaments*, W. de Gruyter, 1972, 276 p. La position de FOHRER est intéressante en ce que, venant après VON RAD qui affichait un grand scepticisme à l'égard des tentatives de retrouver à tout prix une unité de l'A.T., elle essaye néanmoins de voir une unité, mais en refusant de la voir dans un concept ou un mot-clé.

et de garder intacte la tradition, telle est la fonction première du canon.

Un des lieux où se réalisent le mieux la seigneurie de Dieu, la communion avec lui ainsi que l'unité du peuple est incontestablement le culte. En 1950 Gunnar ÖSTBORN [7] a publié une monographie sur *Cult and Canon* qui n'a, semble-t-il, pas reçu toute l'attention qu'elle méritait. Il y proposait de voir comme dénominateur commun du culte et du canon la description et la représentation des grands actes de Yahweh, thème qu'il a développé dans son ouvrage ultérieur *Yahweh's Words and Deeds*,[8] terme qui a été repris depuis et que certains préfèrent à celui d'histoire du salut.[9] Sans doute ÖSTBORN, inféodé à l'idéologie de l'école scandinave, a-t-il eu tort de réduire l'œuvre de Dieu au thème du combat et de la victoire de Dieu, dont il fait une application beaucoup trop schématique en voyant dans la plupart des livres bibliques des liturgies construites à partir de ce thème. On peut aussi estimer qu'il a transposé trop unilatéralement dans un passé ancien les données sur le culte qui n'apparaissent que dans les textes postexiliques. Mais on peut retenir sa thèse générale que le culte était le moment où le peuple prenait le plus fortement conscience de son identité. Les études récentes ont amené à relativiser l'importance du petit credo cultuel de Deutéronome xxvi 5 jadis fortement soulignée par VON RAD;[10] mais on ne saurait sous-estimer le fait que nous sommes là en présence d'une confession de foi récitée dans un cadre cultuel, faite de l'affirmation des actes de Dieu dans l'histoire, ce qui nous autorise à affirmer que l'histoire était en Israel le fondement du culte. En tenant compte de cette donnée fondamentale et des données éparses dans le reste de l'Ancien Testament, nous pouvons dire que le culte comportait trois moments essentiels:

---

[7] *Cult and Canon. A Study in the Canonisation of the Old Testament*, Uppsala 1950, 130 p.

[8] *Yahweh's Words and Deeds. A preliminary study into the Old Testament Presentation of History*, Uppsala 1951, 76 p.

[9] V. entre autres: G. E. WRIGHT: "Reflections concerning Old Testament Theology", dans *Studia Biblica et Semitica T. C. Vriezen dedicata*, 1966, p. 376-388; G. VON RAD: "Das Werk Jahwes", *ibidem* p. 290-298; N. W. PORTEOUS, "Magnalia Dei", qui insiste sur la réalité du canon, dans *Probleme biblischer Theologie, Festschrift von Rad*, 1971, Chr. Kaiser, München, p. 417-427. D'une manière plus radicale James BARR veut détacher l'action de Dieu de l'histoire pour la situer avant tout dans la parole; cf. en particulier *Old and New in Interpretation*, 1964.

[10] Cf. en particulier L. ROST, *Das kleine geschichtliche Credo*, Heidelberg 1965, et A. WEISER, *Einleitung in das AT*, 5me ed., p. 81ss.; ce dernier auteur souligne par ailleurs la grande importance du culte pour la formation de l'Ancien Testament.

a) il était une révélation. Tout culte comportait une théophanie soit exécutée sous forme de rite soit simplement rappelée par la parole du prêtre ou du prophète cultuel, et le contenu en était constitué par l'histoire et par les lois, l'aspect éthique du culte étant conditionné par son fondement historique.

b) le culte était actualisation. Il fallait que le peuple soit transporté dans le passé ou que le passé vienne vers le présent. Certains parlent pour le premier cas de typologie, pour le second de typisation, et pensent que le premier convient aux livres historiques, le second aux prophètes.

c) Le culte était enfin une réponse, se manifestant par la louange, l'acclamation, la prière et les sacrifices.

On pourrait être tenté de faire un parallèle entre cette triple fonction du culte et la forme tripartite du canon, la torah correspondant à la révélation, les nebiim à l'actualisation et les écrits à la diversité de la réponse. Le culte aurait ainsi été la matrice préexistante dans laquelle se serait coulée la matière du canon. Quoiqu'il en soit, la relation entre culte et canon est certaine. L'association étroite de l'histoire et des lois qui caractérise le Pentateuque répondrait fort bien à ce qui était la fonction du culte et du canon, à savoir la réalisation de l'identité du peuple qui ne peut se faire que s'il est régulièrement placé non seulement devant les promesses, mais aussi devant les interpellations et les exigences divines. Le culte pouvait à l'occasion prendre la forme d'une protestation, lorsqu'il était le seul lieu où l'identité du peuple avait la possibilité de se manifester, motif qui n'est absent ni chez l'auteur sacerdotal ni chez le Chroniste.

Le culte a été pour Israel l'occasion régulièrement offerte d'affirmer son identité, mais ce n'était pas la seule. La mémoire d'Israel — et le canon est une mémoire avant d'être une règle — n'était pas confinée au domaine cultuel, elle se traduisait aussi par une intense activité intellectuelle. La mémoire d'Israel a abouti à la création d'ouvrages historiques dont le Sitz im Leben était plus politique que cultuel. Israel a trouvé et retrouvé régulièrement son identité en écrivant son histoire.[11] Il est clair que toute présentation de l'histoire était

---

[11] Une des études les plus récentes et les plus suggestives sur l'historiographie israélite, M. WEIPPERT: "Fragen des israelitischen Geschichtsbewusstseins", *VT* XXIII (1973), p. 415-442, insiste sur cet aspect de l'auto-comprehension d'Israel en tant que peuple, et voit dans les notions de possession d'un pays et dans la conviction de ne pas y avoir toujours vécu, les principes directeurs des grands ouvrages historiques aux origines de la royauté, principes qui n'auraient pas été sans influence sur la vie politique et économique.

inspirée par le souci de l'actualité: le recours au passé sert à expliquer
le présent et à l'assumer. Le Yahviste qu'on situe en général au
temps de Salomon vit à un moment où Israel est en train de perdre
sa spécificité; il subit ce que nous appellerions aujourd'hui une
'crise d'identité'. L'assimilation avait joué à plein, les anciennes
institutions et coutumes sont ébranlées, et c'est ce moment qu'un
auteur, chez qui le profondeur théologique n'a pas étouffé le sens
artistique, choisit pour écrire l'histoire des origines. Il s'attache à
montrer que dès les origines Israel a été menacé dans son existence,
que la vie des patriarches et celle de Moïse ont été une suite de
tentations et d'épreuves qui n'avaient d'équivalent que la validité
des promesses divines. Dès lors l'assimilation, la culture, deviennent
possibles, puisque l'essentiel est maintenu. Et le thème de la bénédiction
qui est à la fois un thème religieux et culturel, et davantage culturel
que religieux puisque relevant de l'ordre de la création, permet au
Yahviste de concilier la spécificité de l'élection et la vocation universaliste d'Israel.

L'affrontement de plus en plus aigu d'Israel aux grands empires
du 9me au 7me siècles risquait de faire perdre à Israel une nouvelle
fois son identité. Israel pouvait-il se maintenir en face des grandes
puissances, et cela d'autant plus qu'au danger extérieur s'ajoutait à
l'intérieur celui du baalisme et de la corruption du droit ancestral.
C'est dans ce contexte qu'un autre historien, celui qu'on appelle
l'Elohiste insiste, dans la révision auquel il soumet l'ouvrage
yahviste, sur la nécessité pour Israel de maintenir son élection; il ne
doit pas oublier qu'il est le "peuple à part qui n'est pas compté
parmi les nations" (Nbs. xxiii 9). En face de toutes les tentations
auxquelles il est exposé, Israel doit non seulement tenir au message
du Yahviste, mais encore pratiquer la crainte de Dieu et l'obéissance.
Un récit comme Genèse xxii, généralement considéré comme
typique de l'Elohiste, sait allier fort bien la foi au dieu exigeant
et au dieu de la promesse. Dès ce moment la reprise des mêmes
thèmes a la force d'une autorité canonique, dès ce moment également
on ne s'oriente pas dans la voie de solutions nouvelles, on cherche
plutôt dans les traditions anciennes le moyen d'assumer des situations
nouvelles. La canonisation de ce qui sera plus tard la Torah est en
germe au 8me siècle, et ce germe devient une plante avec l'apparition
du Deutéronome. Von Rad écrit dans son commentaire du Deutéronome: "La représentation d'un Israel appelé dans les pères, inter-
pellé solennellement au Sinaï, conduit à travers le désert jusqu'à

l'accomplissement de la promesse, était déjà devenue si canonique,
que les époques ultérieures, si elles voulaient se comprendre en tant
qu'Israel, ne pouvaient qu'entrer dans cette représentation et se
comprendre par l'analogie avec l'Israel mosaïque." (A.T.D., *Das
Buch Deuteronomium* p. 21). Quelle que soit l'origine historique
du Deutéronome, que son point de départ se situe plus près de Moïse
ou plus près de Josias, il entend présenter Israel comme le peuple
de Yahweh et Yahweh comme le dieu d'Israel. Beaucoup plus que
ses devanciers qui étaient encore largement tributaires de la narration
légendaire, le Deutéronome fait entrer l'histoire dans un schéma,
les traditions sont stylisées, ramassées dans des formules destinées
à être enseignées et apprises par cœur. Sans se perdre dans les détails
de la narration, il s'agit de montrer qu'Israel est un peuple unique,
qu'il a vécu depuis la sortie d'Egypte sous la conduite de Moïse
une même histoire dirigée par l'élection et concrétisée par l'alliance.
L'action de Yahweh est une comme le peuple est un. Yahweh a
donné à son peuple un pays comme possession permanente et pour
vivre dans ce pays il lui a fait don d'une torah; s'engageant avec
le peuple dans une alliance, il exige en retour un culte sans partage
et qui doit être offert en un lieu unique. Tout cela amène à une
attitude exclusive: le peuple aussi bien que le livre doivent être
préservés de toute altération; la formule dite de Ptah hotep 'ne rien
ajouter, ne rien retrancher' [12] constitue désormais une limite au-delà de
laquelle on risque de tomber dans l'infidélité ou dans l'hérésie. Le
Deutéronome est le point d'aboutissement et de convergence d'une
série de mouvements: renforcement des structures fondamentales
du culte, prédication des Lévites, successeurs qualifiés de Moïse,
effort de réflexion et de pédagogie des sages et bien entendu prédication des grands prophètes. C'est dire que l'ensemble ou du
moins la grande majorité du peuple contribue à la formation de ce
qu'on peut bien appeler le premier canon. Le canon est l'œuvre du
peuple et non d'une minorité ou d'un parti. Dans son très intéressant
et suggestif ouvrage *Palestinian Parties and Politics that shaped the Old
Testament* (1971), Morton SMITH souligne l'importance des partis

---

[12] Selon S. MORENZ (*La Religion égyptienne*, trad. franç., p. 287) ce texte qui
figure vers la fin des maximes de Ptah hotep pourrait être traduit: "Ne dis pas
une fois une chose et une fois une autre, ne confonds pas une chose avec une autre."
Il s'agirait donc d'une exhortation morale propre au genre sapiential, mais qui
aurait pu être interprétée plus tard comme une invitation à garder l'intégrité
d'un texte. Il semble bien que la formulation de ce principe dans le Deutéronome
(iv 2; xiii 1) remonte à une influence égyptienne.

et en particulier du parti de Yahweh pour la composition des livres bibliques; ce parti de Yahweh, exclusif et minoritaire, serait à distinguer nettement de la majorité adonnée au syncrétisme plus ou moins officialisé. Il ne nous semble pas que le Deutéronome soit l'expression d'un parti. Tout en schématisant la réalité existante par des formules qui suppriment les nuances, il est néanmoins l'expression sinon de tout Israel, du moins de la grande majorité du peuple qui avait pris conscience de son rôle de peuple de Dieu. Autrement Josias n'aurait pas pu ériger le Deutéronome en loi d'état et en tirer des conclusions sur le plan national. Ces dernières furent, hélas, éphémères, mais les démentis de l'histoire, bien loin de la supprimer, renforcèrent la prise de conscience de son identité. La présence désormais d'un livre accessible à tous y a puissamment contribué. Il est exact de dire qu'à partir du Deutéronome la religion d'Israel est devenue en partie une religion du livre, mais nous ne donnerons à cette constatation aucune notation péjorative. Nous ne pensons pas qu'avec la prédominance du livre commence pour Israel une période de décadence et il ne faudrait pas tirer d'un passage de Jérémie à l'interprétation difficile (viii 8)[13] sur la plume mensongère des scribes et des sages la condamnation absolue du livre au nom du prophétisme. Il est plus logique de supposer que la cristallisation du principe canonique depuis longtemps présent à l'état latent dans un livre a aidé le peuple à croire et à mieux vivre la formule de l'alliance: "Vous serez mon peuple et je serai votre Dieu."[14] Le livre n'a jamais été, du moins à cette époque, un objet d'idolâtrie ni une cause de sécurisation.

Le passage avec le Deutéronome à une forme concrète de canon marque un certain exclusivisme, autrement il ne serait plus canon, mais l'exclusivisme du Deutéronome reste inclusif. Si le cadre est rigide, il y a place à l'intérieur de ce cadre pour la diversité. L'ouvrage deutéronomiste, dont le livre du Deutéronome devait un jour former l'introduction avant de devenir la conclusion du Pentateuque, applique assez strictement une formule-cadre, mais conserve, à

---

[13] Il ne faudrait pas à partir de ce verset conclure que Jérémie a vu dans le Deutéronome une erreur ou même une pia fraus. Ce n'est pas la plume des scribes qui a été mensongère, mais les auditeurs par leur refus de voir derrière la lettre la parole et de l'écouter pour la mettre en pratique qui l'ont rendue mensongère et vaine pour eux.

[14] Cf. S. Morenz, *La Religion égyptienne*, p. 277n., et les intéressantes considérations de S. Herrmann: "Kultreligion und Buchreligion", dans *Das ferne und das nahe Wort. Festschrift L. Rost*, Berlin 1967, p. 95-105.

l'intérieur du cadre, des traditions multiples parfois en contradiction expresse avec sa propre théologie, car il était trop respectueux de l'histoire pour se permettre de sacrifier les faits à une théologie.

Lorsqu'il arriva que les thèmes essentiels du Deutéronome, terre, royauté, unité, furent impropres à exprimer l'identité d'Israel, ils trouvèrent un refuge dans l'eschatologie où ils ont continué à nourrir la foi. Mais il fallait, pour qu'Israel puisse continuer à se retrouver dans son histoire, une présentation de celle-ci plus conforme aux circonstances de l'exil et de la perte, qui pouvait sembler définitive, de l'indépendance nationale. C'est à cette tâche que se consacre l'auteur dit sacerdotal. Aux vues dynamiques de l'histoire qui sont celles du Yahviste et du Deutéronomiste, il oppose une vue plus statique, à la théologie de la parole il substitue une théologie des institutions, encore que la parole soit pour lui l'institution majeure, ce qui assure la continuité dans le changement. Sous l'influence du courant sapiential déjà largement perceptible dans le Deutéronome et dans toute la tradition prophétique, il met l'accent sur la création, définitivement intégrée à l'alliance, et aussi sur les institutions familiales, généalogie, rites, lois. Les ancêtres du peuple, car le temps des pères reste toujours la période normative, sont présentés comme les initiateurs des institutions: Abraham, le père du peuple en marche, est le père de la circoncision; Moïse le libérateur devient l'organisateur du culte et légitime par là toutes les institutions cultuelles qui n'étaient qu'en partie d'origine israélite. Dieu doit être au moyen de signes visibles présent au milieu du peuple et être une source de sainteté efficace contre le pouvoir dissolvant de ce qui est profane. La mise à part du peuple, conçue jusque là essentiellement comme une mission, est désormais envisagée comme une séparation.

Avec l'auteur sacerdotal le Pentateuque atteint sa forme définitive; c'est vraisemblablement lui que lit Esdras lors d'une cérémonie publique (Néh. viii 5) où l'apparition du livre devant le peuple rassemblé fait le même effet qu'une théophanie. Tout le monde est d'accord pour voir dans cette proclamation la deuxième grande étape sur la voie de la constitution du canon. Résultat étonnant, mais aussi combien déroutant que ce Pentateuque. Pourquoi fallait-il qu'on en revienne toujours à cette période, pourquoi cette fidélité au passé, alors qu'Israel vivait par ailleurs de l'espérance d'un avenir plus beau que le passé? C'est que le passé était la source de tout, du présent et aussi de l'avenir. A travers son histoire si variée et apparemment si discontinue, Israel est toujours resté conscient qu'il n'avait qu'un père, Abraham, et qu'un maître, Moïse. Il y a eu d'autres grands personnages, tout particulièrement David, et, étant donné que l'Ancien Testament a reçu sa forme définitive à Jérusalem, il eût été assez normal que les traditions jérusalémites et davidiques refoulassent à l'arrière-plan celles des pères et du Sinaï. Même si l'on admet que les Psaumes constituent une sorte de réplique au Pentateuque avec la place centrale donnée à David, on ne peut pas parler d'une canonisation de la période davidique. Les possibles conflits entre Moïse et David, Sinaï et Jérusalem ont été résolus non par la voie de l'élimination, mais par celle de l'intégration au Pentateuque. Il eût été anormal que ce dernier qui avait la prétention d'être aussi complet que possible ne fît pas une place à des événements d'une importance aussi vitale que David et Jérusalem. Il le fait discrètement, mais d'une manière suffisamment transparente pour que le lecteur se sente ramené d'Abraham à David et vice versa. Le chapitre xv de la Genèse contient probablement des souvenirs historiques concernant une alliance de Yahweh avec Abraham, mais, ainsi que l'a montré R. E. CLEMENTS,[15] ceux-ci sont dans leur présentation actuelle chargés de traits de l'époque de David, de sorte qu'Abraham est devenu ce qu'il est grâce à sa permanente actualisation, nous pourrions presque dire réincarnation, dans les autres personnages de la tradition qui lui ont donné son sens. Autre exemple: un des buts du récit midrashique de Genèse xiv est d'introduire Jérusalem et la monarchie davidique dans le Pentateuque; elles y revêtent une singulière dignité, puisqu'Abraham s'incline devant le lointain ancêtre de David. Quant à Moïse, sa figure a reçu tant de surcharges venant des rois et des prophètes, sans parler des traits folkloriques, que la reconstitution de sa personnalité historique est une entreprise vouée d'avance à l'échec. Cette canonisation de la période des origines a aussi des raisons politiques; il est certain par exemple qu'on ne pouvait parler de David qu'à mots couverts sous la domination étrangère, mais le motif principal reste le souci de retrouver toujours le commencement, de préserver son identité en évitant de rompre le cordon ombilical qui relie Israel à sa mère . . . qui est la période des pères.

---

[15] *Abraham and David* Studies in Biblical Theology, SCM Press, London 1967. La thèse majeure de CLEMENTS est qu'il y a une relation à la fois historique et théologique entre l'alliance abrahamique de Gen. xv et l'alliance davidique: d'une part la région d'Hébron était le centre de l'histoire d'Abraham et de David, et d'autre part Abraham et David se rejoignent grâce au thème de la promesse et de l'accomplissement.

Telle était l'attitude d'Israel au moment où apparait après la formation définitive du Pentateuque et du canon des prophètes, celui que P. R. Ackroyd a appelé le premier théologien du canon, à savoir le Chroniste.[16] L'intérêt pour les problèmes du canon a pour contrecoup un renouveau d'intérêt pour cet auteur si souvent vilipendé par la critique, car il est, selon le titre de l'ouvrage de T. Willi [17] le premier exégète de la tradition biblique. Les intentions du Chroniste sont peut-être multiples et peuvent être d'ordre politique, messianique, apologétique ou polémique (contre les Samaritains). En tous les cas, si l'histoire a — et cela dès les origines de l'historiographie — pour but non pas de raconter les événements mais de les actualiser, on ne saurait refuser au Chroniste le titre d'historien. Pour cet auteur le personnage central est David et toute sa perspective est sinon messianique du moins davidique, mais il est tellement dépendant des traditions anciennes et en particulier il partage la croyance commune à l'autorité supérieure du Pentateuque qu'il lui arrive de présenter l'œuvre de David d'après l'analogie de celle de Moïse. David transmet à Salomon le modèle du Temple comme Dieu l'avait jadis donné à Moïse (1 Chr. xxviii 19) et les offrandes volontaires pour le Temple (1 Chr. xxix 3) ne sont pas sans rappeler les offrandes des enfants d'Israel pour la construction du sanctuaire du désert (Ex. xxv 1ss., xxxv 4ss.). Bien que la période recouverte par le Pentateuque soit en dehors de son intérêt, il ne conçoit pas d'autre fondement que le Pentateuque.

Maintenir, défendre, préserver l'identité d'Israel, telle était aussi la fonction des prophètes. On peut dire que le seul canon, écrit et non écrit, auquel ils obéissent est de rappeler en tout temps et hors de temps qu'Israel est le peuple de Yahweh, même lorsqu'ils annoncent la rupture provisoire de l'alliance. Il y a apparemment une antinomie entre les termes de "prophète" et de "canon", car le prophète n'est pas l'homme d'un livre, il a reçu une parole valable hic et nunc pour une circonstance bien précise, et qui devient dangereuse et fausse lorsqu'elle est appliquée en dehors de ce contexte particulier; c'est faute d'avoir compris cela qu'a surgi ce qu'on appelle le "faux prophétisme". Mais une parole venant de Dieu, ayant par consé-

---

[16] "The Theology of the Chronicler", *Lexington Theological Quarterly*, VIII, 1973, p. 112. Le même auteur, spécialiste du judaisme postexilique, a insisté dans plusieurs de ses publications sur les problèmes de la tradition, de la continuité et de la réinterprétation.

[17] *Die Chronik als Auslegung*, FRLANT, Vandenhoeck & Ruprecht, 1972, 267 p.

quent une origine surnaturelle, a, bien que dite dans le temps et pour un temps, une dimension qui transcende l'histoire, elle peut donc rester, au delà de son lieu historique, interpellatrice, contraignante, placer devant un choix, à condition de leur faire rejoindre l'actualité. Il y a donc une relation étroite entre les termes de prophète et de canon qui peut s'appuyer sur les témoignages de Ben Sira et de Josèphe qui voient l'un et l'autre dans le canon l'œuvre des prophètes. Il est vrai que jusqu'au rouleau avalé par Ezéchiel, dont il ne faudrait pas oublier qu'il s'agit d'une image, la parole prophétique n'est jamais liée à un livre; les prophètes, du moins ceux d'avant l'exil, ne se réfèrent jamais à une autorité canonique, bien qu'ils soient tous largement dépendants de traditions dont certaines comme le Décalogue devaient avoir valeur normative, mais les paroles des prophètes deviennent pour d'autres un canon, car un prophète, par le simple fait qu'il est prophète, détient en sa personne déjà le sceau de la canonicité. Un point de repère est constitué par Esaie et son cercle de disciples dont l'importance n'a peut-être pas eu l'ampleur que certains ont voulu lui donner,[18] mais dans lequel il faut certainement voir autre chose qu'une simple image. Il semble qu'assez tôt — et cela ne vaut pas seulement pour Esaie — les paroles du prophète ont été mises par écrit et qu'on ait attribué à ces écrits, de dimension modeste sans doute, une fonction qui devait en quelque sorte prolonger et remplacer la présence effective du prophète. Lorsqu'Esaie reçoit l'ordre de sceller une série d'oracles (viii 16) que rien n'autorise à affirmer qu'il n'ait pas vraiment été exécuté, il interrompt momentanément son activité, il se retire, mais il laisse aux mains de ses disciples une parole écrite comme le signe d'une réalité et d'une présence qui sera un jour pleinement dévoilée. Il est intéressant de remarquer que dans la forme actuelle du livre l'appel à la *torah* et à la *te'udah* (*v.* 20) sont opposés à la consultation des esprits des morts; c'est dire que les paroles des prophètes ne sont pas des oracles immédiats et infaillibles comme ceux qu'on demandait aux esprits, mais des signes qui renvoyent à Dieu et qui, dans le cas présent d'Esaie, permettent l'attente et l'espérance, et Habaquq fera écho à cette affirmation (ii 3). Voilà qui nous permet de préciser une

---

[18] Faute de preuves, il est sans doute difficile d'accorder aux disciples des prophètes l'importance que leur donnait naguère MOWINCKEL (*Jesaja-disiplene*, Oslo, 1926). Mais il ne semble pas qu'il faille voir dans les limmudim et les yeladim d'Esaie chargés de conserver les oracles du prophète de simples images comme le supposent entre autres LINDBLOM (*Prophecy in Ancient Israel*, p. 161) et WILDBERGER (*Jesaja*, 3 K, p. 344).

autre fonction du canon: il n'est pas un oracle, mais un signe, mais un signe ayant plus qu'une simple fonction indicative: parlant du canon Franz HESSE a dit qu'il n'indiquait pas seulement une chose, mais qu'il était lui-même déjà une partie de cette chose.[19] Contestées par le plus grand nombre, les paroles des prophètes ont été conservées par de petits groupes qui trouvaient dans leur méditation le moyen de prouver leur identité et la possibilité de jouer un rôle exemplaire pour le peuple. Les groupes des disciples des prophètes ont considéré comme leur mission de rendre les paroles des prophètes, marquées du sceau de leur individualité et des circonstances historiques aux-quelles elles s'appliquaient, utilisables par la communauté en les faisant pénétrer dans la liturgie et la prédication. Les Chroniques qui donnent un écho de la prédication des Lévites nous montrent que celle-ci était inspirée par les prophètes qui devaient jouir d'une autorité canonique semblable à celle du Pentateuque. La parole d'Esaie à Achaz sur la foi (Es. vii 9) est reprise dans 2 Chr. xx 20 dans un discours mis dans la bouche de Josaphat, mais à l'exhortation à la foi en Yahweh est ajouté comme une explicitation: "Croyez en ses prophètes et vous réussirez" (cf. aussi 2 Chr. xxxiii 10, xxxvi 12, 16). Voilà la parole d'Esaie sortie de son contexte historique et revêtue d'une portée générale et, ajouterons-nous, immédiate, car à présent il ne s'agit pas de se plaindre de l'absence ou du silence des prophètes (Ps. lxxiv 9),[20] les prophètes sont présents dans leurs écrits qui sont à portée de main de chacun, et pour les écouter il suffit de les lire. On peut supposer qu'il y a eu des canons partiels de prophètes; ainsi il y a eu un canon d'Esaie, réunissant des éléments divers autour du thème général d'une théologie de Sion curieusement et habilement combinée avec une théologie de l'exode dans la deuxième partie du livre. Il y a eu aussi un canon de Jérémie centré sur une théologie de l'alliance qui était certainement essentielle pour le prophète lui-même. Le pouvoir d'attraction et d'inclusion des prophètes a été très grand; il faut pourtant noter qu'il n'a de loin pas été aussi im-portant que celui du Pentateuque. Le livre d'Esaie a pu devenir pour certains groupes comme les gens de Qumran, une sorte de Bible, mais jamais au point d'éliminer les autres livres, comme

---

[19] "Das Alte Testament als Kanon", *N.Z. syst. Th.*, 1960, p. 327.

[20] Ce texte ne saurait être interprété comme exprimant la disparition du pro-phétisme dans le sens de Josèphe et du Talmud. Il s'agit ici d'un chant national de lamentation du temps de l'exil où parmi d'autres malheurs est déplorée l'ab-sence des prophètes, cf. I Sam iii 1; Ez. vii 26; Lam ii 9.

cela a été possible pour le Pentateuque des Samaritains. De même aucun prophète n'est devenu un "personnage corporatif" au même degré qu'Abraham et Moïse et dans une moindre mesure David. Les traits individuels qui caractérisent la figure collective du serviteur de Yahweh dans le Second Esaie ne sont pas empruntés au prophète Esaie, ce qui eût été assez normal, mais sont inspirés très probablement par la figure de Moïse. Les douze petits prophètes ont très tôt formé un recueil unique, mais dans ce recueil unique l'individualité de chaque prophète a été pleinement respectée, précisément parce qu'il y a avait dans la personne du prophète quelque chose qui résistait à tout nivellement collectif ou abstrait. Il en a été autrement du Pentateuque dont les auteurs restent anonymes, mais les prophètes ne sont pas restés en dehors du courant d'attraction exercé par le Pentateuque. En bien de ses pages la Torah manifeste l'héritage qui lui vient du prophétisme. Abraham et Moïse sont à l'occasion appelés prophètes [21] et c'est peut-être l'importance du prophétisme qui nous vaut de voir à la fin de ce qui constituait un jour le Tétrateuque la curieuse histoire de Balaam, dans laquelle nous avons comme dans 1 Rois xiii et le livre de Jonas, un traité théologique sur le prophétisme. En partant de quelques données historiques, car depuis les textes de Mari nous savons que parler de prophétisme au temps de Moïse n'est pas un anachronisme, ces chapitres traitent du pouvoir contraignant de la parole prophétique, du conflit entre roi et prophète, de la portée prophétique et universaliste de la mission prophétique et de la supériorité de la parole prophétique sur les rites cultuels souvent entachés de magie. Cette conclusion prophétique du Pentateuque donne le ton à l'ensemble et valorise le jugement de Josèphe sur l'origine prophétique du canon. La Torah et son autorité supérieure ne sont pas le résultat du légalisme, avec lequel le terme de Torah n'a rien à voir, mais du prophétisme qui est la vivante démonstration d'un Dieu qui se révèle, qui parle et qui ordonne, ce qu'on saisit dans le Pentateuque peut-être mieux qu'ailleurs. En résumé, ce que les prophètes ont apporté au principe canonique c'est le dynamisme de la parole, ce qui a évité au canon d'évoluer vers une forme exclusive et sclérosée.

Un peuple dont l'identité se manifestait si fortement dans l'audition devait trouver encore d'autres moyens d'écoute, plus réguliers que les prophètes, et cela dès avant l'autorité unique du livre. Or une écoute est d'autant plus efficace qu'elle est dirigée et enseignée.

---

[21] Gn. xx 7; Dt. xviii 15; xxxiv 10.

Les sages ont eu une part non négligeable dans la fonction et dans la formation du canon. Les origines de l'enseignement en Israel sont mal connus; primitivement réservé aux fonctionnaires royaux et fait de connaissances encyclopédiques et de conseils pratiques, il s'est étendu progressivement à des milieux plus larges, et cela d'autant plus facilement que l'élément didactique n'a jamais fait défaut ni au culte ni à la prédication des prophètes. Actualiser l'histoire c'était nécessairement l'enseigner, et l'historien deutéronomiste applique à l'histoire du peuple les mêmes principes pédagogiques que les sages des Proverbes à la vie des individus: la droiture réussit, le péché est source de malheurs. L'importance des sages pour le canon est double: en enseignant le contenu des traditions nationales, ils ont contribué à enraciner le peuple davantage dans celles-ci, mais, revers de la médaille, ils ont eu tendance à ramener toute la tradition à l'enseignement. Le sage qui a laissé sa signature dans le dernier verset du livre d'Osée a sans doute été bien intentionné en écrivant: "Qui est assez sage pour discerner ces choses et assez intelligent pour les connaître? Oui, les chemins de Yahweh sont droits et les justes y marcheront, mais les rebelles y trébucheront" (xiv 10). Ce n'est pas à proprement parler une conclusion au message de conversion et d'amour d'Osée, mais une invitation à la lecture et à la méditation; de même le sage à qui nous devons le Psaume i n'entend pas donner un résumé de tout le Psautier, mais il veut placer le lecteur dans des conditions telles qu'il puisse saisir pleinement la présence de Dieu dans les Psaumes. Une fois les livres donnés, il fallait pouvoir les lire, et les sages ont été les introducteurs à une saine lecture; mais — et c'est le deuxième point que nous voudrions souligner — les sages ont aussi été de véritables créateurs, maniant toutes les ressources de la technique littéraire. Celle-ci déjà sensible dans les ouvrages historiques qui ont vu le jour au temps de l'humanisme salomonien, atteint son degré le plus achevé dans des écrits plus spécifiquement sapientiaux comme Job et Qoheleth. Un disciple de Qoheleth donne de son maître cette caractéristique: "La supériorité de Qoheleth le sage, c'est d'avoir enseigné le savoir aux gens et il a soupesé, creusé, corrigé de nombreux proverbes. Qoheleth cherchait les bonnes formules et les phrases vraies, bien écrites. Les paroles des sages sont des aiguillons et les auteurs de recueils des clous bien enfoncés: ils ont été donnés par un unique pasteur" (Qoh. xii 9). Cette définition caractérise très bien les écrits sapientiaux, mais elle vaut aussi pour l'ensemble du canon: des aiguillons qui poussent en avant et des clous qui ne bougent pas et auxquels on peut s'accrocher, voilà bien l'autorité et le dynamisme des écrits bibliques. On a pu dire que la constitution d'un canon était un frein à la littérature; Franz OVERBECK a parlé du canon comme étant l'acte de décès de la littérature, et WELLHAUSEN se désolait qu'avec la constitution du canon et l'avènement des scribes, ces épigones des prophètes, les eaux vivantes du fleuve aient été enfermées dans des citernes.[22] Nous inclinerions plutôt à penser que le principe canonique, c'est à dire la mise en valeur d'une parole créatrice de mouvement a été aussi bien le moteur que le catalyseur de la littérature; en faisant que la littérature soit toujours engagée, le principe normatif du canon lui a donné une âme. Le souci pour Israel de préserver son identité au cours d'une histoire toujours menacée ne l'a pas amené à une littérature monocorde et à un canon qui ressemblerait à un catéchisme. La littérature n'a pas reculé devant la critique qui mettait en question les fondements mêmes de son existence. Israel ne pouvait pas prétendre être le peuple de Dieu, si Dieu n'était pas vraiment Dieu. C'est à cette suprême crise d'identité que répond le livre de Job, qui traite un problème bien courant dans le monde oriental, mais en l'envisageant sur l'arrière-plan de la vocation spécifique d'Israel, ce qui aboutit à cet aspect dramatique fait de l'association de la critique la plus dure et de la foi la plus pure et qui reste un chef d'œuvre incomparable de la littérature universelle. Il y avait cependant un danger que la sagesse entraînât Israel loin de sa tradition spécifique. Ce qui est dit Prov. viii 22ss. sur la personnification, la transcendance et même la divinisation de la sagesse est proprement révolutionnaire: ni le dabar, ni la torah n'ont connu semblable promotion, et un conflit avec la tradition semblait inévitable. Mais une fois de plus la solution du conflit ne s'est pas faite par la rupture, mais par l'assimilation. Tout d'abord on retint de la sagesse non pas son aspect spéculatif qui ouvrait la porte à la gnose, mais son rôle pratique, non pas son côté divin, mais son aspect humain. En disant et en répétant avec insistance que la sagesse est la crainte de Dieu, on la mettait en accord avec la loi et les prophètes. Quant à la fonction transcendante et révélatrice, elle passa du domaine de la chokmah à celui de la torah. Il est difficile de dire à quel moment précis s'est fait ce passage, l'identité de la chokmah à la torah est en tous les cas attestée par Ben Sira, et elle s'est après cela imposée à l'ensemble de la tradition juive. C'est la torah qui l'a emporté,

---

[22] *Prolegomena zur Geschichte Israels*, p. 426.

mais non sans subir, dans un processus déjà amorcé par le Deutéronome, une assez profonde "sapientialisation".

Le vainqueur a été largement revêtu des dépouilles du vaincu. Le
roi Salomon, patron des sages, mais figure quelque peu hérétique,
cède la place à Moïse qui même dans le livre de la Sagesse attribué
à Salomon, devient le type du sage (Sag. xi 1), et les vrais héritiers
des sages seront les docteurs de la loi. Enfin, lorsqu'une autre forme
de sagesse, la philosophie grecque, fera subir à Israel une nouvelle
crise d'identité, la torah sera déjà suffisamment sapientialisée pour
pouvoir se présenter en face d'elle comme une philosophie non seulement équivalente, mais supérieure, puisque plus ancienne.

L'évolution du peuple et de la tradition israélites concretisées
dans le canon peut être caractérisée par les termes de fidélité et d'ouverture. Fidélité et ouverture insèrent Israel dans un double mouvement, qui d'une part le porte vers le passé, vers le temps des pères,
d'autre part vers l'avenir eschatologique; mais le moteur animant
ce double mouvement ne se trouve pas ailleurs que dans le phénomène
prophétique.[23]

En guise de conclusion à ces considerations où les généralisations
trop peu étayées et la part de l'hypothèse tiennent une trop grande
place, nous voudrions indiquer quelques pistes de recherche vers où
une prise au sérieux de la réalité canonique pourrait orienter.

1. Il serait bon que la science de l'Introduction ne traite plus des
problèmes du canon en appendice. Puisque l'introduction porte
aujourd'hui principalement sur les expressions de la tradition, il
s'agit de retrouver derrière ces expressions les principes fonda-
mentaux qui la régissent et la maintiennent fidèle à elle-même.

2. Il s'agit de vérifier les principes au niveau des textes. Ceux
qui ont établi et transmis le texte des livres bibliques n'ont pas été
de vulgaires copistes dont on se plait à mettre en évidence les nombreuses erreurs, dont certes ils n'ont pas été à l'abri, mais qui étaient
certainement moins nombreuses qu'on veut bien le dire parfois,

---

[23] Le canon est très souvent considéré comme l'épanouissement de la Torah,
mais Ben Sira ne saurait être invoqué en faveur de cette thèse (cf. KOOLE, "Die
Bibel des ben Sira", *OTS*, XIV, p. 370); pour cet auteur les prophètes ne sont
pas les prédicateurs de la loi, annonçant selon le schéma de la loi récompense
et punition. Ben Sira ne fait pas mention d'Esdras le scribe dans l'Éloge des
pères et met au premier plan l'action de l'esprit de Dieu chez les prophètes dans
la ligne de Esd. ix 11; Dan. ix 10; Tob. ii 5, xiv 5 qui prolongent la théologie
deutéronomiste. Cf. aussi J. C. H. LEBRAM, "Aspekte der alttestamentlichen
Kanonbildung", *VT* XVIII (1968), p. 173-189.

lorsqu'on arrive à en déterminer la raison profonde. Les scribes ont eu une herméneutique dont le principe était de montrer l'unité du texte transmis. Il y a quelques années Jean KOENIG [24] et plus récemment Ina WILLI-PLEIN [25] ont montré que les règles herméneutiques d'Eliézer et de Hillel avaient leurs racines dans l'Ancien Testament lui-même. Tenir compte de la méthode analogique, de l'importance des mots-clés, des phénomènes d'homophonie, d'assonance et de métathèse, sur lesquels Martin BUBER avait depuis longtemps attiré l'attention, ne signifie pas qu'il faille totalement changer de méthode, mais simplement que ceci ne doit pas faire négliger cela.

3. En 1935 lors de la rencontre des vétérotestamentaires à Göttingen, H. W. HERTZBERG avait souligné l'importance de la "Nachgeschichte" d'un texte pour sa compréhension.[26] Depuis, l'importance de cette posthistoire qu'on appelle aussi "Wirkungsgeschichte" est de plus en plus reconnue. Tout ce que nous devons à GUNKEL et à son école sur la recherche du "Sitz im Leben" reste valable, mais, pour l'apprécier pleinement, il faudrait mettre l'expression au pluriel, sinon le texte risque de devenir un fossile. Dans le même ordre de recherches, les livres qui se situent au dernier stade de la composition de l'Ancien Testament méritent un intérêt particulier. Sans doute étant davantage reproducteurs que créateurs, ont-ils une originalité moindre, mais précisément le principe canonique nous invite non seulement à constater, mais à se demander pourquoi il en est ainsi. Certains signes nous indiquent que dans les années à

---

[24] "L'activité herméneutique des scribes dans la transmission du texte de l'Ancien Testament", *RHR*, 1961, p. 141-174, et 1962, p. 1-43.

[25] *Vorformen der Schriftexegese innerhalb des Alten Testaments*, *BZAW*, Walter de Gruyter, 1971, 286 p. L'ouvrage ne traite que des livres d'Amos, d'Osée et de Michée. L'enquête très serrée aboutit à réduire considérablement la part des paroles originales de ces prophètes. Tout ce qui est dit sur l'importance théologique des gloses est très important, mais dans toute cette recherche il ne faut pas oublier que les prophètes ont été non seulement créateurs de tradition, mais qu'ils s'insèrent eux-mêmes déjà dans une ou une multiplicité de traditions.

[26] "Die Nachgeschichte alttestamentlicher Texte innerhalb des Alten Testaments", dans *Werden und Wesen des Alten Testaments*, 1936, p. 110-121. Les quatre points mis en avant par HERTZBERG restent toujours valables: a) la première exégèse d'un texte mise en évidence par la posthistoire est toujours d'ordre pratique; c'est bien le principe du midrash. b) les générations postérieures se sont senties interpellées par une parole ancienne qui restait pour elles parole du Dieu vivant. c) la parole de Dieu n'a jamais été envisagée comme intangible; tout littéralisme est exclu pendant cette période de gestation du canon. d) La posthistoire a son importance pour l'histoire de la théologie, en montrant qu'une même parole peut donner naissance à des lectures variées comme la sagesse, l'apocalyptique, le légalisme.

venir des livres comme ceux des Chroniques et de Ben Sira se situeront
au premier plan de la recherche.

4. Avec l'aide de la méthode structuraliste il peut être intéressant
de réfléchir à la structure tripartite du canon. Il y a trois ans, au
Congrès d'Upsala, P. Beauchamp soulignait les phénomènes de
confluence de la loi, de la sagesse et de la prophétie dans le Deutéronome, Ben Sira et les Apocalypses et demandait qu'on étudiât "le
rapport de l'événement avec la fermeture du corpus. L'analyse
structurale doit placer toutes les marques qui concourent à la sig-
nification; le fait d'être dit lui importe autant que ce qui est dit."[27]
Ne peut-on aller plus loin encore et se demander si le rythme ternaire
qui est si important dans l'Ancien Testament et qui est celui du canon,
n'est pas le rythme spécifique de la parole et de l'action de Dieu.[28]

5. En faisant l'exégèse d'un texte isolé, a-t-on tout dit lorsqu'on a
replacé le texte dans son milieu historique, archéologique, littéraire?
N'y aurait-il pas lieu aussi de le soumettre à la critique canonique,
le canon étant lui aussi un milieu susceptible de projeter quelqu'éclai-
rage sur le texte? Par exemple le chant sur la vigne d'Esaie v est tout
d'abord un texte prophétique, mais son genre littéraire de mashal
vient de la sagesse, enfin par son contenu il rappelle toute l'histoire
de l'alliance de Dieu avec son peuple. Constater que le tout se reflète
dans la partie ne doit pas dire que tout se trouve dans tout, et les
progrès que nous avons fait en exégèse devraient nous garder de
retomber dans les erreurs auxquelles l'exégèse juive et chrétienne
n'a pas toujours échappé.

6. C'est surtout au niveau de la théologie que le principe canonique
se révélera important. Une théologie de l'Ancien Testament, et a
fortiori une théologie biblique des deux testaments, se doit de prendre
le canon au sérieux. Encore faut-il trouver la bonne manière de le
faire. Selon les uns, la notion de canon n'est utilisable et valable
que si l'on établit "un canon à l'intérieur du canon".[29] C'est sans
doute ce qu'on fait dans la pratique, et même inconsciemment,

---

[27] *SVT* XXII (Congrès d'Uppsala), p. 125.

[28] On trouvera des indications dans W. M. W. Roth, *Numerical Sayings in the
Old Testament*, *SVT* XIII, 1965, p. 70, et passim, et dans G. Sauer, *Die Sprüche
Agurs*, 3 WANT, Kohlhammer, Stuttgart 1963, mais l'enquête mérite d'être pour-
suivie à l'aide des nouveaux critéres linguistiques.

[29] Sanders (*op. cit.*, p. XV) fait allusion à une discussion entre G. E. Wright
et B. S. Childs, le premier pensant que l'autorité du canon n'est possible que si
l'on établit un canon dans le canon, le second pense qu'on ne peut envisager le
canon que dans sa totalité, et développe sa position dans *Biblical Theology in
Crisis*, Westminster Press, Philadelphia, 1970, p. 255.

porté qu'on est par l'actualité théologique ou par l'actualité tout court. Mais il serait dangereux d'ériger cette manière de procéder en principe, car un "canon dans le canon" peut conduire soit au subjectivisme qui consiste à ramener la Bible à soi, soit à un fondamentalisme partiel qui en privilégiant certains textes amènerait à les faire jouer les uns contre les autres. Nous préférons, pour notre part, ne pas parler de "canon dans le canon". Après ce que nous venons de dire, il apparaît clairement que le canon est avant tout un mouvement, qu'il est le résultat d'une histoire, bien plus qu'il est lui-même histoire et non pas corps de doctrines. C'est donc dans sa totalité qu'il faut l'envisager. Il est vrai que devant la multiplicité des témoignages et les contradictions à l'intérieur du canon, cette position ne peut être que dialectique, mais précisément cette dialectique nous gardera de conférer au canon une valeur absolue, elle nous permettra toujours de voir l'esprit *avec*, non pas derrière, la lettre, et de tenir compte de la richesse de toute la Bible. La pluralité des canons dans la tradition juive et surtout chrétienne ainsi que la prolifération d'une littérature sacrée après la clôture du canon nous garderont de conférer au canon hébraïque une valeur trop absolue, mais nous ne suivrons pas pour autant le Père BARTHÉLÉMY qui voit dans le repli sur la Massora et le canon hébraïque une forme sclérosée et archaïsante alors que le véritable mûrissement de l'Ancien Testament se serait fait à Alexandrie.[30] Pour notre part nous pensons qu'une théologie biblique se fera le mieux à partir du canon hébraïque traditionnel, auquel les écrits postérieurs n'ont rien ajouté de substantiel ni pour ce qui est de la révélation, ni pour ce qui est du dynamisme, ni pour la profondeur, ni même pour la beauté littéraire;[31] c'est le canon hébraïque qui permet le mieux de saisir le mouvement de l'histoire, alors que le canon alexandrin fait voir davantage le développement de la littérature.

Au sujet de l'autorité du canon aujourd'hui, le vétérotestamentaire laissera la parole à la théologie dogmatique et ecclésiastique: la Bible a-t-elle encore, et est-elle la seule autorité normative, et si oui,

---

[30] "L'Ancien Testament a mûri à Alexandrie", *Th Z*, 1965, p. 358-370.

[31] Il faudrait à notre avis faire la distinction entre canonicité et inspiration; la canonicité correspond à une fonction, l'inspiration est une affirmation de la foi; la première peut et doit même être limitée, la seconde échappe à une limitation et déborde la première. On ne saurait dénier aux apocryphes et pseudépigraphes le titre de livres inspirés, mais la présence d'un canon peut être un lieu de référence et de contrôle pour maintenir l'inspiration à l'intérieur de certaines limites.

qu'a-t elle à dire comme parole de Dieu au monde actuel?[32] Peut-être
le travail modeste des biblistes est-il en mesure de rappeler à la
théologie dogmatique le lien du canon avec l'histoire et ainsi de
l'orienter vers une notion du canon plus dynamique. En somme,
il s'agit pour les uns et les autres de se mouvoir à l'intérieur du canon
avec la liberté et l'imagination de l'homme biblique qui ne sait trop
où il va être conduit, tout en prêtant l'oreille à l'écoute de cette
symphonie dont parle Josèphe, et dont les accents parfois discordants
ne sont en fin de compte que l'écho d'une même voix.

---

[32] Cf. James Barr, "The Old Testament and the new Crisis of Biblical Authority" dans *Interpretation*, XXV 1971, p. 24-40, où l'autorité de l'A.T. est envisagée
sur l'arrière-plan de la crise de l'autorité en général.

THE TWILIGHT OF JUDAH: IN THE EGYPTIAN-BABYLONIAN MAELSTROM

BY

A. MALAMAT
Jerusalem

The late seventh century B.C., noted for its reshufflings in the international political sphere, saw the collapse of the Assyrian empire and the subsequent power-struggle between the up-and-coming Babylonia and Egypt over inheritance of the now-orphaned territories spreading from the Euphrates to Sinai. The geopolitical plight of this buffer region swept a most reluctant Kingdom of Judah—like many of her neighbours—into the alternating open conflict and "cold war" which ensued. Indeed, if outside factors were most influential throughout Judah's history, they became overbearing in the two decades following the Battle of Megiddo, in 609 B.C.,—until, in 586 B.C., the little kingdom finally succumbed to international machinations.[1]

A wide range of sources for this tense period provides a particularly detailed insight into much of the political development and internal activities in Judah: besides the Books of Kings and Chronicles, these decades are illuminated by the Book of Jeremiah, and their final years by the Book of Ezekiel. The contemporaneous epigraphical material in Hebrew is plentiful and varied, more so than in earlier periods, and the effects of the political-military events have been revealed in the archaeological excavations on numerous Judean sites. But a proper perspective for evaluating the historical factors underlying the final fate of Judah—factors which determined the policies of its rulers—is to be obtained only from sources beyond Palestine—primarily the Neo-Babylonian Chronicles and, to a lesser degree, Egyptian documentation. The twining of biblical data with external sources—especially the detailed framework of dates they contain—enables a sort of micro-analytic study of this period. Thus,

---

[1] For a complementary study of this period, as treated particularly in the first two sections of the present lecture, see A. MALAMAT, "The Last Kings of Judah and the Fall of Jerusalem", *IEJ* XVIII 1968, pp. 137-156, and the bibliographical references there.

we can trace the historical process in time units much more minute than is generally feasible for the Israelite period—in terms of a specific year, month or even day.

The chronological method applied here has more than once influenced our reconstruction of the chain of events. Though there is a general consensus that the post-dating system, involving accession years, was employed in Judah at this time, another point is still particularly controversial—the month of the Judean regnal new year. Our reckoning is based on an autumnal calendar beginning on 1 Tishri, and not on the spring calendar accepted by many scholars and which was in general use in Babylonia. On previous occasions I have sought to demonstrate the preference of this Tishri reckoning in Judah, and its propensity for reconciling a majority of the variegated data, at least for our period.[2] To facilitate the tracing of the chain of events, a Chronological Table is appended. The months of the year, it must be remembered, were counted from Nisan, in keeping with the Judean civil calendar.

I.

The loss of Josiah at Megiddo in 609 B.C. put an effective end to the prosperity of the Judean kingdom and dispelled all hopes for restored grandeur. Indeed, this tragedy was so deeply felt that a day of remembrance was commemorated for generations (II Chron. xxxv 25; and cf. Josephus, *Ant.* X, 5, 1). The background of Josiah's (639-609 B.C.) clash with Necho II (610-595 B.C.) lies in the geo-

---

[2] See especially *ibid.*, pp. 146ff.; and cf. n. 19 there, for studies adopting a spring calendar, to which now add: K. T. ANDERSEN, *Stud. Theol.* XXIII 1969, pp. 109-114; D. J. A. CLINES, *Austral. Jour. Bibl. Arch.* (= *AJBA*) II 1972, pp. 9-34; idem, *JBL* XCIII 1974, pp. 22-40. In support of the autumnal calendar see the references in *IEJ* XVIII 1968, p. 146, n. 20; and now, with conclusions partly similar to ours: K. S. FREEDY and D. B. REDFORD, "The Dates in Ezekiel . . .", *JAOS* XC 1970, pp. 462-485 (= *Freedy & Redford*); M. WEIPPERT, *Edom*, Tübingen 1971, pp. 351-372, 649-660. WEIPPERT (*ibid.*, pp. 356-357), like E. R. THIELE (*The Mysterious Numbers of the Hebrew Kings*, Grand Rapids 1965, pp. 161-172) and S. H. HORN (*Andrews Univ. Seminary Stud.* V 1967, pp. 12-27) but contrary to our view, assumes that the regnal years of Nebuchadnezzar himself were reckoned in the Book of Kings according to the Tishri calendar, in contrast to official Babylonian practice. He thus seeks to reconcile the discrepancy—illusory in our opinion—between the date of Jehoiachin's exiling as given in II Kings xxiv 12b and as indicated in the Babylonian Chronicle; see below, in section II.

For the conversion of the ancient dates into "absolute" dates, cf. the tables in R. A. PARKER & W. H. DUBBERSTEIN, *Babylonian Chronology 626 B.C.—A.D. 75*, Providence (R.I.) 1956.

political developments which we noted in opening. In the rivalry between Judah and Egypt over the formerly Assyrian territories in Palestine, Psamtik I (664-610 B.C.), Necho's father, had held a clear advantage in time. It would seem that Psamtik gained sway over the cities of Philistia, in the south, and the province of *Magiddu*, which spread over the Jezreel Plain and Galilee, in the north, and thus came into possession of the city of Megiddo.[3] At least as early as 616 B.C., Megiddo must have become a logistics base for the Egyptian forces on the march to the Euphrates in support of their newly-made allies, the Assyrians; it was undoubtedly such a base in 610 and, again, in 609 B.C.[4] Josiah was able to launch his annexation policy only after initiating his reform (around 628 B.C.; cf. II Chron. xxxiv 6), and he seems to have gained control solely over the former Assyrian province of *Samerina* and to have established a corridor reaching the coast in the northern Shephelah, as possibly witnessed by the Hebrew epigraphic finds at Meṣad Ḥashavyahu.

The woeful results of the battle of Megiddo (apparently in Sivan of 609 B.C.)[5] led to rapid political fluctuations in Judah,—and from then till the Destruction of the First Temple,—a mere score years,— the rulers of Judah changed loyalties—to either Egypt or Babylonia—no less than six times. The international scene at this time demanded extreme skill in manoeuvring, and the kings of Judah were repeatedly forced to come to terms with kaleidoscopic situations and astonishingly frequent political dilemmas of a most fateful order. The first exigency was the selection of a successor to Josiah, who apparently had not seen a need to designate his heir. Some

---

[3] For a detailed discussion of the historical circumstances which preceded the Battle of Megiddo, and an analysis of the battle itself, see A. MALAMAT, *The Gaster Festschrift* (*JANES* V 1973), pp. 267-279. For similar general conclusions concerning the rule of Psamtik I over considerable territories in Palestine and Syria, see B. OTZEN, *Studien über Deuterosacharja*, Copenhagen 1964, pp. 78ff.

[4] For the Egyptian expedition to the north, noted in Nabopolassar's Chronicle, see C. J. GADD, *The Fall of Nineveh*, London 1923, pp. 31ff., B.M. 21901, lines 10, 61, 66; D. J. WISEMAN, *Chronicles of Chaldaean Kings 626-556 B.C.*, London 1956 (= *CCK*), pp. 55ff.

[5] Cf. *IEJ* XVIII 1968, p. 139. But note now that the Egyptians required almost a month, rather than two weeks, to cover the distance to the river (which they crossed in Tammuz 609 B.C.), for the actual distance between Megiddo and Carchemish is about 650 km, and the advance of the rushing Egyptian army should be estimated at about 25-30 km *per diem*. See similarly CLINES, *AJBA* II 1972, pp. 30ff.; and also M. VOGELSTEIN, *Biblical Chronology*, Cincinnati 1944, pp. 27f., who, however, considered the march from Megiddo to Carchemish to have taken at least six weeks.

thirty years earlier, Josiah himself had been enthroned by the *'am ha-'areṣ*, that body of landed aristocracy in Judah which is found to be involved wherever the natural succession of the Davidic line was brought in jeopardy. The assassination of Josiah's father, Amon, was undoubtedly of Egyptian instigation, and already then Egypt seems to have been intriguing to install a sympathetic regime in Judah. The *'am ha-'areṣ* managed to suppress the revolt at court (II Kings xxi 19-26), enthrone the young Josiah and surely also set the deeply anti-Egyptian tone of his policy.

The successor to emerge was Josiah's son Jehoahaz (Shallum), in opposition to the principle of primogeniture—Jehoiakim (Eliakim) being the older of the brothers by two years. This irregular enthronement, a sort of *coup d'état*, was again effected by the *'am ha-'areṣ* (II Kings xxiii 30; II Chron. xxxvi 1).[6] The political significance of this step comes into focus when we consider the decidedly anti-Egyptian stand generally taken by the *'am ha-'areṣ* in this period. The choice of Jehoahaz was apparently based on his maternal lineage, for his mother Hamutal "daughter of Jeremiah of Libnah" (II Kings xxiii 31; who is depicted allegorically as a "lioness . . . among lions" in Ezek. xix) was of the Judean rural nobility which comprised the *'am ha-'areṣ*. Eleven years later, Nebuchadnezzar's selection of a ruler seems to have been governed by similar considerations, for Zedekiah was of the same mother and thus also represented the anti-Egyptian faction of the Davidic line. In contrast, Jehoiakim's maternal lineage seems to have been odious to the Judean nobility, for his mother was Zebidah "daughter of Pedaiah of Rumah" (II Kings xxiii 36), the latter a Galilean town in the valley of Beth Netopha, most probably in territory under Egyptian control since the days of Psamtik (as noted above). Thus, in spite of the defeat at Megiddo, the Judean leadership is seen to have continued its anti-Egyptian line, a policy rather premature under the circumstances.

After reigning for only three months, Jehoahaz's fate was put in the balance by Necho's intervention. Jeremiah, for one, was already confident that "he shall return no more to see his native land" (Jer. xxii 10-12; and cf. Ezek. xix 1-4). The king was indeed deposed and exiled to Egypt, probably at the urging of his brother,

---

[6] For the irregularity surrounding the enthronement, see *IEJ* XVIII 1968, pp. 139f. and nn. 6-7 and the bibliography on the *'am hā-'āreṣ* there. For the latter see now also T. Ishida, *Annual of the Japanese Biblical Institute* I 1975, pp. 23-38.

Jehoiakim, who sought recognition of his rights of primogeniture.[7] Jehoiakim's subsequent enthronement by Necho seems to have been based on mutual interests: Pharaoh assisted him in realizing his legitimate claim to the throne (note the specific wording in II Kings xxiii 34: "Necho made Eliakim ... king in the place of *Josiah his father* ..."—which entirely bypasses his brother's reign); in turn, Pharaoh gained a loyal vassal and ally. The punishment meted out to Judah by Necho, apparently hand-in-hand with Jehoiakim, fell poignantly upon the *'am ha-'ares*; with the tables turned, it was the anti-Egyptian faction which had to bear the burden, rather than the palace or Temple treasury in Jerusalem (II Kings xxiii 35).[8] Jehoiakim apparently came to the throne only in Tishri 609 B.C. (though he may have imposed the reckoning of his reign as if he had succeeded his father directly).[9] The summer and autumn of 609 B.C. were thus days of turmoil in Judah, typified by a rapidly changing political situation and the successive reigns of three kings, in rather unusual circumstances.

Necho now controlled the entire area "from the Brook of Egypt to the river Euphrates, all that belonged to the king of Egypt",

---

[7] In I Esdras (i 36) there is a specific tradition that Jehoiakim was behind his brother's arrest, along with other Judean leaders; see J. M. MYERS, *I & II Esdras (Anchor Bible)*, Garden City 1974, pp. 30, 32. Jehoiakim's possible intervention in the overthrow of Jehoahaz has been alluded to in J. SCHARBERT, *Die Prophetie Israels um 600 v. Chr.*, Köln 1967, p. 128.

[8] Professor B. MAZAR has brought to my attention the relatively low sum of the tribute imposed here by the Egyptians (II Kings xxiii 33), in comparison with that exacted from Menahem king of Israel (II Kings xv 19), or Hezekiah, who had to draw upon the royal and Temple treasuries in Jerusalem (II Kings xviii 14). This would seem to confirm that Necho's tribute was to be borne by a particular class rather than by the populace in general, as held in the Commentaries; see J. A. MONTGOMERY, *The Books of Kings (ICC)*, Edinburgh 1951, p. 551; J. GRAY, *I & II Kings* [2], London 1970, pp. 750ff. In any event, the royal palace was hardly affected and Jehoiakim was able to erect splendid royal buildings (cf. Jer. xxii 13ff.).

[9] (a) If Jehoiakim came to the throne only subsequent to 1 Tishri 609 B.C. (as we uphold in *IEJ* XVIII 1968, p. 141, and in the Chronological Table below), a conclusion reasonable in itself, then the period up till Tishri 608 B.C. should be considered his accession year (Akkadian *rēš šarrūti*); this would have been Jehoahaz's first regnal year, in purely chronological terms. (b) On the other hand, if the contemporaneous reckoning of Jehoiakim's years, during his reign, was from Josiah's death—a possibility suggested to me by R. GRAFMAN—1 Tishri 609 B.C. would have ushered in his first regnal year. This would reconcile the chronological difficulty in Jer. xlvi 2 (see n. 11, below), though it raises an outward conflict with II Kings xxiii 36, where the length of Jehoiakim's reign is given as eleven years.

to use the contemporaneous biblical phrase (II Kings xxiv 7).[10] But this period of Egyptian glory was to be short lived. Already in the summer of 605 B.C., Nebuchadnezzar, still Crown Prince, dealt the Egyptians a stunning blow, in the Battle of Carchemish, and subsequently defeated the remnant Egyptian force in the land of Hamath.[11] This, then, truly sealed the fate of Syria and Palestine. But neither then—nor, fatally, even later—did the Judean leaders grasp the full significance of events in the international arena. The traumatic experience of the Battle of Megiddo, and the mutuality of interests between Necho and Jehoiakim may well have shackled the leadership in Jerusalem with the image of a mighty Egypt which would rush to the aid of its allies in time of need. Other states held Egypt in similar regard, as revealed in an Aramaic letter discovered at Saqqara:[12] The ruler of some city, apparently in Philistia, urgently

[10] The Egyptian control of the Lebanon already in the days of Psamtik I is evidenced by an Egyptian stele of 612 B.C.; see *Freedy & Redford*, p. 477; and possibly also by a second inscription, cf. MALAMAT, *Gaster Festschrift*, p. 273, n. 20. Egyptian influence in the Phoenician coastal cities is witnessed by a statue of Psamtik I from the port-city of Arvad; a fragment, possibly also from his reign, discovered at Tyre; and a stele of Necho II at Sidon—for which now see J. J. KATZENSTEIN, *The History of Tyre*, Jerusalem 1973, pp. 299, n. 24; 313, n. 100. KATZENSTEIN also associates the passage in Nebuchadnezzar's Wadi Brisa inscription (col. IX, lines 23-24)—relating of an enemy who had subdued and plundered the Lebanon region—with Egypt. But he assumes that all the above evidence points only to commercial ties between Egypt and Syria, rather than actual Egyptian control; see *ibid.*, pp. 298-304. In contrast, see OTZEN, *Deuterosacharja*, pp. 90ff., who regards the above as proving Egyptian rule in Asia, finding additional support for this in the prophecy in Zech. ix 1-8.

[11] On the Babylonian source, see *CCK*, pp. 66ff. (BM 21946). Jer. xlvi 2 places the Battle of Carchemish in Jehoiakim's fourth regnal year, the only substantial instance of a date conflicting with our Tishri reckoning, which would put this battle in his third year (cf. the Chronological Table). See *IEJ* XVIII 1968, p. 147, n. 21, where we have also cited HORN's suggestion to reconcile the difficulty here by attributing this date to the time of the oracular utterance rather than to the battle itself. Although problematic, this might find support in Jer. xxxvi 1-2, where the date of the Prophet's first scroll, which recorded *inter alia* Oracles on the Nations, is fixed in Jehoiakim's fourth regnal year. The chronological notation at the head of the Oracles on the Nations in Jer. xlvi 2 thus may well have been harmonized with this. WEIPPERT (*Edom*, p. 653, n. 1238) assumes that the Battle of Carchemish and the subsequent Babylonian campaign, which latter took place in the winter of 605/604 B.C., after the enthronement of Nebuchadnezzar, were regarded in Judah as one continuous military episode, which thus would have fallen already in Jehoiakim's fourth regnal year; but Jeremiah's prophecy specifically deals with the defeat of "the army of Pharaoh Necho" which no longer took part in events half a year after the Battle of Carchemish. But for a possible corroboration of the date as given in Jer., see n. 9(b).

[12] Cf. DONNER-RÖLLIG, *KAI*, No. 266; and *IEJ* XVIII 1968, p. 143, n. 11, for additional bibliography. The treaty relations between the vassal king and Pharaoh are inferred in line 8 in the letter: *wtbth* (i.e. a treaty) *ʿbdk nṣr*.

appeals to Pharaoh for military assistance to repell the approaching Babylonians, reminding his suzerain of his treaty obligations.

Thus, we can appreciate all the more such level-headed persons as Jeremiah, possessing deep foresight and historical perspective. A mere few months after the Battle of Carchemish, Jeremiah already proclaimed his steadfast belief in Nebuchadnezzar's impending rule over Judah and Hither Asia in general (Jer. xxv 1-14; and see the Chronological Table).[13] Like Isaiah in his day, or Ezekiel his younger contemporary, Jeremiah strove to smash the popular image of Egypt, which had led to a false sense of security among the Judean leadership and spread a spurious hope of military support (cf., e.g., Egypt as "a staff of reed to the house of Israel ... and when they leaned upon thee thou didst break", in Ezek. xxix 7-8). In Jeremiah's mind, the only way to save the nation was to surrender voluntarily to Babylonia, to which cause he remained loyal to the bitter end (Jer. xxi 8-9; xxxviii 2, etc.). Thus, political orientation became an acute issue among the people of Judah, gradually intensifying the polarity between the pro-Egyptian and pro-Babylonian factions.

The Babylonian subjugation of Judah was not long in coming. The exact date is still a matter of controversy, and even Nebuchadnezzar's Chronicle is indefinite. Military campaigns to the West are recorded for each of the years between 605 and 601 B.C., but no specific names of subjected states are mentioned (except Ashkelon).[14] Briefly, there are several possibilities:

a) Judah was conquered immediately after the Egyptian defeat at the Battle of Carchemish. This is supported by the opening of the Book of Daniel (i 1-4) relating the siege of Jerusalem by Nebuchadnezzar in the third year of Jehoiakim (see Chronological Table), the looting of "vessels of the house of God", and the exiling of

---

[13] The oracle took place "in the fourth year of Jehoiakim ... the first (*ri'šōnît*) year of Nebuchadrezzar" (Jer. xxv 1); if the unusual term for "first" year here refers to Nebuchadnezzar's accession year (*rēš šarrūti*), the prophecy would have been uttered between Tishri 605 and Nisan 604 B.C.; but if it refers to his first actual regnal year, the synchronism covers the period between Nisan and Tishri 604 B.C. (see the Chronological Table). C. F. WHITLEY (*ZAW* LXXX 1968, pp. 38-49) holds that Jer. xxv was the Prophet's earliest oracle and that Jeremiah began his activity only in 605 B.C. (rather than two decades earlier, as recorded in Jer.), but this seems untenable. In support of the traditional dating of Jeremiah's call, see most recently T. W. OVERHOLT, *CBQ* XXXIII 1971, pp. 165-184.

[14] See *CCK*, pp. 66-71. The relevant passage is BM 21946, lines 1-23 and verso ilnes 1-7, from which the following citations are taken.

certain Judeans. Further the last datum is in accord with a tradition related by Josephus (*Ant.* X, 11, 1; *Contra Apionem* I, 19), that Judean captives, amongst others, were carried off to Babylon after the victory at Carchemish. In another passage (*Ant.* X, 6, 1), Josephus even specifies that at this same time Nebuchadnezzar conquered all the lands of the West as far as Pelusium on the border of Egypt— but he explicitely adds: "except the land of Judah". It is difficult, however, to rely upon the chronological accuracy of these traditions (which apparently refer to events occurring several years later).[15] Though Josephus's data largely agree with those of the Babylonian Chronicle, the Chronicle itself does not bear out any widespread conquests in the West while Nebuchadnezzar was still Crown Prince. Immediately after the victory at Carchemish, as we now know, Nebuchadnezzar conquered only the "entire land of Ha[ma]th",[16] and not the "entire land of Hatti" (that is, Syria-Palestine), as formerly read.

b) Judah submitted a year later, when Nebuchadnezzar devastated Ashkelon, in Kislev of his first regnal year (December 604 B.C.). This date corresponds exactly with the ninth month of the fifth regnal year of Jehoiakim, when a general day of fasting was proclaimed in Jerusalem (Jer. xxxvi 9ff.; see the Chronological Table). Jeremiah's foreboding words, brought before an emergency council of ministers on the fastday, warned of the impending national calamity—the full drama of which we can trace today by means of the Babylonian Chronicle.[17] But Jehoiakim, belittling Jeremiah's warning

---

[15] See *IEJ* XVIII 1968, p. 142, n. 10, where we emend in Dan. i 1 "third" year of Jehoiakim to "sixth" year, a minor difference in the Hebrew, and a suitable date for the subjugation of Judah (see below). For the implausibility of the round date of "third year" here, see most recently CLINES, *AJBA* II 1972, pp. 20ff.; and M. DELCOR, *Le Livre de Daniel*, Paris 1971, pp. 59f. The latter assumes that this date was erroneously derived from II Kings xxiv 1, on Jehoiakim's rebellion against Babylonia after three years. Josephus's reference to Judean captives after the Battle of Carchemish may indicate that Judah, like other vassals, had supplied troops in support of the Egyptian army. A list of Egyptian prisoners (?) from Sippar in Babylonia, from the third year of Nebuchadnezzar, may also be noted in this context; see D. J. WISEMAN, *Iraq* XXVIII 1966, pp. 156ff. On the other hand, Josephus may have been telescoping two originally distinct events when he describes Nebuchadnezzar's campaign as far as Pelusium, which would appear, actually, to refer to the Babylonian invasion to the border of Egypt in the winter of 601/600 B.C. (see below).

[16] This restoration was proposed by A. K. GRAYSON, *Bibbia e Oriente* VI 1964, p. 205; B. ODED, *Tarbiz* XXXV 1965, p. 104 (Hebrew).

[17] See A. MALAMAT, *IEJ* VI 1956, pp. 251f. But A. BAUMANN (*ZAW* LXXX 1968, pp. 350-373) now opposes any connexion between Jeremiah's oracles read on the fastday and the Babylonian campaign.

"that the king of Babylon will certainly come and destroy this land" (Jer. xxxvi 29), burned the Prophet's scroll of doom, which leads to the conclusion that Judah at this time was still not subdued.

c) The submission of Judah may have occurred only in the autumn or winter of 603 B.C., during Nebuchadnezzar's campaign in his second regnal year. Unfortunately, the broken state of the Babylonian tablet here does not enable us to confirm this. In this campaign, which was certainly to the West, the Babylonian king set out in the month of Iyyar with a "mighty army" supported by siege machines, indicating that strong opposition was anticipated. Nebuchadnezzar was most probably seeking to subdue all Philistia and gain control of Judah—all as a prelude to his ultimate goal—the conquest of Egypt, his arch-rival. If this be the case, the lacuna here is to be restored with the conquest of a specific city in Philistia, such as Ashdod, Ekron or more probably Gaza [18] (cf. Jer. xxv 20; xlvii 5; Zeph. ii 4); the subsequent missing section of the tablet might then relate to the submission of Jehoiakim (cf. II Chron. xxxvi 6-7; Dan. i 1-2—both apparently relating to this event).[19]

The latter proposal for dating the subjugation of Judah is in good accord with the circumstances which led to Jehoiakim's rebellion against Babylonia. According to II Kings xxiv 1, Jehoiakim submitted to Babylonia for three years; in other words, he submitted to the annual tribute three times. If this tribute was yielded the first time in the autumn or winter of 603 B.C., the third payment would have been made in the autumn or winter of 601 B.C., during the Babylonian campaign in Nebuchadnezzar's fourth regnal year. In Kislev (December) 601 B.C., the King of Babylonia took command of his armies, already mustered in the land of "Hatti" and poised to attack Egypt proper. The ensuing war, in the winter

---

[18] A. F. RAINEY now proposes to restore the name "Gaza" in the lacuna in the Chronicle (BM 21946) at the start of line 22; see his chapter in the forthcoming report by Y. AHARONI on the excavations of the Tel Aviv University at Lachish. The restoration "Ashdod" there is equally possible. This city is signally denoted "the *remnant* of Ashdod" in Jer. xxv 20, among the Philistine cities condemned to fall before the Babylonians. This would suit its reduced status (represented by stratum VI on the site) on the eve of Nebuchadnezzar's conquest, undoubtedly the result of the lengthy siege by Psamtik I; cf. MALAMAT, *Gaster Festschrift*, p. 272 and n. 19 there.

[19] See *IEJ* XVIII 1968, p. 142 and n. 9 there. For a similar dating of the subjugation of Judah, cf. already E. VOGT, *Biblica* XLV 1964, pp. 354f.; and, even prior to the publication of the Babylonian Chronicle, J. T. NELLIS, *RB* LXI 1954, pp. 387-391; while W. F. ALBRIGHT, *JBL* LI 1932, pp. 89ff., brought the surrender of Judah down to 603/602 B.C.

of 601/600 B.C.—an international event of outstanding significance—
was first revealed to us by the Babylonian Chronicle, which makes
no effort to hide the shortcomings of the Babylonian army in its
most ambitious campaign to date. Heavy casualties on both sides
are reported, and the Babylonians were forced to withdraw. It was
this failure, before their very eyes, which most probably encouraged
the Judeans and several neighbouring kingdoms to shake off Babylonian hegemony (see the Chronological Table).[20]

II.

This blow forestalled the Babylonian reaction to Jehoiakim's revolt.
Nebuchadnezzar spend his fifth regnal year (600/599 B.C.) rebuilding
his chariot force. The next year he raided among the Arabs (winter
of 599/98 B.C.), taking much spoil, as finds reflection in Jeremiah's
oracle on "Kedar and the kingdoms of Hazor which Nebuchadrezzar . . . smote" (Jer. xlix 28-33; and see the Chronological Table).[21]
In his seventh year (598/597 B.C.), however, Nebuchadnezzar's full
wrath fell upon Judah, the force of which surely was not lost upon
Egypt and her other camp-followers, as well. Indeed, the Chronicle
entry for this year deals entirely with the conquest of Jerusalem,
the deposing of Jehoiachin and the installing of Zedekiah. This
entry fully substantiates the biblical version, and as *baksheesh* gives
the precise day of the surrender of Jerusalem —2 Adar, 16 March,
597 B.C.—a dating unique in the extra-biblical sources touching
upon Israelite history. This date, and the almost simultaneous
replacement of the Judean ruler, provides a fixed point of reference
for the chronology of this period, as well as a keystone in the matter
of the regnal new year in Judah, a problem extensively treated by
scholars.[22] Moreover, it can guide us toward a fuller understanding
of the actual course of the siege and of the resultant exile.

---

[20] See *IEJ* VI 1956, p. 251; XVIII 1968, p. 142; VOGT, *VTS* IV 1957, p. 90.
On the Babylonian-Egyptian encounter in 601/600 B.C., and further possible
evidence for it, see E. LIPIŃSKI, *AION* XXXII 1972, p. 235-241; and MALAMAT,
Gaster Festschrift, pp. 276f.

[21] See *CCK*, pp. 31f.; and cf. *IEJ* VI 1956, pp. 254f.; VOGT, *VTS* IV 1957,
p. 92. On the various motives which may have been behind the Babylonian
raids on the Arab tribes, see I. EPHAL, *The Nomads on the Border of Palestine . . .*
(Doctoral Dissertation, Jerusalem 1971), pp. 125-129 (Hebrew); and W. J.
DUMBRELL, *AJBA* II 1972, pp. 99-108.

[22] The Babylonian source is BM 21946, verso lines 11-13; *CCK*, pp. 70f.
For the complex chronological problems it raises, see *IEJ* XVIII 1968, pp. 144ff.,
and the bibliography there.

We now know that Nebuchadnezzar mustered his troops and set out for Jerusalem in Kislev (18 December 598-15 January 597 B.C.), and since the march required at least two months, he could have arrived with the bulk of his army only shortly before the city's surrender. But Jerusalem was already under full siege by his "servants" (II Kings xxiv 10-11), probably Babylonian occupation troops and possibly also auxiliary forces (cf. *vs.* 2) stationed in the West. The Chronicle might be supporting this in the entry for the previous year, noting only that the king returned to Babylonia, and thus apparently implying that heavy reinforcements were left in the West.[23]

The biblical sources on the exile of Jehoiachin are in outward contradiction, in both the extent of the exile and its exact date. According to II Kings xxiv, the exile encompassed 10,000 (*vs.* 14) or 7,000 (*vs.* 16) persons, mostly military, to either of which we must add a thousand armourers and sappers.[24] This mass exile, headed by Jehoiachin and his entourage, occurred according to this source in the *eight* year of Nebuchadnezzar's reign (*vs.* 12), the year beginning on 1 Nisan 597 B.C.—at least a month after the surrender of Jerusalem. Moreover, II Chronicles xxxvi 10 also implies that Jehoiachin was exiled around the time of the civil new year, and that Nebuchadnezzar had already returned to his capital, surely for the annual festivities. But according to the list of exiles in Jeremiah lii (based undoubtedly on some official source), a mere 3,023 "Jews" were exiled—in the *seventh* year of Nebuchadnezzar's reign (*vs.* 28). These have generally been regarded as contradicting traditions on one and the same matter, or it has been thought that different chronological systems were employed in the Book of Kings and in Jeremiah lii, respectively [25]—though even then the numbers for the

---

[23] The specific formulation of the Chronicle entry for the sixth year has already been pointed out by WISEMAN, *CCK*, p. 32. On the timing of Nebuchadnezzar's appearance before Jerusalem, see in particular M. NOTH, *ZDPV* LXXIV 1958, pp. 136ff.; and *IEJ* XVIII 1968, p. 144.

[24] The term *masgēr* (paired with *ḥārāš*), usually translated "smith", refers rather to some occupation involved with fortications, as do several other usages of the same root, such as *misgæræt* and the verb *sgr* (cf., e.g., II Sam. xxii 46 || Ps. xviii 46; I Kings xi 27; Micah vii 17). For an Akkadian cognate and a possibly related loanword in Egyptian, cf. W. HELCK, *Die Beziehungen Ägyptens zu Vorderasien im 3. und 2. Jahrtausend v. Chr.²*, Wiesbaden 1971, p. 525, No. 297. In the exiling of the "armourers and sappers", Nebuchadnezzar achieved a double purpose, depriving Judah of elements essential for its defence and, on the other hand, gained a skilled labour force for his own military designs at home.

[25] See, e.g., W. F. ALBRIGHT, *BASOR* CXLIII 1956, pp. 28-33; D. N. FREEDMAN, *BA* XIX 1956, pp. 50-60; both of whom hold that the dates in Jer. lii

deportees disagree. The discrepancies between the two sources can be reconciled, however, by proposing that the exile evolved in two successive deportations: [26]

a) The first phase (already intimated in Jer. xiii 18-19) was a limited deportation prior to or upon the surrender of Jerusalem —still in Nebuchadnezzar's seventh year (Jer. lii 28). The particular appellative here, "Jews"—implying the provincial element of Judah—is brought into perspective by the designation "from Jerusalem", applied to the exiles deported during the final siege, in Nebuchadnezzar's 18th year (vs. 29; and see the Chronological Table). Several years after the destruction of Jerusalem, in Nebuchadnezzar's 23rd year, the deportees are once again, and quite appropriately, called "Jews" (vs. 30).

b) The second, principal phase of the exile, described in the Book of Kings, comprised the cream of Jerusalem and thousands of her defenders, including the armourers and sappers specifically mentioned as exiled from the capital (Jer. xxiv 1; xxix 2). The organization of this mass exile surely necessitated several weeks from the time of the surrender of the city, on 2 Adar, and thus it would have fallen only in Nebuchadnezzar's eighth regnal year, by which time he had already left the country.

The assumption of two separate deportations can also serve to reconcile the discrepancies in the numbers of deportees, as given within II Kings xxiv—10,000 and 7,000 (besides the armourers and sappers, in both cases). There is no need to see here two parallel but conflicting sources, as often presumed. The number 7,000 may well be intended for the main deportation, at the later stage; while the number 10,000 would represent the total of the two deportations, including the 3,000 captives from the initial phase.[27]

28-29 are the only biblical instance of official Babylonian figures, thus identifying the exiles of Nebuchadnezzar's seventh and eighteenth years with those of his eighth and nineteenth years, respectively. W. RUDOLPH, *Jeremia* [3], Tübingen 1968, p. 324, following earlier commentators, emends the "seventh" year of Nebuchadnezzar to "seventeenth", taking the figure (as in the next verse) for the final siege—an emendation which seems unwarranted.

[26] For the following solution, see briefly *IEJ* VI 1956, pp. 253f.; XVIII 1968, p. 154, and n. 32 there. E. THIELE, *BASOR* CXLIII 1956, pp. 22-27, proposed a similar solution which, however, he subsequently abandoned. The 832 deportees of Nebuchadnezzar's eighteenth year (Jer. lii 29), like the 3,023 in his seventh year, represent a minor deportation preceding the major waves in his eighth (see below) and nineteenth years (for which the actual number is missing in the Bible); cf. *IEJ* XVIII 1968, p. 154.

[27] A similar calculation was already made by the early Jewish authors; see

III.

In the last decade of the kingdom of Judah, from the first Baby-lonian conquest of Jerusalem till its final fall, the Bible relates only one incident of international relevance—the anti-Babylonian "con-ference" summoned by Zedekiah. From Jeremiah xxvii we learn that this conspirational meeting in Jerusalem was attended by envoys from the trans-Jordanian states—Edom, Moab and Ammon (who in 599/98 B.C. were still harassing Judah, alongside the Baby-lonians; II Kings xxiv 2), and the Phoenician coastal cities—Tyre and Sidon (Jer. xxvii 3). But besides the states participating in this plot (which conspicuously omit the Philistine cities, already for some time Babylonian provinces), we know little of the particular circumstances leading to the convening of the conference, of the consequences thereof, or even its precise date. The chronological heading to Jeremiah xxvii is, of course, faulty. But the smooth continuity of the events described in Jeremiah xxvii-xxviii (which latter chapter opens with the notation: "In that same year"), would point to Zedekiah's fourth regnal year, that is, between Tishri 594 and Tishri 593 B.C. (see the Chronological Table).[28] Moreover, the

---

Seder Olam Rabba, ch. 25; and cf. Rashi on II Kings xxiv 16 and David Kimchi on vs. 14 there. For a modern approach, close to ours though by a different reconstruction, see VOGELSTEIN, *Chronology*, p. 15; and cf. S. HERRMANN, *Ge-schichte Israels*, München 1973, p. 342. The usual assumption today, however, is of duplicate sources in II Kings xxiv; see e.g. J. A. MONTGOMERY, *Books of Kings*, pp. 554ff.; J. GRAY, *I & II Kings*, pp. 760ff.; and the early treatment of B. STADE, *ZAW* IV 1884, pp. 271ff., who arbitrarily ascribed all the numbers of deportees to 586 B.C. On the number of exiles, see also E. JANSSEN, *Judah in der Exilszeit*, Göttingen 1956, pp. 28ff.

[28] For the textual difficulties of the chronological superscriptions in Jer. xxvii and xxviii, see the Commentaries; for the LXX versions of xxviii 1 (which omit either the phrase "at the beginning of the reign of Zedekiah" or the phrase "in the fourth year"), see now J. G. JANZEN, *Studies in the Text of Jeremiah*, Cambridge (Mass.) 1973, pp. 14f.

For the various chronological attempts to place the anti-Babylonian con-ference, see WEIPPERT, *Edom*, pp. 327ff. Dating it as late as Zedekiah's seventh year, 591 B.C., is untenable; cf. H. SCHMIDT, *ZAW* XXXIX 1921, pp. 138-144. On the other hand, equally unsatisfactory is a date as early as the very beginning of Zedekiah's reign, as proposed by H. G. MAY, *JNES* IV 1945, pp. 217f.; VOGELSTEIN, *Chronology*, p. 32f.; G. R. DRIVER, *Textus* IV 1964, p. 86; and now N. M. SARNA, in *Hagut Ivrit beAmerika*, Tel Aviv 1972, pp. 121-130 (Hebrew). In Jer. xxviii 1, SARNA (*ibid.*) regards the "fourth year" as referring to the Sab-batical cycle, and thus equates it with "the beginning of Zedekiah's reign". But H. SEEBASS (*ZAW* LXXXIII 1970, pp. 449-452) distinguishes between the two notations, relating the "beginning" (597 B.C., in his opinion) only to the prophecy in Jer. xxvii 16-22 (following the LXX version here), on the looting of the Temple vessels at the time of Jehoiachin's exile, whereas the confrontation with Hananiah occurred in Zedekiah's fourth year.

date can probably be pinpointed even more accurately—to only slightly prior to the clash between Jeremiah and the false prophet Hananiah, which occurred in the fifth month of that year, that is, in Ab 593 B.C.—and indeed Jeremiah appears at this confrontation just as he had before the envoys to the conference, with a wooden yoke still about his neck.

The time seemed opportune for the nations of the West to rebel against Babylonia, for the empire had been in straits, at both home and abroad, in the two years prior to the plot, as is apparent from the Babylonian Chronicle.[29] In 596/95 B.C., the King of El[am] marched upon Babylonia, but was repelled—an event which probably inspired Jeremiah's invective against "Elam, in the beginning of the reign of Zedekiah king of Judah" (Jer. xlix 34ff.; and see the Chronological Table). In the winter of 595/94 B.C., revolt broke out even in Babylonia proper, but Nebuchadnezzar was able to suppress it, and immediately after even made a brief campaign to the West. Less than a year later, in Kislev of his eleventh regnal year (December 594 B.C.), Nebuchadnezzar set out once again to the West—the last event mentioned in the Chronicle prior to its breaking off. If our above assumption is correct—that the plot was hatched in Jerusalem several month later—then this Babylonian campaign, of which we have no detailed information, was indecisive and may well have even encouraged the ferment in the West. During his fourth regnal year, Zedekiah went to Babylon, or at least sent his "quartermaster" (Jer. li 59), but we do not know the precise date. It may have occurred prior to or in conjunction with Nebuchadnezzar's campaign to the West, or it may have been a corollary to the Babylonian reaction to the conspiracy, and therefore took place in the late summer of 593 B.C.[30]

The anti-Babylonian conference in Jerusalem provoked the sharp encounter between Jeremiah and the faction of false prophets who preached open revolt against Nebuchadnezzar, not only in Judah (Jer. xxvii 9-15; xxviii) but also among the Judean exiles in Babylonia (Jer. xxix 8-9). In Jeremiah's epistle to the exiles he even mentions

---

[29] For the following citations from the Babylonian Chronicle, see *CCK*, pp. 72ff.

[30] *Freedy & Redford*, p. 475, assume that Zedekiah was obliged to accompany Nebuchadnezzar upon his return to Babylon, but that in Ab he had already come back to Jerusalem and found the time ripe to rebel. According to the LXX version, Zedekiah himself did not go to Babylon, but merely sent a deputation; see RUDOLPH, *Jeremia*, p. 317.

the names of two prophets executed by Nebuchadnezzar, and a third who had made libellous accusations against him (Jer. xxix 21-32). These increased prophetic activities, we maintain, were the context for Ezekiel's call: his inaugural vision occurred on the fifth day of the fourth month in the fifth year of Jehoiachin's exile, that is, on 31 July 593 B.C. (see the Chronological Table).[31] If this is converted to the calendric system then used in Judah, according to Zedekiah's regnal years (from 1 Tishri 597 B.C.), it took place on the fifth day of the fourth month of Zedekiah's fourth year—a mere few weeks before Jeremiah's confrontation with Hananiah. Thus, it must have occurred at about the time of, or possibly even during, the anti-Babylonian meeting being held at Jerusalem. Could it have been this parley—portentous for the Babylonian exiles no less than for Judah—which aroused Ezekiel to his mission?

The ideological platform of the false prophetic faction was aptly conveyed by Hananiah, proclaimed in Yahwe's name, during his encounter with Jeremiah at the Temple in Jerusalem: "I have broken the yoke of the king of Babylon. In another ($be^c\bar{o}d$)[32] two years I will bring back to this place all the vessels of the Lord's house, which Nebuchadnezzar king of Babylon took away from this place and carried to Babylon. I will also bring back to this place Jeconiah the son of Jehoiakim, king of Judah, and all the exiles from Judah who went to Babylon . . ., for I will break the yoke of the king of Babylon" (Jer. xxviii 1-4). In his slighting response to this prophecy, Jeremiah entirely bypasses the specific notion of the return of King Jehoiachin (Jer. xxviii 6). This may well have been a deliberate cut, reflecting a bone of contention between the "true" and "false" prophetic circles in the political-ideological controversy over re-

---

[31] For the date, combining data in Ezek. i 1-2, see the commentaries, and recently W. ZIMMERLI, *Ezechiel* I, Neukirchen-Vluyn 1969, pp. 40ff. Cf. also C. G. HOWIE, *The Date and Composition of Ezekiel*, Philadelphia 1960, pp. 27ff. Of all the commentators of Ezekiel, as far as is known to me, only G. HÖLSCHER (*Hesekiel*, *BZAW* XXXIX 1924, pp. 12ff.) noted the proximity in dates between Ezekiel's call and the superscription in Jer. xxviii 1, and the significance of this correspondance.

[32] The word $be^c\bar{o}d$ is generally translated "*within* (two years)"; however, in biblical usage it often connotes "after", and hence our translation "*in another* (two years)". Cf., e.g., Gen. xxx 13, 19; Josh. i 11. Whereas Hananiah set a specific time for the return of the sacred vessels, etc., the other false prophets used the more general phraseology "now shortly" (Jer. xxvii 16). This latter phrase is omitted here in the LXX, as in the second instance of "in yet two years", in Jer. xxviii 11. These two instances may have been inserted into the MT on the basis of Jer. xxviii 3.

lations with Babylonia—the legitimacy of the royal succession in Judah.[33] This controversy derived from the co-existence of two kings of the Davidic line in the last decade of the First Temple period—the exiled Jehoiachin and his uncle Zedekiah, appointed in his stead; both had supporters in Judah, further splitting the people. This duality, of course, tarnished the standing of the last of the kings of Judah, undermined his authority and restricted his manoeuvrability. On the other hand, it might throw light on Zedekiah's paradoxical behaviour in rebelling—contrary to his own interests—against the very power which installed him.[34] Jeremiah countenanced Zedekiah, despite his drawbacks, and thoroughly rejected the legitimacy of Jehoiachin (or for that matter any of Jehoiakim's seed; cf. Jer. xxxvi 30), as advocated by the false prophets, with Hananiah at their head.

In Hananiah's prophecy, he boldly sets the fulfillment date for the release of the exiles and the return of Jehoiachin, even repeating it after symbolically breaking the wooden yoke on Jeremiah's neck: "Even so will I break the yoke of Nebuchadnezzar king of Babylon from the neck of all the nations in yet ($b^{e c} \bar{o}d$) two years" (Jer. xxviii 11). Since this prophecy was uttered in the fifth month of the fourth regnal year of Zedekiah (see above), the fulfillment date fell in the fifth month of Zedekiah's sixth regnal year, that is, in Ab 591 B.C. In the chronological terms employed among the exiles, as manifest

---

[33] See A. MALAMAT, *PEQ* LXXXIII 1951, pp. 81-87; and cf. also K. BALTZER, in *Studien zur Theologie der alttest. Überlieferungen* (*G. von Rad Festschrift*, ed. R. RENDTORFF and K. KOCH), Neukirchen 1961, pp. 33-43.

[34] See *PEQ* LXXXIII 1951, pp. 86f., where we further assume that the change of Mattaniah's name to Zedekiah, upon his appointment by Nebuchadnezzar, occurred under the inspiration of Jeremiah's prophecy on the Messianic King (Jer. xxiii 5-6; xxxiii 14-16)—in direct reversal of the usual interpretation, regarding this prophecy as based on accomplished fact. Recognition of the legitimacy of Zedekiah's rule is intimated even after the destruction of Jerusalem in Lam. iv 20. The theory of ALBRIGHT (*JBL* LI 1932, pp. 72-106) and his followers (e.g. H. G. MAY, *AJSL* LVI 1939, pp. 146-148), that even after his deportation Jehoiachin in effect remained king *de jure* of Judah, and that Zedekiah was only regent or *locum tenens*, is not sufficiently supported in the sources. The seal-impression "(Belonging) to Eliakim servant (*na'ar*) of Yaukin" lends no support, for the seals of the *na'ar* class are not indicative necessarily of royal officials; see now N. AVIGAD, "New Light on the *Na'ar* Seals", *G. E. Wright Volume* (in press). Palaeographically, too, it would seem that the above seal should be dated long before Jehoiachin's reign (F. M. CROSS, JR.—orally). Further, the designation of Jehoiachin as "King of the land of Judah" in the Weidner Tablets, like that of other deposed kings in exile, is not decisive in this matter; see the several documents in *ANET*, p. 308a and b.

in the Book of Ezekiel, this was in the fifth month of the seventh year of Jehoiachin's exile (reckoned from 1 Nisan 597 B.C.). How surprising, then, that so similar a date should appear in the superscription to Ezekiel xx: "In the seventh year, in the fifth month, on the tenth day of the month [that is, on 10 Ab, 14 August 591 B.C.], certain of the elders of Israel came to enquire of the Lord ..." (Ezek. xx 1; and see the Chronological Table).

Is this correspondence in dates, hitherto unnoticed, merely coincidental, or—as in Ezekiel's other chronological notations—is there some underlying significance? Though the object of the enquiry of the elders of Israel is not specified here,—as in other cases where the leadership sought divine tidings, it certainly concerned some pertinent national issue. In contrast to the prevailing interpretations of Ezekiel xx, ZIMMERLI has recently suggested that the enquiry might have concerned the release of the exiles of Jehoiachin, but he made no connection with Hananiah's prophecy. FREEDY and REDFORD have connected it with the hopes for redemption raised among the exiles by the campaign of Psamtik II to Asia, which they date in 591 B.C.[35] But this latter dating is spurious, as we shall see below.

Would it not be much more reasonable to assume that the enquiry was related specifically to Hananiah's prophecy of redemption "in yet two years"? The acute question at that time—at exactly the term of the prophecy—would have been whether, indeed, redemption was to come. The absolute refusal of the Lord ("Is it to enquire of me that you come? As I live ..., I will not be enquired of you"; Ezek. xx 3, 31), and the prophet's chastisement of the elders, instead of the expected words of salvation, both show that Ezekiel in exile, like Jeremiah in Judah, was totally opposed to the oracles of early redemption uttered by Hananiah and those like him.

The elders turned to Ezekiel, probably on this same matter, on another occasion as well, and were then, too, rejected by the Lord (Ezek. xiv 1-3: "Should I let myself be enquired of — at all

---

[35] For these views, see ZIMMERLI, *Ezechiel* I, p. 441; *Freedy & Redford*, pp. 469f., 480. Anticipating these was the medieval commentator David Kimchi, who regarded the elders in Ezek. xx 1 as seeking knowledge of the return to Judah. M. GREENBERG—in *Oz leDavid* (*D. Ben-Gurion Festschrift*), Jerusalem 1964, pp. 433-442 (Hebrew)—in contrast, regards the rebuke in Ezek. xx as the prophet's reaction to the exiles' acceptance of their fate. In his opinion, the visit of the elders to Ezekiel occurred a year after (!) Hananiah's prophecy had proved false (*ibid.*, p. 439), but we cannot accept this dating.

by them?"). Moreover, on that occasion they were clearly warned
that if a "prophet be deceived and speak a word, I, the Lord, have
deceived that prophet . . ., and will destroy him from the midst
of my people Israel" (Ezek. xiv 9). Indeed, this was the very fate
which soon befell Hananiah (cf. Jer. xxviii 16-17).[36]

One last chronological notation remains in the Book of Ezekiel
prior to the final siege of Jerusalem (Ezek. xxiv 1), for which no
historical circumstance has been found—the heading of Ezekiel
viii: the fifth day, in the sixth month (LXX: fifth month) of the
sixth year of Jehoiachin (that is, 17 September 592 B.C.). This is
also the third and only other notice of the leaders of the community
in exile coming to Ezekiel (in contrast to the two other instances,
here they are specifically denoted the elders of *Judah*, not Israel; in
Ezek. xxxiii 30ff., no mention is made of leaders *per se*). Again we
may assume that the elders came to the prophet on some particular
occasion which was considered fateful for the nation. In his trance,
Ezekiel was transported to Jerusalem and he luridly depicts the
abomination of the Temple cult. In the syncretistic cult described,
Egyptian elements are prominent, alongside other foreign features
(e.g. Tammuz worship), as has been noted often.[37] These elements
seem to include typical animal symbolism—"And there, portrayed
upon the wall round about, were all kinds of creeping things, and
loathsome beasts . . ." (Ezek. viii 10); the mysteries performed by
"the elders of the house of Israel . . . in the dark, every man in his
room of pictures" (*vs.* 12); and the worship of the sun (*vs.* 16), in
which "they put the branch (*zᵉmōrāh*) to my nose" (*vs.* 17; the last
word of the phrase here in MT, *appam*, "their nose", is a *tiqqun
soferim* for *appi*, "my nose", that is, presenting the branch to the

---

[36] The conceptual bond between the type of prophet mentioned in Ezek.
xiv 9 and the prophetic faction which Hananiah represented has been alluded
to by J. W. MILLER, *Das Verhältnis Jeremias und Hesekiels Sprachlich und Theologisch Untersucht*, Assen 1955, p. 164.

[37] See especially G. FOHRER, *Ezechiel*, Tübingen 1955, pp. 51f.; and for the
numerous earlier commentators who emphasized the Egyptian cultic elements
in this chapter, see G. FOHRER, *Die Hauptprobleme des Buches Ezechiel*, Berlin
1952, p. 175, n. 48. To them we might add H. SCHMIDT, *Die grossen Propheten*
(*Die Schriften des Alten Testaments* II, 2), Göttingen 1915, pp. 39ff.; idem, *ZAW*
XXXIX 1921, pp. 140f., who distinguishes between the overtness of the Babylonian worship here and the clandestine nature of the Egyptian; and, in part,
W. EICHRODT, *Der Prophet Hesekiel*, Göttingen 1966, pp. 59f. And cf. also:
W. F. ALBRIGHT, *Archaeology and the Religion of Israel* [2], Baltimore 1946, pp. 165ff.

deity, similar to the presentation of flowers or papyrus garlands to Egyptian gods; and see below).[38]

In a previous study we have already noted that the dates in Ezekiel, besides being of intrinsic value, are "Judah-centric", that is, they are oriented upon events which took place at home, in Palestine. Thus, we sought to show that the chronological notations heading oracles of doom on Egypt correspond with the despatch and subsequent failure of the Egyptian expedition to Judah during the final Babylonian siege of Jerusalem, in the spring of 587 B.C. (see the Chronological Table).[39] Might not the above-mentioned date heading Ezekiel viii be ascribed to another stirring development which befell Palestine—the campaign of Psamtik II to Kharu (that is, Palestine and the Phoenician coast) in his fourth regnal year, and its political and religious implications? Psamtik II's fourth year essentially corresponds with 592 B.C., rather than 591 (or even 590) B.C., as generally still held (see the Chronological Table).[40] From the Egyptian source, it is apparent that this was more of a

---

[38] For the various explanations of the word $z^e m \bar{o} r \bar{a} h$, and the foreign cult described in this context, see—besides the commentaries on Ezekiel—the studies devoted specifically to this matter, e.g.: R. GORDIS, *JThS* XXXVII 1936, pp. 284-288; H. W. F. SAGGS, *ibid.*, NS XI 1960, pp. 318-329; N. M. SARNA, *HThR* LVII 1964, pp. 347-352, all of which appear to fall wide of the mark. More convincing than SAGGS' attempt—to explain the passage on the basis of a Mesopotamian rite—is FOHRER's view (*loc. cit.*), which regards the $z^e m \bar{o} r \bar{a} h$ (a vinebranch) as a local Palestinian manifestation of the Egyptian ritual of presenting plants to gods, especially the sun-god; such would explain the close connections of this verse with the preceding *vs.* 16, specifically mentioning sun worship.

[39] See *IEJ* XVIII 1968, p. 152.

[40] For the revised Egyptian chronology of the Twenty-sixth Dynasty, retarding the initial year of each reign by a year, see: R. A. PARKER, *MDAIK* XV 1957, pp. 208-212 (and cf. E. HORNUNG, *ZÄS* XCII 1965, pp. 38f.). These dates have been accepted in such histories as A. GARDINER, *Egypt of the Pharaohs*, Oxford 1961, p. 451; W. HELCK, *Geschichte des alten Ägypten*, Leiden-Köln 1968, pp. 253ff.; and now also F. K. KIENITZ, *Fischer Weltgeschichte* IV, Frankfurt 1967, pp. 269f.—in contrast to his previous *Die politische Geschichte Ägyptens von 7. bis zum 4. Jahrhundert vor der Zeitwende*, Berlin 1953, pp. 25ff., 158.

Thus, Psamtik II ruled from 595 to 589 B.C.—rather than in 594-588 B.C., and Hophra began his reign already in February 589 B.C. Psamtik II's fourth year would have fallen between 18 January 592 and 17 January 591 B.C., as Prof. HORNUNG has kindly informed me. The obsolete figures for the dates of Psamtik II's reign have unfortunately been retained by, e.g., *Freedy & Redford*, p. 476. In any event, it is now clear that Psamtik II came to the throne more than two years prior to the anti-Babylonian conference in Jerusalem, and thus we can no longer accept a direct connection between these two events, as has been assumed by various scholars.

cultic "showing of the flag", than a military campaign, a sort of tour or pilgrimage to holy sites in the land of Kharu.[41]

Accompanying Pharaoh on this tour were priests bearing garlands (specific mention is made of a priest of Amun and of garlands of this deity), probably for the cult of the local or Egyptian gods in the temples of Kharu. Psamtik's destination has been regarded as the city of Byblos and the cult of Osiris there, but shrines in Palestine may well have been visited too. In the autumn of the same year, Ezekiel had his vision on the defiled Temple of Yahwe (see the Chronological Table). Could the touring Pharaoh, or at least his priests, have come to the Temple in Jerusalem? Could the abominous ritual blasted by Ezekiel—the proffering of the $z^e m\bar{o}r\bar{a}h$ within the Temple—be a reflection of the rite involving such cultic garlands as those brought by the Egyptian priests?[42]

Ezekiel's harsh oracle of doom on Jerusalem and its Temple (Ezek. viii-xi) should have served to preclude as vain any illusions among the Judean leadership—whether in Jerusalem or in exile—which may have been raised by Pharaoh's campaign. The appearance of Psamtik II in Kharu certainly had diplomatic overtones and undoubtedly fanned the anti-Babylonian sentiments already held by many local rulers, including the King of Judah. But it was only after the ambitious Hophra had acceded to the Egyptian throne (in early 589 B.C., and not 588 B.C.) that Judah openly rebelled, thus goading Babylon to war.

---

[41] See now the inscription, published by F. L. GRIFFITH in 1909, in *ibid.*, pp. 479f. (and the bibliography there). In contrast to the oft-held assumption that Psamtik II carried out a basically military campaign to Kharu, *Freedy & Redford* justly stress the peaceful character of this Egyptian undertaking (cf. similarly the two works of F. K. KIENITZ, mentioned in n. 40, above; and WEIPPERT, *Edom*, p. 376), and further assume that political contacts were then made with Zedekiah. M. GREENBERG (*JBL* LXXVI 1957, pp. 304-309) even assumed that Zedekiah was stirred into open rebellion against Babylon already by Psamtik II's appearance in Kharu.

[42] For the Egyptian ritual of presenting garlands of flowers or papyri to the gods (including by Pharaoh), see G. ROEDER, *ZÄS* XLVIII 1910, pp. 115-123; A. DE BUCK, *OTS* IX 1951, pp. 18-29; H. BONNET, *Reallexikon der ägypt. Religionsgeschichte*, Berlin 1952, pp. 120f., s.v. *Blumen*; D. B. REDFORD, *Orientalia* XXXIX 1970, p. 36, n. 1. and, most recently, E. BRUNNER-TRAUT, *Lexikon der Ägyptologie* I, Wiesbaden, 1974, pp. 836-9, s.v. *Blume*; *Blumenstrauss*.

From the many Egyptian depictions of the presentation of plants to the face of the god, we may call attention to an example from Palestine—on a stele from Beth Shean, showing a lotus being presented to the nose of a goddess; see *ANEP*, No. 475.

At this juncture Judah's plight was extreme: politically, her diplomatic efforts to achieve an anti-Babylonian front had collapsed, and the frailty of Egyptian support left her virtually isolated. Militarily, the Babylonian subjugation a decade earlier had deprived her of the cream of her fighting potential. Internally, the nation was divided over the dilemma of facing Babylon or giving in to fate. But the stand of the political leadership, which had inevitably drawn Nebuchadnezzar to the gates of Jerusalem once again, now spurred the remarkable resistance which enabled the city to withstand the two and a half years of siege prior to its fall (see the Chronological Table).[43]

In final analysis, the policy advocated by the "true" Prophets —Jeremiah and Ezekiel—could have steered Judah clear of the maelstrom which, as we know, did engulf her.

---

[43] On the final siege of Jerusalem and its duration, basing on a Tishri calendar, see *IEJ* XVIII 1968, pp. 150ff.

POSTSCRIPTUM

I was unable to refer to the article of E. Kutsch, "Das Jahr der Katastrophe: 587 v. Chr.", *Biblica* LV 1974, pp. 520-543, which reached me while the present paper was in proofs. The article is a careful and comprehensive defense of the alternative dating of the fall of Jerusalem, but I have not found its arguments of sufficient weight to alter my stand as set forth in this paper.

CHRONOLOGICAL TABLE OF THE LAST DECADES OF THE KINGDOM OF JUDAH

Events mentioned in the Babylonian Chronicles	Julian year B.C. beginning in January	Regnal years in Babylonia beginning in Nisan (Ist mo.)	Regnal years in Judah beginning in Tishri (VIIth mo.)	Events mentioned in the Bible
		Nabo-polassar	Josiah	
Egyptian army crosses Euphrates ⟶	609 ---	17-IV ---	31 --- ⟶ Battle of Megiddo (2 Kings 23: 29; 2 Chron. 35: 20-23)	
			*Jehoahaz (1)	
	608	18	*Jehoiakim 1	
	607	19	2	
	606	20		
Battle of Carchemish Conquest of "entire land of Ḥamath" ⟶	605 ===	21 === *Nebuchadrezzar	3 --- ⟶ Oracle on Battle of Carchemish (Jer. 46: 1-2; date in vs. 2 problematic)** [Subjugation of Judah according to Dan: 1:1ff.]	
	604	1 --- IX	4 --- ⟶ Oracle on Nebuchadrezzar's rule over Hither Asia (Jer. 25: 1ff.)	
Sack of Ashkelon ⟵	603	2	or --- IX 5 --- ⟶ Fast and emergency council (Jer. 36: 9)	
Campaign to West (?) [text broken] ⟵	602	3	6 --- ⟶ Subjugation of Judah?	
	601	4	7	
Babylonian invasion ⟵			8	Oracle "about the coming of Nebuchadrezzar..."

Copyright A. MALAMAT, 1974

Left-hand event labels:

- Raids against Arabs
- Conquest of Jerusalem
- War against Elamites
- Rebellion in Babylonia
- Troops mustered against West = [Chronicle breaks off]
- Psamtik's tour to Palestine, in his fourth year
- Hophra's accession in Egypt

Exile beginning in Nisan 597 B.C. (year column):

Exile yr	Date
1	-(I)
2	
3	
4	
5/(IV)	(31 July)
6 - 5/VI	(27 sept.)
7 - 10/V	(14 Aug.)
8	
9 - 10/X	
10	
11 - 12/X	7/I
12 - 5/X	

Regnal / calendar column:

- 10 · IX
- 7 · 2/XII
- Jehoiachin
- *Zedekiah · 8
- 1 · 9
- 2 · 10
- IX–X · 3 · 11
- (IV/V) · IX · 4 · 12
- 5 · 13 · 18 Jan
- 6 · V · 14 · 17 Jan
- 7 · 15
- 8 · 16 · 8 Feb
- 9 · 10/X · 17 · 15 Jan
- 10 · 18 · 7 Jan · 29 Apr
- 9/IV · 11 · 19 · 18 July · 14 Aug
- 7/V · 585 · 8 Jun

Central event descriptions:

- Oracle on Kedar and the kingdoms of Hazor "which Nebuchadrezzar... smote" (Jer. 49; 28ff.)
- Siege and surrender of Jerusalem (2 Kings 24; 10ff.); deportation of 3032 "Jews" (Jer. 52;28); Exile of Jehoiachin and elite (2 Kings 24; 12; 2 Chron. 36; 10)
- Oracle against Elam "in the beginning of the reign of Zedekiah" (Jer. 49; 34ff.)
- Anti-Babylonian conference in Jerusalem (Jer. 27; date, Jer. 28; 1)?
- Ezekiel's call (Ezek. 1;1-2)
- Ezekiel's vision of foreign abominations in Temple (Ezek. 8;1)
- Elders come to Ezekiel to enquire of the Lord (Ezek. 20; 1)
- "Fulfillment" date of Hananiah's prophecy (Jer. 28; 1ff.) — 2 years
- Start of final siege of Jerusalem (2 Kings 25; 1; Jer. 52; 4; Ezek. 24; 1-2)
- Egyptian relief and defeat (Ezek. 29; 1; 30; 20); Jeremiah in prison, buys field (Jer. 32; 1); Exile of 832 deserters (Jer. 52; 29)
- Breach of walls of Jerusalem (Jer. 39; 2; 52:6-7); Destruction of Temple (2 Kings 25;8-9; Jer. 52;12); Refugee in Babylonia reports Destruction (Ezek. 33; 21)

* Accession year.
** For date, see notes 9 and 11.

OLD TESTAMENT WISDOM LITERATURE AND DUALISTIC THINKING IN LATE JUDAISM

BY

BENEDIKT OTZEN
Aarhus

It is well known that at the end of the second volume of his Theology of the Old Testament GERHARD VON RAD has tried to show that the idea of Apocalyptic ought first and foremost to be regarded as a descendant of Wisdom thinking. Among the arguments he adduces, the most important refers to the conception of a divine order which permeates nature and history, a conception that has deep and firm roots in Wisdom thinking, and which in Apocalyptic is developed into the idea of determination of the exact time of the end. From here there are—still according to VON RAD—lines to eschatology as a secondary element and further on to the "period-thinking" and to the apocalyptic-dualistic thought of the two aeons, the latter idea being dependent upon the notion of the division of time into periods of weal and periods of woe, which is also found in Wisdom tradition.[1]

VON RAD only touches on dualism in this apocalyptic form. But the idea of the two aeons is not the only representative of dualistic thought in Late Judaism, and Apocalyptic is not the only genre in Late Judaistic literature. Both in apocalyptic texts and in texts not belonging to Apocalyptic proper, we meet with a kind of dualism that is not, principally, cosmic and eschatological, but which should rather be characterized as *psychological* and *ethical*—even if it also has cosmic and eschatological connotations. Conspicuous traits in this kind of dualistic teaching include the following: "the two ways" mentioned more or less clearly in Ethiopic Enoch xci 4,

---

[1] GERH. VON RAD, *Theologie des Alten Testaments*, Band II, 5. Aufl., München 1968, 316-331; cf. *Weisheit in Israel*, Neukirchen 1970, 337-63. Earlier attempts to understand Apocalyptic as dependent on Wisdom (HÖLSCHER, PFEIFFER) seem rather hesitant; see J. M. SCHMIDT, *Die jüdische Apokalyptik. Die Geschichte ihrer Erforschung von den Anfängen bis zu den Textfunden von Qumran*, Neukirchen 1969, 13f., 258-60; 298-302. VON RADS conception is sharply criticized by P. VON DER OSTEN-SACKEN, *Die Apokalyptik in ihrem Verhältnis zu Prophetie und Weisheit*, (Theologische Existenz heute CLVII) München 1969, 9-12 and 53-63.

19; xciv 1-4; Sirach ii 12; xxxiii 11; Testament of Asher i and Slavonic Enoch xxx 15. Further: the antithesis "light-darkness" as it is found in Ethiopic Enoch xli 8; cviii 11-15; Sirach xxxiii 14; Testaments of the Twelve Patriarchs *passim*; Slavonic Enoch xxx 15; Book of Wisdom vii 29f; Fourth Ezra xiv 20.[2] As a third example of such dualistic ideas we could refer to the notion of "the two inclinations in man", a conception dominating the Testament of Asher and occurring also in Sirach xv 14-20 (where, by the way, the Hebrew text uses the word יצר and thus indicates the relationship to the later Jewish idea of the two יצרים).[3]

Everybody knows that since the discovery of the Qumran texts scholarly interest in the dualistic thought of Late Judaism has grown immensely. The reason is not that dualism is a Qumran invention— we have just seen that dualistic ideas of different kinds are quite widespread in texts known long before 1947. But the remarkable thing about Qumran is the fact that we have here a whole theological system that is so to speak founded on dualistic thinking. In the Qumran texts dualism is present not only as certain conceptions lying on the fringes of religious thinking; it is the very foundation of the theological system and can be considered under three aspects, namely as a *psychological-ethical dualism* (the nature of man is constituted of two opposite powers or "spirits"), a *cosmic-ethical dualism* (man and the world divided into two groups led respectively by the "prince of light" and the "angel of darkness"), and an *eschatological dualism* (the present world, under the rule of Beliar or the "angel of darkness", will be succeeded by a new world under the dominion of God). This third aspect, by the way, is next to the apocalyptic idea on which VON RAD concentrated. The whole system is set forth in the Qumran Manual of Discipline page III-IV.[4]

---

[2] Cf. Sv. AALEN, *Die Begriffe 'Licht' und 'Finsternis' im Alten Testament, im Spätjudentum und im Rabbinismus*, Oslo 1951, 170-75 and 178-83.

[3] Cf. W. BOUSSET, *Die Religion des Judentums im späthellenistischen Zeitalter*, 3. Aufl. hrsg. von H. GRESSMANN, Tübingen 1926, 402-404; J. BONSIRVEN, *Le Judaïsme Palestinien au Temps de Jésus-Christ*, Tome II, Paris 1935, 18-23; with inclusion of the Qumran-material: R. E. MURPHY, "Yeser in the Qumran Literature", *Biblica* XXXIX, 1958, 334-44 and O. J. F. SEITZ, "Two Spirits in Man", *New Testament Studies* VI, 1959-60, 82-95.

[4] About the different aspects of Qumran dualism see B. OTZEN, "Die neugefundenen hebräischen Sektenschriften und die Testamente der zwölf Patriarchen", *StTh* VII, 1953, 135-36. Not least P. WERNBERG-MØLLER, "A Reconsideration of the Two Spirits in the Rule of the Community (1Q Serek III, 13-IV, 26)", *RQ* III, 1961-62, 413-41, has tried to show that the dualism in 1QS is to be conceived totally on the psychological level. His attempts have been criticized

The Qumran texts are not typical apocalyptic literature, even if they contain apocalyptic elements. They stand next to the Testaments of the Twelve Patriarchs, but on the whole they have their own character and represent a special kind of piety dominated by the ethical-dualistic system on which we shall concentrate here. VON RAD found, as mentioned, some connection between the apocalyptic idea of the two aeons and Wisdom tradition. He does not mention the more elaborate Qumran ethical dualism in this context. But there seem to be certain links between the ethical dualism in Qumran on one side and Wisdom literature on the other, and this might throw a certain sidelight on VON RAD's idea of a connection between Apocalyptic as such and Wisdom thinking.

I am not trying to say that Late Judaistic dualism in its different forms can be derived exhaustively from Wisdom. I hardly think that any scholar would deny foreign influence in Late Judaistic dualistic thinking—whether one assumes Persian or Greek influence.[5] The interesting question must be how strong the foreign influence has been—whether it has been universal and total, or whether it rather has played the role of a catalyst in the further development of biblical ideas. Thus the task must be to try to draw the line of demarcation between foreign elements in dualism and original Jewish or Old Testament ideas. It sounds rather simple, but is not so at all. For even if quite a large number of things in Late Judaistic dualism can be explained one way or another as a development of biblical ideas, the problem of influence and dependence in such matters is always evasive and elusive.

It is for reasons of space out of the question to give a survey of the different scholarly opinions about this problem. But three scholars, who most recently have been treating the problem of

by several scholars (f. instance H. G. MAY, "Cosmological Reference in the Qumran Doctrine of the Two Spirits and in Old Testament Imagery", *JBL* LXXXII, 1963, 1-6, and J. H. CHARLESWORTH, in the article mentioned in note 6, page 82-85). I am also unable to accept the main result of WERNBERG-MØLLER's article; nevertheless, his investigation into 1QS III-IV is one of the most profound in recent years and deserves close attention; several "standard-conceptions" about 1QS III-IV will have to be reconsidered in the light of this article.

[5] Regarding Persian influence, see note 6. Greek or "Jewish-gnostic" influence is found by K. SCHUBERT, "Der Sektenkanon von En Feshcha und die Anfänge der jüdischen Gnosis" *ThLz* LXXVIII, 1953, 495-506 and H. J. SCHOEPS, "Das gnostische Judentum in den Dead Sea Scrolls", *ZRGG* VI, 1954, 276-79. More recent views by K. RUDOLPH, "Gnosis und Gnostizismus, ein Forschungsbericht", *ThRu* XXXVI, 1971, 101-104 and M. HENGEL, *Judentum und Hellenismus*, (Wiss. Unters. z. NT X) 2. Aufl., Tübingen 1973, 394-453.

origin and character of Qumran dualism, are rather typical in their different approaches: JÜRGEN BECKER follows KUHN and DUPONT-SOMMER in assuming a Persian origin of the dualistic elements— except for the thought of God as creator of both spirits in man.[6] PETER VON DER OSTEN-SACKEN, on the other side, thinks that the dualism in the War Scroll represents the primordial form and is developed from Old Testament ideas (the Holy War, the Day of Yahweh, and certain conceptions in the Book of Daniel), whereas Persian influence is perceptible in the Manual of Discipline and other later Qumran writings.[7] ROBERT LEANEY, the British scholar, will not deny foreign influence, but rather follows AALEN in thinking that the origin of the dualistic system is to be found in the contrast light-darkness which, as he says, "seems to provide a fundamental antithesis in all poetry, religion and primitive philosophy". LEANEY traces this antithesis back in the Old Testament, but thinks that the idea of the two spirits in man may be based on later speculation due to foreign influence.[8] In such efforts to search for at least some of the sources of dualistic thought in Qumran and in Late Judaism in general, it is seen that Wisdom literature has played no

---

[6] J. BECKER, *Das Heil Gottes*, (Studien zur Umwelt des Neuen Testaments III) Göttingen 1964, 83-103, specially 96-99. Cf. A. DUPONT-SOMMER, "L'instruction sur les deux Esprits dans le 'Manuel de Discipline' ", *RHR* CXLII, 1952, 5-35 and "Le Problème des influences étrangères sur la secte juive de Qumran", *La Bible et l'Orient*, (Cahiers de la RHPhR XXXIV), Paris 1955, 75-94 (in the latter article Greek-syncretistic (pythagoraean) influence is stressed as well); K. G. KUHN, "Die Sektenschrift und die iranische Religion", *ZTK* XLIX, 1952, 296-316; similarly H. WILDBERGER, "Der Dualismus in den Qumrānschriften", *Asiatische Studien* VIII, 1954, 163-77, H. RINGGREN, *Tro och liv enligt Döda-havs-rullarna*, Stockholm 1961, 66f. and others; survey of recent opinions: JAMES H. CHARLESWORTH, "A Critical Comparison of the Dualism in 1QS 3:13-4:26 and the "Dualism" Contained in the Gospel of John", *John and Qumran* (ed. by J. H. CHARLESWORTH), London 1972, 76-89.

[7] PETER VON DER OSTEN-SACKEN, *Gott und Belial*, (Studien zur Umwelt des Neuen Testaments VI), Göttingen 1969, 84-87 and 138-41.

[8] A. R. C. LEANEY, *The Rule of Qumran and its Meaning*, London 1966, 37-56. Cf. Sv. AALEN, *Die Begriffe 'Licht' und 'Finsternis' im Alten Testament, im Spätjudentum und im Rabbinismus*, Oslo 1951, 170ff. In a more general way other scholars have isolated certain passages in the Old Testament which could be considered as starting point of a dualistic way of thinking (Jer. xxi 8 and Is. xlv 7 are often mentioned); cf. for instance G. MOLIN, *Die Söhne des Lichts*, Wien 1954, 129, and H. G. MAY, (the article mentioned in note 4), 6-14, the latter concentrating on the antithesis chaos-cosmos in the Old Testament. The first monograph about Qumran dualism (H. W. HUPPENBAUER, *Der Mensch zwischen zwei Welten*, Zürich 1959) represents an interior analysis of the dualism; he says that the problem of origin and of relations to Old Testament teaching require a special nvestigation (pp. 12f.).

important role. JAMES SANDERS in his edition of the Qumran Psalms from Cave 11 regrets that "no work has been done on Wisdom thinking generally in Qumran literature".[9] This is strange; for RINGGREN is right when he says that in the Qumran texts we find "the whole gamut of terms for wisdom, insight, and understanding, which we know from the OT Wisdom literature, used more or less interchangeably with *da'at* and the verb *yāda'*".[10] NÖTSCHER has shown that these notions in the Qumran texts are not gnostic but first and foremost oriented towards the Law—like the notion "wisdom" in Sirach and other Late Judaistic sapiential writings. [11] On the whole, looking for connections between Qumran and Wisdom literature, we find that the similarities to the contemporary Sirach are the most conspicuous—which should not surprise us. WERNBERG-MØLLER, CARMIGNAC, and M. R. LEHMANN have listed the similarities which are mostly found in single expressions, and especially in the ethical teachings. There is, however, a single passage in Sirach observed by PAUL WINTER which seems to have a closer connection with dualistic thinking, and to which we shall revert.[12]

Eventually, we come to the OT Wisdom literature. Is it possible in OT Wisdom literature to find ideas akin to the ethical dualism in Late Judaism? The situation is more or less the same as it was, as far as Sirach is concerned: scholars have observed similarities in vocabulary and in isolated expressions. WERNBERG-MØLLER and LEANEY, in their commentaries on the dogmatic essay on dualism page III-IV of the Manual of Discipline, both list about twenty references to OT Wisdom Literature—mostly comparing single expressions in the catalogues of virtues and vices in the Manual of Discipline with expressions in Job and Proverbs.[13]

---

[9] J. A. SANDERS, *The Psalms Scroll of Qumran Cave 11*, (Discoveries in the Judaean Desert of Jordan. IV), Oxford 1965, 69.

[10] H. RINGGREN, "Qumran and Gnosticism", *The Origins of Gnosticism*, (Supplements to Numen XII) Leiden 1967, 379.

[11] F. NÖTSCHER, *Zur theologischen Terminologie der Qumran-Texte*, (Bonner Biblische Beiträge X), Bonn 1956, 38-79.

[12] P. WERNBERG-MØLLER, *The Manual of Discipline*, (Studies on the Texts of the Desert of Judah I), Leiden 1957, 16f. J. CARMIGNAC, "Les rapports entre l'Ecclésiastique et Qumran", *RQ* III, 1961-62, 209-18. M. R. LEHMANN, "Ben Sira and the Qumran Literature", *RQ* III, 1961-62, 103-16. A comparison between Qumran texts and the Wisdom of Solomon is, from our point of view, of less interest, as most scholars will agree that the Wisdom of Solomon is later than the Qumran texts and dependent upon them; a very thorough investigation into the question is made by C. LARCHER, *Études sur le Livre de la Sagesse*, Paris 1969, 112-32.

[13] See the indices in the works mentioned in notes 8 and 12, and LEANEY's

However, in his introduction to the commentary, LEANEY has an interesting observation. In his treatment of the light-darkness imagery—which, as already mentioned, according to LEANEY is at the bottom of dualistic thinking—he says in a footnote: "In the OT an embryonic form of dualism appears in such passages as Deut. 30.15-20; Jer. 21.8; Ps. 1; Prov. 2.13; 7-8".[14] What is of interest to our investigation is the reference to Psalm i and Proverbs. And we can again put the question: to what degree can dualistic thinking in Late Judaism be traced back to OT Wisdom literature?

I will take as my point of departure the catalogues of virtues and vices that we find closely connected with dualistic theology both in The Testaments of the Twelve Patriarchs (TestAsher v; TestBenj. vi-vii, etc.) and in the Qumran Manual of Discipline (p. IV), all of which characterize good and evil respectively. As mentioned earlier, WERNBERG-MØLLER and LEANEY find certain similarities in vocabulary between the Qumran catalogues on the one hand, and OT Wisdom Literature on the other. Two German dissertations about the NT catalogues both delve into the Qumran- and Testament-catalogues and emphasize the close connection of both texts with dualistic theology. As far as the question of origin of the catalogue-tradition in Late Judaism and in the NT is concerned, the two Germans do not agree. EHRHARD KAMLAH above all seeks the origin in syncretistic, Greek-oriental traditions,[15] whereas SIEGFRIED WIBBING assumes two roots: one which goes back into Hellenistic popular philosophy, especially the Stoic diatribe, and the other root which extends back into the OT. WIBBING points to lists of ethical precepts in the OT lawbooks (the decalogue, collections like Lev xvii-xix, etc.), reflections of such lists in Psalms (Ps. xv), and to prophetic imitations of such lists (Hos. iv and Jer. vii); he also mentions two passages in the Book of Proverbs, namely vi 17-19 and viii 13. Nevertheless, he does not want to talk about catalogues of virtues and vices in the OT, as the lists he has mentioned are not,

---

diagram pp. 51f. As for the *Hodayot*—where dualistic theology again is a constitutive element—references to Wisdom literature seem very sparse; see Sv. HOLM-NIELSEN, *Hodayot. Psalms from Qumran*, Aarhus 1960, 310f.

[14] A. R. C. LEANEY, *The Rule of Qumran and its Meaning*, London 1966, 47.

[15] E. KAMLAH, *Die Form der katalogischen Paränese im Neuen Testament*, (Wiss. Unters. z. NT VII), Tübingen 1964, 53-150. Like WIBBING (see note 16) he also mentions certain passages in Proverbs (vi 16-19; viii 13; further: iii 16f. and iv 10f.) as a possible source of inspiration of Tannaitic catalogues and the Qumran- and Testament-catalogues (pp. 152 and 173f.).

from a form-critical point of view, exactly like the Late Judaistic and NT catalogues.[16]

But this is certainly to attach too much weight to form-criticism. I think that precisely WIBBING's reference to the verses from Proverbs is of great value. Not only are the catalogues of virtues and vices in Proverbs—especially in Proverbs i-ix—far more numerous than WIBBING thinks, but, according to my view, we have in the descriptive lists of virtues and vices in Proverbs the best Old Testament parallels to the dualistic catalogues in the Manual of Discipline and in the Testaments. And furthermore, not only the catalogue *form* can be traced back to Proverbs, and not only single expressions in the vocabulary of the later catalogues can be traced back to Proverbs, but also—and of more importance—some of the *ideas* behind the catalogues in Proverbs point to dualistic ideas as they are developed in the Late Judaistic writings. We may in Proverbs have some germs of dualistic thinking, if not, as LEANEY puts it, dualism in an embryonic form.

Already in the introduction to Proverbs i we find a catalogue of human qualities typical of the person who has adopted Solomonic wisdom (Prov. i 2-6). Here we have catchwords, most of which are also found in the Qumran catalogue of virtues: צדק, משפט, ערמה, שכל, בינה, חכמה, and דעת. These notions are the common property of all Wisdom literature. But in Proverbs ch. ii we meet with more special concepts: verses 6-10 of the chapter comprise a list of qualities typical of the "righteous", the one who knows wisdom and is צדיק

---

[16] S. WIBBING, *Die Tugend- und Lasterkataloge im Neuen Testament und ihre Traditionsgeschichte unter besonderer Berücksichtigung der Qumran-Texte*, (BeihZNW XXV), Berlin 1959, 24-26. In an unprinted dissertation (Humboldt-Universität, Berlin), P. HARTMUT ASCHERMANN, *Die paränetischen Formen der "Testamente der Zwölf Patriarchen" und ihr Nachwirken in der frühchristlichen Mahnung. Eine formgeschichtliche Untersuchung*, Berlin 1955, the author treats from a form-critical standpoint the rather numerous catalogues spread all over The Testaments of the Twelve Patriarchs. He follows VON RAD ("Die Vorgeschichte der Gattung von 1. Kor. 13, 4-7", *Ges. Studien*, München 1958, 281-96) in assuming a cultic-liturgic origin in the Old Testament for the catalogue-form (Deut. etc.) and thinks that it is also found in what he calls Wisdom literature with a strong poetical stamp, namely certain psalms and some passages in the book of Job; he refers to passages in Ps x; xxxvi; lxiv; lxxiii and in Job xv; xviii; xx; xxi; xxiv; xxvii; xxx but admits that these texts do not represent catalogues proper but rather descriptions of the fate of the godless (pp. 37f. and 48f.). From the Book of Proverbs he mentions some conditional phrases (i 10-11, 15 and xxiii 1; p. 85) and some admonishing sentences (iii 1f.; iii 27-35; iv 20-27; vi 20.25; vii 1-4.24-25; ix 18f.; xxii 17-29 etc. — p. 90), not all of which can be said to be typical of the catalogue-form.

and יָשָׁר. In these verses we have some of the same notions that we had in the introduction in ch. i, but throughout this chapter the righteous are said to be walking in "the paths of right", in "the way of God's loyal ones", in "the way of good men", and in "the paths of the righteous" (*vv.* 8 and 20). The second half of the chapter is a catalogue of vices typical of the רָשָׁע, "the godless", who is said to walk in "the evil way" and in "the ways of darkness" (*vv.* 12-13). The two last verses of the chapter sum up with a slight eschatological note: "The upright shall dwell on earth and blameless men remain there; but the wicked shall be uprooted from it and traitors weeded out" (*vv.* 21-22). With these notations we are a step nearer to the Qumran theology and, of course, as early as BROWNLEE it was observed that the expression "way of darkness" was taken from the Book of Proverbs.[17]

Whereas the parenetic catalogues in ch. iii are not quite typical, we have in ch. iv a kind of catalogue in verses 10-19 that is half parenetic and half descriptive; the notions "way of wisdom" and "tracks of righteousness" again function as parallels to "the paths of the godless" and "the way of evil". But the ending is interesting in our connection: "The course of the righteous is like morning light, growing brighter till it is broad day; but the ways of the wicked are like darkness at night, and they do not know what has been their downfall". LEANEY, who thinks that the light-darkness idea is at the bottom of Late Judaistic theology, lists these verses in his diagram (p. 51).

A very typical catalogue of vices is found in vi 16-19 (mentioned by WIBBING): "Six things the Lord hates, seven things are detestable to him: a proud eye, a false tongue, hands that shed innocent blood, a heart that forges thoughts of mischief, and feet that run swiftly to do evil, a false witness telling a pack of lies, and one who stirs up quarrels between brothers". Also this catalogue has a certain interest because it links up the different vices with parts of the human body—exactly like the catalogue of vices in the Manual of Discipline which also talks about the vices of hands, heart, tongue, eyes, ears, and neck (1QS IV, 9-11) and the more "scientific" lists of TestReuben iii and TestNaphtali ii 8. Once more in ch. viii wisdom is described in a list of virtues ending with: "I walk in the path of righteousness, in the tracks of justice" (Prov. viii 12-20).

[17] W. H. BROWNLEE, *The Dead Sea Manual of Discipline*, (BASOR Suppl. Studies X-XII), New Haven 1951, 15.

Of course there are quite a large number of exegetical and form-critical problems attached to these lists or catalogues, which we cannot treat here. I can only refer to the commentaries.[18] But even if the delimitation of the sections can be discussed, the mentioned passages could have been conceived as ethical catalogues by a reader in Late Judaistic times. In Sirach, by the way, the catalogue-form is not typical. Sir. xxli 21-xlii 2 may be the best example; perhaps also the beginning of ch. xv.

What are the deeper ideas behind these catalogues in the Book of Proverbs which so strongly resemble the Late Judaistic catalogues in dualistic setting? We observe that the catalogues in Proverbs are confined to chapters i-ix, which by many recent scholars are not considered to be much younger than the rest of the Book, as they were in earlier scholarship.[19] The following chapters consist of isolated utterances; but what we might call the dualistic note is dominant as well, although in a different way. We have here—not least in ch. x-xii—an endless row of antithetic sayings about the צדיק and the רשע: it would not be an exaggeration to say that any human act or attitude is taken as characterizing the person as being either "righteous" or "godless". In his book *Wesen und Geschichte der Weisheit*, HANS HEINRICH SCHMID, the Swiss scholar, says that in these antitheses mankind is divided into two groups, and each of them is referred either to the positive or to the negative half of reality. These antitheses express, SCHMID says, a special "Wisdom" understanding of world-order: not only mankind but the world as such is divided into two spheres, the sphere of good and the sphere of evil.[20] I mentioned earlier a noteworthy passage in Sirach observed by PAUL WINTER and brought into connection with Qumran dualism. This well-known passage seems to represent a further development of this fundamental Wisdom idea; it is Sir. xxxiii (xxxvi) 14f., which runs: "Over against evil stands the good, and against death, life; likewise, over against the godly, the sinner.

---

[18] F. ex. H. RINGGREN, *Sprüche*, (ATD XVI), Göttingen 1962 and W. MCKANE, *Proverbs*, London 1970.

[19] Cf. R. N. WHYBRAY, *Wisdom in Proverbs*, (Studies in Bibl. Theology XLV), London 1965; CHRISTA BAUER-KAYATZ, *Einführung in die alttestamentliche Weisheit*, (Bibl. Studien LV), Neukirchen 1969, 37f.; B. LANG, *Die weisheitliche Lehrrede*, (Stuttgarter Bibel-Studien LIV), Stuttgart 1972, 46-60. Cf. also W. MCKANE, *Proverbs*, London 1970, 1-10, and G. VON RAD, *Weisheit in Israel*, Neukirchen 1970, 24 and 152.

[20] H. H. SCHMID, *Wesen und Geschichte der Weisheit*, (BeihZAW CI), Berlin 1966, 159.

Even thus look upon all the works of God, each different, one the opposite of the other". In Sirach's optimistic view, the sentence is intended to demonstrate the harmony of creation.[21] But the antitheses in Proverbs that may have inspired Sirach have their centre of gravity in the experience that each human act works in its own sphere,[22] so that man through his actions is placed either in one sphere or in the other. Thus the antitheses throw a sharp light on the catalogues in the first nine chapters in Proverbs and indicate that the deeper meaning of the catalogues is the characterization of two different kinds of man belonging to two different spheres.

By continuously seeking the deeper meaning of the catalogues in Proverbs, we are drawing near to a very essential complex of ideas in Wisdom tradition. The urge to divide mankind and the world into two spheres that lies behind both the catalogues and the antitheses has its origin in the craving for order that is the motive power of all Wisdom thinking. The immense spiritual strength that is hidden in Wisdom tradition emanates from a need to understand the surrounding world and to arrange it according to its immanent laws. As VON RAD has it: "Die Weisheit . . . (ist) das Bemühen des Volkes Israel, die Gesetzmässigkeiten seines Lebensraumes zu erfassen und zu ordnen". [23] The catalogues and the antitheses serve this purpose.

This urge for order that lies behind what we have called the dualistic note in these chapters in Proverbs does not make up the whole characterization of Wisdom literature. Not least GESE and ZIMMERLI—but also VON RAD—have shown that in Wisdom tradition certain limits are set to these efforts to understand the laws of existence. These limits are set by the fundamental Israelite faith in Yahweh and could be indicated by the notions "creation" and

---

[21] PAUL WINTER, "Ben Sira and the Teaching of 'Two Ways' ", *VT* V, 1955, 315-18. Not least M. HENGEL, *Judentum und Hellenismus*, (Wiss. Untersz.NT X), 2. Aufl., Tübingen 1973, 261-64, emphasizes that the theme of such passages in Sirach is a demonstration of the "Zweckmässigkeit" of creation. Like WINTER he also refers to Sir. xlii 24 ("everything is double, one thing opposite the other . . ."). Cf. also J. MARBÖCK, *Weisheit im Wandel*, (Bonner Biblische Beiträge XXXVII), Bonn 1971, 152-53, and L. SCAZZOCCHIO, "Ecclesiastico, Tobia, Sapienza di Salomone alla luce dei testi di Qumran", *RSO* XXXVII, 1962, 205, who also refers to Sir. xv 14-18.

[22] Cf. the expression "schicksalwirkende Tatsphäre" coined by K. KOCH, "Gibt es ein Vergeltungsdogma im Alten Testament?", *ZTK* LII, 1955, 2-10.

[23] G. VON RAD, *Theologie des Alten Testaments*, Band II, München 1960, 319 (expressed in other words in 5. Aufl., 1968, 318).

"determination". Taken together these two ideas express the thought that even if Yahweh has established laws for the world-order, and even if man through wisdom can gain insight into these laws, man cannot dispose of ("verfügen über") these laws. God as creator and sustainer is the sovereign ruler of the immanent laws of his creation. Fear of God as the beginning of wisdom (Prov. i 7; ix 10) is not fear of the God of covenant and commandments, but is the recognition of God as creator and Lord of world-order. And this leads to the thought of determination, that is expressed in various ways in Proverbs—most clearly in the well-known passage: "Man plans his journey by his own wit, but it is the Lord who guides his steps" (Prov. xvi 9)—a group of sentences that have their quite special meaning in the Wisdom setting and leads on to Qohelet.[24]

We must content ourselves with a mere indication of these motifs in Wisdom literature and return to the Late Judaistic texts. We could refer to certain passages in The Testaments of the Twelve Patriarchs, but for reasons of time we shall have to concentrate on the most typical passage, the Qumran Manual of Discipline III-IV. We have already dwelt for some time on the catalogues of virtues and vices on page IV, and we have seen a connection from them back to similar lists in Proverbs. If we go back a bit, we meet on page III the fundamental ideas of Qumran dualistic thought, and we are able to observe that the similarities between Wisdom literature and the dualistic ideas of Late Judaism extend beyond the catalogues.

After the introductory phrase למשכיל להבין וללמד—all of them genuine Wisdom expressions—there follow some all-encompassing terms which show that the teaching has a cosmic character and is about the whole order of world and man: the teaching is about "the order of genealogy of all the sons of men, about their different spirits with their characteristics corresponding to their deeds in their generations, and about the visitation of them with afflictions and their end in peace" (1QS III, 13-15). According to most scholars, this section talks about the two groups of mankind, their "order of genealogy" (תולדות), their characteristics (further developed in the

---

[24] Cf. H. GESE, *Lehre und Wirklichkeit in der alten Weisheit*, Tübingen 1958, 38-41 and 46-48; W. ZIMMERLI, "Ort und Grenze der Weisheit im Rahmen der alttestamentlichen Theologie", *Les Sagesses du Proche-Orient ancien*, Paris 1963, 127-31. Cf. G. VON RAD, *Weisheit in Israel*, Neukirchen 1970, 131-48. Sentences like Prov. xvi 9, by the way, are often quoted in the Qumran Psalms; cf. RINGGREN, *Sprüche*, (ATD XVI), Göttingen 1962, 68.

catalogues), and their final fate (also mentioned in the catalogues)[25]. In the following lines we meet with two ideas that we have already met in Wisdom literature: the thought of determination ("From the God of Knowledge is all the present and future, and before they came to be, he prepared all their pattern, etc."—III, 15-17). The creation thought is subsequently expressed and combined with the idea of the two spirits in man. This thought develops directly into the seminal concept of mankind divided into two groups: בני צדק and בני עול, reminding us of the sharp distinction in Wisdom teaching between צדיק and רשע. The characteristics of בני צדק and בני עול respectively are listed in the two catalogues on the first half of page IV, whereas the eschatological ideas are developed on the rest of page IV.

We must renounce a detailed investigation into the section, but what we have seen should be enough to indicate that influence from Wisdom tradition is perceptible and conspicuous in this dualistic theology and that the influence should not be confined to vocabulary. Nevertheless, it must not be exaggerated. It is clear from what we have elaborated that Wisdom influence can be traced only in what we have called cosmic-ethical dualism (the idea of the world and mankind divided into two spheres or groups), whereas the psychological-ethical (the two spirits in man) and the eschatological dualisms have no connection with Wisdom tradition. The same holds good as far as the mythologizing tendency in both Qumran and The Twelve Testaments is concerned (Beliar and his spirits etc.). It is difficult to decide how much of all this is due to foreign influence—but certainly a considerable amount.[26] In general, the foreign influence in the Twelve Testaments seems stronger than in Qumran, as the Testaments contain only psychological-ethical dualism.[27]

I mentioned earlier that JAMES SANDERS indicates the need for a general treatment of Wisdom influence in the Qumran literature. I think he is right—and furthermore I think that the investigation should be extended to certain groups of pseudepigraphic literature as well. There is much to do in this field, and this paper has, I hope, provided a modest contribution to this work.

---

[25] P. WERNBERG-MØLLER (article mentioned note 4) thinks that תולדות can mean "natures" (p. 419-21). This conception—with right, I think—is criticized by MAY (article mentioned note 4, p. 2).

[26] Cf. M. HENGEL, *Judentum und Hellenismus*, (Wiss. Unters. z. NT X) 2. Aufl., Tübingen 1973, 422-27.

[27] Further treatment of this difference between Qumran and the Testaments: B. OTZEN, "Die neugefundenen hebräischen Sektenschriften und die Testamente der zwölf Patriarchen", *StTh* VII, 1953, 136-41.

DER "JAHWIST" ALS THEOLOGE?
ZUM DILEMMA DER PENTATEUCHKRITIK

VON

R. RENDTORFF
Heidelberg

In der neueren alttestamentlichen Forschung ist eine bemerkens-
werte Wandlung in der Beurteilung der 'Quellen' des Pentateuch
erkennbar. Frühere Generationen waren bemüht gewesen, möglichst
sorgfältig und genau die *literarische* Abgrenzung zwischen den
einzelnen Quellenschriften vorzunehmen, ihren Sprachgebrauch zu
erforschen, ihre Entstehungszeit zu bestimmen und schließlich den
Vorgang ihrer redaktionellen Zusammenfügung zu beschreiben. In
neuerer Zeit sind alle diese Probleme auffallend in den Hintergrund
getreten; stattdessen herrscht ein sehr ausgeprägtes Interesse an der
Theologie der Quellenschriften bzw. ihrer Autoren, ja, vielfach wird
gerade das Charakteristische der Quellenschriften darin gesehen, daß
sie theologische Werke sind. Trotzdem werden aber weiterhin die
traditionellen Bezeichnungen 'Jahwist', 'Elohist', 'Priesterschrift'
usw. verwendet, und zur Abgrenzung wird auf die traditionellen
Argumente verwiesen. Darin zeigt sich, daß vielen Forschern die
Veränderung der Fragestellung offenbar nicht deutlich bewußt ist.

Es handelt sich aber in der Tat um eine grundsätzliche Veränderung
der Fragestellung. Am Anfang dieses Jahrhunderts war trotz aller
Bemühungen um exakte Abgrenzung der Pentateuchquellen vielfach
eine deutliche Skepsis erkennbar gegenüber der Frage, ob diese
Abgrenzung überhaupt genau und zuverlässig durchgeführt werden
könne und ob sich insbesondere ein klares Profil der einzelnen
Pentateuchquellen herausarbeiten ließe. So bezeichnete etwa Hermann
GUNKEL in der Einleitung zu seinem Genesiskommentar die 'Quellen'
als "Sammlungen, die nicht aus *einem* Gusse sind und nicht mit
einem Male fertig gewesen sein können, sondern die *im Laufe der
Geschichte entstanden sind*".[1] Deshalb folgerte er: "'J' und 'E' sind
also *nicht Einzelschriftsteller, sondern Erzählerschulen*".[2] GREẞMANN

---

[1] H. GUNKEL, *Genesis übersetzt und erklärt*, Göttingen (³1910, ⁷1966), LXXXIV.
[2] AaO, LXXXV.

ging noch einen Schritt weiter, wenn er in seinem Buch *Mose und seine Zeit* (1913) schrieb: "In vielen Fällen sind JE weiter nichts als Etiketten, die man beliebig vertauschen darf".[3] Es ließen sich zahlreiche weitere Zitate anderer Forscher hinzufügen.

Wie konnte es angesichts dieser Skepsis dazu kommen, daß heute wieder ein so großes Interesse an den *Persönlichkeiten* der Quellenautoren besteht? Der entscheidende Grund dafür ist offenbar die schon erwähnte Tatsache, daß die Quellenautoren als *Theologen* betrachtet werden und daß deshalb ihre jeweilige theologische Konzeption das Interesse auf sich zieht. Aber wie kam es zu dieser neuen Sicht der Dinge? Wenn ich recht sehe, war eine der wesentlichen Voraussetzungen dafür die neue Konzeption vom Werden des Pentateuch bzw. Hexateuch, die Gerhard VON RAD entwickelt hat. In seinem Buch *Das formgeschichtliche Problem des Hexateuchs* (1938)[4] hat er die Entstehung des 'Hexateuch' als eine große Kompositionsarbeit dargestellt, bei der aus zahlreichen ursprünglich selbständigen Traditionskomplexen ein neues Ganzes entstand. Diese Komposition geschah nach der Auffassung VON RADS unter ganz bestimmten theologischen Leitgedanken und ist deshalb auch als die theologische Leistung eines einzelnen zu verstehen.

Hier muß deutlich betont werden, daß es sich bei dieser These VON RADS um einen grundsätzlich neuen Ansatz zur Lösung der Probleme des Pentateuch (bzw. Hexateuch) handelt, der mit der Fragestellung und insbesondere mit der Antwort der Quellenscheidung zunächst nichts zu tun hat. Die Quellenscheidung geht ja von der vorliegenden *End*gestalt des Pentateuch aus und stellt die Frage nach der literarischen Einheitlichkeit des uns heute vorliegenden Textes. Dabei kommt sie in der Gestalt der 'klassischen' Urkundenhypothese zu einer Lösung, bei der der ganze Stoff des Pentateuch in mehrere parallele *Längsschnitte* zerlegt wird, von denen jeder mehr oder weniger das Ganze der Darstellung von der Schöpfung oder jedenfalls von der Vätergeschichte bis zur Landnahme oder jedenfalls bis zum Tod des Mose umfaßt haben soll. VON RADS Fragestellung ist eine gänzlich andere: Er fragt gerade nicht nach *parallelen* Strängen, die den gesamten Stoff umfassen, sondern nach Traditionskomplexen, die jeweils *ein* Thema oder

---

[3] H. GRESSMANN, *Mose und seine Zeit. Ein Kommentar zu den Mose-Sagen*, Göttingen (1913), 368.
[4] Wiederabgedruckt in: *Gesammelte Studien zum Alten Testament*, München (1958, ⁴1971), 9-86.

einen Themenbereich enthalten. Durch die Zusammenfügung dieser
Komplexe entsteht dann ein neues Ganzes mit einer neuen, umfassenden Thematik. Von RAD wollte also den Pentateuch gerade
wieder als ein *einheitlich* konzipiertes Gesamtwerk verstehen, hinter
dem ein starker theologischer Gestaltungswille steht.

Daß dieser grundlegende Wechsel in der Fragestellung nicht
deutlich wurde und daß von RAD selbst sich seiner vielleicht nicht
ganz bewußt geworden ist, hat seinen Grund offensichtlich darin,
daß von RAD zu sehr ein Kind seiner Zeit war und sich nicht ohne
weiteres von der traditionellen Sicht der Quellenscheidung lösen
konnte. Denn als er einen Namen wählen mußte für den Theologen,
der diese Kompositionsarbeit geleistet hat, sprach er wie selbstverständlich vom 'Jahwisten'. Es scheint so, als ob von RAD hierin
nie ein Problem gesehen habe, obwohl doch dieser 'Jahwist' mit
dem der Urkundenhypothese kaum etwas zu tun hat. Vor allem ist
dieser 'Jahwist' für von RAD nicht *einer* von mehreren Quellenautoren. Im Gegenteil! Von RAD hat selbst klar ausgesprochen,
daß die traditionelle Quellenscheidung in seiner Konzeption keinen
Platz hat: "Nicht, daß das Dazukommen von E und J ein für uns
durchsichtiger, ja überhaupt befriedigend erklärbarer Vorgang wäre!
Die Frage nach dem Woher und Wozu dieser beiden Werke, nach
ihrer Entstehungsart und ihren Lesern ist nach wie vor offen und
wird es vermutlich bleiben. Aber diese Probleme sind anderer Art
als das von uns hier Behandelte".[5] Zugespitzt gesagt, bedeutete das
Nebeneinander verschiedener Quellen für von RAD eine Störung
seiner Sicht der Dinge und war mit ihr im Grunde unvereinbar.

Daraus geht m.E. hervor, daß es ein historischer Zufall war, daß
von RAD den Theologen, dem er die Gestaltung des Pentateuch
bzw. Hexateuch im ganzen zuschrieb, als 'Jahwisten' bezeichnet hat.
Er hätte genauso gut — oder sogar besser und zutreffender — einen
anderen, nicht vorbelasteten Namen wählen können. Er hätte dann
im übrigen auch nicht mit diesem Namen die ganze Problematik
der traditionellen Quellenscheidung als Hypothek mit übernehmen
müssen.

In der nachfolgenden Forschung hat sich nun noch eine interessante
Verschiebung ergeben. Martin NOTH hat zwar die These von RADS
im Grundsatz aufgenommen, hat sie aber entscheidend verändert,
indem er dem Jahwisten einen viel kleineren Anteil an der Gestaltung
des Pentateuch zuschreibt. Trotzdem hält er daran fest, daß der

---

[5] AaO, 67[= 81].

Jahwist primär Theologe sei. Er sieht nun aber dessen theologische Arbeit im wesentlichen im Anfang seines Werkes, in der Voranstellung der Urgeschichte und in der Formulierung des Abschnittes Gen xii 1-3. "Im folgenden hat er sich dann fast ausschließlich an das überkommene Gut der Pentateucherzählung gehalten, ohne ändernd oder erweiternd in dessen Substanz einzugreifen. Es genügte ihm, im Eingang eindeutig gesagt zu haben, wie er alles weitere verstanden wissen wollte".[6]

Ähnlich wie NOTH suchen viele Forscher die Theologie des 'Jahwisten' in dem, was er *gesagt* hat — ganz anders als VON RAD, für den die theologische Leistung in der Gestaltung und Komposition des ganzen Pentateuch aus den verschiedenen Traditionskomplexen lag. Dabei ist die Frage der *literarischen* Abgrenzung und Charakterisierung fast ganz hinter der Frage nach der 'Theologie' zurückgetreten. Dies gilt insbesondere für den 'Jahwisten'. Vielfach werden einfach die Bestandteile, die zur 'Priesterschrift' und zum 'Elohisten' (oder den 'elohistischen Fragmenten') gehören sollen, ausgeschieden; der Rest gehört dann mehr oder weniger zum 'Jahwisten' (sofern nicht noch eine weitere Quelle angenommen wird). Es ist also eine Art Subtraktionsmethode, bei der am Schluß der 'Jahwist' übrigbleibt. Die Frage nach seinen literarischen Kennzeichen wird kaum noch gestellt. Im Gegenteil: es wird oft gesagt, daß sich der Jahwist als einheitliche *literarische* Größe gar nicht fassen lasse, da er weithin auch Sammler sei und deshalb der Stil der Darstellung vielfältig wechsle. Aber wie will man die Theologie des 'Jahwisten' feststellen, wenn man nicht zuvor die literarischen Kriterien dafür angeben kann, was zu seinem Werk zu rechnen ist?

Hier wird das Dilemma der neueren Pentateuchforschung erkennbar. Es liegt vor allem darin, daß zwei Fragestellungen miteinander verbunden werden, die sich nicht verbinden lassen. Die Literarkritik hat mehr und mehr die innere Uneinheitlichkeit der 'Quellen' erkennbar werden lassen; gleichwohl werden diese Gebilde auf ihre einheitliche theologische Konzeption hin befragt. Das Ergebnis ist entsprechend unbefriedigend, was sich schon darin zeigt, daß in der neueren Literatur gänzlich verschiedene Antworten auf die Frage nach der Theologie des 'Jahwisten' gegeben werden. Offenbar reicht das Instrumentarium nicht aus, um diese Frage eindeutig zu beantworten.

---

[6] M. NOTH, *Überlieferungsgeschichte des Pentateuch*, Stuttgart (1948), 258.

Was lassen sich aus dieser Analyse der gegenwärtigen Situation für Folgerungen ziehen? Es ist offenkundig, daß das Interesse an der *theologischen* Gestaltung des Pentateuchstoffes im Vordergrund steht. Dieses Interesse ist durchaus berechtigt; wir werden aber nach besseren und sachgemäßeren Wegen suchen müssen, um die damit aufgeworfenen Fragen zu beantworten.

Wenn es zutrifft, daß die 'Quellenschriften' in sich uneinheitlich sind, weil sie verschiedenartiges Material aufgenommen haben, dann müßte ihre theologische Intention in der Bearbeitung dieses Materials gesucht werden. Diese Bearbeitung könnte zunächst in der bloßen Anordnung und Komposition des Stoffes liegen. Wir haben aber im Alten Testament viele Beispiele dafür, daß die Bearbeiter sich nicht mit solcher Kompositionsarbeit begnügten, sondern daß sie ihre theologische Absicht deutlich zu erkennen gaben. Wir müssen deshalb die Frage stellen, ob wir im Pentateuch deutliche Spuren einer planvollen theologischen Bearbeitung erkennen können.

Wenn wir dieser Frage nachgehen, dann zeigt sich bald, daß sich in den verschiedenen Bereichen des Pentateuch ganz verschiedene Bearbeitungsspuren finden. Dabei werden wir wieder auf die einzelnen thematischen Komplexe zurückgeführt, die VON RAD herausgearbeitet hat. Die theologische Bearbeitung der Väterüberlieferung ist offenbar von ganz anderer Art als die der Mose- und Exodustradition, diese ist wiederum anders als die der Sinaiüberlieferung und der Traditionen von Israel in der Wüste. Wir müssen uns deshalb diesen einzelnen Traditionskomplexen zuwenden.

In dem begrenzten Rahmen dieses Vortrags will ich mich jetzt darauf beschränken, einige Beobachtungen zur theologischen Bearbeitung der Vätergeschichten in der Genesis vorzutragen. Es fällt sofort ins Auge, daß theologische Aussagen hier in großem Umfang in der Form der göttlichen *Verheißungsrede* gemacht werden. Es legt sich deshalb die Vermutung nahe, daß wir in ihnen ein Element theologischer Bearbeitung finden können.

Die Verheißungsreden sind bekanntlich sehr vielfältig und vielschichtig, sowohl hinsichtlich ihrer Themen als auch in der Form. Zur Klärung der damit gegebenen Probleme hat Claus WESTERMANN einen wesentlichen Beitrag geleistet mit seiner Studie "Arten der Erzählung in der Genesis" (1964).[7] Wir können seine Ergebnisse aufnehmen und fortführen. Inhalt der Verheißung sind vor allem:

---

[7] In: C. WESTERMANN, *Forschung am Alten Testament. Gesammelte Studien*, München (1964), 9-91.

das Land, die Nachkommenschaft, der Segen — und m.E. auch die "Führung" als selbständiges Verheißungsthema. Die Formen, in denen die Verheißungen ausgesprochen werden, und die Verbindungen der verschiedenen Themen untereinander sind vielfältig, und es erscheint sehr schwierig, in dieser Vielfalt ein System zu erkennen. Es lassen sich aber doch bestimmte Beobachtungen dazu machen. Ich beschränke mich jetzt auf die Frage nach der Gliederung und dem Rahmen der Vätergeschichten.

In der *Isaakgeschichte* finden sich zwei Verheißungsreden, eine am Anfang und eine gegen Ende der Sammlung (xxvi 2-5, 24). Beide haben keinen engeren Zusammenhang mit dem erzählerischen Kontext, gehören also offenbar einer bestimmten Bearbeitungsschicht an. Beide werden mit der Formel "da erschien ihm Jahwe" eingeleitet; beide enthalten eine Führungszusage ("ich will mit dir sein"); am Anfang findet sich eine ganze Sammlung von Verheißungsthemen, wobei die Landverheißung betont im Mittelpunkt steht; am Schluß steht nur die Verheißung zahlreicher Nachkommenschaft. Hier sind also offensichtlich die Verheißungsreden als ein planmäßiges Mittel der Rahmung und theologischen Interpretation der Isaakgeschichte eingesetzt worden.

In der *Jakobgeschichte* durchzieht die Zusage der Führung die ganze Sammlung der Erzählungen: Am ersten entscheidenden Wendepunkt, auf der Flucht vor Esau in Bethel, heißt es: "Ich will mit dir sein und will dich beschützen, wohin du gehst" (xxviii 15); vor dem Entschluß Jakobs zur Flucht aus Haran wird der Erzählungszusammenhang unterbrochen durch ein kurzes Jahwewort, das wiederum die Zusage der Führung enthält (xxxi 3); und schließlich empfängt Jakob ganz am Ende seiner Lebensgeschichte vor seiner Reise nach Ägypten noch einmal die Zusage der Führung (xlvi 2-4). Auch in der Jakobgeschichte findet sich, wie bei Isaak am Anfang innerhalb einer komplexen Verheißungsrede die Landverheißung (xxviii 13) und gegen Ende der Sammlung in einer betont herausgestellten Verheißungsrede, die vom erzählerischen Kontext unabhängig ist, noch einmal die Verheißung der zahlreichen Nachkommenschaft (xxxv 9-12, besd. 11f.).

In der *Abrahamgeschichte* schießlich bildet die Landverheißung ein zentrales Thema, das vor allem im ersten Teil der Sammlung häufiger auftaucht (xii 7; xiii 15, 17; xv 7). Am Ende steht dann noch einmal in einer zur Erzählung von der Opferung Isaaks hinzugefügten Verheißungsrede die Zusage der zahlreichen Nachkommenschaft (xxii 17), genau wie bei Isaak und Jakob!

Hier zeigt sich aber gleich noch ein weiteres Element: die Zusage
der Segenswirkung für alle Völker. Sie wird hier am Schluß der
Abrahamgeschichte noch einmal aufgegriffen: "In dir sollen Segen
finden alle Geschlechter der Erde" (xxii 18), nachdem sie schon
ganz betont am Anfang stand (xii 3). Sie findet sich aber auch in der
Isaakgeschichte und in der Jakobgeschichte — und zwar jeweils
nur einmal, betont am Anfang (xxvi 4; xxviii 14). Damit ist also
offenbar eine zusammenfassende und übergreifende theologische
Bearbeitung aller drei Vätergeschichten erfolgt.

Ich will hier noch auf ein interessantes Detail aufmerksam machen:
Die Zusage der Segenswirkung erscheint bekanntlich in zwei verschiedenen grammatischen Formen — im Niphal und im Hitpael;
bei den beiden Niphalformen in xii 3 und xxviii 14 heißt es: "in dir
sollen gesegnet werden *alle Geschlechter der Erde*", bei den Hitpael-
formen in xxii 18 und xxvi 14 hingegen: "*alle Völker der Welt*"; das
Zitat im göttlichen Selbstgespräch in xviii 18 nimmt eine Zwischen-
stellung ein. Wichtig ist nun vor allem folgendes: In xii 3, dem ersten
Vorkommen dieser Formel, ist sie auf Abraham selbst bezogen:
"*in dir* sollen Segen finden", ebenso in xviii 18: "*in ihm* . . ."; in xxviii
14 der weiteren Niphalformel, heißt es zunächst ebenfalls: "*in dir*
sollen Segen finden alle Geschlechter der Erde", dann ist aber
hinzugefügt: "*und in deinem Samen*". Es ist ganz deutlich, daß es sich
hier um eine nachträgliche Hinzufügung handelt. In den Hitpael-
formeln ist die Sache jedoch anders. Hier heißt es beide Male: "es
sollen Segen finden in *deinem Samen* alle Völker der Welt". Offenbar
ist also die Entwicklung hier schon eine Stufe weitergegangen. Erst
bezog sich die Verheißung auf den Erzvater selbst, dann wurde der
"Same" hinzugefügt, und schließlich trat dieser an die Stelle des
Erzvaters, so daß nun gar nicht mehr der Erzvater selbst, sondern
nur noch der "Same" Empfänger der Verheißung ist.

Derselbe Vorgang läßt sich in den Verheißungsreden der Vätergeschichten noch mehrfach deutlich erkennen. Ich muß mich jetzt
auf *ein* Beispiel beschränken: bei der Landverheißung heißt es
mehrfach: "dir will ich das Land geben", z.B. xv 7 und xiii 17; in
einigen Fällen ist dann wieder nachträglich die Ausweitung auf den
"Samen" hinzugefügt, so in xiii 15; xxviii 13; xxxv 12; und schließlich
hießt es in einer Reihe von Fällen: "deinem Samen will ich dieses
Land geben", so in xii 7; xv 18; xxiv 7 u.ö. Hier hat sich also eine
Verschiebung der Verheißung von den Erzvätern selbst auf die
Nachkommenschaft, den "Samen" vollzogen. Und offenbar handelt

es sich dabei um einen Vorgang *innerhalb* der theologischen Bearbeitung der Vätergeschichten. Diese Bearbeitung ist also demnach nicht in einem Zuge erfolgt, sondern es lassen sich in ihr selbst verschiedene Stadien oder Schichten erkennen. Ich muß mich aber hier mit diesen wenigen Beispielen begnügen.

Jedenfalls zeigt sich ganz eindeutig, daß die Verheißungsreden ein Element der planmäßigen theologischen Bearbeitung der Vätergeschichten sind — und zwar einerseits zur Gliederung und Rahmung jeder einzelnen Vätergeschichte, andererseits aber auch zur Zusammenfassung aller drei Vätergeschichten unter einem übergreifenden theologischen Leitgedanken. Im Blick auf unser Thema ergibt sich nun die Frage, ob es sich dabei um eine Bearbeitung handelt, die den ganzen Pentateuch umfaßt.

Die Antwort auf diese Frage ist ganz offenkundig negativ. Das Element der Verheißungsrede, das in den Vätergeschichten eine so bedeutende Rolle spielt, findet keine Entsprechung in den folgenden Themenkomplexen des Pentateuch. Die Verheißungsinhalte kommen aber auch nicht in anderer Form zum Ausdruck. Das ist besonders auffallend bei der Landverheißung. In den Vätergeschichten spielt sie eine zentrale Rolle, und es ist alles auf ihre künftige Erfüllung hin angelegt. Umso überraschender ist es, daß im ganzen Umkreis, der Exodustradition in den älteren Schichten des Textes mit keinem Wort darauf Bezug genommen wird. Im Gegenteil! Bei der ersten Erwähnung des Landes in den Ankündigungen der Herausführung aus Ägypten wird von ihm gesprochen, als sei es völlig unbekannt: "Ich will euch führen in ein gutes und weites Land, in ein Land, das von Milch und Honig überfließt, an die Stätte der Kanaanäer, der Hethiter, der Amoriter, der Peresiter, der Hewiter und der Jebusiter" (Ex iii 8). Kein Wort von den Vätern! Kein Wort davon, daß die Väter schon generationenlang in diesem Land gelebt hatten, und daß Gott ihnen zugesagt hatte, ihnen und ihren Nachkommen dieses Land als dauernden Besitz zu geben. Es ist zwar ein gutes und fruchtbares, aber ein unbekanntes, fremdes Land, in dem viele fremde Völker leben. (Erst die jüngere, priesterliche Schicht erwähnt den 'Schwur' Gottes an die Väter, ihnen das Land zu geben, Ex vi 2ff).

Nachdem wir einmal auf diesen Sachverhalt aufmerksam geworden sind, zeigt sich gleich noch mehr: Die Erzväter und die an sie ergangenen Verheißungen werden in den Büchern Exodus und Numeri an keiner Stelle, die von der traditionellen Quellenscheidung zum sicheren Bestand einer der älteren Quellen gerechnet wird, erwähnt —

außer in der formelhaften Rede vom 'Gott der Väter'. Eindeutiger
kann kaum die Tatsache zum Ausdruck kommen, daß die Vätergeschichten und die folgenden Themenkomplexe nicht einer gemeinsamen, übergreifenden theologischen Bearbeitung unterzogen worden
sind. Wenn es den 'Jahwisten' als theologischen Bearbeiter und
Gestalter gäbe, dann müßten hier die Spuren seiner Arbeit erkennbar
sein. Denn es ist schlechterdings undenkbar, daß ein Theologe von
solchem Rang, wie es nach der herrschenden Auffassung der 'Jahwist' sein soll, nach dem gewaltigen Aufwand, der in den Vätergeschichten mit den Verheißungsreden getrieben worden ist, später
davon geschwiegen haben sollte. Die Tatsache, daß die Herausführung aus Ägypten nicht als die Rückführung in das Land der
Väter dargestellt wird, läßt nur den einen Schluß zu, daß die beiden
Berichte unabhängig voneinander konzipiert und theologisch be-
arbeitet worden sind — und daß sie auch vor der Phase der 'priesterlichen' Endredaktion nicht theologisch zueinander in Beziehung
gesetzt worden sind.

Es ist klar, daß für den 'Jahwisten' als Theologen hier kein Platz
mehr ist. Es gibt ihn nicht. Es ist aber ebenso klar, daß die Vätergeschichten für sich genommen einer sehr intensiven, offenbar
mehrschichtigen theologischen Bearbeitung unterzogen worden
sind — einer Bearbeitung, für die gewiß nicht zutrifft, was Noth über
seinen 'Jahwisten' gesagt hat: daß es ihm genügt habe, am Anfang
einmal gesagt zu haben, wie er alles Weitere verstanden wissen
wollte. Wer die theologischen Intentionen erkennen will, die hinter
der Sammlung und Bearbeitung der pentateuchischen Stoffe stehen,
muß vielmehr sehr genau und ins einzelne gehend den Spuren dieser
Bearbeitung nachgehen. Er wird dabei auf vielfältige, gewichtige und
theologische Aussagen stoßen; den Verfassern der 'Quellen' im Sinne
der klassischen Urkundenhypothese wird er dabei aber nicht begegnen.

Das Dilemma der neueren Phase der Pentateuchkritik besteht
darin, daß sie die neu aufgetauchte Frage nach den *theologischen* Intentionen der Sammlung und Bearbeitung der alten Überlieferungen
mit einem Instrumentarium zu beantworten versucht, das zur Be-
antwortung völlig anders gearteter Fragen entwickelt worden ist
und das sich deshalb als gänzlich ungeeignet erweist. Wenn die Frage
nach den theologischen Intentionen ernsthaft gestellt werden soll,
muß sie sich von diesen althergebrachten Methoden freimachen und
neue, adäquate Methoden entwickeln. Damit könnte eine neue
Phase der Pentateuchforschung eingeleitet werden.

DER BIBLISCHE UND DER HISTORISCHE ELIA

VON

RUDOLF SMEND

Göttingen

I.

"Keine biblische Persönlichkeit hat das religiöse Denken des nachbiblischen Judentums so stark beschäftigt wie diejenige des Propheten Elias".[1] Aber auch in der Theologie und im Kultus des Christentums spielt diese Gestalt bekanntlich eine besondere Rolle, und daneben darf die Bedeutung nicht vergessen werden, die sie für den Islam hat.[2] Das alles kann nicht verwundern, wenn man bedenkt, daß das Alte Testament von Elia erzählt, er sei nicht gestorben, sondern im Sturm in den Himmel aufgefahren, und daß es erwartet, er werde als Vorläufer und Wegbereiter des Endes wiederkommen.[3] Neben diesem Außerordentlichsten hat natürlich auch das, was das Alte Testament vom irdischen Wirken des Elia erzählt, immer großen Eindruck gemacht und außer der Religion die künstlerische Phantasie in allen ihren Gattungen angeregt. Auch heutigen Lesern erschließen sich die Erzählungen von Elia oft eher als andere — nicht durch leichte Verständlichkeit, wohl aber durch die Gewalt, die hinter ihnen steht, und den Zauber, den sie ausüben.

Nun lassen sich Zeugnisse dafür beibringen[4], und die Erfahrung wird den meisten von uns hier oder an verwandten Gegenständen geläufig sein, daß solche Leser einen kleineren oder größeren Schreck bekommen können, wenn sie erfahren, daß die so imposante Gestalt des Elia geschichtlich durchaus nicht leicht greifbar ist und daß die Erzählungen, die von ihr handeln, großenteils als sagenhaft oder legendar angesehen werden müssen. Der biblische Elia, aus dem die Elias der drei Religionen hervorgingen bis zum Elia Felix MENDELSSOHNS oder zum Elia Martin BUBERS, ist nicht der historische; allerdings ist er seinerseits — das verneint nur übergroße Skepsis,

---

[1] J. JEREMIAS, *ThWNT* II, pp. 930f.
[2] Vgl. das Sammelwerk *Élie le prophète* I/II, Paris 1956.
[3] 2 Reg. ii 11; Mal. iii 23f.
[4] Vgl. etwa E. HIRSCH, *Das Alte Testament und die Predigt des Evangeliums*, Tübingen 1936, pp. 2f.

der man nicht oft begegnet — aus dem historischen Elia hervor-
gegangen. Die Unterscheidung zwischen beiden ist ein neuzeitliches
Problem.

Ein ziemlich schwieriges Problem. Ein gut orientierter Außenseiter
hat kürzlich im Blick auf die vorhandenen Versuche gemeint, es sei
offenbar nicht zu lösen; man könne "nicht hinter den biblischen
Bericht zurückgehen, ohne daß man sich in einen Wald von subjek-
tiven Hypothesen verirrt".[5] Da der Historiker hier keine sicheren
Lösungen anzubieten vermag, kann es niemandem übelgenommen
werden, wenn er dann lieber ganz auf den Versuch verzichtet, den
Weg vom biblischen zum historischen Elia zu gehen; dies um so
mehr, als dieser Verzicht auch sonst ehrenwerte Motive für sich in
Anspruch nehmen kann, ästhetische, aber auch theologische [6] —
mutatis mutandis ebenso wie bei anderen Gestalten und Vorgängen
der biblischen Geschichte.

Trotzdem bleibt uns jener Versuch aufgegeben, mag der Wald
der Hypothesen auch noch so groß und dunkel sein, durch den der
Weg vom biblischen zum historischen Elia führt, und mögen wir
auch nur unter vielen Schwierigkeiten oder überhaupt nicht in der
Lage sein, ihn zu Ende zu gehen. Den Versuch gibt uns nicht nur die
historische Neugier auf, eine Eigenschaft, deren wir uns auch in der
Bibelwissenschaft weniger schämen sollten, als es oft geschieht.
Wichtiger ist, daß uns gerade das Bemühen um den historischen
Elia helfen kann, den biblischen Elia besser zu verstehen. Wenn,
neuzeitlich und darum ganz unangemessen ausgedrückt, der biblische
Elia der historische zu sein beansprucht, entbindet uns das nicht
von der Pflicht, das in Wahrheit sehr komplizierte Verhältnis zwischen
beiden so genau wie möglich zu erfassen, um beiden gerecht zu werden.
Das Bemühen um den historischen bedeutet also keine Preisgabe
des biblischen Elia, sondern eher das Gegenteil. So wollen auch die
folgenden Ausführungen verstanden sein.

Ich bitte Sie dabei möglichst wenig zu erwarten. Es kann sich
nach Lage der Dinge kaum um mehr handeln als darum, einerseits
möglichst illusionslos die Grenzen unseres gegenwärtigen Wissens
und andererseits möglichst vorsichtig die einigermaßen festen
Punkte zu fixieren, die wir besitzen. Eine Bestandsaufnahme dieser
Art ist, wie mir scheint, um so nützlicher, je weniger Sensationen
sie bietet.

---

[5] W. NIGG, *Drei große Zeichen. Elias, Hiob, Sophia*, Olten 1972, p. 17.
[6] Vgl. außer NIGG C. A. KELLER, *ThZ* XVI, 1960, p. 313.

II.

Die erste und allgemeinste Reduktion, die die neuzeitliche Historiographie an der Geschichte des Elia vorgenommen hat, betrifft deren übernatürliche Züge. Da, wie mit Recht gesagt worden ist, der Reiz des biblischen Eliabildes gerade in der Mischung des Transzendenten mit dem Immanenten liegt,[7] steht zu erwarten, daß diese Reduktion hier noch tiefer einschneidet als an vielen anderen Stellen der Bibel. Sie läßt keine der Erzählungen von Elia unbetroffen, fast alle berührt sie nicht nur an der Peripherie, sondern im Kern. So erstaunt es nicht, daß seit J. G. EICHHORN [8] die Beschäftigung mit Elia zu einem sehr großen Teil eine Beschäftigung mit dem im weitesten Sinne Wunderhaften in diesen Erzählungen ist. Schon eher erstaunt es, daß dabei, ebenfalls seit EICHHORN, die natürliche Erklärung der Wunder kaum je gefehlt, manchmal sogar ganz das Feld beherrscht hat. Ernsthafte Forschung wird die Phänomene möglichst sorgfältig registrieren,[9] aber auch feststellen, daß sie in der Hauptsache jenseits der Grenzen historischer Erkenntnis liegen; diese kann sie zumindest unmittelbar nicht verwenden.

Was bleibt dann? Nach einer beachtlichen, immerhin von B. DUHM vertretenen Auffassung kaum etwas. Elia war, so DUHM, wie Elisa gewiß eine große Persönlichkeit mit gewaltiger Wirkung, aber diese Wirkung ist nur indirekt daran zu ermessen, daß diese Gestalten wie Magneten "Vorstellungen und Geschehnisse wie Eisenspäne" angezogen haben, "die überall in der Welt aus dem gleichen Boden erwachsen sind und der gleichen Kultur so natürlich entsprießen wie die Vegetation dem Acker. Sie sind etwas Wirkliches wie Gras und Halm, aber nicht etwas Historisches, wie Gras und Halm es auch nicht sind". Historischen Wert haben diese Geschichten also nicht, indem sie Elia, sondern indem sie die Volksreligion erkennen lassen.[10] Die Sicht auf Elia wird durch ihr kaum differenziertes Helldunkel so gut wie unmöglich gemacht.

Man kommt nur weiter, wenn es gelingt, in diesem Helldunkel wenigstens an einigen Stellen Helles und an anderen Dunkles zu finden. Die Kriterien, die dabei bewußt und unbewußt, oft wohl einfach gefühlsmäßig, angewendet werden, sind nach der negativen

---

[7] G. Rösch, ThStKr LXV, 1892, p. 551.

[8] Vgl. den Aufsatz "Über die Propheten-Sagen aus dem Reiche Israel" in EICHHORNS Allg. Bibliothek der biblischen Litteratur IV, 2, Leipzig 1792, pp. 193ff.

[9] Vgl. etwa G. FOHRER, Elia, [2]Zürich 1968, pp. 59f.

[10] B. DUHM, Israels Propheten, [2]Tübingen 1922, p. 84.

Seite vor allem natürlich das Auftreten volkstümlich-wunderhafter, legendarer Motive (mehrfach in direkter Parallele oder gar Abhängigkeit zur Überlieferung von Elisa oder auch Mose), nach der positiven Seite vor allem das Vorkommen von wirklichen oder leicht denkbaren historischen Personen und Situationen, daneben aber auch von allgemeineren theologisch-religiösen Motiven, die aus der Schriftprophetie bekannt sind und in denen man dann den Unterschied des Elia zu der ihn umgebenden Volksreligion meint greifen zu können. Man kommt dann in der Regel auf den Kampf gegen den Baal einerseits, gegen die königliche Ungerechtigkeit im Falle des Naboth andererseits als die Themen und Ereignisse, auf 1 Reg. xviii und xxi und dazu etwa noch 2 Reg. i als die Texte.[11] Aber es gibt auch schärfere Eingrenzungen. So beurteilt Ed. MEYER[12] 1 Reg. xvii-xix insgesamt als Erzeugnis ziemlich freier Phantasie; davon unterscheidet er aber "die beträchtlich ältere und rein historische Erzählung von Nabot" 1 Reg. xxi, für deren Historizität er auch die Anspielung des Jehu auf den Vorgang in 2 Reg. ix 25f. ins Feld führt. Damit sind zwei weitere Kriterien genannt: das Alter der Erzählungen und die Möglichkeit, sie an Hand von Daten zu kontrollieren, die von ihnen unabhängig sind. Wieviel läßt sich nun heute, in möglichst wenig einseitiger Anwendung dieser Kriterien über den historischen Elia ausmachen?

III.

Natürlich kommt viel auf das Alter der Erzählungen an. Hier herrscht wenig Sicherheit. Schon für EICHHORN[13] ist alles, "was wir in den Büchern der Könige vom Staat Israel lesen, fern von der Scene der Begebenheiten erst im Reiche Juda aufgezeichnet worden — nicht blos in der Form, in welcher wir es gegenwärtig finden, sondern selbst nach den Quellen, die dabei gebraucht sind". Dieses Urteil haben seitdem mehrere Gelehrte mit geringfügigen Varianten wiederholt.[14] Es dürfte indessen nur für die gegenwärtige Gestalt der Erzählungen zutreffen. In ihr finden sich Wendungen, die mit

---

[11] Vgl. beispielsweise H. GREẞMANN, SAT ²II, 1 pp. 272f. 282; H. RINGGREN, *Israelitische Religion*, Stuttgart 1963, p. 239.

[12] *Geschichte des Altertums* II, 2, ³Stuttgart 1953, pp. 329, n. 1, 350, 352.

[13] l.c., p. 209.

[14] Genannt seien B. STADE, *Geschichte des Volkes Israel* I, Gießen 1887, p. 522, n. 3; *Theologie des Alten Testaments* I, Tübingen 1905, p. 72; RÖSCH, l.c., pp. 557ff.; A. B. EHRLICH, *Randglossen zur hebräischen Bibel* VII, Leipzig 1914, p. 262; H.-C. SCHMITT, *Elisa*, Gütersloh 1972, pp. 119ff., bes. 126.

großer Wahrscheinlichkeit in die Zeit nach dem Untergang des Nordreichs gehören und die wir meist dem Bereich zuordnen können, den wir in Ermangelung eines besseren Ausdrucks als deuteronomistisch zu bezeichnen pflegen.[15] Wenn man also auch nicht mehr mit M. Noth [16] sagen kann, die Erzählungen von 1 Reg. xvii-xix hätten noch ihren überlieferten Wortlaut, so läßt sich andererseits doch gerade in diesen Kapiteln die Redaktionsschicht mit so großer Wahrscheinlichkeit abheben, daß der überlieferte Wortlaut deutlich genug zu Tage tritt.[17] Bei ihm handelt es sich um eine gewiß schriftlich vorhanden gewesene Quelle, die dem deuteronomistischen Geschichtswerk einverleibt wurde. Diese Quelle halbwegs sicher zu datieren will einstweilen nicht gelingen. Vordeuteronomistisch: ja, das beweist die deuteronomistische Bearbeitung. Vorexilisch: auch dagegen gibt es keine gewichtigen Einwände.[18] Weniger glatt kommt man in die Zeit vor 722 zurück. Der Ausdruck "König von Samaria", der in 1 Reg. xxi 1 für Ahab und in 2 Reg. i 3 für Ahasja gebraucht ist, könnte die assyrische Okkupation voraussetzen.[19] Sicher ist das freilich nicht, und außerdem sollte man, schon weil geringfügige Gestaltveränderungen bei solchen Literaturwerken leicht möglich sind, aus einer derartigen Einzelheit keine allzu weit reichenden Schlüsse ziehen, zumal nicht auf 1 Reg. xvii-xix, die mit 1 Reg. xxi und 2 Reg. i literarisch nicht zusammengehangen haben müssen. Ebensowenig sollte man aber auch umgekehrt, wie es oft geschieht,[20] schon aus dem "Beerscheba, das in Juda liegt" von 1 Reg. xix 3 die Herkunft aus dem Nordreich folgern. Zwingende Einzelargumente in der einen oder anderen Richtung scheint es also nicht zu geben, die allgemeinen Erwägungen, die man anstellen kann, bleiben Ermessenssache. Das bedeutet aber, daß sich die Zeit vor 722 für die Entstehung der schriftlichen Gestalt der Eliaerzählungen, namentlich des zusammenhängenden Komplexes 1 Reg xvii-xix, nicht ausschließen läßt. Jedenfalls das 8. Jahrhundert muß dafür zumindest

---

[15] Vgl. die Zusammenstellung bei Fohrer l.c., pp. 53ff.

[16] *Überlieferungsgeschichtliche Studien*, ³Tübingen 1967, p. 82.

[17] Vgl. R. Smend, "Das Wort Jahwes an Elia. Erwägungen zur Komposition von 1 Reg. xvii-xix", *VT* XXV, 1975, pp. 525ff.

[18] Das argumentum e silentio wird zu stark beansprucht, wenn man mit Schmitt, l.c., p. 126, n. 265 für eine Datierung des Motivs der Prophetenverfolgung in die Zeit vor Jojakim (oder Manasse) ausdrückliche und präzise Zeugnisse über derartige Vorgänge in älterer Zeit verlangt.

[19] Schmitt, l.c., p. 27, n. 56.

[20] Seit J. Wellhausen, *Die Composition des Hexateuchs und der historischen Bücher des Alten Testaments*, ³Berlin 1899, p. 281.

hypothetisch offengehalten werden, vielleicht aber auch die letzten Jahrzehnte des neunten. Der Hinweis auf unrichtige Angaben über die Zeit Ahabs widerlegt das nicht; gegen den Kanon, es könne in einer Erzählung des 9. Jahrhunderts "keine Angabe enthalten sein, deren historische Unrichtigkeit im 9. Jahrhundert noch allgemein bekannt sein mußte",[21] ließen sich sogar aus unserem so wohlinformierten 20. Jahrhundert leicht Gegenbeispiele anführen. Mit Sicherheit aber gilt, daß hinter die Zeit Jehus unter keinen Umständen zurückzugelangen ist; diese wird in 1 Reg. xvii-xix deutlich vorausgesetzt, nicht nur in den Schlußversen, wo Jehu mit Namen am Horizont erscheint (xix 16f.), und auch kaum als etwas ganz Neues. Der terminus ante quem non ist also etwa die zweite Hälfte der Regierung Jehus, d. h. das letzte Viertel des 9. Jahrhunderts kommt noch in Betracht — aber eben nur als die früheste der Möglichkeiten, die sich von da an doch wohl über volle zwei Jahrhunderte erstrecken.

Das heißt: die relative Stabilität schriftlicher Überlieferung reicht auf einen Abstand von bestenfalls reichlich zwei Jahrzehnten, schlimmstenfalls reichlich zwei Jahrhunderten an Elia heran. Auch der beste dieser Fälle ist für den Historiker alles andere als gut. Denn wie will er auch nur über ein Vierteljahrhundert hinwegkommen, wenn die Brücke in einer mündlichen Überlieferung besteht, von der er mit Sicherheit nur das schriftlich fixierte Endergebnis kennt, dessen Bild von den Vorgängen sich ihm in vielen Zügen als unhistorisch, dagegen kaum irgendwo mit Sicherheit als historisch präsentiert? Die Möglichkeiten des Überlieferungshistorikers und vollends des Historikers sind hier ziemlich gering. Ich sage das mit Respekt und Bewunderung für O. H. STECKS scharfsinniges Unternehmen, in den Eliaerzählungen bis in letzte Details hinein den sukzessiven Niederschlag einer schon vorliterarischen Denkbewegung zu finden, die sich jeweils mit Ereignissen der Zeitgeschichte in Verbindung bringen läßt.[22] Sowohl was die Erzählungen als auch was die Zeitgeschichte betrifft, ist hier viel gesehen und viel Anregung gegeben. Aber — auf Einzelheiten kann hier nicht eingegangen werden — dabei liegt eine Voraussetzung zugrunde, die von vornherein und dann auch im Vollzug der Exegese nicht ohne Probleme ist: daß nämlich in 1 Reg. xvii-xix (und xxi) der mündliche Überlieferungsprozeß in allen seinen Stadien noch meist wortgetreu

---

[21] SCHMITT l.c., p. 125, vgl. auch p. 26, n. 54.

[22] O. H. STECK, *Überlieferung und Zeitgeschichte in den Elia-Erzählungen*, WMANT XXVI, Neukirchen-Vluyn 1968.

greifbar ist und die Literaturwerdung lediglich die schriftliche
Fixierung von Vorhandenem war.[23] Ich frage mich, ob hier nicht
der Traditionsbildung in der mündlichen Periode zu viel, in der
schriftlichen zu wenig zugetraut wird. Es scheint mir danach nicht
möglich, einfach von dem STECKschen Gesamtbild auszugehen.
Vielmehr wird man nur einzelnes herausgreifen können, wo die
Umstände eine historische Einordnung zu gestatten oder doch
mindestens nicht zu verbieten scheinen.[24]

IV.

Den wichtigsten Versuch in dieser Richtung hat bekanntlich
A. ALT [25] für die von ihm so genannte Erzählung vom Gottesurteil
auf dem Karmel unternommen. Er sah in 1 Reg. xviii 17-40 einen
Vorgang berichtet, der in die Geschichte der politischen Beziehungen
zwischen Israel und Phönikien gehöre: der Karmel, erst durch
David dem Reich Israel einverleibt, sei als südliche Grenze der
Ebene von Akko möglicherweise bereits unter Salomo, sonst unter
seinen Nachfolgern in phönikischen Besitz gelangt, dann aber infolge
eines Ausgleichs der Interessen zur Zeit des Freundschaftsver-
hältnisses zwischen Phönikien und Israel unter Omri oder Ahab an
Israel zurückgefallen; bei der Besitzergreifung des Karmel durch
Israel habe Elia den Machtkampf zwischen dem dortigen Baal und
Jahwe, dem Gott Israels, und die Entscheidung des Volkes und des
Königs für die alleinige Verehrung Jahwes auf dem Karmel er-
zwungen. Die These ALTS läßt sich heute nur noch modifiziert
wiederholen. Wie E. WÜRTHWEIN gesehen hat,[26] kommt Ahab in
der ursprünglichen Erzählung nicht vor; es hat sich also nicht, wie
ALT meinte, um eine "Haupt- und Staatsaktion" gehandelt. Über
WÜRTHWEIN hinaus wird man feststellen müssen, daß die Szene in
1 Reg. xviii nicht die ursprüngliche Erzählung ist und auch nicht
ohne weiteres durch Streichung von 40 und anderem dazu gemacht
werden kann; die Szene, wie wir sie jetzt haben, ist vielmehr nach
der Revolution Jehus für den Zusammenhang von 1 Reg. xvii-xviii
(xix) konzipiert worden.[27] Das heißt aber nicht, daß dieses erzähle-

---

[23] Vgl. besonders STECK, l.c., pp. 7f.

[24] Die Schwierigkeit des Unternehmens zeigt sich übrigens auch daran, daß
sich auch STECK aus seiner Analyse der Erzählungen noch nicht ohne weiteres
eine Antwort auf die Frage nach Elia selbst ergibt (l.c., pp. 4, 131).

[25] *Kleine Schriften* II, München 1953, pp. 135ff.

[26] *ZThK* LIX, 1962, pp. 132, 143.

[27] Vgl. *VT* XXV, 1975, pp. 537ff.

rische Manifest für den Ausschließlichkeitsanspruch Jahwes in
Israel auch abgesehen von seiner jetzigen Gestaltung einfach ein
schriftstellerisches Produkt aus der Zeit der Dynastie Jehus wäre
und daß sein Inhalt nichts mit dem historischen Elia zu tun hätte.
Mag es auch mit der Rückgewinnung des Karmel unter Omri oder
Ahab stehen, wie es will — ALT hat sich hier übrigens etwas vor-
sichtiger ausgedrückt als gelegentlich seine Nachfolger [28] —, so
bleiben doch die beiden grundlegenden Tatbestände: einmal die
Grenzlage des Karmel, die sich inzwischen auch von anderer Seite
her bestätigt hat,[29] zweitens die Religionspolitik der Omriden.
Sie scheint im Zusammenhang mit deren allgemeiner Politik im
ganzen darauf angelegt gewesen zu sein, dem Baal zu geben, was des
Baal war, und Jahwe zu geben, was Jahwes war. Die Quellenlage
erlaubt uns keine sicheren Aussagen darüber, wie sich das auf die
staatlichen und religiösen Institutionen auswirkte,[30] und auch nicht
darüber, welches die Politik jedes einzelnen der omridischen Könige
war. Immerhin wird man bei Ahab jedenfalls der Intention nach von
einem Versuch der Gewährung der religiösen Rechte an den kanaanäischen wie an den israelitischen Bevölkerungsteil im Sinne der eben
formulierten Maxime reden dürfen,[31] dagegen bei seiner Witwe
Isebel als der Königinmutter unter — oder besser: über — den
Königen Ahasja und Joram von entschiedener Förderung des
Kanaanäertums und gewiß auch seiner Religion, mögen nun die
alttestamentlichen Angaben über blutige Verfolgungen im Recht sein
oder — vielleicht eher — nicht[32]. Für die Religionspolitik des Ahasja
ist die Befragung des Baal Sebub von Ekron (2 Reg. i) noch kein
zuverlässiger Anhaltspunkt;[33] immerhin spricht der Vorgang zumindest nicht dagegen, in dieser kurzen Regierung mit der deuteronomistischen Redaktion (1 Reg. xxii 53f.) die Linie Ahabs und auch
die Isebels fortgesetzt zu sehen. Im Unterschied zu Ahasja wird sein
Bruder und Nachfolger Joram von der Redaktion positiv gegen die
Eltern abgesetzt, unter Berufung darauf, daß er die von Ahab er-

---

[28] Vgl. etwa FOHRER l.c. p. 66. Kritisch SCHMITT l.c. p. 184 n. 29.
[29] Vgl. Y. AHARONI in: *Archäologie und Altes Testament*. Festschrift für Kurt
Galling, Tübingen 1970, pp. 1ff.
[30] A. ALTS These vom Stadtstaat Samaria (*Kleine Schriften* III, München 1959,
pp. 258ff.) versucht von diesen Auswirkungen ein präzises Bild zu geben.
[31] Vgl. ALT, l.c., pp. 272ff.
[32] Dazu STECK, l.c., p. 70 (und überhaupt pp. 53ff.) einerseits, SCHMITT,
l.c., pp. 124f. andererseits.
[33] Vgl. ALT, l.c., p. 282.

richtete Baalsmassebe beseitigt habe (2 Reg. iii 2). Wie es sich mit
diesem Hin und Her auch genauer verhalten haben mag, dahinter
müssen Auseinandersetzungen über die Frage gestanden haben,
die in 1 Reg. xviii 21-40 auf dem Karmel verhandelt und entschieden
wird. Es ist danach nicht wahrscheinlich, daß man sich diese Szene
nach dem Umsturz unter Jehu einfach aus den Fingern gesogen hat;
vielmehr wird die Überlieferung von einem wirklichen Vorgang
zugrundeliegen. Eine Kombination wie die A. JEPSENS,[34] Joram sei
durch diesen Vorgang zu seiner Tat gegen die Baalsmassebe veranlaßt
worden, kann durchaus das Richtige treffen. Dagegen scheinen mir
JEPSENS Argumente für seine weitergehende Vermutung, der Vorgang habe sich bei Samaria und nicht auf dem Karmel abgespielt,[35]
weder gegen die Tradition noch gegen die Erwägung aufzukommen,
daß der Karmel in seiner israelitisch-kanaanäischen Grenzlage für
eine derartige Auseinandersetzung geradezu prädestiniert war.[36]

Wie man den Vorgang erzählt hat, bevor er nach dem Umsturz
durch Jehu in großer Ausweitung der Szene und des Aufgebots
bis hin zur Abschlachtung der Baalspropheten durch Elia Literatur
wurde, und wie er sich vielleicht einmal abgespielt haben mag,
darüber können wir nichts Sicheres sagen. Einen Anhaltspunkt
bietet die Geschichte von der Zerstörung des Baalsaltars durch
Gideon Jud. vi 25-32.[37] Dort wie hier handelt es sich um einen Baals-
und einen Jahwealtar, einen Stier bzw. zwei zum Brandopfer, die
dem Baal zumindest ironisch als einem Gott eingeräumte Möglichkeit,
für sich zu streiten. Führt hier Elia die Sache Jahwes, so tut es dort
Gideon mit zehn Männern, freilich nachts, in Furcht vor dem Haus
seines Vaters und den Männern der Stadt, die denn auch nach Gideons
Tat die Gegenpartei bilden, sozusagen als die Baalspropheten und
das Volk der Karmelszene in eins. Die geographische Situation

---

[34] In: *Near Eastern Studies in Honour of W. F. Albright*, Baltimore-London
1971, p. 303.

[35] l.c., pp. 304f.

[36] Daß die Fragen nach dem genauen Ort des Vorgangs und nach dem auf
dem Karmel verehrten Baal verschiedene Antworten zulassen, schließt die dortige
Lokalisierung keineswegs aus. Auch die 450 Baalspropheten tun das nicht; sie
gehören zum Ensemble der Haupt- und Staatsaktion, als die der Vorgang in
seinem jetzigen literarischen Zusammenhang stilisiert ist. Auf die geringe Be-
weiskraft der von ihm zugunsten seiner Vermutung herangezogenen Eliatradition christlicher Zeit aus der Gegend von Samaria weist JEPSEN bereits selbst
hin.

[37] Zusammenstellung und Diskussion des Materials bei H. D. PREUẞ, *Ver-
spottung fremder Religionen im Alten Testament*, BWANT XCII, Stuttgart 1971,
pp. 67ff., 80ff.

erzwingt, wo immer man das manassitische Ophra zu suchen hat,[38] in das doch wohl auch diese Gideongeschichte gehört, auch dort die enge Berührung mit den Kanaanäern. Mag uns diese Geschichte hinsichtlich ihrer Komposition, der Datierung ihrer Elemente [39] und gerade auch hinsichtlich ihrer Beziehung zur Karmelszene noch in manchem rätselhaft sein, so gibt sie doch eine plastische Vorstellung davon, wie ein solcher lokaler Konflikt zwischen den beiden Religionen aussehen konnte und wie er vielleicht auch auf dem Karmel ungefähr ausgesehen hat.

Wir haben mit alledem noch kaum von Elia gesprochen. Wie gehört er in diese Dinge hinein? Gehört er überhaupt in sie hinein? Kürzlich ist das für die ursprüngliche Erzählung von dem Ereignis auf dem Karmel in Frage gestellt worden: es sei nicht auszuschließen, daß hier "den anonymen Baalspropheten ein anonymer israelitischer Gottesmann gegenüberstand, der erst im Laufe der Traditionsentwicklung mit Elia gleichgesetzt wurde".[40] Gewiß ist das — wie in diesen Bereichen außerhalb sicherer quellenmäßiger Bezeugung sehr vieles — nicht auszuschließen; es hat aber angesichts der schlechterdings zentralen Rolle, die dieser Jahweprophet hier spielt,[41] keinerlei Wahrscheinlichkeit. Setzen wir aber einmal den unwahrscheinlichen Fall: dann erhebt sich die Frage, warum der Anonymus ausgerechnet mit Elia gleichgesetzt wurde. Solche Übertragungen von Geschichten auf bestimmte Personen erfolgen ja nicht zufällig und meist auch nicht nur darum, weil es sich um eine besonders bekannte Person handelt; die Gründe sind im allgemeinen spezifischer. Zu fragen ist also, welche Anhaltspunkte wir außerhalb jener Karmelszene dafür haben, wer und was Elia war.

Mir scheint, daß man dabei mit größerer Zuversicht, als es zu geschehen pflegt, ein Element heranziehen darf, das doch wohl das persönlichste ist: den Namen Elijjahu. Die Aussage dieses "Bekenntnisnamens"[42] trifft in sehr auffälliger Weise mit dem Satz

---

[38] Vgl. Y. AHARONI, *The Land of the Bible*, London 1967, pp. 240f.

[39] Auch über die (sicher nicht für das Ganze zutreffende) Annahme deuteronomistischer Herkunft (A. KUENEN, Historisch-critisch onderzoek I, ²Leiden 1887, p. 342, n. 5) wird man nicht mehr so schnell hinweggehen dürfen, wie das früher zu geschehen pflegte.

[40] SCHMITT, l.c., p. 185, n. 29.

[41] Weitere Vermutungen über diese Rolle bei H. SEEBAß, *ZThK* LXX, 1973, pp. 121ff.

[42] Vgl. M. NOTH, *Die israelitischen Personennamen*, Stuttgart 1928, pp. 140f. Die Frage, ob das i zwischen den beiden Bestandteilen des Nominalsatzes Suffix oder bloßer Bindevokal ist, sowie die nach Subjekt und Prädikat in diesem Satz können hier offenbleiben.

zusammen, auf den die Karmelszene zusteuert: יהוה הוא האלהים
(1 Reg. xviii 39). Der Name, so ist gesagt worden, drückt bereits das
Programm der ganzen Bewegung, nämlich des Kampfes für Jahwe
in Nordisrael, aus.[43] Wie erklärt sich dieses Zusammentreffen? Man
scheut sich, einfach einen Zufall anzunehmen, ebenso wie bei Obadja
in 1 Reg. xviii 3-16 [44] oder auch bei Jehu. Das andere Extrem wäre
die Annahme, Elia sei eine erdachte Figur, die ein Programm repräsen-
tieren soll. Dagegen spricht, daß die Person des Elia in der Überlieferung doch viel Farbe hat und daß auch die Herkunftsangabe in
1.Reg. xvii 1 unerfunden aussieht; sie ist ja auch für weitere Schlüsse
auf die Person des Propheten ganz unergiebig. Man hat dann die
Wahl zwischen den beiden Möglichkeiten, daß er den Namen schon
von Geburt an trug, also vermutlich einer besonders jahwetreuen
Familie entstammte,[45] oder daß er ihn später angenommen hat.[46]
Das letztere würde zur Koinzidenz von Namen und überliefertem
Handeln am besten stimmen und darf daher, so wenig es sich natürlich beweisen läßt, doch wohl eine gewisse Wahrscheinlichkeit
beanspruchen. Singulär ist es im Alten Testament ja nicht, daß
jemand einen neuen Namen bekommt. Als naheliegendes Beispiel
nenne ich den Schluß der eben schon herangezogenen Geschichte
von Gideons Aktion gegen den Baalsaltar, wo Gideon auf Grund
dieses Ereignisses Jerubbaal genannt wird (Jud. vi 32).[47] Daß es
sich dabei wohl um einen Zusatz handelt, der die verschiedenen
Personen Gideon und Jerubbaal zusammenbringen soll und der
außerdem die ursprüngliche Bedeutung von Jerubbaal mißver-
steht, nimmt der Analogie nicht ihren Wert; für den Verfasser des
Zusatzes war ein solcher Vorgang möglich, und das genügt. Uns
aber ist es nun wohl erlaubt, bei der weiteren Durchsicht der für den

---

[43] G. HÖLSCHER, *Die Profeten*, Leipzig 1914, p. 177. Weitere Stimmen bei
L. BRONNER, *The Stories of Elijah and Elisha as Polemics against Baal Worship*,
POS VI, Leiden 1968, pp. 22f.

[44] Vgl. HÖLSCHER, l.c., p. 175, n. 2; H. GUNKEL, *Elias, Jahve und Baal*, Tübingen
1906, p. 14.

[45] Vgl. A. ŠANDA, *Die Bücher der Könige*, EH IX, 1, Münster 1911, p. 414;
R. KITTEL, *Die Bücher der Könige*, HK I, 5, Göttingen 1900, p. 138; BRONNER, l.c.

[46] Zu dieser Möglichkeit neigen O. THENIUS, *Die Bücher der Könige*, KeH IX,
²Leipzig 1873, p. 216; J. A. MONTGOMERY (-H. S. GEHMAN), *The Books of Kings*,
ICC, Edinburgh 1951, p. 296 ("the name may have been an assumed religious
alias"); J. STEINMANN in: *Élie le prophète* I, Paris 1956, p. 97 ("très probablement
un surnom, un 'nom de religion'"); J. GUTMANN in: *Encyclopaedia Judaica* VI,
Jerusalem 1971, col. 633; J. GRAY, *I & II Kings*, ²London 1970, p. 402 (unter
Hinweis auf die abrupte Einführung ohne Vatersnamen in 1 Reg. xvii 1).

[47] Vgl. auch BRONNER, l.c., p. 23.

historischen Elia in Betracht kommenden Tradition mit aller Vorsicht als eine Art Kanon das zu benutzen, was der Name sagt: (mein) Gott ist Jahwe — und nicht Baal, wie man gewiß sachgemäß zu ergänzen hat.[48]

Der Blick fällt dabei sogleich auf 2 Reg. i, die Erzählung von der Befragung des Baal Sebub von Ekron durch den kranken König Ahasja, dem daraufhin durch Elia ergangenen Wort Jahwes an den König und dessen Tod.[49] Der Einschub der schaurigen Wunderpassage 9-16 macht das Alter der Erzählung in ihrem Grundbestand sozusagen perspektivisch deutlich, und dafür spricht auch unser Wissen von der kurzen Regierungsdauer des Ahasja, der zu Anfang sicherlich mit Recht als das königliche Gegenüber des Elia genannt ist. Nicht weniger fest ist Elia selbst in der Erzählung verankert. Nebenbei hören wir, daß er an seinem langen Haar und einem ledernen Schurz zu erkennen war (8). Der Einschub setzt ihn wie selbstverständlich "auf dem Gipfel des Berges" sitzend voraus (9); das erinnert an die Szene bzw. die Szenen auf dem Karmel in 1 Reg. xviii, hat aber, da es im Grundbestand der Erzählung zumindest dem jetzigen Wortlaut nach fehlt, keinen selbständigen Zeugniswert.[50] Was die Erzählung sagen will, wird zweimal in der rhetorischen Frage formuliert, ob es denn keinen Gott in Israel gebe, daß man hingehe, Baal Sebub, den Gott von Ekron, zu befragen (3, 6, vgl. 16). Das aber ist eine Variation dessen, worin die besprochene Karmelszene mit der doppelten Akklamation "Jahwe ist der Gott" ihr Ziel fand, und ebenso des Namens Elijjahu. Wir sind berechtigt, im Grundbestand von 2 Reg. i ein Zeugnis vom Wirken des historischen Elia zu sehen, und zwar ein unmittelbareres Zeugnis als in 1 Reg. xviii 21-40, wo wir die Existenz einer entsprechenden alten Erzählung zwar sicher voraussetzen, deren Gestalt aber nicht mehr greifen können.

Um noch etwas weiter zu kommen, muß man sich vor Augen halten, daß die religiöse Alternative ja nicht nur in Sätzen formuliert wurde, zu denen ja oder nein zu sagen war, sondern daß es dabei wahrlich um Inhalte ging, und um Mächte und Gewalten. Von da her läßt sich in der Eliatradition die Alternative Jahwe/Baal als wichtiges Motiv im Hintergrund auch dort vermuten, wo sie nicht ausdrücklich genannt wird, wo aber der Prophet machtvoll in

[48] Vgl. W. CASPARI, *Die israelitischen Propheten*, Leipzig 1914, p. 48.
[49] Außer den Kommentaren vgl. O. H. STECK, *EvTheol* XXVII, 1967, pp. 546ff.
[50] Dasselbe gilt von dem Feuer, das vom Himmel fällt (10, 12, 14).

Bereichen tätig ist, die als Domäne der Baalsreligion galten, also dort, wo es um Natur, Vegetation, Leben geht. In diesem Zusammenhang wird man auch den Vorfall mit Ahasja sehen dürfen. Im übrigen lassen sich bestimmte Personen in diesen Bereichen für den Historiker meist weniger leicht greifen, und für Elia gilt das hier besonders wegen der mehrfachen Überschneidung der Überlieferung von ihm mit derjenigen von Elisa. Trotzdem scheint eine Erzählung sehr ernsthaft für ihn in Betracht zu kommen, nämlich die von der Wiederkehr des Regens 1 Reg. xviii 41-46.[51] Sie ist jetzt fest in den Zusammenhang von xvii und xviii eingebunden, aber doch wohl als ein von Hause aus selbständiges Stück, dessen Exposition in den beiden Kapiteln entweder gar nicht oder nur noch modifiziert in einzelnen Elementen erhalten ist.[52] Das Fragment scheint den Gegensatz zwischen Elia und Ahab (xviii 17f.; xxi 20; doch wohl auch xvii 1) noch nicht zu kennen. Elia ist ein machtbegabter Mann, dessen Fähigkeiten sich beim Wiederkommen des Regens zur Geltung bringen und der vor dem König her nach Jesreel laufen kann. Der Ort seiner Wirksamkeit ist wiederum der Karmel; der Berg und das Meer gehören in die Geschichte unlöslich hinein.

Der letzte Text, auf den hier eingegangen werden soll, ist 1 Reg. xxi, die Erzählung von Naboths Weinberg. Sie hat in der Eliatradition eine wichtige Stelle und wird für das Bild des historischen Elia meist unbedenklich herangezogen. Ja, man glaubt hier am sichersten auf historischem Boden zu stehen; ich zitierte schon Ed. MEYER und könnte beispielsweise noch einige pathetische Sätze von M. BUBER anführen.[53] Aber es bleiben auch Gegeninstanzen zu bedenken. Zunächst gibt es gattungsmäßig keinen Unterschied zwischen dieser Erzählung und den anderen Eliaerzählungen, der es erlaubte, gerade sie in besondere Nähe zur Geschichtsschreibung zu rücken.[54] Sodann steht bei dem Vorfall um Naboth zwar der Gegen-

---

[51] Freilich liegt auch hier Berührung mit der Elisaüberlieferung vor; vgl. SCHMITT, l.c., p. 186, n. 37 (mit ansprechender Vermutung über das Prioritätsverhältnis).

[52] Vgl. *VT* XXV, 1975, pp. 535f. und die dort genannte Literatur.

[53] "Durch den Schleier der Sage erkennt man den Mann der heiligen Unruhe, zwischen Botschaftserfüllung und der an die Welt verzweifelnden Suche nach seinem Gott. Dann aber zerreißt der Schleier, und im klaren geschichtlichen Licht steht er Ahab gegenüber (21, 17ff.), in der rechten geschichtlichen Haltung des Künders JHWHs zum 'König von Israel' (V. 18) ... Hier hat der harte theopolitische Sachverhalt allen Versuchen der Tradition, ihn legendär zu verklären, widerstanden" (*Der Glaube der Propheten*, Zürich 1950, p. 114 = *Werke* II, München-Heidelberg 1964, p. 317).

[54] Vgl. GUNKEL, l.c., pp. 40ff.; STECK, l.c., pp. 142ff.

satz zwischen dem israelitischen und dem kanaanäischen Bodenrecht im Hintergrund;[55] aber es ist doch nicht so präzise der Kampf Jahwes gegen den Baal, der hier geführt wird, daß wir berechtigt wären, auf Grund des Kriteriums des Namens Elijjahu gerade hier eine spezifisch elianische Geschichte zu finden. Schließlich und am wichtigsten: es fragt sich, ob Elia überhaupt von Anfang an in diese Geschichte hineingehört hat. Schon C. F. BURNEY hat darauf hingewiesen,[56] daß er hier nicht wie in xvii-xix die Zentralfigur ist; er erscheint erst in 17, und auch da nicht so spezifisch, wie es sein könnte.[57] Dazu kommt das Zeugnis von außen, das Wort Jehus an seinen Adjutanten Bidkar 2 Reg. ix 25f. Man tut sicher recht, dadurch die Historizität der Nabothgeschichte im wesentlichen bestätigt zu finden.[58] Das gilt aber, wie man seit G. HÖLSCHER [59] wissen kann, nicht für die Rolle des Elia. Daß Jehu den Spruch Jahwes gegen Ahab anonym zitiert, wiegt um so schwerer, als Elia offenbar im übrigen als Inaugurator oder doch Vorläufer dessen in Anspruch genommen wurde, was Jehu tat; ich verweise außer auf den Salbungsbefehl 1 Reg. xix 16 auch auf die Abschlachtung der Baalspropheten am Kison 1 Reg. xviii 40.[60] Die Erzählung von Naboths Weinberg dürfte danach, wenn es um die Quellen für den historischen Elia geht, eher in die zweite Reihe zu stellen sein.

V.

Die grobe, kaum auf Einzelheiten eingehende Sichtung des Materials, die hier nur möglich war, erlaubt die folgenden Aussagen über den historischen Elia:

---

[55] Vgl. K. BALTZER, *WuD* NF VIII, 1965, pp. 73ff.; zur ganzen Perikope zuletzt P. WELTEN, *EvTheol* XXXIII, 1973, pp. 18ff.

[56] *Notes on the Hebrew Text of the Books of Kings*, Oxford 1903, p. 210.

[57] Die Beobachtung, "daß Elia mit seiner Person mehr und mehr Mittelpunkt der Erzählungen wird" (A. JEPSEN, *Nabi*, München 1934, p. 67), trifft zwar für das Werden der Gesamtüberlieferung durchaus zu, läßt sich aber auf den vorliegenden Fall nicht anwenden.

[58] So schon H. EWALD, *Geschichte des Volkes Israel*, III, ²Göttingen 1866, p. 538, n. 2; heute etwa FOHRER, l.c., pp. 69ff.

[59] *Die Profeten* p. 177; *Geschichte der israelitisch-jüdischen Religion*, Gießen 1922, p. 95, n. 3; vgl. schon die Bedenken bei B. STADE, *Geschichte des Volkes Israel* I, Berlin 1887, p. 527, n. 1; seitdem J. M. MILLER, *VT* XVII, 1967, pp. 315f.; O. EIßFELDT, *Kleine Schriften* V, Tübingen 1973, p. 28; SCHMITT, l.c., p. 122, n. 246; WELTEN, l.c., p. 28.

[60] Daß hier Jehus Vorgehen gegen die Baalsverehrer gerechtfertigt werden soll, steht schon in populärwissenschaftlicher Literatur zu lesen: W. HINKER-K. SPEIDEL, *Wenn die Bibel recht hätte . . .*, Stuttgart 1970, pp. 109ff.

Elia stritt dafür, daß allein Jahwe als Gott zu verehren sei. Er tat das, indem er auf dem Karmel den Jahwekult gegen den Baalskult durchsetzte, indem er die Anfrage des Königs Ahasja beim Baal Sebub in Ekron zurückwies und indem er als Diener Jahwes und nicht des Baal für das Kommen des Regens zuständig war. Scharfer Gegensatz zu einem König ist nur im Falle des Ahasja belegt; im Falle des Ahab zwingt nichts, ihn anzunehmen, so wenig er natürlich auch durch 1 Reg. xviii 41-46 schon ausgeschlossen ist.

Ort der Handlung ist in einer der Erzählungen, die für uns die Grundlage bilden, mit Sicherheit, in einer zweiten sehr wahrscheinlich der Karmel, in der Erweiterung der dritten sitzt Elia auf "dem Gipfel des Berges". Wir dürfen danach vermuten, daß dieser Berg sein häufiger oder regelmäßiger Aufenthaltsort oder Wohnsitz war.[61] Sein für den Historiker im Dunkeln liegender, aber natürlich im Zusammenhang der hinter 1 Reg. xvii-xviii stehenden Ereignisse leicht vorstellbarer Aufenthalt im phönikischen Zarpath (1 Reg. xvii 7ff.) würde dem nicht widersprechen, sondern geographisch durchaus dazu passen.

Mit dem, was wir über die Herkunft des Elia wissen, können wir kaum etwas anfangen. Elijjahu braucht nicht sein Geburtsname gewesen zu sein, der Name seines Vaters wird nicht genannt. Die Herkunftsbezeichnung מִתֹּשָׁבֵי גִלְעָד (1 Reg. xvii 1 MT) ist mit hoher Wahrscheinlichkeit (vgl. LXX) Textfehler für מִתִּשְׁבֵּי גִלְעָד, also für die Angabe des (nicht lokalisierbaren) Ortes, nach dem Elia der Thisbiter heißt (1 Reg. xvii 1; xxi 17, 28; 2 Reg. i 3, 8; ix 36).[62] Es ist also ohne Grundlage, wenn man über die "Beisassen von Gilead" spekuliert [63] oder aus dem Fehlen eines Herkunftsortes auf nomadische Existenz und Zugehörigkeit zu Kenitern oder Rechabitern schließt.[64]

Was überhaupt das Verhältnis des Elia zu diesen und anderen Gruppen [65] angeht, so wissen wir davon kaum etwas. Wenn sich die Bewegung des Jehu auf Elisa, auf die Rechabiter und eben

---

[61] Für SCHMITT, l.c., p. 186, hat er geradezu am dortigen Heiligtum fungiert; vgl. auch J. LINDBLOM, *Prophecy in Ancient Israel*, Oxford 1963, pp. 79f.

[62] Vgl. M. NOTH, *Aufsätze zur biblischen Landes- und Altertumskunde* I, Neukirchen-Vluyn 1971, pp. 519ff., aber auch S. MITTMANN, *Beiträge zur Siedlungs- und Territorialgeschichte des nördlichen Ostjordanlandes*, ADPV, Wiesbaden 1970, p. 222, n. 34.

[63] E. TÄUBLER, *Biblische Studien*, Tübingen 1958, p. 250.

[64] Vgl. GUTMANN, l.c., col. 632. Auf Zugehörigkeit zu den Rechabitern kommt RÖSCH, l.c., pp. 571f., nach seiner scharfen Kritik der Quellen hinaus.

[65] JEPSEN, *Nabi*, p. 72, n. 1, p. 168, n. 1 denkt wegen der langen Haare daran, daß Elia Nasiräer war.

auf Elia berief, dann muß das über das Verhältnis dieser drei Größen untereinander (und übrigens auch zur vierten) noch nicht viel besagen. Aber auch gegenüber dem noch engeren Verhältnis, das die Tradition zwischen Elia und Elisa behauptet, ist dem Historiker Vorsicht geboten. Der Mantel, den Elia auf Elisa wirft (1 Reg. xix 19) und mit dem vor seiner Entrückung er und danach Elisa den Jordan zerteilt (2 Reg. ii 8, 13f.), ist in dieser — magischen — Bedeutung ein Requisit der Überlieferung von Elisa, nicht von Elia; in der Eliaüberlieferung kommt der Mantel nur einmal ganz unspezifisch vor (1 Reg. xix 13),[66] und als die Boten dem Ahasja das Aussehen des Elia beschreiben (2 Reg. i 8), da erwähnen sie den Mantel gerade nicht.[67] Was von dem Mantel gilt, gilt vom Verhältnis zwischen Elia und Elisa überhaupt.[68] Daß sich Elisa als Nachfolger des Elia betrachtete, und womöglich in dieser oder jener Hinsicht zu Recht, und auch daß zwischen beiden eine persönliche Beziehung bestand, ist damit nicht ausgeschlossen; es liegt aber außerhalb dessen, was wir wissen. Richtig wird der oft ausgesprochene Eindruck sein, während Elisa mit einer prophetischen Gruppe oder mehreren mindestens in enger Verbindung gestanden habe, sei Elia eine Einzelfigur gewesen.[69] Dieser Umstand rückt Elia näher an Micha ben Jimla als an Elisa heran;[70] auch das aber könnte ein Grund dafür sein, in der gänzlichen Isoliertheit seiner Position das Ergebnis einer gewissen Überzeichnung durch spätere Tradition zu sehen.[71]

Kein Grund aber wäre es dafür, und einen solchen Grund gibt es auch sonst schwerlich, die Gestalt des Elia zu nivellieren. R. KITTEL [72] hat seinem Kollegen GUNKEL geradezu genüßlich vorgerechnet, wie bei ihm das Bild des Propheten, das er zunächst so

---

[66] Nach SCHMITT, l.c., p. 75, n. 18, der WÜRTHWEIN folgt, sind hier die Elisa-Stellen bereits vorausgesetzt.

[67] Vgl. die überzeugenden Ausführungen von PH. VIELHAUER, *Aufsätze zum Neuen Testament*, München 1965, pp. 49ff.

[68] SCHMITT sieht die speziell hierher gehörenden Texte in einer "Sukzessor-sammlung" zusammengefaßt (l.c., p. 75f., 102ff., 109ff., 180ff.).

[69] Ihn einen Nabi zu nennen, ist problematisch; vgl. JEPSEN, l.c., pp. 58ff., auch J. FICHTNER, *Das erste Buch von den Königen*. Die Botschaft des AT XII, I, Stuttgart 1964, pp. 269f.

[70] Vgl. J. WELLHAUSEN, *Israelitische und jüdische Geschichte*, [7]Berlin 1914, p. 74, aber auch M. BUBER in seinem Mysterienspiel: *Werke* II, pp. 1211ff., 1223f. — Übrigens hat der Name des Micha ungefähr dieselbe Bedeutung wie der des Elia.

[71] Vgl. ALT, *Kleine Schriften* III, p. 283.

[72] *Die Bücher der Könige*, p. 162.

gut wie vollständig kritisch zersetzt habe, dann unversehens doch
wieder in großer Mächtigkeit dastehe. In der Tat haben gerade
kritische Forscher gern in Superlativen von Elia gesprochen, Kate-
gorien wie die des Heroischen auf ihn angewendet [73] und ihn einzig
dem Mose nachgeordnet.[74] So fragwürdig das in manchem für
heutigen Geschmack und heutige Theologie sein mag, man kann
es doch nicht einfach als Heldenverehrung im Stile des 19. Jahrhunderts abtun, die sich auf sekundäre Quellen stütze. Nicht nur
unser Interesse, sondern auch unsere Fähigkeit, Individuelles zu
erfassen, ist gegenwärtig bemerkenswert gering und wird das auf
diesem Felde bleiben, solange unsere Methoden kaum mehr her-
geben als die Subtraktion von Nichtindividuellem. So stehen wir
etwas hilflos vor der Frage nach der persönlichen Eigenart des Elia,
ja einige unter uns werden sogar das Recht und den Sinn dieser
Frage bezweifeln. Unter dem Vorbehalt besserer Belehrung möchte
ich aber meinen, daß das eigentümlich "Meteorische" [75] im Auftreten des Propheten, das uns gerade in den sekundären Stufen der
Tradition entgegentritt und das dann je länger desto mehr, aber
doch wohl in einem tiefen Sinne nicht unsachgemäß ins gänzlich
Unhistorische projiziert wurde (entscheidender Vorgang die Entrückung), auf den originalen Eindruck zurückgeht. Und das stimmt
zur Sache des Elia, wie schärfere Kritik sie doch wohl noch genauer
erkennen kann als R. KITTEL, der etwas pauschal zu der "guten
Zuversicht" aufrief, "daß die Hauptzüge . . . auf historischem Grunde
ruhen". Die Sache des Elia wird nach dem, was wir ermittelt haben,
von der Tradition sehr präzise umschrieben, wenn sie dem Propheten,
nicht zufällig auf dem Horeb, die Worte in den Mund legt, er habe
für Jahwe, den Gott Zebaoth, "geeifert" (1 Reg. xix 14). Darin,
daß sie ihn hier und anderwärts offenbar mit Mose in Beziehung
setzt, ja fast als zweiten Mose erscheinen läßt,[76] haben es ihr nicht
wenige Gelehrte nachgetan. Und das geschah bei allen Vorbehalten,
die man hier machen muß, mit Recht. Das "Jahwe oder Baal" auf
dem Karmel interpretiert in weitergerückter Zeit das "Jahwe" auf
dem Sinai. Ob Elia die Alternative als erster ausgesprochen hat,
wissen wir nicht.[77] Aber für sie eingetreten ist er mit großer Wahr-

[73] Vgl. außer GUNKEL etwa WELLHAUSEN, l.c., p. 73: "die grandioseste Hel-
dengestalt in der Bibel".
[74] Vgl. etwa GREßMANN, l.c., p. 270.
[75] Den Ausdruck gebraucht WELLHAUSEN, *Die Composition des Hexateuchs*, p. 282.
[76] FOHRER, l.c., pp. 55ff.
[77] Positiv z.B. O. EIßFELDT, *Kleine Schriften* I, Tübingen 1962, pp. 7f.; negativ

scheinlichkeit, mit welchen Worten auch immer, und hat damit der
Folgezeit einen Orientierungspunkt auch dann gegeben, wenn er
unmittelbar keine dauernde Wirkung erzielte. Er "glich einem Vogel,
der vor dem Morgen singt", sagt WELLHAUSEN.[78] Als der Tag
angebrochen war, nahm man diesen Gesang als Ouvertüre und
gestaltete ihn in diesem Sinne weiter aus, so daß er nun, ohne uferlos
zu werden, doch die großen Themen der kommenden Prophetie
anklingen läßt, auch das Thema der prophetischen Existenz selbst
(dies besonders in 1 Reg. xix).[79] So wurde aus dem historischen der
biblische Elia. Wenn es zutrifft, daß die Grundvoraussetzung des
Alten Testaments in dem Satz ausgesprochen ist, Jahwe sei der Gott
Israels, und Jahwe allein, dann war das ein legitimer Vorgang;
dann rechtfertigt aber auch die Bedeutung des Mannes, Elia in einem
Atem mit Mose zu nennen.

W. H. SCHMIDT, *Alttestamentlicher Glaube und seine Umwelt*, Neukirchen-Vluyn
1968, p. 207.

[78] *Grundrisse zum Alten Testament*, München 1965, p. 90.

[79] Hierzu K. SEYBOLD, *EvTheol* XXXIII, 1973, pp. 3ff.

Art ZOBEL

ANCIENT ISRAELITE POETRY AND ANCIENT "CODES" OF LAW, AND THE SOURCES 'J' AND 'E' OF THE PENTATEUCH

BY

J. ALBERTO SOGGIN

Roma

1. Among the majority of scholars, who since the end of the last century have used the Documentary Hypothesis in their approach to the Pentateuch,[1] there has often been a feeling of uneasiness, sometimes of uncertainty, as to where to situate within the sources 'J' and 'E' the ancient poetical texts, a few of which are explicit quotations from older sources, and the ancient law "codes" which do not belong either to 'D' or to 'P'.

I refer to the following texts:[2]

'J': a) Ancient poetry: Gen. iv 23-24; ix 25-27; xvi 12; xxvii 27b-29, 39b-40; xlix 1-27; Ex. xv 1-18; Num. xxiv 3-9, 15-19.

    b) Ancient law "codes": Ex. xxxiv 10-26.

'E': a) Ancient poetry: Ex. xv 21; xvii 16; Num. x 35-36; xxi 14-15, 17-18, 27-30; xxiii 7-10, 18-24; Deut. xxxii 1-43; xxxiii 1-29.

    b) Ancient law "codes": Ex. xx 1-17; xx 22-xxiii 33.

This uneasiness, sometimes uncertainty, appears often quite clearly, as soon as one tries to relate more closely one of these texts to its source with a certain measure of exactness and detail, or whenever a discussion starts on the source to which a text ought to be, or cannot be, assigned. In these fields there is anything but agreement among the scholars.

---

[1] For the limits of this approach today and presumable directions of future research, see R. RENDTORFF, "Traditio-historical method and the Documentary Hypothesis", in *Proceedings of the Fifth World Congress of Jewish Studies*, 1969, vol. I, Jerusalem 1973, pp. 5-11. In these lines see further "Der 'Jahwist' als Theologe? Zum Dilemma der Pentateuchkritik", this volume pp. 158-66.

[2] This classification is derived from A. WEISER, *Einleitung in das Alte Testament*, Göttingen ⁶1966 (Engl. transl. London—New York 1961), § 14-15.

2. It has often been recognized, and so it appears in many standard works, that the solution of the two problems I have just touched is at least uncertain. It would go beyond the scope of this paper to give a complete and accurate review and classification of current scholarly opinions on this theme: I shall limit myself, therefore, to presenting only a selection of opinions which strike me as the most typical and qualified at the same time, in order to clarify what I am trying to expose.

a) Already at the time of J. WELLHAUSEN and A. KUENEN, the matter of assigning some of our texts to 'J' or to 'E' was anything but settled. J. WELLHAUSEN [3] was doubtful as to the possibility of assigning Gen. xlix to 'J', although it could hardly belong to 'E'; the Decalogue he assigned to 'E', Ex. xxxiv to 'J'. But the difficulties in assigning these texts to certain sources appear clearly in his discussion with A. KUENEN, who considers the 'Book of the Covenant' neither 'J' nor 'E' and Ex. xxxiv partially 'E'. Sections of Num. xxi are considered by WELLHAUSEN to belong to 'J', while on the Bil'am oracles he holds an opinion quite different from that of most contemporary scholars: Num. xxiii goes to 'J', Num. xxiv to 'E'!

b) R. H. PFEIFFER [4] considers the ancient poems only "embedded" in the documents and grants a notable autonomy to the legal texts. The general conclusions about the latter reached by this author (who has been considered, by the way, one of the major, most radical followers of WELLHAUSEN and sometimes even the last of the representatives of Pentateuchal higher criticism in its classical form [5]) are the following: ". . . of the narrative sources of the Pentateuch, only D and P, combining history and legislation, contained originally any law whatsoever". [6]

Another extreme representative of the Documentary Hypothesis is

c) A. LODS; [7] according to him, all legal texts that do not belong

---

[3] *Die Composition des Hexateuch*, Berlin [3]1899 = [4]1963, pp. 60, 84, 108, 110ff., 113ff., 329ff., 334. On the 'Book of the Covenant' see H. CAZELLES, *Études sur le Code de l' Alliance*, Paris 1946, pp. 11ff.

[4] *Introduction to the Old Testament*, New York [2]1948, pp. 210ff. and 217ff.; cp. pp. 147ff. and 220f.

[5] I. ENGNELL, "The Call of Isaiah", *UUÅ* 1949: IV, p. 47; S. MOWINCKEL, *VT* V (1955), p. 15.

[6] *Op. cit.*, p. 211.

[7] *Histoire de la littérature hébraïque et juive*, Paris 1950, pp. 23ff., 51ff., 200ff., 204ff. For reviews, all stressing their criticism of his rather static adherence to the theories of J. WELLHAUSEN, cp. i.a. R. DE VAUX, *RB* XLVII (1950), pp. 443-447; R. H. PFEIFFER, *JBL* LXIX (1950), pp. 402-404; É. JACOB, *RHPhR* XXX (1950), pp. 305-310 and W. F.ALBRIGHT, *BASOR* CXX (1950), p. 29.

either to 'D' or to 'P', are to be assigned: to 'J' Ex. xxxiv 10ff.; or to 'E' Ex. xx to xxiii. The 'Book of the Covenant' belongs to a more recent stratum of the latter. That ancient poetry can also be divided between the two ancient sources, seems probable to him.[8]

d) Aa. BENTZEN [9] assigns the major poetical and legal text to 'JE' and accepts that Gen. xlix has "important connections with 'J' "; the problem remains open for the minor texts.

e) O. EISSFELDT [10] shows a rather high degree of uncertainty: ancient poetry and legal texts are basically assigned to 'J' and 'E' according to the traditional pattern of the Documentary Hypothesis; but elsewhere in his monumental Introduction he shows a considerable reserve in matters of detail: Gen. xlix is called "an expansion of basic materials found in the L strand" (*Auswertung eines im L Faden gegebenen Grundbestandes*); about Deut. xxxii, xxxiii and Ex. xv he is not quite certain whether they have been "found by him ['J'] and taken into his work . . ." or "inserted into it secondarily" (*Aufgenommen oder sekundär eingesetzt*); the Decalogue is probably to be assigned to 'E', while in the 'Book of the Covenant' there are elements of both sources. Num. xxi is classified as belonging to 'J'.

f) G. FOHRER [11] accepts the original independence of the ancient poetical and legal materials from the sources; they were "taken over" (*aufgenommen*) by them. This position had been intiated years before by A. WEISER,[12] to whom I owe the above suggested classification. He considers our texts as having been "mainly *earlier material*, which has been taken over" (*übernommen*) by the sources. Both authors thus agree on the thesis that our texts had an autonomous existence

---

[8] The inadequacy of this way of assigning texts to the sources (which is widespread, so that A. LODS can be in no way considered responsible for it): e.g.: it cannot be 'D' or 'P', therefore it must be 'J' or 'E'; it cannot be 'J', so it must be 'E' and *vice versa*, has been recently emphasized by R. RENDTORFF, *art. cit.*, pp. 6ff.

[9] *Introduction to the Old Testament*, Copenhagen ³1957, vol. I, pp. 139ff.; vol. II, pp. 44ff. and 58.

[10] *Einleitung in das Alte Testament*, Tübingen ³1964, pp. 250ff. and 265ff.; cp. pp. 72ff., 190, 279ff., 286ff., 304ff. etc. Engl. transl.: *The Old Testament: an Introduction*, Oxford 1965, pp. 188ff. and 199ff.; cp. p. 54ff., 143ff., 210ff., 215ff., 229ff. etc.

[11] E. SELLIN—G. FOHRER, *Einleitung in das Alte Testament*, Heidelberg ¹⁰1965 = ¹¹1969, pp. 146ff., 149, 159ff., 166ff. etc., Engl. transl. New York—Nashville 1968, London 1970, pp. 132ff., 136ff., 146ff. 152ff. etc.

[12] *Einleitung* . . . cit., § 14-15. I have myself leaned heavily on A. WEISER's work, cp. *Introduzione all' Antico Testamento*, vol. I, Brescia 1968, pp. 118ff. and 123ff.; ²1974 (in one vol.), pp. 151ff. and 156ff.

in an archaic phase of their transmission, which antedates their present inclusion into the sources.

g) The most recent Introduction to the Old Testament, edited by H. Cazelles, [13] follows the current attribution of our texts to the sources.

h) As far as I can see, there has been only one lonely, but very authoritative, dissenting voice, which has questioned altogether the possibility of relating many of our texts to the sources 'J' and 'E': Martin Noth.[14] He does not assign Gen. xlix, Ex. xv, Num. xxiii-xxiv, Deut. xxxiii; Ex. xx 22-xxiii 33, cp. Ex. xvii 16 to any of the ancient sources, while Num. x 35f. and xxi 14ff. are supposed to belong to 'J' instead of to 'E' for various reasons.

i) But also among those who accept in principle that these texts do belong to the ancient sources, there is anything but an agreement as to the source to which each text ought to be assigned. This seems to be, at least, a sympton that objective elements for classifying them are lacking.

W. F. Albright [15] is, like so many scholars before and after him, quite uncertain as to the source to which Gen. xlix ought to be

---

[13] H. Cazelles (ed.), *Introduction critique à l'Ancien Testament* (Introduction à la Bible, vol. II), Paris-Tournay 1973, pp. 178ff. and 213ff. This important work has been available to me for too short a time, to allow my making full use of it.

[14] *Überlieferungsgeschichte des Pentateuch*, Stuttgart 1948, pp. 18, 32, 39, 81f., 107, 223ff. etc., Engl. transl. *A History of Pentateuchal Tradition*, Englewood Cliffs 1972. Cp. M. Noth's Commentaries: *Das zweite Buch Mose*, ATD V, Göttingen 1960 and *Das vierte Buch Mose*, ATD VII, Göttingen 1966 (both in Engl. transl.), *ad loc.* On Num. xxi see: "Nu 21 als Glied der 'Hexateuch'-Erzählung", *ZAW* LVIII (1940-41), pp. 161-189 = *Aufsätze* . . ., Neukirchen 1971, pp. 75-101. See further G. von Rad, *Das erste Buch Mose*, ATD II-IV, Göttingen ⁹1972, p. 347: there is no evidence suggesting that Gen. xlix should be connected with 'J'; even more strongly R. de Vaux, *Histoire ancienne d'Israël*, vol. II, Paris 1973, pp. 40f.: "This composition does not belong to any of the sources of the Pentateuch". Contra H. Cazelles, *op. cit.*, p. 189. Two of the more recent monographs on the 'Book of the Covenant' and Ex. xxxiv 10ff.: S. M. Paul, *Studies in the Book of the Covenant in the Light of Cuneiform and Biblical Law*, SVT XVIII, Leiden 1970, and H. Horn, "Traditionsgeschichten in Ex. 23, 10-33 und Ex. 34, 10-26", *BZ* n.F. XV (1971), pp. 203-222, avoid carefully assigning these texts to any of the sources. For S. H. Paul these laws relate much better to ancient oriental law than to any source of the Pentateuch; according to H. Horn, the two parallel texts derive from the same source, which is neither 'J' nor 'E'. I have not been able to see the work by F.-E. Wilms, *Das jahwistische Bundesbuch in Exodus 34*, München 1973.

[15] "Jethro, Hobab and Reuel in Early Hebrew Traditions", *CBQ* XXV (1963), pp. 1-11; and *Yahweh and the Gods of Canaan*, London 1968, p. 29.

assigned,[16] while he endeavors to prove that the whole of the Bil'am oracles, Num. xxiii-xxiv, ought to be given to 'E'; Deut. xxxii and xxxiii he considers "rather 'J' than 'E' ". As for Ex. xv 1ff., while NOTH thinks at most of a late stage of 'J', F. STOLZ[17] considers the poem as post-exilic, a deduction he draws from his previous, "oben geäusserten *Vermutungen*" (italics mine), rejecting without discussion its early dating by W. F. ALBRIGHT, F. M. CROSS and D. N. FREEDMAN. R. H. PFEIFFER [18] considers Ex. xxxiv 10ff. deuteronomistic, while H. KOSMALA [19] points out that "the general ascription . . . to the various sources . . . does not help us any further": the text is obviously related to Ex. xxiii 14ff. and not to other texts. F. HORST [20] does not assign either the Decalogue or the 'Book of the Covenant' to any of the ancient sources; H.-W. WOLFF and W. BRUEGGEMANN,[21] who have recently studied 'J' and 'E' from a historical and systematic

---

[16] For an analysis of this very peculiar composition, see H.-J. KITTEL, *Die Stammessprüche Israels*, Diss. Berlin—K. H. 1959.

[17] F. STOLZ, *Jahwes und Israels Kriege*, ATANT LX, Zürich 1972, pp. 91ff. (the quotation is from footnote 4. Working mainly with "suppositions" seems to be a characteristic of this author); see however F. M. CROSS, *Canaanite Myth and Hebrew Epic*, Cambridge, Mass. 1973, pp. 121ff.

[18] *Op. cit.* p. 221; quite similar has been recently L. PERLITT, *Bundestheologie im Alten Testament*, WMANT XXXVI, Neukirchen 1969, p. 216ff., but already A. ALT, *Die Ursprünge des israelitischen Rechts*, 1934 (*Kl. Schr.* I, pp. 278-332: p. 317, n. 1) had denied that this text can be assigned to 'J', cp. earlier the discussion between WELLHAUSEN and KUENEN, quoted above, p. 186.

[19] "The so-called Ritual Decalogue", *ASThI* I (1962), pp. 31-61, esp. p. 38 n. 16 and 58.

[20] Art. "Bundesbuch" and "Dekalog", *RGG* II (³1957), c. 1523-25 and III (³1958), c. 69-71; W. J. HARRELSON, art. "Ten Commandements", *IDB* IV (1962), p. 569-573: a few decades ago the Decalogue was generally taken as "most closely related to . . . 'E' "; today connections with sources or traditions of the Pentateuch are generally dropped. Cp. O. PLÖGER, Art. "Elohist", "Jahwist" and "Pentateuch", *RGG* II (³1958), c. 435f., III (³1959), c. 516f. and V (³1961), c. 211-217. According to him, 'P' is only a narrative source, while in 'E' the Decalogue and the 'Book of the Covenant' are additions. Silent about sources is J. J. STAMM, Art. "Bundesbuch", "Dekalog" and "Dodekalog", *BHH* I (1962), c. 289, 331f. and 346; for a review of scholarly work on the Decalogue see, by the same author: *Der Dekalog im Lichte der neueren Forschung*, Bern ²1962, Engl. transl. with additions by M. E. ANDREW: *The Ten Commandments in Recent Research*, SBTh II, 2, London 1967. The same caution, if not silence alltogether, we find in most encyclopaedical works: *LThK, BL, EKL* etc.

[21] H.-W. WOLFF, "Das Kerygma des Jahwisten", *Ev. Theol.* XXIV (1964), pp. 73-98 = *Ges. Stud.*, München ²1973, pp. 345-373, Engl. transl. "The Kerygma of the Yahwist", *Interpr.* XX (1966), pp. 131-158; W. BRUEGGEMANN, "David and his Theologian", *CBQ* XXX (1968), pp. 156-181; H.-W. WOLFF, "Zur Thematik der elohistischen Fragmente im Pentateuch", *Ev. Theol.* XXIX (1969), pp. 59-72 = *Ges. Stud.*, cit. p. 402-417, Engl. transl. "The Elohistic Fragments in the Pentateuch", *Interpr.* XXVI (1972), pp. 158-173.

point of view, include in the sources the ancient poetry, but do not mention the legal texts.

3. Many of these positions, with the exception of M. Noth, voice therefore certain perplexities on matters of detail. There is, however, a more substantial factor, which can hardly be overlooked: that the situation of 'J' and 'E' in this field is fundamentally different from that of 'P', which seems to me an adequate illustration for what I am trying to prove.

It is widely accepted today [22] that 'P' is essentially a narrative source, like 'J' and 'E'. Nevertheless, legal and ritual sections ('P', as is well known, has no ancient poetry), show often, and on fundamental matters, a clear relationship to the narrative sections. A few examples should be sufficient: in Gen. ii 1-3 we have a report on how and why the Sabbath was instituted by God; Ex. xxxi 12-17 and other texts give us the rules for its observance. Gen. ix 1-4 introduce the first, fundamental dietary law, forbidding the consumption of blood; Lev. vii 26f.; xvii 10-14; xix 26 and other texts repeat the commandement or give some detailed rules for its upkeeping. Gen. xvii 1ff. give an accurate and complete report on circumcision: why and how it was instituted, how and when it is supposed to be practised; the wealth of information contained in this narrative text allows only short references to circumcision further on in the source, such as Lev. xii 3. Ex. xii 1-20, 43-50 report on the institution of the festival of Pesaḥ and the feast of Unleavened Bread, while Num. ix 2-5, 10-14 and other texts detail the rules governing its celebration.

Now we all know that there is considerable evidence for the independent origin of certain legal and ritual sections of 'P': Lev. i-vii, xi-xv, the 'Code of Holiness'; but there can be hardly any doubt that, whatever differences or even inconsistencies in matters of detail can be found (e.g. the age for ordination of priests, the number and type of altars), there seems to have been an overall planning which gave an organic connection between the narrative and the legal-ritual sections. Further, as far as I can see, this picture is in most cases confirmed by a consistency of vocabulary and style.

---

[22] M. Noth, *Überlieferungsgeschichte* ... cit. p. 7ff.; K. Elliger, "Sinn und Ursprung der Priesterlichen Geschichtserzählung", *ZThK* XLIX (1952), pp. 121-143 = *Kl. Schr.*, München 1966, pp. 174-198; W. Brueggemann, "The Kerygma of the Priestly Writers", *ZAW* LXXXIV (1972), pp. 397-414; N. Lohfink, "Die Abänderung der Theologie des Priesterlichen Geschichtswerkes ...", *Festschr. K. Elliger*, Neukirchen 1973, pp. 129-136; and the Introductions to the Old Testament.

If we turn now to 'J' and to 'E', there is no difficulty in ascer-
taining that there is a lack of connection between the narrative
sections of the former and Ex. xxxiv 10-25; and those of the latter
and Ex. xx 1-17 or xx 22-xxiii 33. If we accept therefore that these
materials belong to 'J' and to 'E', we ought to admit also that they
were introduced into the sources without any reference to their
narrative counterparts. With the ancient poems the situation appears
different, as relevant theological and conceptual elements can be
isolated, which are found in the narrative sections of 'J' and 'E';
this is more difficult for the latter, owing to the scarcity of the texts
transmitted.[23]

One radical way to solve the problem in the case of the legal and
ritual materials would be to assume that the narrative sections of
'J' and 'E' constitute in fact the historical prologues to the body
of a covenant formula expressed in legal stipulations,[24] but such a
solution, besides being rather complex and offering a covenant
formula where the prologue is disproportionly long as compared
to the body, hardly recommends itself after the latest investigations
on the word and the concept of *berît*,[25] or at least not in the customary,
wholesale way.

Thus the problem of relating the legal-ritual materials to the
narrative sections of 'J' and 'E' remains unsolved. The situation
of the early poetry appears considerably more easy to deal with.

4. As is well known, certain detailed criteria have been elaborated
during the last 100 years, since the Documentary Hypothesis was
proposed in its definitive form, to assign texts to the sources of the
Pentateuch. They are, taken alone, not always conclusive and thus
prove insufficient to assign a text to a source without appeal; nevertheless, they have led to a certain consensus as far as most of the
narrative sections are concerned. Among these criteria let me quote

---

[23] This is justly emphasized by H. CAZELLES, *Introduction* ... cit. pp. 178ff.
and 213ff.

[24] So e.g. the important article by H. B. HUFFMON, "The Exodus, Sinai and
the Credo", *CBQ* XXVII (1965), pp. 101-113, anticipated without details by
W. J. HARRELSON, Art. "Covenant, Book of the", *IDB* I (1962), p. 723. Essentially on the same lines is H. CAZELLES, *Introduction* ... cit., p. 210ff.

[25] Cp. L. PERLITT, *Bundestheologie* ... cit. and E. KUTSCH, *Verheissung und
Gesetz*, BZAW CXXXI, Berlin 1973. But see also M. WEINFELD, Art. "ברית
b^erît", *ThWbAT* I (1973), c. 781-801 and "Covenant Terminology in the Ancient
Near East and its Influence on the West", *JAOS* XCIII (1973), pp. 190-199;
and recently W. SELB, "Διαθήκη im Neuen Testament", *JJSt* XXV (1974),
pp. 182-198.

just the following two: first the lexicographical one, which allows
a considerable degree of objectivity, especially in the case of parallel
texts, i.e. the use of certain proper or common names instead of
their synonyms for the same persons and/or functions;[26] to the
other one I have shortly referred above (p. 190): the recurrence of
certain theological and other ideological elements which are held
to be typical for one source, but are mostly lacking in the other;
this second criterion suffers, as ought to be obvious, from a rather
high degree of subjectivity, especially where theological elements
are involved.[27] What do these criteria have to contribute to the
solution of our problem?

a) Lexicography. An investigation of the occurrence of certain
words which are considered typical respectively of 'J' and 'E' yields
the following results:

"Yahweh" is found also in texts which are currently assigned
to 'E': Ex. xvii 16; xx 2, 5, 7, 10, 11, 12; xxii 19; xxiii 17, 25; Num.
x 35-36; Deut. xxii 3, 9; xxxiii 2, 7, 11, 12, 13, 29; the same happens
to *ēl* and *'elōhîm*, which appear in the following texts, mostly considered 'J'[28]: Gen. xlix 25; Ex. xv 2; Num. xxiv 4, 6 (*'ēl*), and Gen.
ix 26; Ex. xv 2; xxxiv 23, 24, 26 (*'elōhîm*).[29] However, as is well
known:

I. After Ex. iii there is nothing strange in finding "Yahweh"
in 'E'-texts, although the same cannot be said about *'ēl* *'elōhîm* in
'J'-texts.

II. Divine names and titles are generally considered the least
adequate criterion to assign a text to a source. So we may drop it
altogether.

But the names "Sinai" and "Canaanite(s)", which are currently
considered part of the vocabulary of 'J', are found also in the fol-

---

[26] See the classical exposition by C. STEUERNAGEL, *Lehrbuch der Einleitung
in das Alte Testament*, Tübingen 1912, pp. 214ff.; cp. further A. LODS, pp. 176ff.;
E. SELLIN—L. ROST, *Einleitung in das Alte Testament*, Heidelberg 81949, pp. 48
and 54; O. EISSFELDT, pp. 243f.; G. FOHRER, pp. 163ff. and 171ff., all *op. cit.*

[27] Besides the works quoted in the preceeding footnote, see also H. CAZELLES,
op. cit., pp. 178ff. and 210ff.

[28] Excluded have been, of course, those texts where these words stand for
"other/foreign Gods" or for "God" as an attribute of Yahweh.

[29] In several cases, however, we deal with idioms and compound expressions:
in Gen. ix 26, where *'elōhê šēm* could hardly be rendered according to the classical
lexicography of 'J'; in Gen. xlix 25, where we have the expression "The God
of your father...", or in Ex. xv 2b, where "God" is an attribute of Yahweh,
so also Ex. xxxiv 23, 26.

lowing texts considered 'E': "Sinai" in Deut. xxxiii 2; "Canaanite(s)" in Ex. xxiii 23, 28. On the other hand "Amorite", considered a typical 'E'-synonym for 'J'-"Canaanite" when describing the pre-Israelite population of Palestine, appears in Ex. xxxiv 11, a text attributed to 'J' by many authors, who consider it the 'J' counterpart of the 'E' Decalogue (but see below). To be sure, the investigation yields only one case in which the vocabulary confirms traditional assignment of texts to a source: *'āmāh*, typical for 'E', appears in fact in Ex. xx 10; xxi 7, 26, 27; xxiii 12.

Other classical terms for the vocabulary of 'J': *šifḥāh, pilégeš, saq, ṣā'îr*; and of the vocabulary of 'E': *Ḥóreb, Yéter/Yitrô, 'amtáḥat, qāṭōn* do not appear at all in our texts. [30]

There thus seems to be one obvious conclusion, although hampered by the scarcity of the evidence: on a lexicographical basis, only the Decalogue and the 'Book of the Covenant' can be asigned to 'E', but only for one word, while the use of "Yahweh" in both texts and of "Canaanite(s)" in the former, which do refer rather to 'J', sets a limit even to this conclusion; a further difficulty with *'āmāh* here is that any parallel is lacking, so that one can hardly speak of a synonym for the same person and function. In other words, we may suggest that the lexicographical evidence for assigning these texts to one of the sources is lacking or else extremely scanty.

b) Theological and ideological elements, although less objective, are fundamental for our investigation. It ought to be obvious that such elements are lacking altogether in Ex. xxxiv 10ff. if we compare this text with the narrative sections of 'J': the anti-Canaanite emphasis of *vv.* 10-16 would point rather to 'E' or even to 'D', while the "neutral" agricultural atmosphere one breaths in *vv.* 17-26 hardly proves anything, unless we find some substancial evidence that 'E' had a wholly negative, "Rechabite" attitude towards agriculture.[31] But the same seems to be true, *mutatis mutandis*, also for the 'Book of the Covenant' and even more, of course, for the Decalogue: the former has nothing especially anti-Canaanite or orthodox-Israelite features which are currently related to 'E'; rather the opposite is true: Ex. xxi 6; xxii 7, 8 use *'elōhîm* to indicate quite generically "the Godhead" and could be used by any religion. We are reminded

---

[30] Some of these words do not appear, of course, simply because there is no use for them in the context. Still, for this reason the evidence is lacking.

[31] Further evidence against an attribution of Ex. xxxiv 10ff. to 'J' are found in L. PERLITT, *op. cit.* pp. 216ff.

of the above mentioned (p. 186) statement by R. H. Pfeiffer that only 'D' and 'P' had legal sections.

The situation seems quite different as far as the ancient poetry is concerned: there we find some relevant items which can be connected with 'J' and 'E'. Gen. xlix 1ff.; Ex. xv 1ff.; Num. xxiv 3-9, 15-19 are rich in elements that are considered typical of the theological and ideological frame of 'J': pre-eminence of Judah in function of the pan-Israelite, Davidic, "imperial" frame of thought. From this point of view it is therefore to be taken seriously into consideration that these texts *could* have been transmitted through the source 'J'. Quite similar is the situation of Num. xxiii 7-10, 18-24; Deut. xxxii 1ff. and xxxiii 1ff. in relation to 'E': these texts refer often to motives such as the exclusiveness of Israel among the nations, its separation from the other peoples, its religious exclusiveness and strictness; such elements are generally connected with the theological frame of 'E'.

It must be said therefore that in these cases we have a reasonable probability that 'J' and 'E' respectively were the channels through which these texts entered the Pentateuch. However, a reasonable probability cannot mean in any case conclusive evidence, and this seems even more true for those smaller poetical compositions where all elements of proof are lacking: if 'J' and 'E' have quoted them, which is quite possible, no traces of this procedure are left, so that we are in no position to say *who* transmitted them and for what reason. Gen. iv 23f. and ix 25ff. *could* have been used by 'J' in order to back its theological thesis about progressive degeneration of mankind; but we can hardly proceed beyond this conditional.

5. This paper wishes to draw attention to a problem which cannot be ignored; it cannot solve the problem here. It would like, however, to present an alternative to the way in which higher criticism has currently handled these texts.

There can be hardly any doubt that, on the whole, the ancient poetical texts in the Pentateuch have far greater affinities, formal and substantial, with similar texts outside the Pentateuch (Judg. v 1ff.; 1 Sam. ii 1ff.; 2 Sam. i 19ff.; xxii 1ff. || Ps. xviii 1ff.; 2 Sam. xxiii 1-7; Ps. xxix 1ff. etc.) than with any material of the sources 'J' and 'E'. This is particularly evident if we compare, for example, the tribal oracles of Gen. xlix and Deut. xxxiii with those of Judg. v 14ff. and Ps. lxviii 28ff.;[32] or Ex. xv 1-18 with xv 21, the former

---

[23] For a comparative analysis of these materials, see H.-J. Zobel, *Stammesspruch und Geschichte*, BZAW XCV, Berlin 1965.

allegedly 'J', the latter 'E': on what objective grounds can we separate the refrain from the song, assigning each to a different source?
It seems therefore convenient to consider the ancient Israelite poems
as something on their own. We may call them "Ancient Yahwistic
Poetry", a title proposed about a quarter of a century ago.[33] The
theological and ideological parallels with 'J' and 'E', which we find
in some cases, do not prove anything else but that these texts originated in a similar *Sitz im Leben*: the need to legitimate from a Yahwistic
point of view the rise of the united monarchy in Israel; the struggle
with syncretism at the time of the great Prophets.

As far as the ancient legal texts are concerned, the evidence seems
to contradict much more than it proves their traditional attribution
to the sources 'J' and 'E'. I suggest therefore a new denomination:
"Ancient legal and ritual texts", or, as S. H. Paul [34] has put it recently: "Early Israelite Jurisprudence".

Parallels which can sometimes be found between certain ancient
poems (e.g. between Gen. xlix and Deut. xxxiii) or between ancient
legal and ritual texts (e.g. Ex. xxiii 14ff. and xxxiv 10ff.) do not
point to different sources, but rather to the same, or a similar, origin,
differentiation being the product of their independent transmission.

---

[33] F. M. Cross, Jr., *Studies in Ancient Yahwistic Poetry*, Diss. Johns Hopkins
University, Baltimore 1950.

[34] *Studies in the Book of the Covenant* . . . cit., p. 102.

CENTENAIRE DE LA MORT DE FIRKOWICZ

PAR

S. SZYSZMAN
Paris

Notre congrès coïncide avec le centenaire de la mort d'Abraham FIRKOWICZ qui s'éteignit le 7 juin 1874 à Kalé en Crimée. C'est pourquoi il nous a paru bon d'évoquer devant vous ce personnage dont la vie très mouvementée et l'activité sont toujours l'objet de controverses; leur violence ne s'apaise pas avec le temps. Une immense littérature est née autour des problèmes très complexes que ses recherches ont posés. On ne saurait les exposer tous, ni dans le cadre d'une simple conférence, ni dans celui d'un article. Aussi, nous bornerons-nous à présenter quelques points, à titre d'introduction à une étude plus approfondie.[1]

Abraham FIRKOWICZ, fils de Samuel, est né le 27 septembre 1787 à Loutzk en Volhynie dans une famille de petits agriculteurs. Il commença d'ailleurs sa carrière comme agriculteur et meunier. Ayant perdu, par suite de fléaux naturels, toute sa fortune, FIRKOWICZ, à l'âge de 25 ans, déjà marié et père de famille, se mit à étudier à l'école paroissiale karaïte de Loutzk; par la suite il y devint maître.

FIRKOWICZ était un érudit de type médiéval qui existe encore en Orient et qui s'est conservé chez les karaïtes jusqu'à notre époque. Nous nous rappelons encore avoir connu dans notre jeunesse des vieillards qui avaient reçu cette ancienne formation. Prodigieusement érudits en Ecriture Sainte, ils étaient capables d'en réciter par cœur

---

[1] D'autres problèmes posés par les découvertes de FIRKOWICZ sont examinés dans nos articles: "Les passionnants manuscrits d'Abraham Firkowicz", *Archéologia* LXXVIII, janvier 1975, p. 61-69; "A. Firkowicz, faussaire de génie ou collectionneur hors pair?" (communication présentée le 14 décembre 1974 à la Société Ernest Renan, résumé à paraître dans le *Bulletin de la Société*, annexe à la *Revue de l'histoire des religions*); "Les collections Firkowicz: leur intérêt pour les études philologiques et linguistiques" (communication présentée le 18 décembre 1974 au GLECS, texte à paraître dans les *Comptes rendus*, tome XIX); "La collection samaritaine de Firkowicz" (communication présentée le 29 janvier 1975 au GLECS, texte à apraître dans les *Comptes rendus*, tome XIX); "Les inscriptions funéraires découvertes par Firkowicz" (communication présentée le 9 mai 1975 à la Société asiatique, résumé à paraître dans le *Journal asiatique*).

des chapitres entiers. Ils possédaient une excellente mémoire et étaient une mine inépuisable de renseignements précieux. Mais, en même temps, il leur manquait les notions les plus élémentaires de la méthode scientifique moderne ainsi que l'esprit critique. Ces braves gens acceptaient de la meilleure foi du monde tout ce qu'on leur présentait et, avec la même naïveté, transmettaient tel quel tout ce qu'ils avaient appris, ce qui provoquait des sourires de commisération chez les personnes pourvues d'une véritable formation universitaire.

S'étant pris de querelle avec les supérieurs de la communauté de Loutzk, FIRKOWICZ partit en Crimée, puis à Istamboul, où il fut également maître d'école dans les communautés karaïtes. Ici encore il ne put se maintenir longtemps. Il faut dire que FIRKOWICZ avait un caractère difficile et ne pouvait rester quelque part sans se quereller avec tous et à propos de tout. Il en résulta, au cours de sa longue vie, de solides inimitiés dans tous les milieux. Après avoir fait un pèlerinage en Terre Sainte, selon une coutume toujours en honneur chez les karaïtes, FIRKOWICZ fonda à Eupatoria, qui était à l'époque le principal siège des karaïtes en Crimée, une maison d'édition afin de publier les œuvres des classiques karaïtes. Mais bientôt il cessa ce genre d'activité car il en avait trouvé une autre qui allait donner à ce modeste meunier une renommée mondiale.

En 1839 avait été fondée à Odessa la Société d'histoire et des antiquités qui avait comme président d'honneur le comte Michel VORONTZOV, gouverneur général de la Nouvelle Russie.[2] Formé par les meilleurs maîtres en Angleterre, où son père avait été ambassadeur, c'était un homme de haute culture, amateur de littérature latine, protecteur des artistes et des littérateurs. VORONTZOV possédait en Crimée plusieurs domaines où il passait une grande partie de son temps. Lors de ces séjours, les rapports entre sa famille et les karaïtes étaient fréquents et amicaux. C'est ainsi que naquit chez VORONTZOV et son entourage un réel intérêt pour les karaïtes.[3] Aussi, tout au début de son activité, le 31 janvier (12 février nouveau style) 1839, la nouvelle Société adressa aux autorités karaïtes de Crimée, dont le siège était à Eupatoria, une lettre pour leur demander des renseignements sur leur origine, leurs croyances et leur histoire. Comme l'a dit l'historien de la Crimée, le professeur V. D. SMIRNOV, de telles questions au-

---

[2] Province comprenant la Crimée et les territoires situés sur le littoral nord de la mer Noire.

[3] Sur la vie culturelle et scientifique à Odessa, sur le personnage de Vorontzov et sur les rapports entre sa famille et les karaïtes, cf. "L'affaire Firkowicz" (en préparation).

raient embarrassé n'importe qui.[4] De fait, elles embarrassèrent la communauté karaïte qui s'était comme figée au niveau de la science médiévale et qui était depuis longtemps en pleine décadence culturelle, au point d'ignorer sa propre histoire.

Ayant reçu cette lettre, Sima BOBOVITCH, le chef des karaïtes, interrogea sans succès les personnes les plus érudites. C'est alors que FIRKOWICZ fut chargé d'entreprendre des recherches de documents et de mener une enquête auprès des personnes âgées. Pour accomplir sa mission, pendant plus de trente ans, presque jusqu'à sa mort, FIRKOWICZ parcourut de nombreuses localités du Proche Orient ou d'Europe centrale et orientale qui étaient, ou avaient été, habitées par les karaïtes. Il recueillit ainsi d'énormes quantités de manuscrits, parfois plus que millénaires, des estampes reproduisant des inscriptions et d'autres documents de différents genres. On peut avoir une idée de leur volume si l'on sait qu'ils ont rempli deux grandes salles de la Bibliothèque Publique Impériale de Saint-Pétersbourg (aujourd'hui Bibliothèque Publique d'Etat M. E. SALTYKOV-CHTCHEDRIN de Leningrad). Selon les dates de leur entrée, on les divise en trois parties: première collection, deuxième collection et collection samaritaine. Quelques pierres tombales avec inscriptions sont entrées au Musée asiatique de l'Académie russe (actuellement Institut d'orientalisme de Leningrad, dépendant de l'Académie des sciences).

On ne pourra connaître le nombre exact de ces manuscrits avant l'achèvement de la mise en ordre et l'inventaire de l'ensemble. A partir de 1863, les rapports annuels publiés par le directeur de la Bibliothèque [5] ont donné de brèves notices sur les travaux de clas-

---

[4] *Sbornik starinnykh gramot i uzakonenij Rossijskoj Imperii kasatel'no prav i sostojanija russko-poddannykh karaïmov*, St.-Pétersbourg, 1890, Préface, p. VIII.

[5] *Otčet Imperatorskoj Publičnoj Biblioteki za ... god*, St.-Pétersbourg; *Imperatorskaja Publičnaja Biblioteka za sto let, 1814-1914*, St.-Pétersbourg 1914, p. 243-244, 347-349, 395, 438; *Zapiski Odesskago obščestva istorii i drevnostej* I, Odessa 1844, p. 640-649; E. M. PINNER, *Prospectus der der Odessaer Gesellschaft für Geschichte und Alterthümer gehörenden ältesten hebräischen und rabbinischen Manuscripte*, Odessa 1845; *Zapiski Imperatorskoj Akademii nauk* 15, St.-Pétersbourg, 1869, p. 252-264; *Žurnal Ministerstva narodnago prosveščenija* 178, St.-Pétersbourg 1875, p. 5-49; A. HARKAVY, H. L. STRACK, *Catalog der hebräischen Bibelhandschriften der Kaiserlichen Öffentlichen Bibliothek in St. Petersburg*, St. Petersburg-Leipzig 1875 (cité: *Catalog*); A. HARKAVY, *Opisanie samaritjanskikh rukopisej khranjaščikhsja v Imperatorskoj Publičnoj Biblioteke*, St.-Pétersbourg, 1875; idem, "Die Samaritanische Handschriftensammlung in St. Petersburg", *Russische Revue* IV, St. Petersburg, 1874, p. 74-80; K. B. STARKOVA, "Rukopisi kollekcii Firkoviča Gosudarstvennoj Publičnoj Biblioteki im. M. E. Saltykova-Ščedrina", *Pis'mennye pamjatniki Vostoka*, Annuaire 1970, Moscou 1974, p. 165-192.

sement des collections. On peut en conclure que le nombre des manuscrits (entiers ou fragmentaires) triés avant la première guerre mondiale approchait de dix mille ce qui ne représentait qu'une partie de l'ensemble. Il n'est sans doute pas exagéré de dire que, lors d'un classement définitif, ce nombre pourra atteindre une vingtaine de mille. A. HARKAVY qui, en qualité de conservateur, a étudié pendant de nombreuses années les collections FIRKOWICZ, en a rédigé un catalogue de quelque quatre mille pages. Ce manuscrit a disparu de la Bibliothèque après la Révolution russe; il paraît qu'il se trouverait actuellement en Occident. Quand verra-t-il la lumière et la verra-t-il jamais?

D'après leur genre, on peut approximativement classer les manuscrits FIRKOWICZ de la manière suivante:

I Manuscrits bibliques

Ces manuscrits constituent les exemplaires les plus nombreux, les plus précieux et, avant les récentes découvertes dans le désert de Juda, les plus anciens du monde: entre autres le fameux *Codex B 19a*, œuvre des Ben Asher, et le *Codex Babylonicus*. En plus des textes en langue originale, on y trouve également des traductions en araméen, en turc, en arabe, en persan et, probablement, en d'autres langues encore.

II Manuscrits samaritains

Ces documents, qui concernent tous les domaines, aussi bien religieux que profanes, sont uniques en leur genre, plus anciens, plus importants et plus nombreux que ceux des fonds samaritains de toutes les autres bibliothèques du monde pris ensemble.

III Ouvrages d'auteurs karaïtes et écrits divers

Ce sont des commentaires bibliques, dont beaucoup étaient inconnus ou considérés comme perdus; des ouvrages d'exégèse, de philosophie, de poésie; des *peshers* karaïtes du Xe et du XIe siècles, contenant des récits sur la situation contemporaine en Orient; des ouvrages historiques; des traités relatifs à la jurisprudence, aux sciences exactes et naturelles; des estampes ou des photographies d'inscriptions. Certains de ces ouvrages sont susceptibles d'apporter de nouvelles lumières relatives aux esséniens: ainsi, un des commentaires karaïtes du Xe siècle donne des précisions sur le dualisme dans les croyances des Fils de Sadok.

Cet aperçu préliminaire devra être complété lorsque sera enfin achevé le dépouillement des documents que FIRKOWICZ a sauvé d'une destruction certaine.

Les premières conclusions tirées de l'étude de ces collections étaient si inattendues et si contraires aux conceptions admises que certains ont été amenés à nier immédiatement l'authenticité des documents réunis par FIRKOWICZ. En effet, la première moitié du XIXe siècle, période du romantisme, fut marquée, aussi bien en Occident que dans les pays slaves, par l'apparition de plusieurs faux. Cela a provoqué, dans la deuxième moitié de ce siècle, une réaction et une attitude hypercritique des savants officiels à l'égard de toutes les découvertes faites par les chercheurs considérés comme des amateurs, ne possédant pas de titres universitaires. Cela a permis à certains milieux, inspirés par des motifs complètement extra-scientifiques, de déclencher *après la mort de Firkowicz* une campagne acharnée et bien orchestrée visant à disqualifier ses découvertes.

Au début, ces attaques furent lancées et dirigées surtout par Albert (Abraham) HARKAVY qui appartenait à une famille d'illustres savants talmudistes [6] et qui était conservateur en chef du Département des manuscrits orientaux de la Bibliothèque Publique Impériale de St.-Pétersbourg. Par malchance, c'est Daniel CHWOLSON, professeur à la Faculté des langues orientales et à l'Académie de théologie orthodoxe de St.-Pétersbourg, qui défendit FIRKOWICZ, ce qui irrita encore davantage HARKAVY. En effet, HARKAVY avait été autrefois l'élève de CHWOLSON, et celui-ci avait fait refuser sa thèse de doctorat en montrant que c'était un plagiat des travaux de Chr. M. VON FRÄHN et de Fr. B. CHARMOY.[7] HARKAVY fut donc obligé de renoncer à une chaire universitaire et de se contenter de la situation de bibliothécaire. Sans doute pour se venger, HARKAVY redoubla ses attaques contre FIRKOWICZ, afin de montrer qu'en prenant pour argent comptant les découvertes faites par celui-ci, CHWOLSON était un ignorant et un parfait idiot (selon les expressions de CHWOLSON lui-même). [8] HARKAVY ne ménageait ni injures ni humiliations à son ancien professeur.[9] Il y eut des moments où CHWOLSON, péniblement touché par ces

---

[6] *The Jewish Encyclopedia* VI, 1904, p. 234-236; S. WININGER, *Grosse jüdische National-Biographie* III, Cernâuti 1928, p. 1-2.

[7] D. CHWOLSON, *Corpus inscriptionum hebraicarum, enthaltend Grabschriften aus der Krim und andere Grab- und Inschriften in alter hebräischer Quadratschrift, sowie auch Schriftproben aus Handschriften vom IX. - XV. Jahrhundert*, St. Petersburg 1882, Vorwort, col. IX (cité: *Corpus*).

[8] CHWOLSON, *Corpus*, col. IX, 13: "Fast aus jeder Zeile seines Buches leuchtet sein Streben durch, mich als beispiellosen Ignoranten, ja selbst als Idioten darzustellen, und zwar geschieht dieses auf eine so gehässige Weise, wie dies zu thun einem gebildeten und einigermaassen anständigen Menschen unmöglich wäre".

[9] CHWOLSON, *Corpus*, col. III, IV, IX.

attaques incessantes, pensait à abandonner l'affaire pour retrouver sa tranquillité. C'est dans ces moments de découragement qu'il a laissé échapper quelques mots amers à l'adresse de FIRKOWICZ. Cette querelle scandalisa la science pendant de longues années.[10] Toutefois, vers la fin de sa vie, CHWOLSON s'est reconcilié avec HARKAVY, ce qui n'a pourtant pas empêché le nom de FIRKOWICZ d'entrer dans l'histoire comme synonyme de faussaire sans scrupule.

Pourtant il aurait fallu à FIRKOWICZ des forces herculéennes et un véritable génie pour accomplir les exploits qu'on lui attribuait.[11] On l'a accusé d'avoir fabriqué, inscrit et transporté des dizaines et même des centaines de pierres tombales dans les anciens cimetières karaïtes de Crimée, que ce soit à Théodosia, à Staryï Krim, à Eupatoria, à Mangoup et surtout à Kalé.[12] Cette dernière localité, située dans la banlieue de Bakhtchisaraï, forteresse rocheuse naturelle et autrefois imprenable, était jusqu'au début du XIXe siècle la capitale des karaïtes de Crimée. Après l'annexion du Khanat par la Russie et le changement des conditions économiques, la population émigra de Kalé vers d'autres localités, surtout à Eupatoria. L'abandon fut complet après la guerre de Crimée, et la ville est alors entièrement tombée en ruines.[13] Néanmoins, Kalé fut toujours considérée comme un centre spirituel du karaïsme. Près de la ville se trouve un vaste cimetière, très vénéré, où, jusqu'à la Révolution, on transportait même les corps des karaïtes morts dans les plus lointaines régions de Russie. Par suite de sa ressemblance avec celui de Jérusalem, ce cimetière fut appelé la *vallée de Josaphat*. On y trouve des chênes séculaires appelés "Balta tiymez" (= ceux que la hache ne peut pas toucher). Ces arbres sont l'objet d'une vénération toute particulière, et, pendant la sécheresse, on fait près d'eux des prières.[14]

---

[10] Préface de la Société Archéologique à l'édition russe du *Corpus*; Zapiski Imperatorskago Russkago Arkheologičeskago Obščestva, nouvelle série, I, 1886, Procès-verbaux, p. III.

[11] D. E. RIEHM, "Schlussbemerkungen", *Theologische Studien und Kritiken* XLVII, 1874, p. 192.

[12] A partir du XVIIe siècle appelé parfois également Tchouft-Kalé, cf.: *Žurnal Ministerstva narodnago prosveščenija* CXCII, juillet 1877, p. 103; *Evrejskaja enciklopedija* IX, col. 288.

[13] Seuls sont restés intacts: la maison qu'habitait FIRKOWICZ et dans laquelle il mourut et deux sanctuaires. C'est dans leur geniza que Firkowicz a commencé ses recherches et a découvert le *Codex Babylonicus* et le *Codex B19a*.

[14] P. S. PALLAS, *Bemerkungen auf einer Reise in die südlichen Statthalterschaften des russischen Reichs in den Jahren 1793 und 1794* II, Leipzig 1801, p. 35. C'est là une survivance d'un ancien culte des arbres que l'on considérait surtout comme dispensateurs de la pluie, culte qui est attesté dans cette région par la *Vie de Saint*

HARKAVY affirmait que FIRKOWICZ gravait des inscriptions sur des pierres tombales qui provenaient d'un ancien cimetière tatar et qu'il aurait transformées.[15] C'est une accusation insoutenable. En effet, dans le proche voisinage du cimetière de Kalé, il n'existe aucun cimetière tatar. Ensuite, HARKAVY omet ce fait: c'est que les pierres tombales des karaïtes et des tatars de Crimée se distinguent les unes des autres par leurs formes.[16] De plus, les pierres des tombeaux tatars ont, en règle générale, des dimensions beaucoup plus faibles que celles des karaïtes. D'une stèle karaïte, on peut tailler dix stèles tatares, mais même vingt pierres tatares ne donneront jamais la possibilité de fabriquer une pierre karaïte monolithe. HARKAVY est même allé jusqu'à affirmer que, pour fabriquer les pierres tombales, FIRKOWICZ se serait servi d'un dépôt de pierres taillées destinées à la construction et laissées inutilisées depuis plusieurs siècles.[17] Comment fabriquer des pierres tombales géantes, ayant souvent des dimensions supérieures à 2 mètres,[18] avec les pierres de taille destinées à la construction des maisons, cela est resté pour jamais le secret de HARKAVY.

Quoique HARKAVY ait affirmé avoir parfaitement exploré sur place le cimetière de Kalé, CHWOLSON, se basant sur les témoignages de nombreuses personnes présentes à Kalé pendant le séjour de HARKAVY et de STRACK,[19] constata que ceux-ci s'étaient contentés tout sim-

---

Cyrille. Cf.: A. BASCHMAKOFF, *Cinquante siècles d'évolution ethnique autour de la mer Noire*, Paris 1937, p. 151; FR. DVORNIK, *Les légendes de Constantin et de Méthode*, Prague 1933, p. 205-207, 370-371.

[15] A. HARKAVY, *Altjüdische Denkmäler aus der Krim* (*Mémoires de l'Académie Impériale des sciences de St.-Pétersbourg*, VIIe série, tome XXIV, n° 1), St.-Pétersbourg 1876, p. 268-269, cité: *Denkmäler*; idem, *Evrejskaja enciklopedija* IX, col. 287; A. KUNIK (Ernst-Eduard), *Tokhtamyš i Firkovič* (Annexe au volume 27 des *Zapiski Imperatorskoj Akademii nauk*), St.-Pétersbourg 1876, p. 33; CHWOLSON, *Corpus*, col. 36-38.

[16] PALLAS, *Bemerkungen*, *Album*; CHWOLSON, *Corpus*, col. 29-33, 37; P. KEPPEN, *Krymskij sbornik*, St.-Pétersbourg 1837, p. 29-35; FR. DUBOIS DE MONTPÉREUX, *Voyage au Caucase . . . et en Crimée*, *Atlas*, Neuchâtel, 1843.

[17] *Evrejskaja enciklopedija* IX, col. 287-288.

[18] CHWOLSON, *Corpus*, col. 30-32.

[19] Au début, H. STRACK a fidèlement assisté HARKAVY en attaquant violemment CHWOLSON et la mémoire de FIRKOWICZ. Ils se sont cependant vite brouillés et HARKAVY n'a pas craint d'accuser de plagiat son meilleur ami et collaborateur, STRACK. Cette accusation fut formulée pour la première fois à la séance du 27 août (8 septembre nouveau style) 1876 du IIIe Congrès international des orientalistes tenu à St.-Pétersbourg, où elle suscita un vrai scandale, et fut répétée ensuite dans plusieurs publications. A la suite de cet incident, STRACK rompit avec HARKAVY et présenta des excuses à CHWOLSON en lui avouant que s'il avait agi ainsi ce n'était que pour complaire à HARKAVY. Cf.: HARKAVY, *Denkmäler*, p. VI, 270, note; CHWOLSON, *Corpus*, col. 12-14 et notes; H. L. STRACK, *A. Firkowitsch und seine Entdeckungen*, Leipzig 1876, p. 41.

plement de deux ou trois courtes promenades à travers cet immense champ des morts.[20] D'après HARKAVY, le cimetière serait situé à 20 pas de la porte de la forteresse de Kalé,[21] tandis qu'en réalité cette distance est d'un demi kilomètre.[22] Le cimetière, dit encore HARKAVY, occupe une ancienne place destinée aux revues militaires; en réalité, il est situé sur les pentes cahoteuses d'une montagne où il n'aurait jamais été possible d'organiser une revue.[23]

Voici par contre la description du cimetière faite par CHWOLSON qui l'a étudié à fond et y a exécuté des fouilles: le cimetière de Kalé est situé sur les deux pentes assez abruptes d'une montagne peu élevée, ayant la forme d'un croissant; son terrain est presque complètement couvert par des arbres et des buissons qui empêchent de le parcourir dans sa plus grande partie. Parfois CHWOLSON était forcé de recourir à l'aide d'ouvriers pour sortir des fourrés dans lesquels il s'était aventuré. Les pierres tombales colossales sont enfoncées profondément dans la terre. Elles sont les unes sur les autres; tout est enchevêtré, couvert de buissons; les racines d'arbres ont souvent la grosseur de la main.[24] Il n'y a pas d'allées dans ce cimetière, mais un sentier étroit à peine suffisant pour laisser passer une seule personne.[25] La voie d'accès permet tout juste le passage d'une voiture légère.[26] Comment alors, dans ces conditions, peut-on parler d'un dépôt clandestin de pierres fabriquées? Quels moyens de transport et quelles équipes d'ouvriers aurait-il fallu pour déplacer même quelques pierres? Cela n'aurait pu échapper à l'attention des habitants des localités avoisinantes. Il est cependant établi et hors de doute que FIRKOWICZ procédait à ses fouilles en solitaire et n'était que rarement aidé d'un manoeuvre. Une autre affirmation de HARKAVY révèle son ignorance complète du terrain. Il dit que les pierres nouvelles, par leur apparence, ne se distinguent pas du tout des anciennes. Mais CHWOLSON a montré des dessins de pierres datant de différentes époques et qui se distinguent parfaitement entre elles au premier coup d'œil.[27] CHWOLSON raconte, comment, pendant ses fouilles, des ouvriers complètement

---

[20] CHWOLSON, *Corpus*, col. 29.
[21] HARKAVY, *Denkmäler*, p. 268; CHWOLSON, *Corpus*, col. 35.
[22] CHWOLSON, *Corpus*, col. 35-36.
[23] CHWOLSON, *Corpus*, col. 22-35.
[24] CHWOLSON, *Corpus*, col. 22, 26, 37, 38.
[25] CHWOLSON, *Corpus*, col. 22.
[26] CHWOLSON, *Corpus*, col. 37-38.
[27] D. CHWOLSON, *Achtzehn hebräische Grabschriften aus der Krim* (*Mémoires de l'Académie Impériale des sciences de St.-Pétersbourg*, VIIe série, tome IX, n° 7), St.-Pétersbourg 1865, p. 6-8; idem, *Corpus*, col. 29-33.

analphabètes distinguaient eux-mêmes facilement les objets intéres-
sants.[28]

Ceux qui ont attaqué FIRKOWICZ ne se sont jamais résolus à soumettre ces pierres à un examen sérieux dans des laboratoires de minéra-
logie. Cependant, B. DORN de l'Académie russe, les ayant étudiées
d'un point de vue archéologique et ayant trouvé que leur aspect ne
laissait place à aucun doute quant à leur anthenticité, poussa la
prudence jusqu'à demander à un spécialiste, Ad. GOEBEL, une étude
minéralogique et pétrographique. Bien que les résultats aient été
publiés dans le *Bulletin de l'Académie de St.-Pétersbourg*,[29] on les a
passés sous silence.[30] Or, l'étude de GOEBEL donne la possibilité de
distinguer les inscriptions anciennes de celles qu'on aurait gravées
récemment. Aussi, est-on autorisé à se demander: pourquoi cette
méthode précise et objective de l'examen de l'authenticité a-t-elle
été négligée par les professeurs renommés et les illustres académiciens
qui se sont acharnés contre FIRKOWICZ ? Pourquoi toute leur ar-
gumentation repose-t-elle sur de pures spéculations au lieu de prendre
pour base des réalités objectives ?

Une des premières découvertes faites par FIRKOWICZ à Kalé fut la
pierre tombale d'Isaac Sangari [31] qui, au VIIIe siècle, convertit au
karaïsme le roi khazar Bulan, et avec lui une branche de la dynastie
et une partie du peuple khazar. Quand la nouvelle de cette découverte est parvenue à S. J. L. RAPOPORT, éditeur de la revue *Kerem
Hemed* à Prague, celui-ci s'adressa à B. STERN, maître à l'école juive
d'Odessa, en l'invitant à vérifier la découverte sur place. La Société
d'histoire et des antiquités d'Odessa a donné, en effet, à STERN la
mission d'aller en Crimée pour y effectuer cette vérification. Dans
son compte rendu, STERN a donné un avis favorable et a même men-
tionné plusieurs autres pierres anciennes inconnues de FIRKOWICZ,

---

[28] CHWOLSON, *Corpus*, col. 29-30.

[29] *Bulletin de l'Académie Impériale des sciences de St.-Pétersbourg* VII 1864, p. 378-
391; *Mélanges asiatiques* V, St.-Pétersbourg 1868, p. 128-146. Cf. aussi CHWOLSON,
Achtzehn hebräische Grabschriften, p. 8-9.

[30] Seul HARKAVY s'est référé une fois à l'étude de GOEBEL en détachant toutefois
la citation de son contexte. Cela donne une conclusion contraire à celle de GOEBEL.
Cf.: HARKAVY, *Denkmäler*, p. 288.

[31] Limité par la place, nous ne reprenons pas ici le problème de la pierre tombale
de Sangari et renvoyons à nos études précédentes: "Le roi Bulan et le problème
de la conversion des Khazars", *Ephemerides theologicae lovanienses* 33, 1957, p. 68-
76; "Les Khazars, problèmes et controverses", *Revue de l'histoire des religions*
CLII, 1957, p. 174-221; "Où la conversion du roi khazar Bulan a-t-elle eu lieu?",
Hommages à André Dupont-Sommer, Paris, 1971, p. 523-538.

notamment celle de Sangarite, vraisemblablement la femme de Sangari.

Evidemment, HARKAVY ne tarda pas à mettre en doute l'authenticité de la pierre tombale de Sangarite. Son argument est que l'inscription ne contient qu'un seul mot (forme féminine de Sangari) sans aucun prénom.[32] Cependant, cet argument peut être retourné contre son auteur. En effet, par le fait de son succès dans la conversion d'un roi, Isaac Sangari devint tellement célèbre que son surnom seul suffisait à l'identifier et à distinguer sa femme. Si FIRKOWICZ a vraiment fabriqué cette inscription, pourquoi n'est-il pas allé jusqu'au bout, pourquoi s'est-il arrêté à mi-chemin en laissant ainsi la possibilité de douter de son authenticité?

Par ailleurs, un fait a paru extrêmement suspect à HARKAVY, à savoir que STERN n'a présenté son compte rendu ni à RAPOPORT ni à une revue juive, mais à la Société d'Odessa qui l'a publié dans ses *Memoires*.[33] Mais à qui un chargé de mission [34] doit-il présenter son rapport sinon à l'institution qui lui a confié une telle mission?

L'authenticité des pierres de Sangari et de Sangarite fut aussi combattue par HARKAVY pour une autre raison: il avait une théorie selon laquelle il n'y aurait pas à Kalé de pierres authentiques antérieures au XIIIe siècle. Et même celles-ci ne pouvaient, selon lui, qu'avoir été apportées au XVIIe siècle par des karaïtes qui, en venant s'installer à Kalé, se seraient déplacés avec des pierres tombales de leurs ancêtres dans leurs bagages! [35] Cependant, après la mort de FIRKO-WICZ, CHWOLSON effectua pendant quelques semaines des fouilles à Kalé. Il travailla seul, aidé par un de ses fils et par quelques manœuvres sans disposer des moyens techniques nécessaires. Même dans ces conditions, n'ayant exploité qu'une partie infime de cet immense champ des morts, il a pu découvrir plusieurs dizaines de pierres inconnues de FIRKOWICZ et ayant des dates très antérieures au début du XIIIe siècle. CHWOLSON en a d'ailleurs trouvé d'autres, encore plus anciennes, et même, selon lui, allant parfois jusqu'au IIIe siècle de l'ère chrétienne. Il a même trouvé une pierre non

---

[32] HARKAVY, *Denkmäler*, p. 172-182.

[33] *Zapiski odesskago obščestva istorii i drevnostej* I, Odessa 1844, col. 648-649.

[34] Cette mission de STERN a donné l'occasion à HARKAVY de mettre en doute "le comportement loyal de Stern" et à STRACK de jeter une suspicion sur les rapports de Stern avec les karaïtes. Cf. HARKAVY, *Denkmäler*, p. 126; STRACK, *A. Firkowitsch*, p. 9, note 9.

[35] HARKAVY, *Denkmäler*, p. 268-269; CHWOLSON, *Corpus*, col. 35. On peut se demander d'ailleurs pourquoi les karaïtes auraient attaché plus d'importance aux pierres tombales qu'aux restes de leurs défunts qui reposaient sous ces pierres.

datée que, pour des raisons paléographiques, il attribu au IIᵉ siècle de l'ère chrétienne.[36]

Selon HARKAVY, les dates des pierres antérieures au xiiiᵉ siècle auraient été transformées par FIRKOWICZ à partir de dates plus récentes. Mais, l'authenticité des dates peut être vérifiée si le jour de la semaine figure dans le texte, car, dans le cas d'une transformation de date, les jours de la semaine ne coïncideraient qu'exceptionnellement. En 1912, Yu. D. KOKIZOV a composé les tables chronologiques pour 2200 ans d'après le calendrier karaïte (de l'année 240 à l'année 2440 de l'ère chrétienne). A titre d'essai, on a vérifié quelques dizaines de dates qui, à l'exception de 2 ou 3 cas incertains, donnaient des résultats complètement en accord avec les prévisions contenues dans ces tables.[37] Bien que les accusateurs de FIRKOWICZ aient souvent déclaré que la rédaction de telles tables devrait le confondre complètement, ils ont passé sous silence les travaux de KOKIZOV. En outre, KOKIZOV a attiré l'attention sur les particularités de la computation karaïte qui peuvent expliquer plusieurs points douteux de datation. Les spécialistes des problèmes de calendrier devraient approfondir ces questions afin d'établir des critères d'authenticité tout à fait sûrs. De façon générale, tous les critères employés jusqu'ici ont d'ailleurs été établis autoritairement par les seuls accusateurs afin, et seulement afin, d'accabler davantage Firkowicz. Tous ces critères doivent donc être réexaminés scientifiquement.

Ainsi, HARKAVY met en doute toute inscription funéraire contenant le mot *est mort* (מת); d'après lui c'est une expression "cynique et prosaïque".[38] Or CHWOLSON a trouvé dans différents coins du monde une dizaine d'inscriptions semblables, dont les dates s'échelonnent entre le VIIème et le IXème siècles. Composées dans un style élégant et savant, elles contiennent précisément cette expression suspecte.

---

[36] CHWOLSON, *Corpus*, col. 243-267.

[37] YU. D. KOKIZOV, *Karaimskij kalendar' na 2200 let*, St.-Pétersbourg 1912; idem, *44 nadgrobnykh pamjatnika*, St.-Pétersbourg 1910; "V zaščitu pamjati Firkoviča", *Karaimskaja žizn'* VII, Moscou 1911, p. 52-62; idem, "Novye dokazatel'stva protiv starykh obvinenij", même revue 1, 1911, p. 40-53; idem "Otvet Evrejskoj starine", même revue XII, 1912, p. 50-53; D. KOKIZOV, *Čemakh David*, St.-Pétersbourg, 1897. Cf. aussi: B. HOCHSTÄDTER, "Chronologische Bemerkungen über die durch Herrn A. Neubauer veröffentlichten Firkowitz'schen Abdrücke von alten hebräischen Grabinschriften aus der Krim", *Ben Chananja* VII, Szegedin, 1864, p. 851-855, 898-901, 984-986, 1013-1014; KUNIK, *Tokhtamyš i Firkovič*, p. 59; T. S. LEVI-BABOVIČ, *Tri stranički*, Sébastopol 1928, p. 31-44; CHWOLSON, *Corpus*, col. 283-286, 373-374; CHWOLSON, *Achtzehn hebräische Grabschriften*, p. 5.

[38] HARKAVY, *Denkmäler*, p. 133, 252.

Mais si *est mort* est "cynique et prosaïque", une autre expression est pour HARKAVY "incorrecte", une troisième "biblique" ou "trop artificielle pour des temps si reculés". Comment alors, nous demandons-nous avec CHWOLSON,[39] ces pauvres gens auraient-ils dû désigner la fin de notre existence terrestre pour satisfaire aux exigences de HARKAVY?

HARKAVY déclarait faux les renseignements que l'on peut tirer des documents découverts par FIRKOWICZ, s'ils ne sont pas confirmés par ailleurs. Et si le renseignement concorde avec d'autres sources, il est évident pour HARKAVY que FIRKOWICZ l'a fabriqué en se servant de celles-ci. En réalité, pour utiliser ces sources et même pour connaître leur existence, une bonne connaissance des langues classiques anciennes et des langues occidentales modernes était indispensable, ce qui n'était absolument pas le cas pour FIRKOWICZ: il ne connaissait même pas bien le russe.[40] Dans ses accusations, HARKAVY se servait de méthodes qui auraient dû éveiller la suspicion, même chez des personnes peu critiques. Ainsi, formule-t-il une accusation dans son catalogue [41] à la page 39 et promet d'en apporter les preuves à la page 42. Puis, à la page 42, il répète la même accusation en renvoyant pour les preuves à la page 39. Parfois la façon de procéder est même plus compliquée: la page XXI renvoie à la page 141, 141 à 109 et 109 de nouveau à 141. Le lecteur s'y perd finalement, mais le climat de méfiance est instauré, ce qui est le but de HARKAVY. Souvent même HARKAVY ne se donne pas autant de peine. Il écrit tout simplement: "cela est pour moi douteux", "cela me semble être faux" ou "c'est faux" et cette affirmation doit suffire pour clore toute discussion.[42]

HARKAVY use encore d'un autre argument contre FIRKOWICZ. Comme on le sait, les encres qui ont servi à la confection des manuscrits anciens ont souvent pâli. Or, à l'époque, on ne disposait pas encore de moyens perfectionnés tels que la photographie et les rayons spéciaux; on se servait de certaines solutions que l'on étendait sur les endroits illisibles. FIRKOWICZ faisait publiquement un large usage de ces produits.[43] Il n'était du reste pas le seul. C'est ainsi que sur la demande de CHWOLSON, A. A. MENCHOUTKIN, professeur de chimie à St.-Pétersbourg, utilisait le même procédé pour rendre lisibles certains

---

[39] CHWOLSON, *Corpus*, col. 280, 468-469.
[40] CHWOLSON, *Corpus*, col. 6.
[41] A. HARKAVY, H. L. STRACK, *Catalog der hebräischen Bibelhandschriften*; CHWOLSON, *Corpus*, p. 203-204.
[42] *Catalog*, p. 30, 79, 85, 93, 126, 230, 239; CHWOLSON, *Corpus*, col. 193, 280.
[43] CHWOLSON, *Corpus*, col. 510.

passages.[44] Les taches laissées par les produits révélateurs sur les manuscrits ont donné à HARKAVY une excellente occasion de mettre en doute l'authenticité des passages qui ne lui convenaient pas [45] en acceptant cependant ceux qui paraissaient devoir lui servir, alors même qu'ils portaient des marques analogues.[46]

Il ne faut pas non plus oublier que les manuscrits de FIRKOWICZ ne lui venaient pas directement de l'atelier des scribes, mais qu'ils avaient derrière eux un passé parfois millénaire, qu'ils avaient été lus par plusieurs générations, corrigés, annotés, usés, frottés, froissés et enfin déposés dans les genizas, où, évidemment, ils n'étaient pas protégés. Comment donc s'étonner qu'ils soient parfois tachés, raturés, déchirés, etc.? Les examens effectués récemment avec des moyens modernes ont révélé de nombreuses ratures et modifications également dans les manuscrits samaritains de FIRKOWICZ. Faut-il en rejeter sur lui la responsabilité? Quel intérêt aurait-il eu à agir ainsi?

Des ratures faites à l'époque moderne ne sont pas non plus exclues, mais il faut établir qui les a faites et dans quel but. Un exemple de telles modifications intentionnelles est très instructif et donne à réfléchir. Pendant son dernier voyage en Orient, FIRKOWICZ trouva en Egypte un manuscrit qui contenait la version longue de ce qu'on appelle la *Lettre du roi khazar Joseph*. CHWOLSON, qui a examiné soigneusement ce manuscrit, l'a reconnu absolument authentique. Une autorité aussi compétente en la matière que P. KAHLE le considère comme n'étant pas postérieur au XIIe siècle.[47] Le document en question contient des données sur la géographie de l'Etat khazar et, entre autres, mentionne la localité de Mangoup (מאנגוף). L'apparition de ce vocable dans un document aussi ancien était très gênante pour HARKAVY car il affirmait que cette ville ne portait pas ce nom avant l'invasion mongole (XIIIe siècle) et, sur cette base, avait déclaré faux tous les textes anciens contenant le nom de Mangoup.[48]

En 1875, HARKAVY a publié la *Lettre khazare* dans une traduction

---

[44] CHWOLSON, *Corpus*, col. 511.

[45] Ainsi, par exemple, HARKAVY déclara falsifié un passage taché d'un certain manuscrit. Le passage en question ne lui convenait pas, car il prouvait que la famille des massorètes Ben Asher était karaïte; il déclara tout simplement que c'était une "invention de Firkowicz". Cf. *Catalog*, p. 141, n° 107. Pour l'origine de la famille Ben Asher voir la *Revue biblique* LXXVIII, 1966, p. 531-551.

[46] C'est ainsi que H. GRÉGOIRE a remarqué à juste titre en 1937 que HARKAVY savait s'arrêter à temps quand il y avait intérêt. Cf. *Byzantion* XII, 1937, p. 235.

[47] *Byzantion* XII, 1937, p. 740.

[48] *Catalog*, p. 10.

allemande[49] et a fait remarquer que la lettre *pe* serait une modi-
fication de la lettre *ṭet* (ט). En 1879, HARKAVY a publié l'original
hébreu [50] dans lequel ce nom figure déjà sous la forme Mankhoup
(מאנכופ) avec *pe* ordinaire (פ). CHWOLSON avait eu le manuscrit
entre les mains en 1870 et, le 1ᵉʳ juillet (19 juin ancien style) il en
avait préparé une copie exacte. Après lecture de l'édition faite par
HARKAVY en 1879, CHWOLSON s'est rendu à la Bibliothèque Publique
et a demandé à voir le manuscrit. On ne l'a pas trouvé à sa place habi-
tuelle, mais dans le tiroir du bureau de HARKAVY. CHWOLSON s'est
reporté au passage en question, et à son grand étonnement, il trouva
que celui-ci de toute évidence avait fait l'objet d'un grattage et que
le nom de Mankhoup (מאנכופ) avait été substitué à celui de Mangoup
(מאנגופ), et, au surplus écrit avec une encre différente. Qui donc
pouvait avoir intérêt à faire mettre en doute l'authenticité de ce document par une transformation aussi grossière? Est-ce FIRKOWICZ,
qui depuis plusieurs années était déjà dans la tombe? Rappelons ce que
HARKAVY a écrit au sujet de ce manuscrit, en 1875, *après la mort de
Firkowicz*, dans un rapport officiel publié dans le *Journal officiel* du
Ministère de l'Instruction Publique (que nous citons mot à mot):
". . . je considère nécessaire de remarquer que le manuscrit en question aussi bien du point de vue de son aspect extérieur que de celui
de son contenu porte en lui tous les signes d'une grande ancienneté
et ne donne pas le moindre prétexte à des doutes ni à des soupçons".[51]

Une accusation tellement grave formulée par le savant renommé
et l'homme de moralité impeccable que fut CHWOLSON,[52] publiée
en allemand sous l'égide de la Faculté des langues orientales de St.-
Pétersbourg[53] et en russe sous l'égide de la Société Impériale Archéo-

---

[49] *Russische Revue* VI, 1875, p. 87.
[50] Annexe N° 8 à la revue *Hameliz*, 1879, p. 165 et suivantes. Le *pe* final (ף)
ne convenait pas à HARKAVY, car, selon la théorie qu'il avançait, מנגופ avec un *pe*
ordinaire (פ) est une orthographe karaïte tardive. Cf. *Catalog*, p. 10 et 54.
[51] *Žurnal Ministerstva narodnago prosveščenija* 178, mars 1875, p. 39. Pour éviter
tout malentendu, nous tenons à préciser que nous soutenons l'ancienneté et
l'authenticité du manuscrit et non pas l'authenticité des faits que son texte relate.
En effet, ce texte fut rédigé à des fins apologétiques et complété au cours des
siècles par plusieurs interpolations tendancieuses. Il est possible que l'auteur du
texte primitif de la *Lettre* ait utilisé quelques ouvrages authentiques relatifs aux
Khazars. Cependant tout fut ensuite noyé par de nombreuses additions tendancieuses. Aussi, doit-on apporter un réel esprit critique pour bien utiliser un tel
document.
[52] S. WININGER, *Grosse jüdische National-Biographie* I, Cernăuti 1925, p. 554-557.
[53] CHWOLSON, *Corpus*, col. 519-522.

logique Russe,[54] aurait dû normalement disqualifier n'importe qui, et plus encore un bibliothécaire à qui la conservation des manuscrits était confiée. Cependant tout cet épisode est passé inaperçu. Aucune enquête n'a été ouverte ni aucune sanction prise contre HARKAVY qui, jusqu'à la fin de sa vie, est resté seul maître des collections FIRKOWICZ. Pourquoi, dans toute cette affaire, faisait-on deux poids et deux mesures? D'une part, la moindre suspicion suffisait pour condamner sans appel le petit meunier, d'autre part de graves méfaits imputés à une personne ayant fait des études supérieures dans les écoles modernes, chargée de fonctions importantes et faisant partie des hautes sociétés scientifiques, n'étaient pas relevés.

Aussi, est-on autorisé à se demander: combien d'autres textes, gênants pour lui, HARKAVY a-t-il mutilés ou, tout simplement, détruits dans cette masse de papiers non inventoriés, non catalogués, dont le nombre, même approximatif, n'est connu de personne? Pour effectuer de telles manipulations, HARKAVY avait toute facilité, ses fonctions lui donnant la responsabilité, sans aucun contrôle, des collections FIRKOWICZ.

Qu'une telle destruction fût non seulement possible, mais ait eu effectivement lieu, est prouvé dans le cas d'un certain Ephraïm DEINARD. Ce pauvre garçon, originaire de Courlande, était venu de sa bourgade natale de Sasmaken tenter sa chance en Crimée. Par pitié, FIRKOWICZ l'hébergea dans sa maison. DEINARD lui servit d'homme à tout faire allant même jusqu'à remplir les fonctions de secrétaire, si l'on peut dire, car FIRKOWICZ ne connaissait même pas correctement le russe.[55] Bien que n'étant que serviteur, DEINARD était cependant considéré comme faisant presque partie de la famille. Lorsque, *après la mort de Firkowicz*, la campagne contre sa mémoire a commencé, DEINARD s'est dépêché d'y apporter sa contribution en publiant toute une série de libelles, dans lesquels il accusait son bienfaiteur de tous les crimes imaginables, y compris d'assassinat dans sa famille. Cette activité de DEINARD a provoqué du dégoût même chez certains de ses coreligionnaires, comme par exemple M. KAHAN, qui lui a consacré un article sous le titre significatif "Le vautour sur les cadavres".[56]

DEINARD a détruit un texte absolument authentique [57] qui mention-

---

[54] D. CHWOLSON, *Sbornik evrejskikh nadpisej, soderžaščij nadgrobnyja nadpisi iz Kryma i nadgrobnyja i drugija nadpisi iz inykh mest*, Sanktpeterburg 1884, col. 499-502.

[55] Cf. ci-dessus, p. 207, note 40.

[56] M. H. KAGAN, "hʿiṭ ʾl hfgrim", *Meerev ad orev I*, Vilno 1904, p. 281-286.

[57] CHWOLSON, *Corpus*, col. 517 et suivantes. Ce document n'ayant jamais appartenu à FIRKOWICZ, il n'était pas possible de mettre en doute son authenticité

nait deux villes qui seraient situées sur le littoral nord-est de la mer
Noire: l'une Matarkha (probablement l'actuelle Taman') dont la
communauté utilisait une ère particulière, et l'autre Sefarad (probablement identique à l'actuelle Kertch'). Cela a permis d'ajouter encore
deux accusations: FIRKOWICZ aurait inventé (on n'expliquait pas
dans quel but) l'existence, d'une part, d'une ère inconnue par ailleurs,
et, d'autre part, l'existence en Crimée d'un toponyme qui est propre
à l'Espagne.[58] On a même trouvé la source où FIRKOWICZ aurait
puisé ce renseignement. Ce serait un passage de Saint Jérôme.[59]
Mais pour cela on attribuait à FIRKOWICZ une connaissance du latin
qui lui manquait complètement.[60] Pourtant le fait que le nom de
Sefarad désigne l'Espagne ne peut pas l'empêcher de paraître également en Crimée. Les cas de toponymes parallèles ne sont pas rares. Par
exemple, un autre nom de l'Espagne, à savoir Ibérie, était appliqué
depuis les temps anciens et est encore appliqué à un pays voisin de la
Crimée, la Géorgie.[61]

Le sommet de l'activité de DEINARD fut la fabrication d'une lettre
qu'il a attribuée à FIRKOWICZ. Dans cette lettre, celui-ci, avant même
de commencer ses recherches, aurait dressé un plan détaillé des "falsifications" qu'il avait l'intention de commettre au cours des années à
venir. Cet apocryphe est devenu la pierre angulaire des accusations
contre FIRKOWICZ et STERN, considéré comme son complice. Or
DEINARD n'a jamais présenté le texte original, qui aurait dû être en
karaïte,[62] mais seulement deux traductions (sensiblement différentes
entre elles) en hébreu.[63] Il a donné deux versions (en désaccord
évident entre elles) de la manière dont cette lettre serait venue en sa
possession.[64] Mais ce qui confond définitivement Deinard, c'est la

---

sous prétexte que celui-ci l'avait falsifié. Pour d'autres altérations de la vérité
dans les témoignages de DEINARD, cf. *Corpus*, col. 522-524, note.

[58] HARKAVY, *Catalog*, p. 35, 289; idem, *Denkmäler*, p. 37-39.

[59] "Ubi nos posuimus *Bosphorum*, in Hebraico habet SAPHARAD (ספרד)".
Cf. "S. Eusebii Hieronymi Commentariorum in Abdiam prophetam liber unus",
J.-P. MIGNE, *Patrologia* XXV, Paris 1845, col. 1115.

[60] Voir ci-dessus, p. 207, note 40.

[61] Un autre pays du Caucase est également désigné par deux noms: *Azerbaïdjan*
et *Albanie*.

[62] La langue karaïte est un dialecte turc archaïque. DEINARD n'étant pas lui-
même karaïte était incapable de rédiger quoique ce soit dans cette langue.

[63] Traduit de l'hébreu en allemand et publié par H. STRACK, *A. Firkowitsch und
seine Entdeckungen*, Leipzig 1876, p. 16 et suivantes; E. DEINARD, *Massa Krim*,
Varsovie 1878, p. 20-40.

[64] STRACK, *A. Firkowitsch*, p. 16; CHWOLSON, *Corpus*, col. 524; DEINARD,
Massa Krim, p. 2, p. 20, note.

date qu'il a donnée à son œuvre. Etant trop sûr de lui et sans réfléchir, il a choisi une date de plusieurs mois antérieure à celle où la lettre de la Société d'Odessa, qui aurait dû provoquer la réaction de FIRKOWICZ et être à l'origine de sa lettre, est parvenue à Eupatoria.

Ce n'est pas contre FIRKOWICZ seul que HARKAVY s'est acharné, mais contre l'ensemble des karaïtes. Ces tendances anti-karaïtes, HARKAVY les expose tout à fait franchement dans son article de l'édition russe de la *Jewish Encyclopaedia* [65] qui est comme le résumé de toute son activité anti-karaïte (dans laquelle FIRKOWICZ n'était qu'un prétexte) et qui révèle les raisons trop évidentes qui inspirent cette campagne diffamatoire. En effet, les découvertes de FIRKOWICZ mettent en relief l'importance des doctrines karaïtes et le rôle que le karaïsme a joué dans l'histoire, en particulier dans l'histoire religieuse et culturelle. Cela ne pouvait être aucunement admis. En compromettant FIRKOWICZ, on cherchait dès le début et on cherche toujours à compromettre du même coup l'ensemble des karaïtes.

Pour expliquer les motifs de ces prétendues falsifications, on a accusé FIRKOWICZ d'avoir voulu tirer un bénéfice matériel de ses découvertes et d'avoir voulu élever la position sociale des karaïtes afin d'obtenir pour eux la plénitude des droits civiques ainsi qu'une situation privilégiée dans l'Empire Russe.[66] Or, quelle était en réalité la situation juridique des karaïtes en Russie au moment où FIRKOWICZ commençait ses recherches? Les deux groupes de karaïtes européens, celui de Crimée et celui de Lituanie et de Pologne, se sont trouvés presque simultanément et presqu'entièrement sous l'égide de l'Empire russe, pendant le règne de Catherine II, à la fin du XVIIIe siècle, par suite de l'annexion du Khanat de Crimée, d'une part, et des partages de la Pologne et de la Lituanie, d'autre part. [67] Dans le *Statesman's Handbook for Russia*, publication officielle du Comité des ministres, nous lisons à leur sujet: "... les karaïtes, qui sont un élément très utile et très laborieux, jouissaient, à partir de l'époque de Catherine II, de tous les droits qui appartiennent aux sujets russes d'origine".[68]

Une telle situation résultait du "Règlement", sorte de loi fonda-

---

[65] *Evrejskaja enciklopedija* IX, col. 285-290.

[66] KUNIK, *Tokhtamyš i Firkovič*, p. 17, 19-20, 22; HARKAVY, *Denkmäler*, p. 95, 210; STRACK, *A. Firkowitsch*, p. 39; HARKAVY-STRACK, *Catalog*, p. XXII.

[67] Quelques communautés en Galicie se sont trouvées sous la domination autrichienne. Cf. *Zeitschrift für Ostforschung* VI, 1957, p. 48.

[68] *Statesman's Handbook for Russia*, edited by the Chancery of the Committee of Ministers, St. Petersburg 1896, I, p. 48.

mentale promulguée par Pierre le Grand le 28 février 1727 et qui statuait que dans les provinces nouvellement acquises par la Russie, pour établir la situation juridique de chaque peuple, on devait tenir compte des privilèges dont il jouissait sous le pouvoir précédent.[69]

Quelle était donc la situation des karaïtes sous les pouvoirs qui ont précédé celui de la Russie? En Crimée, ils appartenaient à la classe privilégiée des tarkhans et gardaient entre leurs mains une puissante forteresse, Kalé, reste d'une principauté karaïte qui, ayant reconnu la souveraineté du Khanat, avait conservé une large autonomie. La garnison et le commandant de cette forteresse étaient toujours karaïtes; lors de son séjour en Crimée de 1666, le fameux voyageur turc Evliya Çelebi fut étonné et indigné que, dans le centre d'un pays musulman, tout près de sa capitale, des "infidèles" possèdent une telle puissance. Ch. Peysonnel, consul de France près du Khan de Crimée au XVIIIème siècle, fait état d'une "infinité de privilèges" dont les karaïtes jouissent dans cet Etat.[70] En Lituanie et en Pologne, les karaïtes qui appartenaient à la noblesse partageaient tous les droits de cette classe: possession de biens fonciers, postes dans l'administration d'Etat, régiment karaïte dans l'armée lituanienne. Les karaïtes de la classe bourgeoise étaient régis par la législation dite de Magdebourg. Cette législation, établie au Moyen Age d'après les privilèges accordés à cette ville, était très appréciée en Europe centrale et orientale. En règle générale, on ne l'accordait qu'aux catholiques, rarement aux orthodoxes. Le cas des karaïtes est le seul connu où la législation de Magdebourg ait été accordée à des non-chrétiens. Les karaïtes bourgeois étaient administrés par leur chef, nommé par le roi et responsable devant lui seul. Les litiges entre les karaïtes et les chrétiens étaient jugés en commun par ce chef et par le voïvode (gouveneur de province).[71] C'est donc en conformité avec ces lois que, comme l'écrit l'historien de la Crimée, V. D. Smirnov, professeur à la Faculté des langues orientales de Saint-Pétersbourg, "...le Gouvernement Impérial russe considérait les karaïtes, à partir du moment de leur inclusion dans l'Empire russe, comme étant égaux en droits avec tous les autres citoyens de cet empire et jouissant de la même protection

[69] *Polnoe sobranie zakonov Rossijskoj Imperii* VI, St.-Pétersbourg 1830, p. 150-151.

[70] *Observations historiques et géographiques, sur les peuples barbares qui ont habité les bords du Danube & du Pont-Euxin.* Par M. de Peyssonnel, ci-devant Consul pour Sa Majesté auprès du Khan des Tartares, Paris 1765, p. 106.

[71] Pour la situation juridique des karaïtes en Lituanie et en Pologne, cf. *Zeitschrift der Deutschen Morgenländischen Gesellschaft* 102, 1952, p. 215-228; *Zeitschrift für Ostforschung* VI, 1957, p. 24-54.

des lois communes".[72] Mieux encore dans les années 1827-28, c'est-
à-dire douze ans avant que FIRKOWICZ ait commencé ses recherches,
les karaïtes de Russie étaient déjà assimilés à la classe privilégiée: on les
avait dispensés, comme les autres classes supérieures de la population,
du devoir de fournir des recrues, ce qui, à l'époque, était extrêmement
pénible, du fait que le service militaire durait 25 ans. Pourquoi donc
eut-il fallu que les karaïtes aient cherché à enfoncer une porte ouverte et
à demander ce qu'ils possédaient déjà légitimement et à un degré
supérieur à ce qu'on pouvait souhaiter?

D'ailleurs, cette situation est reconnue par DEINARD lui-même.
Dans le pamphlet où il accuse FIRKOWICZ et les karaïtes, en général,
de tous les méfaits possibles, il termine son "exposé" en s'adressant
au Gouvernement russe et en exprimant le vœu que ses "révélations"
l'incitent à *supprimer* les droits civiques des karaïtes, car, dit-il, ce sont
"des Tatars, des Tsiganes, des Mongols".[73]

S'ils ne pouvaient pas atteindre leur but et supprimer les droits
civiques des karaïtes, HARKAVY et ceux qui le suivaient espéraient tout
au moins les ridiculiser et les compromettre aux yeux de l'opinion
publique. Et de nos jours encore, on continue de se servir du nom de
FIRKOWICZ comme d'un moyen infaillible pour combattre les karaïtes et exciter contre eux d'autres peuples. Ainsi, par exemple, tout
récemment encore, dans le périodique "Alef-Bet" que l'administration
israélienne publie à Naplouse pour les samaritains, on menait toute
une campagne contre FIRKOWICZ (et contre les karaïtes en général)
en l'accusant d'avoir privé les samaritains de leurs manuscrits anciens.

Bien que FIRKOWICZ et ses collections semblent être ainsi discré-
dités, cela n'empêche pas les accusateurs de se servir des collections
qu'il a réunies quand celles-ci leur conviennent. On déclare alors tout
simplement: il est vrai que le document en question provient d'une
source suspecte, mais il faut espérer que précisément dans ce cas
la main du "faussaire" ne l'a pas touché.[74]

Le problème FIRKOWICZ est devenu une arme classique pour tous
ceux qui cherchent à combattre les karaïtes; on s'en sert même quand
il s'agit de questions qui ne peuvent avoir aucun rapport ni avec sa
personne ni avec ses découvertes. La méthode est simple et infaillible:
quand on n'a aucun argument pour faire tomber un témoignage favo-

---

[72] *Sbornik starinnykh gramot i uzakonenij Rossijskoj Imperii kasatel'no prav i sostojanija russko-poddannykh karaïmov*, St.-Pétersbourg 1890, Préface, p. XIX.
[73] DEINARD, *Massa Krim*, p. 2, 37, 58-61, 63, 76, 78.
[74] *Revue biblique*, LXXIII, 1966, p. 547, note 71.

rable aux karaïtes, on évoque alors le spectre de "Firkowicz, le faus-saire, l'homme sans scrupule. . . " . L'effet est immédiat. Comme la culpabilité de Firkowicz est devenue un axiome indiscutable, on s'acharne sur cette brebis galeuse, on la condamne une fois de plus, mais surtout, on oublie le point de départ du débat.

On peut se poser une question légitime: pourquoi les karaïtes ne se sont-ils pas défendus et ont-ils permis le développement de toute cette campagne? Pour y répondre, il faut se rendre compte de la situation culturelle du karaïsme à cette époque. Ce qu'il faut bien dire, c'est que le xixe siècle est déjà une époque de décadence évidente pour les kara-ites, d'oubli total de leur propre passé et d'absence complète d'intérêt pour tout ce qui aurait dû les toucher de près. Au début du xixe siècle, toute l'instruction commençait et se terminait, chez les karaïtes, dans les écoles paroissiales, où l'on enseignait encore selon des méthodes médiévales. Dans la deuxième moitié du xixe siècle, un intérêt pour l'instruction moderne s'éveille chez les karaïtes. Le nombre des gens qui obtiennent des diplômes universitaires augmente de plus en plus, mais ils s'intéressent de moins en moins aux problèmes de leur milieu d'origine, l'abandonnant à son propre sort. On peut compter sur les doigts de la main les cas où les karaïtes ont essayé de prendre la parole dans la discussion relative au problème Firkowicz. Tous ces essais naïfs, faits sans connaître même la bibliographie élé-mentaire et publiés en province, sont passés complètement inaperçus.

Quand en 1877 Chwolson est arrivé en Crimée, il fut frappé par le manque absolu de toute compréhension et d'intérêt quelconque pour l'affaire Firkowicz de la part de la masse et des chefs karaïtes. Il lui a fallu beaucoup de peine pour faire comprendre aux responsables de la communauté que l'action organisée contre Firkowicz touchait à l'honneur de tous les karaïtes. "Puisqu'on accuse Firkowicz, que ses enfants le défendent donc" — telle était leur réaction.[75] Il y avait même pire: Sultanski, prêtre karaïte de Sébastopol, d'ailleurs proche parent de Firkowicz, nourrissait, comme son père l'avait fait, une forte inimitié à l'égard de celui-ci. Il s'est montré fort mécontent des recherches de Chwolson qui auraient pu réhabiliter son parent et ne cachait pas qu'un échec lui aurait fait plaisir.

Nous ferons une dernière remarque: si l'on revient constamment sur cette affaire, si les accusations sont sans cesse reprises, c'est qu'on veut à tout prix compromettre définitivement l'œuvre de Firkowicz.

---

[75] Chwolson, *Corpus,* col. 15-18, 238.

Ses découvertes remettent trop de choses en question. Tout homme
qui cherche à lever le voile est immédiatement suspecté et bientôt
injurié: tel François LENORMANT, archéologue et historien des religions, professeur à la Sorbonne et membre de l'Institut, savant respectable et bien connu à l'époque, parce qu'il s'était prononcé en
faveur de FIRKOWICZ,[76] fut aussitôt, lors de la réunion de la Société
Archéologique Russe de Saint-Pétersbourg, qualifié de *charlatan* par
HARKAVY.[77]

Pourtant, parmi ceux qui osaient aller à contre-courant dans cette
affaire, on comptait de grands noms de l'époque. Nous ne citerons
que les paroles de RENAN:[78] "La Crimée a fourni un trésor, je veux
parler de ces inscriptions funéraires publiées et commentées par M.
CHWOLSON; on y reviendra bientôt dans ce journal. Il serait fort à
désirer que l'Académie de Saint-Pétersbourg fît exécuter en Crimée
quelques fouilles qui, en fournissant des données archéologiques au
débat, couperaient court à toutes les objections."

Ce vœu reste toujours lettre morte et depuis un siècle l'affaire
FIRKOWICZ tourne autour de discussions absolument stériles. Elle a
causé un très grave préjudice non seulement à la mémoire de FIR-
KOWICZ, mais également au bon renom de l'ensemble des karaïtes.
Cependant, le préjudice est encore plus grave pour la science, car
cette campagne diffamatoire n'a pas permis aux chercheurs d'apprécier à leur juste valeur ces documents dont l'importance ne doit pas
être sous-estimée.

Il est donc grand temps de résoudre ce problème d'une façon
réaliste et de reprendre son examen en commençant par une étude
des documents eux-mêmes, aussi bien du point de vue de leur contenu
que de celui de leur état matériel.

---

[76] FR. LENORMANT, *Essai sur la propagation de l'alphabet phénicien*, Paris 1872,
I, p. 268 et suivantes; idem in *The Academy* 400, le 3 janvier 1880, p. 16.

[77] CHWOLSON, *Corpus*, col. 3, note 1.

[78] "Rapport sur les travaux du conseil de la Société asiatique pendant l'année
1867-1868, fait à la séance annuelle de la Société, le 9 juillet 1868", *Journal asiatique*,
6ème série, 1868, XII, p. 79.

COMMON SENSE AND HYPOTHESIS
IN OLD TESTAMENT STUDY

BY

MATITIAHU TSEVAT
Cincinnati

The study of the Old Testament in modern times is marked by a progressing reduction of the influence of dogma, tradition, legend, and concern of the authority of Church or Synagogue and by a concomitant increasing emphasis on common-sense arguments. Looking back over a history of almost two centuries it would seem that biblical scholars have reason to take pride in biblical philology's having reached the status of a science. It is the burden of this paper to question the extent to which this notion is justified.

Arguments based on common sense as such have little or no place in the sciences, the humanities included. (For the convenience of argument I subsume philology under science.) And this failure to achieve place is due to this: that common sense does not assess the available evidence on which its conclusions are or should be properly based. The case for common sense is further weakened by its tendency to engage in a search for apparently plausible "first principles" whose disclosure may be used to account for so-called "facts" or postulate the very existence of such "facts".[1]

An examination of the procedures of Old Testament philology will reveal that this branch of learning all too often does not submit its cognitive claims to the challenge of such evidence as exists or might theoretically exist. This tendency is especially to be remarked in provinces to which I shall direct attention here, higher criticism and, to a lesser degree, history of text.[2] Questions typical in these

---

[1] This definition-by-description of common sense follows E. NAGEL, *The Structure of Science*, 1961, pp. 12f. Different but not incompatable statements are those of E. E. HARRIS, *Hypothesis and Perception*, 1970, pp. (296-298), 299; and K. R. POPPER, *Objective Knowledge*, 1972, pp. 33f., 60, and elsewhere.

[2] Attention to other provinces of Old Testament study will probably reveal that the statement applies to a wider area than is treated here. It should be clear, however, that the extensions of its applicability must stop short of studies which stand in ancillary relation to Old Testament philology, e.g., history of Israel, geography of Palestine, the Hebrew linguistics.

areas are: 'Is a given segment of a book genuine?' 'Is it unified or composite?' 'Did the original author utilize existing material?' 'What reconstruction of the prehistory of a text receives support from its ancient witnesses?'

Biblical scholarship has commonly answered such questions by having implicit recourse to "first principles" possessing prima facie plausibility, principles such as putative universal characteristics of such phenomena as the writing of books, the behavior of authors, or the operation of literary influences. It is presupposed that authors do this and do not that; that books have not a variety of fates but only fates a, b, or c, whereas d, e, and f are not options granted by philology. In like vein, it may not be allowed that several parts of a work by one author may use different names for the same person; that he may freely project different aspects of religion; further, that the descendants of an official text, themselves official, may appear multicolored as did Laban's flock before Jacob set up his regulative rods. That scholars do not ordinarily state these principles explicitly does not affect the ubiquitous use of such principles.

The place of the common-sense notion in a reasoned argument is a matter of no little importance, which prompts a brief digression. A reasoned argument, the primary example of which, in science, is an explanation broadly speaking, has two main parts: one, the premises and two, the conclusion. Among the premises one distinguishes universal statements or propositions and particular statements. The former may range from loose generalizations to lawlike formulations or hypotheses; the latter are the data, namely, the object under investigation and pertinent information about it.[3] To concretize with an example from Hebrew palaeography. I wish to establish the age of a manuscript. Universal statement: Hebrew script after A.D. 400 consistently uses the final letters kaf, mem, etc. Particular statement: The manuscript under investigation has no final letters. Conclusion: The manuscript is earlier than A.D. 400.[4]

---

[3] A notable exposition of the subject is that of C. G. HEMPEL and P. OPPEN-HEIM, "Studies in the Logic of Explanation", *Philosophy of Science* XV (1948), pp. 135-175; several times republished, e.g., (with some changes and an addition) in C. G. HEMPEL, *Aspects of Scientific Explanation and Other Essays* . . ., 1965, pp. 245-295. In note 7 (p. 251 [1965]), the authors disclaim novelty for their approach and refer to predecessors.

[4] This proposition does not rest only on the absence of contrary evidence ('All ravens are black,' for no nonblack raven has ever been seen); it receives considerable support from the testimony of the talmudic insistence (e.g., jMegilla 1:9 [71d]; bShabbat 104a) upon the obligatory use of these letters. There are

Turning now to the question of the place and the function of a common-sense notion in an argument one observes that, whereas in our illustration the universal proposition is either true or subject to refutation, the common-sense notion is featured in this role of a universal proposition with this crucial difference: for all its seeming plausibility its truth is far from corroborated, and there are no criteria for putting it to a test.

The failure of Old Testament philology to probe its universal premises, so far stated in a general way, is reinforced by a special circumstance. Let such a premise be a hypothesis about the behavior of authors. Realistically speaking, the Old Testament critic develops this hypothesis in the course of his work with a limited class of objects, say the Old Testament narratives, and he formulates it with a view to the totality of this class. Now it is obvious that the data which serve as material for the framing of a hypothesis cannot be employed for testing this hypothesis. For the hypothesis will be so formulated and the data so presented that the hypothesis and the data will not contradict each other. Contradictions thus ruled out, it goes without saying that the need for testing will never be asserted. This is a radical weakness of modern Old Testament research.

Scholars engaged or interested in the areas of study to which this paper invites attention, if they would remedy the situation will find that they must go outside the biblical field for part of their scholarly endeavor. And this not in order to broaden their horizon nor to learn new tricks but rather to perform work abroad that cannot be performed at home. Indeed, it is likely that they will have to travel to distant shores. For while the biblical scholar may understandably be attracted to the early literature of ancient Greece, especially Homer and Homeric philology, he will find that, external though these be to the Old Testament, they are not far enough afield. The Old Testament and Homer have several features in common as have Old Testament and Homeric studies. During the past two hundred years the two disciplines have gone through similar phases. The similarity of the objects of study and of methods employed and results achieved are, to be sure, enlightening and have proved useful to biblical scholarship; the writings of DORNSEIFF,

---

various traditions about the age of this prescription, but the third century A.D. seems to be a reasonable terminus post. For the subject consult N. H. TUR-SINAI, *Hlšwn whspr* I (1954), pp. 4-5(ff.); and N. AVIGAD in *Scripta Hierosolymitana* IV (1958), pp. 64, 66, 70, 72f.

to mention only one author, are impressive testimony.[5] But essentially, Homer is not the text with which the Old Testament scholar can successfully check his methods and explanations because, in crucial aspects, Homer and the Bible are too similar. Explanations of Homeric phenomena and hypotheses about them are marked by a comparable lack, or very low degree, of internal testability. The kinds of things which are uncertain in the Bible are often uncertain also in Homer. A biblicist who attempts to answer critical questions in biblical philology by invoking Homeric philology risks interpreting *ignotum per ignotum*.

There is no hope for progress unless he breaks out of these charmed circles and reaches bases of testable facts. These he will discover in modern literature. It is in and about modern works that he will find sufficient information for checking arguments put forth in Old Testament philology mainly by testing their universal premises. The information consists of drafts, autographs, and the like, documented biographies of authors and their friends, and so on. It is simply a matter of extant information, the happy accident of available sources.

In the following section a number of examples from literature and music will be deployed. With one exception, which is from the ancient Near East, they are from late eighteenth century Germany. The purpose of the presentation is to test the quality of hypotheses current in Old Testament scholarship and to cast an occasional glance at the conclusions derived from the hypotheses and the manner of derivation.

The *Magic Flute* of MOZART and his librettist SCHIKANEDER features two camps, the powers of good and the powers of evil, the former represented by the Queen of the Night and her retinue, the latter by Sarastro and his. This holds for the first third of the work. With the beginning of the first finale a volte-face takes place: The Queen of the Night now represents the evil principle and Sarastro the good one. No reason is given for the change, no attempt made to harmonize the parts. Scholars have had a field-day with this matter.[6] The very existence of the break and the consequent contradiction have been denied or explained away; alternatively, the break has been acknowledged but justified in terms of a putative

---

[5] F. DORNSEIFF, *Antike und Alter Orient*, 1959.

[6] "Toujours inexpliqué" [T. DE WYZEWA and] G. DE SAINT-FOIX, *W. A. Mozart; sa vie musicale* . . . V [1946], p. 220).

profound symbolism; others have responded to the esthetic problem by picturing a pitiable MOZART, a great musician helpless in the clutches of an inferior librettist.[7]

We need not dwell on these speculations. What we need to do is to note the universal premise common to criticisms of MOZART and the Old Testament: Imperfections, such as contradictions, just do not occur in a work of art produced by a single creator. The modern biblical critic seeing the explanations offered by MOZART critics would likely be reminded of exegetical essays that were in vogue in his own field in centuries past but are renounced today, and properly so. He does not explain away or harmonize or resort to mystification. He stipulates several independent strands in a text which as a whole is not compatible with his propositions. Now this approach of the biblicist presents the one answer which is not available to the MOZART philologian. For the latter the background of the *Magic Flute* and its composition are illumined by the bright light of documented history; flight into the shelter of source conjecture is the one avenue barred to him.

We now turn from opera with its literary ingredient to literature proper. The first example has its focus on a modern author's comment on one of his own works, a comment made against the background of hypotheses which had been proposed about ancient literature. In a letter drafted to SCHILLER and dated July 7, 1796, GOETHE writes about his novel in progress *Wilhelm Meister*: "I myself scarcely believe that one will find in the book a unity other than that of steadiness in progress (der fortschreitenden Stetigkeit), but we shall see; and since it is the work of so many years ... I am in this—if one may compare the little with the great—both Homer and Homerid at one and the same time". GOETHE is commenting on the unsatisfactory integration of *Wilhelm Meister*. Such a shortcoming, detected in the Homeric epics by the then nascent criticism of Homer, would— GOETHE implies—be charged to Homerid meddling with the pristine

---

[7] A rich bibliography of the *Magic Flute* between 1911 and 1962 is contained in L. VON KÖCHEL, *Chronologisch-thematisches Verzeichnis sämtlicher Tonwerke W. A. Mozarts* in the 6th ed. by F. GIEGLING a.o., 1964, pp. 713f. Comments on the above problem will be found in many of its items. Later literature is listed in the annual MOZART bibliography of the subsequent volumes of the *Mozart-Jahrbuch*. F. KLINGENBECK, *Die Zauberflöte*, 1966, discusses the theme on pp. 70-92. Examples of contrived profundity or mystification are the writings of E. SCHMITZ, in *Festschrift Max Schneider*, ed. W. VETTER, 1955, p. 210; and, a more intelligent and refined specimen, J. CHAILLEY, *Mozart-Jahrbuch 1967*, 1968, pp. 100-110.

original.[8] This is double-edged criticism on the part of GOETHE: explicit criticism of his own novel and implicit criticism of the studies of Friedrich August WOLF, the father of modern Homer criticism in Germany. GOETHE means to convey that lack of integration in a work of literature is an esthetic phenomenon, which cannot be interpreted as a clue to the prehistory of that literature. This point he substantiates by reference to his own work.

This example is not given with the intention of invoking GOETHE as an ultimate authority for the evaluation of the critical philology of Homer and, by extention, of the Bible. But the issue of testing hypotheses about ancient literature by means of exemplars from modern literature looms behind this epistolary passage of his, and this author is as well qualified as any to offer such critical comments.

The next example features another aspect of premises and their operation in the study of literature. Its subject matter is the forerunner of *Urfaust* as discussed in GOETHE philology. *Urfaust* is the conventional name for that version of *Faust* that GOETHE brought to Weimar when he settled there in 1775; it was the only *Faust* known, and at that only to a small circle of friends, before the publication in 1790 of the next version, *Faust; a Fragment*. Not meant for publication and never published during its author's lifetime, *Urfaust* was discovered in 1877, half a century after his death. Now in the opinion of a number of scholars, the very title *Urfaust* is a misnomer. For they hold that *"Urfaust"* was itself preceded by one or more yet earlier if rather incomplete versions of the work; this hypothesis they flesh out with a partial description of that proto-*Urfaust*. For its reconstruction they employ elements and produce results which, in essence and up to a point, resemble those appearing in Old Testament higher criticism: prose versus poetry and various types of poetry versus one another; uncertainty as regards the identity and image of personae; apparently gratuitous duplications; and the unsettled question regarding the focus of the drama, its aim and conclusion. The constituents of the argument comprise both facts and constructs which, properly formulated and organized, are said to lead to the hypothesis of proto-*Urfaust*.[9]

---

[8] The Homerids are the post-Homeric rhapsodists.

[9] A detailed (313 pages) overview of *Urfaust* research is given by V. NOL-LENDORFS, *Der Streit um den Urfaust*, 1967. (Out of the great number of passages which highlight different sides of the problem I mention pp. 83f., 103, 136-140, 220.) After NOLLENDORFS there appeared a book which deserves listing: H. REICH, *Die Entstehung der ersten fünf Szenen des Goethischen 'Urfaust'*, 1968. For

The invitation to compare the criticism of the Old Testament and of *Faust* is obvious. In respect to the Old Testament the examination of a class of features of a text, a part of the Old Testament, results in one or the other of several hypotheses: the text is a fabric woven from different recognizable strands; the text represents a main constituent complemented by a number of additions; or, in the case of certain narratives, the text is a recast of an ancient Hebrew epic. In respect now to *Urfaust*, its examination, supplemented by an examination of other *Faust* versions, culminates in the hypothetical onetime existence of a vaguely describably earlier stage of the text, and this text like the extant ones is the work of the one author.

For reasons similar to those which obtained in the case of the *Magic Flute*, the student of *Faust* explains a type of features in a way markedly different from that of the student of the Old Testament. The rich number of particular premises available to *Faust* research, i.e., the known facts about *Faust* and its sources and GOETHE and his time, precludes the type of answers yielded in Old Testament research. Biblical research has at its disposal, beyond the texts themselves and whatever little information can be culled from them, only a very small number of particular premises. Therefore the possibility here of a rather wide variety of explanations and answers, a possibility uncommon in many other branches of philology. (That not all of these possibilities are realized in Old Testament study is more a matter of trends and fashions in scholarship than of logical requirements or exclusions.) Given this state of the science, the question as to the worth of these explanations becomes all but rhetorical. To put it differently: The failure to test universal statements together with the paucity of particular statements is the reason for the common-sense prescientific nature of part of Old Testament scholarship.

Our next example, Friedrich HÖLDERLIN's poem "Brot und Wein", will be instructive for yet another reason. This elegy exists in three authentic versions. In any single one, the incongruities, while present, are not overwhelming. But when we compare all three versions (all written shortly after 1800), we are faced with a difference, which is momentous. The earliest version, called "Der Weingott", and the last version both build up to a culmination in a reference to Dionysus, which is as unambiguous as it is impactful. In the climax of the second version, however, Christ, unmistakable

---

first acquaintance with the problem I suggest E. STAIGER, *Goethe* I, 1952, "Urfaust" (pp. 204-244, especially the first half of the chapter).

for all his not being so named, takes the place of Dionysus. His appearance is anticipated and reinforced in the poem's new title "Bread and Wine", a likely allusion to the Last Supper.[10] The incongruity inhering in the poem is compounded in the third version, where Christ has all but disappeared; at best, only faint traces are left.

Now HÖLDERLIN was unquestionably not frivolous as artist or thinker. He did not toy with the divine, nor were the names of the Greek gods for him arbitrary symbols, capriciously chosen. To the extent that I understand him, I may own that I know of no writer of postclassical times who was so piously drawn to the Greek gods as he. And as regards Jesus Christ, let us note that HÖLDERLIN repeatedly strove to integrate him into what is essentially a Greek pantheon; this, too, is piety, and here, too, he is altogether serious.

Imagine now the reaction of scholars should there come to light an ancient duplicate of a biblical text with Baal appearing where now we have YHWH. Our received text would by unanimous pronouncement be declared to be an Israelite adaptation of a Canaanite original. But we need not appeal to imagination when, in fact, a biblical text, Psalm xxix, has been[11] and is, with mounting frequency, being identified as such in the absence of that imaginary duplicate or any other textual evidence deserving this name.

Interpreters of HÖLDERLIN are at pain to understand both the thrust and the complex of ideas in "Bread and Wine" and in his other Christ poems.[12] Their proposals, while often less than convincing, represent serious philological efforts, generally more sober than the Papageno-like stabs by some musicologists in the murk of the *Magic Flute* problem. The interpreter of the Old Testament might well view HÖLDERLIN philology with wistful envy, not only its material basis, that is to say, its particular premises (texts based on autographs and some authentic editions as well as biographical information) but also the general sobriety of its speculations—for speculations they are. When he then looks again at his own discipline,

---

[10] The change from "Der Weingott" to "Brod und Wein" is made in a correction of the autograph of the second version; see F. BEISSNER in the large Stuttgart edition II 2, p. 592.

[11] Since 1936: H. L. GINSBERG, *Ktby 'wgryt*, pp. 129-131.

[12] The following studies are significant for the problem at hand (disregarding general interpretations of the poem and essays on the so-called Christ hymns): Primarily F. BEISSNER, *Hölderlins Götter*, 1969, pp. 26-36; then P. BÖCKMANN, "Friedrich Hölderlin: Brod und Wein . . .," in B. WIESE, ed., *Die deutsche Lyrik* I, 1959, pp. 394-413.

he cannot be oblivious to the facility of its stipulations of universal premises and the consequent eventuation of assorted assumptions fulfilling these stipulations.

The final illustration is a group of texts from the ancient Near East. It will bring us close in place and time to the provenience of biblical literature, whose study is the subject of our discussion. A prefatory word: Given our very limited knowledge of the lives of authors and of the earliest histories of their works in that region and era, we can hardly expect to find ancient Near Eastern literary works with which we might test other and unrelated works of that civilization, be it in regard to matters of higher criticism or to the issue of complexes of ideas. In respect, however, to the history of the Old Testament text the conditions for comparison must be seen more favorable. Therefore, for the examination of Frank M. Cross's hypothesis about early biblical text types, which follows, Near Eastern texts may be utilized.

Cross arranges pre-Christian texts of the Old Testament in a stemmatological fashion. This he does by assigning three different text types, respectively, to three countries. Two of these types he assigns by index fossils to Egypt and Palestine, respectively.[13] The third he places in Babylonia on the strength of the following argument: Egypt and Palestine have been preempted, and the possibility that different "textual traditions ... can exist side by side in the same ... locality for centuries" must be "brusquely" rejected.[14] I think Cross is overly assertive in his claim for this as a principle of textual history. The prima facie plausibility which he discerns for the rejection of the centuries-long common domicile of different textual traditions may be refuted by any number of instances to the contrary in the case of ancient Near Eastern texts. I cite but a few examples.

(1) Text 1 of Shalmaneser I (1274-1254) in Weidner's publication. It has quite a number of variant readings other than simple matters of phonetics and morphology.[15] All manuscripts of this text come from the temple of the god Ashur in the city of Assur.

(2) The eleventh tablet of the Epic of Gilgamesh. This features

---

[13] The merit of the placements is not assessed here. They are accepted for the sake of the argument.

[14] F. M. Cross, *HTR* LVII (1964), pp. 297-299.

[15] The variants are from [E. Ebeling ...] E. F. Weidner, *Die Inschriften der altassyrischen Könige*, 1926: p. 112, vars. e, o, u, x; p. 116, var. l'; p. 120, vars. l, a'; p. 122, vars. m, s; p. 124, vars. b, w, f'; p. 126, var. a.

variants of the kind found in the Shalmaneser I text.[16] Virtually all of the manuscripts are from Assurbanipal's library in Nineveh, seventh century.

(3) The Phoenician inscriptions from Karatepe. For this eighth century monumental text G. D. YOUNG's conclusions in regard to its variants [17] are in full agreement with those advanced in this paper.

(4) The Hittite Laws. Almost all known texts are imperial copies, probably thirteenth century, of originals of some four centuries earlier; all come from the capital Hattusas. Here, too, the variants conform to the types of variants in the previously mentioned specimens.[18]

The variants in these examples are approximately of the order of the variants in the Pentateuch and Samuel that are featured in CROSS's hypothesis. The texts in which they appear are official documents— one of them, Gilgamesh, is even characterized as canonical. The last text as well as the text of the Hittite Laws own a history of centuries' duration. The Assur and Karatepe texts are equally pertinent in spite of their lack of prehistory; for they did not evolve gradually from popular, divergent, uncontrolled material, but were, from the moment of their composition, official in every respect—for all this no one apparently was concerned about a uniform version.

In summation, this is another case of a universal lawlike statement refuted by testing. My purpose for citing it, however, is not to single out its author for criticism. This case, in common with all the others, is typical of an ambience in which such statements with their rami-

---

[16] The list is from R. C. THOMPSON, *The Epic of Gilgamesh*, 1930: p. 62, vars. 7, 32f., 36, 37; p. 63, vars. 1, 12; p. 65, vars. 8, 26; p. 66, vars. 12-13.

[17] G. D. YOUNG, *OS* VIII (1950), pp. 291-299.

[18] As a sampling there follows an incomplete listing of variants from §§ 41-46 of the first tablet; text KBo VI 4 (whose sections are conventionally Roman-numbered), which has more variants, is not included in the overview. Reference is according to FRIEDRICH's main text (KBo VI 3:II), which applies also to the editions of F. IMPARATI, *Le leggi ittite*, 1964, and R. HAASE, *Die Fragmente der hethitischen Gesetze*, 1968. (For easier identification I have added the numbers of the footnotes of J. FRIEDRICH, *Die hethitischen Gesetze*, 1959).

On the age of one text containing these sections (FRIEDRICH's text A) see H. G. GÜTERBOCK, *JCS* XVI (1962), p. 17. § 41:47 (n. 36) *danzi/pianzi* "one takes/one gives" (a difference of the order "to wind up/to wind down" [as, a campaign]). § 42:49 (n. 5) *nu Ú-UL sarnikzi/sarnikzil* [NU.GÁL] "he does not make restitution/there is no restitution." § 43:52 (n. 14) GUD-*ŠU*/GUD.ḪI.A (his)ox/oxen." § 44b:56 (n. 34) a pair of somewhat extended variants. § 46:59 (nn. 43f.) A.Š[À.ḪI.A *sa]ḫḫana*/A.ŠÀ.ḪI.A-*an/saḫḫanas* A.ŠÀ.ḪI.A "field(s) and fief/a field/a field of fief." § 46:59, 60 (nn. 46, 49) *takkussi/takku* "if him/if."

fications well-nigh represent the norm, an ambience from whose influence no one is immune.

At this juncture we must anticipate an objection as to the validity of the analogical illustrations which we have adduced.[19] All of our illustrations, with the exception of the last, appear to be open to the objection that examples from Western civilization are not appropriate for, and have no bearing on, the interpretation of ancient Near Eastern phenomena. More specifically, one might quarrel with the analogy of literary inconsistencies in modern Western works, which may be a relatively rare phenomenon, for the critical analysis of the Old Testament, where this phenomenon is frequent. The employment of this analogy may appear as an attempt to disprove a hypothesis formulated for one area by applying it to another area for which it was not intended and for which it is irrelevant; this is to say, that it was formulated for an area which features a large number of occurrences, occurrences which it—presumably—explains, while the latter area features a small number of similar occurrences (mere exceptions), which it admittedly fails to explain. To state it differently: The criticism is that undue significance is accorded to exceptions which, at that, are extraneous. Such criticism would be cogent but for the following considerations.

First, in regard to the quantitative element in this criticism. I readily agree that inconsistencies are more frequent in the Old Testament than in modern literature. The question is "How much more?" Erroneous ideas about true proportions abound, that is, precision beyond the rudimentary comparatives "more" and "less", and in particular as regards relative frequencies of occurrences. And scholars are not unsusceptible to such aberrance. One example. The rarity of the assimilation of the Hebrew consonant nun in the preposition *min* before the article (e.g., *mehabbayit*) is stressed in BAUER-LEANDER and supported demonstratively by the citation of

---

[19] Our listing of various literary incongruities which may not be utilized for higher criticism is far from comprehensive; attentive readers of modern literature will find that they can extend it considerably. Long ago E. STEMPLINGER, *Studien zur vergleichenden Literaturgeschichte* VII (1907), pp. 194-203, assembled material of this kind (not included here), but not all his examples are impressive. See also DORNSEIFF (n. 5), p. 5. Professor M. DAHOOD has reminded me kindly that *The New Yorker*, a weekly well-known to American readers, regularly carries a collection of writers' foibles: short quotations, many from current newspapers, which it accompanies with its own caustic comments. The individual entries are normally nonliterary, but they may alert the reader to what happens in literature.

just three instances. SPERBER counters this assumption of impressionistic scholarship, listing ninety instances.[20]

Further, where the elements to be quantified are stylistic or structural inconsistencies, divergent religious modalities, traces of foreign influence, or similar literary imponderables, the very count will depend crucially upon the precision of the analysis of the text and the judgmental acumen of the quantifier with specific reference to the range and order of his literary criteria for the imponderables. The determining factors will depend on the setting of the threshold for the admission or exclusion of individual phenomena; hence, widely differing results may be expected.

Again, the dubiety of the quantification of criteria presents a problem to literary research in general. But the problem is considerably sharpened in biblical philology. The Old Testament is the more diligently researched as to literary tensions and inconsistencies, differing religious outlooks within narrow literary confines, varying stylistic features, and other potential material for higher criticism. The reason for this is clear: the researcher's labors are rewarded with the discovery of elements making for impressive hypotheses about the origin and growth of the literature. In the case of modern literature, the reward for those who engage in such enterprise is, generally speaking, substantially less. The smaller or the less likely the reward, the less awareness of these imponderables and the less energetic the search for them. It is an old and unphilological story: the hope for reward creates proof texts.

These three points taken together render far less formidable the quantitative aspect of the objection to the use of modern examples for the study of ancient literature. But the objection in its essential aspect is altogether without merit for the following reasons.

One. In what is probably the majority of cases, the critical analysis of Old Testament texts takes its departure from what may broadly be called literary faults and incongruities: unmotivated changes of names, contradictions, repetitions, and the like. Now the proportionately few occurrences of inconsistencies in modern Western texts must be seen greatly to outweigh the proportionately many in the ancient Near East, for standards of consistency (like other features of rationalism) are the property of the heirs of Aristotle's Poetics to a degree far beyond that characterizing the heirs of other cultures. Therefore it is that an argument based on even a few cases

[20] A. SPERBER, *JBL* LXII (1943), pp. 140-143.

of violation of these standards in the West is potent, and even a few Western cases may supply legitimate controls for the testing of universal propositions of Old Testament study.

Two. Any standard brought to bear on Old Testament literature for the purpose of higher criticism is a Western standard; no such standard is formulated in the Old Testament itself and none can be derived from it (as opposed to some noncritical philological standards which can; for instance, standards of poetical parallelism). If this be granted, works of modern Western literature may not be deemed unsuitable for the critical assessment of ancient Israelite literature; especially if, for considerations discussed before, quantitative proportions must be heavily weighted in favor of Western literature. Unless we are prepared to propose the frivolous notion that only Western authors are privileged to disregard Western standards, we shall be constrained to accept that the literary standards applied to the Old Testament by modern research for the purpose of higher criticism—standards which are generally not so applied in the criticism of modern Western literature—are unreasonably stringent.

Here the reader might take issue with the recommendation following from the preceding paragraphs to relax critical standards for certain kinds of exegesis and rethink the critical approach of Old Testament philology. He might be concerned lest such rethinking impair the ability of the exegete to understand his literature. Such concern, however, would not be well founded. If it is true that the prevailing standards of Old Testament scholarship are too stringent, operations shaped and directed by them are likely to be deformed and misdirected. Therefore, the standards are to be relinquished; no impairment to the understanding can possibly follow from the relinquishment of inappropriate standards. This simple logical cognition is complemented by a philological consideration. To look at the text one is studying with an anticipation of finding perfection is unhelpful when it is not misleading. The philologist ought not to maximize for his text an expectation of consistency and unflawed esthetics.

The concluding remarks, I confess, represent more my personal stance than philosophy of philology. I am aware that I may be criticized for counselling underinterpretation. My response: underinterpretation, while bad, is a shade better than overinterpretation. Overinterpretation breeds a host of untestable hypotheses; like the hoped-for nuclear fusion reactor it produces its own fuel. Yet facile hypotheses (in the biblicists' jargon, "bold hypotheses") are more a hindrance than a furtherance of Old Testament science.

Rigor is a requisite ingredient of Old Testament philology as of all science. Rigor, however, may not be posited as existing in the object under investigation but should be recognized as an ideal to be realized in the operations, the methods and, foremost, the epistemological foundations of science. As wrong as it is to expect the authors studied to be always rigorous, so wrong is it to permit the scholar ever to be less than rigorous. Adherence to this principle is indispensible if we are to raise Old Testament philology above the level of common-sense reasoning and set it on what KANT called *den sicheren Gang einer Wissenschaft*.[21]

---

[21] *CPR*, 2nd ed., preface.

"A PEOPLE COME OUT OF EGYPT"

An Egyptologist looks at the Old Testament

BY

R. J. WILLIAMS

Toronto

Many years ago, the pioneer studies of Gunkel,[1] Gressmann,[2] Causse,[3] Humbert,[4] Baumgartner,[5] and Fichtner [6] demonstrated in a most convincing fashion that Israel's literary heritage, especially in the area of Wisdom literature, was an integral part of the cultural continuum of the ancient Near East. This was inevitable, since geographical and political factors combined to preclude Israel's isolation from her neighbours. Not only did she share the same cultural *milieu*, but she was continually exposed to influences from the much older and more highly developed civilizations which surrounded her.

By the very nature of their training, Old Testament scholars are more likely to have acquired a first-hand knowledge of the Canaanite and cuneiform sources than they are to have mastered the hieroglyphic and hieratic materials of Egypt. For this reason they have had to depend to a greater degree on secondary sources for the latter. It is not surprising, then, that Israel's heritage from Western Asia in such areas as mythology, psalmody, theodicy, proverb collections, legal "codes" and practices, suzerainty treaties and royal annals has been more thoroughly investigated. Yet Egypt's legacy is by no

---

[1] H. Gunkel, "Ägyptische Parallelen zum Alten Testament", *ZDMG* LXIII (1909), pp. 531-539, repr. in *Reden und Aufsätzen* (Göttingen, 1913), pp. 131-141.

[2] H. Gressmann, *Israels Spruchweisheit im Zusammenhang der Weltliteratur* (Berlin, 1925).

[3] A. Causse, "Sagesse égyptienne et sagesse juive", *RHPR* IX (1929), pp. 149-169.

[4] P. Humbert, *Recherches sur les sources égyptiennes de la littérature sapientiale d'Israël* (Neuchâtel, 1929).

[5] W. Baumgartner, *Israelitische und altorientalische Weisheit* (Tübingen, 1933), and "Die israelitische Weisheitsliteratur", *ThR* N.F. V (1933), pp. 259-288.

[6] J. Fichtner, *Die altorientalische Weisheit in ihrer israelitisch-jüdischen Ausprägung: eine Studie zur Nationalisierung der Weisheit in Israel*, BZAW LXII (Giessen, 1933).

means negligible, and a greater appreciation of this fact has been achieved during the past half century.

Israel was always conscious of her ties with Egypt, and the traditions of her sojourn there were indelibly impressed on her religious literature. But long before the Hebrews became a nation Egypt had exerted an economic supremacy over Syria-Palestine during the Middle Kingdom (ca. 2052-1786 B.C.). The inscribed vessels and figurines known as Execration Texts [7] testify to the Egyptian presence in Palestine, and both wall-paintings and texts bear witness to the continual movements of Semitic nomads to and from Egypt.[8] After the Hyksos invasion Egyptian influence waned somewhat, but during the New Kingdom Thutmose III began ca. 1482 B.C. to carve out an Asiatic empire which was later to contest the control of Syria-Palestine with the Hittites. During this period we find Semites in positions of authority in Egypt, some even serving at the royal court.[9]

Although Egyptian power reached a low ebb some four centuries later, relations between the Hebrews and the Egyptians became increasingly important during the Twenty-first Dynasty (ca. 1085-945 B.C.). This was the era of David and Solomon, when Egypt became a sanctuary for the Edomite crown-prince Hadad (I Kings xi 14-22) and the later rebel Jeroboam (I Kings xi 40). The biblical reference to Solomon's relations with the pharaoh Siamun who became his father-in-law is tantalizingly brief (I Kings ix 16), but there can be no doubt that the marriage alliance itself is evidence of a close association between Egypt and the Hebrew kingdom.

The Twenty-second Dynasty ruler Shoshenq I (ca. 945-924 B.C.) sent an army into Palestine which claimed to have subdued 156 cities among which was Jerusalem where the temple was plundered (I Kings xiv 25f.). The recent studies of KITCHEN have contributed to a better understanding of the actual route of this campaign as it can

---

[7] K. H. SETHE, *Die Ächtung feindlicher Fürsten, Völker und Dinge auf altägyptischen Tongefässscherben des Mittleren Reiches nach den Originalen im Berliner Museum herausgegeben und erklärt*, *APAW* 1926, 5; G. POSENER, *Princes et pays d'Asie et de Nubie: Textes hiératiques sur les figurines d'envoûtement du Moyen Empire* (Brussels, 1940); W. HELCK, *Die Beziehungen Ägyptens zu Vorderasien im 3. und 2. Jahrtausend v. Chr.*, Äg. Abh. V, 2nd ed. (Wiesbaden, 1971), pp. 44-67.

[8] G. POSENER, "Les Asiatiques en Égypte sous les XIIe et XIIIe dynasties", *Syria* XXXIV (1957), pp. 145-163.

[9] J. M. A. JANSSEN, "Fonctionnaires sémites au service de l'Égypte", *CdÉ* XXVI (1951), pp. 50-62; S. SAUNERON and J. YOYOTTE, "Traces d'établissements asiatiques en Moyenne-Égypte sous Ramsès II", *RdÉ* VII (1950), pp. 67-70.

be reconstructed from the valuable topographical list preserved in the temple at Karnak.[10]

In 853 B.C. Ahab of Israel received military support from Osorkon II against the Assyrians at Qarqar. The Assyrian threat led many Israelites to seek refuge in Egypt (Hos. vii 11, ix 6), but so weakened by internal strife was the latter kingdom that the pleas of King Hoshea for aid fell on deaf ears (II Kings xvii 4). From this time on Assyria was the dominant power in Palestine. During the reign of Hezekiah of Judah, however, some still looked longingly to Egypt for help (Isa. xxx 1-5, xxxi 1-3).

Contacts with Egypt became still closer as an increasing number of emigrants made their way there. Under Psammetichus I (664-610 B.C.) a Jewish military garrison was established at Elephantine, and other colonies in both the Delta and Upper Egypt are mentioned in the Old Testament (Jer. xxiv 8, xliv 1). On the capture of Jerusalem by Nebuchadrezzar in 587 B.C. more refugees fled to Egypt, dragging with them the prophet Jeremiah (Jer. xli 16-18, xliii 5-7).

In the light of these long-standing connexions, it is only to be expected that the venerable and highly advanced civilization of Egypt would leave its imprint on that of Israel. It is not my purpose here to survey in detail the ways in which this was accomplished, for this has been done elsewhere.[11] Rather would I seek to draw attention to a few topics which are still controversial.

One of the results of modern Old Testament studies is the increased recognition of the importance of the age of David and Solomon for the development of Hebrew literature, a period which von Rad has characterized by the term *Aufklärung*, or "enlightenment". This was a crucial time during which Israel first achieved a national consciousness, and was transformed from a loose confederacy of tribes to a highly centralized and wealthy state.

The most notable accomplishment was the establishment of the monarchy. It has been observed by Bright that some elements of

---

[10] K. A. Kitchen, *The Third Intermediate Period in Egypt (1100-650 B.C.)* (Warminster, 1972), pp. 294-300, 432-447.

[11] S. Morenz, "Ägypten und die Bibel", in *Die Religion in Geschichte und Gegenwart*, Vol. I, 3rd ed. (Tübingen, 1957), cols. 117-121, and "Die ägyptische Literatur und die Umwelt", in B. Spuler (ed.), *Handbuch der Orientalistik*, I, 2, 2nd ed. (Leiden, 1970), pp. 226-239; R. J. Williams, "Egypt and Israel", in J. R. Harris, ed., *The Legacy of Egypt*, 2nd ed. (Oxford, 1971), pp. 257-290, and "Ägypten und Israel", in the forthcoming *Theologische Realenzyklopädie*, ed. G. Fohrer; R. Grieshammer, "Altes Testament", in *Lexikon der Ägyptologie*, ed. W. Helck and E. Otto, Vol. I (Wiesbaden, 1972ff.), cols. 159-169.

Israelite kingship were derived from neighbouring Canaanite states.[12]
This may well be true, but it should be remembered that Egyptian
influence was strong throughout Palestine and Phoenicia, and many of
the features can be traced ultimately to this source. For instance,
the description of Solomon's throne (I Kings x 18-20) indicates a
design found in Ugarit and Phoenicia which is based on a prototype
peculiar to the New Kingdom in Egypt.[13] BRUNNER has pointed out
that this Egyptian throne was mounted on a pedestal identical with
the Egyptian hieroglyph for *m3ʿt*, "righteousness", "justice", and
ingeniously suggested that this was the basis for such an assertion
as the biblical line "Righteousness and justice are the foundation
of thy throne" (Ps. lxxxix 14 [Heb. 15], xcvii 2; cf. Prov. xvi 12,
xx 28 [LXX], xxv 5).[14]

It has been claimed by VON RAD that the coronation ritual was
modelled on that of Egypt.[15] In II Kings xi 12 (= II Chr. xxiii 11),
before the new king is anointed, the נֵזֶר, "crown", and עֵדוּת, "testimony", are conferred on him. These two items are equated by
VON RAD with the Egyptian *ḫʿw*, "crown", and *nḫbt*, "titulary", with
which the pharaoh was similarly endowed.[16] He regards the עֵדוּת as
a protocol by means of which the ruler's claim to the throne is
legitimized, and points to the fact that the Egyptian royal titulary
proclaims the ruler as the "Son of Reʿ." KITCHEN has taken exception
to this view and rightly insists that the *nḫbt* is only the titulary and
nothing more.[17] The Hebrew term עֵדוּת probably refers rather
to the characteristically Israelite concept of the covenant which
was introduced into the ritual.

This does not, however, exclude the use of a titulary in the Israelite ceremony. Like the Egyptian and other Near Eastern rulers,
the Hebrew king adopted a throne-name. Now the Egyptian style
of a fivefold titulary seems to lie behind the use of the epithets in

---

[12] J. BRIGHT, *A History of Israel* (London, 1960), pp. 205f.

[13] F. CANCIANI and G. PETTINATO, "Salomos Thron, philologische und
archäologische Erwägungen", *ZDPV* LXXXI (1965), pp. 88-108, espec. pp. 103ff.

[14] H. BRUNNER, "Gerechtigkeit als Fundament des Thrones", *VT* VIII (1958),
pp. 426-428.

[15] G. VON RAD, "Das judäische Königsritual", *TLZ* LXXII (1947), cols.
211-216, repr. in *Gesammelte Studien zum Alten Testament* (Munich, 1958), pp. 205-
213; Eng. trans. in *The Problem of the Hexateuch and Other Essays* (Edinburgh/
London, 1966), pp. 222-231.

[16] E.g. Thutmose III, as described in *Urk.* IV, 160, 10-161, 12, trans. in *BAR* II,
§§ 142-147.

[17] K. A. KITCHEN, *Ancient Orient and Old Testament* (London, 1966), pp. 106-111.

Isa. ix 2-7 (Heb. 1-6), as VON RAD was the first to recognize. The significance of this was further elaborated by ALT and WILDBERGER.[18] A similar rhetorical usage appears in the Egyptian *Tale of the Eloquent Peasant* (BI, 64-68), as RANKE first pointed out.[19] The use of this convention elsewhere in Western Asia is attested by the titles of King Niqmepaʿ recorded on a tablet from Ugarit.[20] Indeed, the phrase "to make a great name" in II Sam. vii 9 probably reproduces the Egyptian *irỉ rn wr*, "make a great name", which is the technical expression for proclaiming the titulary.[21]

The third part of the ritual mentioned in II Kings xi 12, namely the anointing of the king, which was practised elsewhere in Syria-Palestine, has been traced by DE VAUX to the Egyptian custom of anointing vassal rulers.[22] The theological significance of this in the Hebrew coronation ceremony is apparent: the king was to be viewed as a vassal of Yahweh. That he was also regarded as an adopted son of the Deity is claimed by COOKE, who cites the relevant Egyptian parallels.[23]

The creation of a state required an efficient administrative structure, and it seems probable that again Egyptian models were adopted. These would certainly be familiar from the long domination of Palestine by Egypt. Two of the high officials were the סוֹפֵר and the מַזְכִּיר (II Sam. viii 16f., xx 24f., I Kings iv 3). These have been compared with the Egyptian titles *sš nsw*, "royal scribe", and *wḥmw*, "herald", respectively.[24]

It should be noted, however, that the former title was a common one in Egypt, and has been likened by HELCK to an academic degree.[25]

---

[18] A. ALT, "Jesaja 8, 23-9, 6: Befreiungsnacht und Krönungstag", in *Festschrift für Alfred Bertholet* (Tübingen, 1950), pp. 29-49, repr. in *Kleine Schriften zur Geschichte des Volkes Israel*, Vol. II (Munich, 1953), pp. 206-225; H. WILDBERGER, "Die Thronnamen des Messias, Jes. 9, 5b", *ThZ* XVI (1960), pp. 314-332.

[19] H. RANKE, "Zu Bauer I, 64ff.," *ZÄS* LXXIX (1954), pp. 72f.

[20] C. F.-A. SCHAEFFER (ed.), *Le palais royal d'Ugarit*, Vol. II (Paris, 1957), pp. xvif.; text on p. 20.

[21] S. MORENZ, "Ägyptische und davididische Königstitulatur", *ZÄS* LXXIX (1954), pp. 73f.

[22] R. DE VAUX, "Le roi d'Israël, vassal de Yahvé", in *Mélanges Eugène Tisserant* Vol. I (Rome. 1964), pp. 119-133, repr. in *Bible et Orient* (Paris, 1967), pp. 287-301.

[23] G. COOKE, "The Israelite King as Son of God", *ZAW* LXXIII (1961), pp. 202-225.

[24] R. DE VAUX, "Titres et fonctionnaires égyptiens à la cour de David et de Salomon", *RB* XLVIII (1939), pp. 394-405, repr. in *Bible et Orient* (Paris, 1967), pp. 189-201; J. BEGRICH, "Sōfēr und Mazkīr", *ZAW* LVIII (1940/1), pp. 1-29, repr. in *Gesammelte Studien zum Alten Testament* (Munich, 1964), pp. 67-98.

[25] W. HELCK, *Zur Verwaltung des Mittleren und Neuen Reichs* (Leiden/Cologne, 1958), p. 61.

CODY has made the helpful suggestion that the strange name שִׁישָׁא
and its variant spellings (II Sam. xx 25, I Kings iv 3, I Chr. xviii
16) might be an attempt to reproduce the Egyptian title *sš š't*, "document-scribe", which appears in cuneiform as *šaḫšiḫa* (EA 316, 16).[26]
The head of the royal secretariat in the New Kingdom bore the
full title *sš š't (n) nsw n pr-ʿ3*, "royal document-scribe of Pharaoh",[27]
and there is clear evidence that only one official held this high office
at any one time. He was a private secretary to the king, responsible
for state correspondence and royal annals, and might be regarded
as a Secretary of State.[28]

The second title, *wḥmw*, was both a civil and a military one, granted
to a number of persons. The fuller designation *wḥmw nsw tpy*, "first
royal herald", on the other hand, was accorded to only one high
official who acted as the king's representative and was responsible
for court ceremonial. His duties are outlined on the stela of Inyotef,
the First Royal Herald of Thutmose III.[29] The Hebrew מַזְכִּיר was
therefore probably, among other things, a chief of protocol.[30]

Another title current at the Hebrew court was רֵעֶה (הַמֶּלֶךְ) (II
Sam. xv 32 [LXX], 37, xvi 16, I Chr. xxvii 33, I Kings iv 5). This
has been equated with Egyptian *smr*, "companion", a very common
title,[31] but the term *rḫ nsw*, "royal confidant", seems more suitable.[32]
The Egyptian origin of this office is somewhat less convincing than
the others, but the first element in the cuneiform equivalent *ruḫi
šarri* (EA 288, 11) seems to be an Egyptian loanword which is translated in the title *mūdu šarri* found at Ugarit. The role of such persons
was probably that of adviser.

One further functionary was known as "the one over the household" (I Kings iv 6), which appears to have been a low rank under
Solomon but became a high office by the time of Hezekiah (Isa.
xxii 15), and was in existence throughout the monarchy, as the seal
of Gedaliah shows. Since this title was applied to Joseph also (Gen.
xli 40), it has been identified with the Egyptian office of vizier, but

---

[26] A. CODY, "Le titre égyptien et le nom propre du scribe de David", *RB* LXXII
(1965), pp. 381-393.

[27] W. HELCK, *Verwaltung*, pp. 277f.

[28] T. N. D. METTINGER, *Solomonic State Officials*, Coniectanea Biblica, O.T.
Ser. V (Lund, 1971), pp. 25-51.

[29] *Urk.* IV, 963-975; trans. *BAR* II, §§ 763-771; cf. HELCK, *Verwaltung*,
pp. 65-70.

[30] METTINGER, *op. cit.*, pp. 52-62.

[31] H. DONNER, "Der 'Freund des Königs'," *ZAW* LXXIII (1961), pp. 269-277.

[32] METTINGER, *op. cit.*, pp. 63-69.

this is quite out of the question. The proper parallel would be the Egyptian *imy-r3 pr wr*, usually rendered as "High Steward". The incumbent of this office was the administrator of the royal domains,[33] and this would be an appropriate function at the Hebrew court.[34]

David is also said to have surrounded himself with a group of thirty men (II Sam. xxiii 18-39). ELLIGER equated these with the Egyptian *m'b3yt* which was a high tribunal, and maintained that they formed an élite corps.[35] Objections have properly been raised against this identification,[36] since the Egyptian institution was not a military but a legal body of thirty men. Nevertheless, it would be just as fitting to regard David's men as a group of advisers who functioned as a sort of Privy Council, for which the Egyptian comparison is not inappropriate.

A convincing example of Egyptian influence may be seen late in Solomon's reign when he apportioned the land into twelve districts under prefects for the purpose of taxation and the provision of monthly supplies (I Kings iv 7, 27 [Heb. v 7]). This was none other than the system instituted by his contemporary Shoshenq I, as REDFORD has demonstrated.[37] If we may trust Herodotus (ii 124), Solomon's division of the labour force into shifts of three months each (I Kings v 13f. [Heb. 27f.]) was also an Egyptian custom.

Further evidence of close links with Egypt in administrative practices is the fact that five Palestinian sites have yielded inscribed Hebrew ostraca of the eighth and seventh centuries B.C. which employed hieratic numerals for writing dates, to which must be added the growing number of shekel weights also bearing hieratic numerals.[38] It has been argued that the hieratic numeral for "two" occurs as early as the late tenth century Gezer Calendar,[39] but the sign in question may well be a *waw*. The Hebrew system of weights,

---

[33] A. H. GARDINER, *Ancient Egyptian Onomastica* (Oxford, 1947), Vol. I, pp. 45*-47*.

[34] METTINGER, *op. cit.*, pp. 70-110.

[35] K. ELLIGER, "Die dreissig Helden Davids", *PJB* XXXI (1935), pp. 29-75.

[36] B. MAZAR, "The Military Élite of King David", *VT* XIII (1963), pp. 310-320; D. B. REDFORD, in J. W. WEVERS and D. B. REDFORD (eds.), *Studies on the Ancient Palestinian World* (Toronto, 1972), pp. 141f.

[37] REDFORD, *op. cit.*, pp. 154-156. The statement of METTINGER, *op. cit.*, p. 127, that "contemporary Egypt did not levy any taxes" flies in the face of the evidence.

[38] Y. AHARONI, "The Use of Hieratic Numerals in Hebrew Ostraca and the Shekel Weights", *BASOR* CLXXXIV (1966), pp. 13-19, and "A 40-Shekel Weight with a Hieratic Numeral", *BASOR* CCI (1971), pp. 35f.

[39] J. B. SEGAL, " '*yrḥ*' in the Gezer 'Calendar'," *JSS* VII (1962), pp. 212-221.

moreover, was made to conform to that of Egypt, so that eight shekels were equated with one *dbn*, and the numerals appearing on the weights represent the number of Egyptian *qdt*.[40] The standard measure of length, the cubit, was likewise adjusted early in the ninth century B.C. to the longer Egyptian "royal cubit".[41]

The new state which emerged under David and Solomon made it imperative that there should be an ever increasing body of trained civil servants to carry out the complicated and demanding requirements for the maintenance of the courts, the army, the labour force for Solomon's extensive programme of building, the assessment and collection of taxes, the conduct of international trade on a large scale and the needs of diplomacy. This brings us to our next topic, that of education.

That schools existed in Syria-Palestine long before the Hebrew conquest is a known fact. When Akkadian was the *lingua franca* of Western Asia, the city-states had need of men skilled in the difficult and complicated cuneiform script. From the late fifteenth and early fourteenth centuries B.C. we have archaeological evidence for a school at Ugarit.[42] Contemporary with this is a cuneiform letter discovered at Shechem in which a teacher protests that payment has not yet been received.[43]

By the time of David, however, the Semitic alphabet was the prevailing script in Palestine, and hence the methods of instruction would naturally be different.[44] Again it was logical to turn to the Egyptians for guidance, since they were accustomed to write with pen and ink on ostraca and papyrus, employing a script which indicated only consonants and was at least partially alphabetic rather than syllabic. It is worthy of note that the Hebrew word קֶסֶת is a borrowing of the Egyptian word *gstỉ*, "scribal kit", and that the Hebrew term דְּיוֹ, "ink", if its sole occurrence in Jer. xxxvi 18 is

---

[40] R. B. Y. Scott, *PEQ* 1965, p. 135.

[41] Y. Aharoni, *BA* XXXI (1968), p. 24.

[42] A. F. Rainey, "The Scribe at Ugarit: His Position and Influence", *Israel Acad. of Sciences. Proc.* III, 4 (1968), pp. 126-139; J. Krecher, "Schreiberschulung in Ugarit: Die Tradition von Listen und sumerischen Texten", *Ugaritforschungen* I (1969), pp. 131-158.

[43] W. F. Albright, "A Teacher to a Man of Shechem about 1400 B.C.," *BASOR* LXXXVI (1942), pp. 28-31.

[44] For schools in Mesopotamia see A. Falkenstein, "Die babylonische Schule", *Saeculum* IV (1953), pp. 125-137; J. J. A. van Dijk, *La sagesse suméro-accadienne* (Leiden, 1953), pp. 21-27; W. W. Hallo, "New Viewpoints in Cuneiform Literature", *IEJ* XII (1962), pp. 13-26.

a copyist's error for רִין, might also be an Egyptian loanword.[45]

We are now fairly well acquainted with Egyptian schools and methods of education.[46] For the situation in ancient Israel, on the other hand, we are left with little more than conjecture.[47] Nevertheless, since the appearance of BRUNNER's masterly treatment of the Egyptian material, Old Testament scholars have been stimulated to re-examine the biblical sources.[48]

Before we do that, let us first survey the materials used for instruction in ancient Egypt. A mass of evidence is available in the form of schoolboy copies on potsherds, limestone flakes, wooden writing tablets and papyri. These usually contain excerpts from larger works, the execution of which exhibit varying degrees of proficiency. They may be readily identified as schoolboy exercises not only by the indications of inexperience and carelessness natural to beginners in the art of writing, but also by the occasional marginal corrections of the teacher. Frequently the exercises are provided with the date on which they were written. From their contents we can deduce the works that were regarded as suitable not only for training in calligraphy and orthography, but also for inculcating those attitudes of mind and spirit which were deemed desirable for those who would aspire to the ranks of educated officials.

Foremost among them were didactic treatises, the earliest of which date back to the Old Kingdom. These were designed specifically for those who were to be trained for government service, and their purpose was to develop the ability to express oneself in felicitous speech and to instil in youthful minds the rules of etiquette and ethical conduct. Surviving students' copies reveal that such use was made of the compositions attributed to Ḥardjedef and Ptaḥḥotpe[49] of the Old Kingdom, and Any, Amennakhte and Amenemope [50] of

---

[45] Thus T. O. LAMBDIN, *JAOS* LXXIII (1953), p. 149.

[46] H. BRUNNER, *Altägyptische Erziehung* (Wiesbaden, 1957), and "Die harte Erziehung der alten Ägypter", *Das Altertum* VI (1960), pp. 67-77; E. OTTO, "Bildung und Ausbildung im alten Ägypten", *ZÄS* LXXXI (1956), pp. 41-48; R. J. WILLIAMS, "Scribal Training in Ancient Egypt", *JAOS* XCII (1972), pp. 214-221.

[47] For earlier discussions see A. KLOSTERMANN, "Schulwesen im alten Israel", in *Festschrift Th. Zahn* (Leipzig, 1908), pp. 193-232; L. DÜRR, *Das Erziehungswesen im Alten Testament und im antiken Orient, MVAG* XXXVI, 2 (Leipzig, 1932).

[48] H.-J. HERMISSON, *Studien zur israelitischen Spruchweisheit*, WMzANT XXVIII (Neukirchen-Vluyn, 1968), pp. 97-136; METTINGER, *op. cit.*, pp. 140-157.

[49] Trans. in W. K. SIMPSON, ed., *The Literature of Ancient Egypt* (New Haven-London, 1972), pp. 159-176.

[50] Trans. ibid., pp. 241-265.

the New Kingdom, as well as other partially preserved texts whose authorship is still unknown. These were supplemented by a work entitled *Kemyt*, meaning "Completion", which was a simple manual of idioms and epistolary formulae, compiled in the Eleventh Dynasty. The abundant citations of this text bear witness to its popularity in the schools for a period of a thousand years.

In the following dynasty a noted scribe by the name of Khety composed a work which broke new ground. This was the much copied *Satire on the Trades*,[51] in which the office of scribe was extolled above all other occupations. It was to spawn a multitude of compositions of like nature in later ages. The same author was by tradition credited with two more writings which also had a great vogue in the schools: the *Hymn to the Nile* [52] and the *Instruction of Amenemhet*.[53] The latter was a work of political propaganda, and was supplemented in the curriculum by three similar texts of the Middle Kingdom: the *Prophecies of Neferti*,[54] the *Loyalist Teachings* [55] and the *Tale of Sinuhe*.[56]

In addition to these compositions, during the New Kingdom various collections of model letters, hymns, eulogies, etc., were produced which ERMAN has termed *Schülerhandschriften*.[57] These furnished still more material for practice in writing. The so-called *Scribal Controversy*,[58] best known from Pap. Anastasi I, offers us a sarcastic *viva voce* of an apprentice scribe, suggesting perhaps the manner in which pupils were examined. As in Mesopotamia, lexicographical lists of natural phenomena, flora and fauna, place-names and titles were drawn up for the use of students, to which we are accustomed to give the title "onomastica". Finally, grammatical paradigms and collections of problems in mathematics and geometry were available for instructional purposes.

The meagre yield of ostraca and papyri from the soil of Palestine,

---

[51] Trans. in *ANET*, p. 432-434.
[52] Trans. in *ANET*, pp. 372f.
[53] Trans. in SIMPSON, *op. cit.*, pp. 193-197.
[54] Trans. ibid., pp. 234-240.
[55] Trans. ibid., pp. 198-200.
[56] Trans. ibid., pp. 57-74; on the subject of propaganda literature in Egypt see G. POSENER, *Littérature et politique dans l'Égypte de la XIIe dynastie*, Bibl. de l'École des Hautes Études CCCVII (Paris, 1956); R. J. WILLIAMS, "Literature as a Medium of Political Propaganda in Ancient Egypt", in W. S. McCULLOUGH, ed., *The Seed of Wisdom: Essays in Honour of T. J. Meek* (Toronto, 1964), pp. 14-30.
[57] Trans. R. A. CAMINOS, *Late-Egyptian Miscellanies* (London, 1954).
[58] Trans. in *ANET*, pp. 475-479.

in contrast to the rich harvest from Egypt, prevents us from making a similar catalogue for schools in Israel. Indeed, only one object has been discovered in Palestine which would possibly be associated with a school. This is the Gezer Calendar, a small inscribed limestone plaque to be dated palaeographically to the latter part of the tenth century B.C. It is probably a palimpsest, and because of this and the mnemonic form of its contents it has been regarded by ALBRIGHT as a schoolboy exercise,[59] although this view has been challenged.[60] We must perforce scrutinize the limited body of Hebrew literature which the religious community of Israel saw fit to preserve in the pages of sacred Scripture.

The obvious place to begin is with the Book of Proverbs which is a collection of instructions, proverbs and wise sayings bearing a striking resemblance to the "teachings" familiar from both Egypt and Mesopotamia. We should note that there is an interesting difference between the two latter bodies of material. The Egyptian *sbōyet*, "teaching", consisted mainly of formal instructions, and only in the latest demotic compositions from the Persian or Ptolemaic period, *viz.* the *Instruction of 'Onkhsheshonqy* and Pap. Insinger, do we also find a large proportion of aphorisms. In Mesopotamia, on the other hand, in addition to a few works containing formal instruction, there are substantial compilations of proverbs and maxims, even including the occasional fable. In form, Prov. i-ix and xxii 17-xxiv 34 belong almost exclusively to the genre of instructions, while x-xxii 16 and xxv-xxix resemble the Mesopotamian and very late Egyptian "proverb" collections. Incidentally, in the light of the early appearance of both types in the ancient Near East it can no longer be maintained that the instruction form is later than the compilations of aphorisms, as KAYATZ affirms.[61]

The recognition of the fact that the greater part of the Book of Proverbs is pre-exilic, although subject to editing and revision in the post-exilic period, is the result of a greater appreciation of its close relationship to Egyptian sapiential literature. The foremost representative of this is the section contained in Prov. xxii 17-xxiv 22 which is today generally accepted as based in part on the *Instruction of Amenemope*. I do not believe that this can be reasonably doubted.

---

[59] W. F. ALBRIGHT, *BASOR* XCII (1943), p. 21.

[60] J. B. SEGAL, *JSS* VII (1962), pp. 220f.

[61] C. KAYATZ, *Studien zu Proverbien 1-9*, WMzANT XXII (Neukirchen-Vluyn, 1966), p. 3.

We must digress a little at this point in order to discuss the date
and original form of this Egyptian composition. The British Museum
manuscript which contains the only complete copy of the text was
earlier given various dates on the basis of palaeography ranging
from the Twentieth to the Twenty-sixth Dynasty. We can now assign
it more precisely to the Twenty-sixth or Twenty-seventh Dynasty,
i.e. to the sixth century B.C. This, of course, merely provides a
terminus ad quem for the original work.

However, in addition to this we possess three wooden writing
tablets. One, located in Turin, is of a slightly earlier date, but probably comes from the Twenty-sixth Dynasty; a second now in Moscow
is likely to be from the Twenty-fifth or Twenty-sixth Dynasty, but
the third, which is in the Louvre, is much earlier and must come from
the Twenty-first or more probably the Twenty-second Dynasty.[62]
Recently a second fragmentary papyrus copy has come to light in
Stockholm which can be attributed to the Twenty-first or Twenty-
second Dynasty.[63] To this we must add an unpublished ostracon in
Cairo which Černý dated to the late Twenty-first Dynasty. Since the
new papyrus and the ostracon are both schoolboy copies, the original
composition can hardly be later than the Twentieth Dynasty. We may
then assign it with some confidence to the twelfth or even thirteenth
century B.C. Hence there is no reason to suppose that the text was
unknown in the days of Solomon.

But what is the nature of the relationship of the *Instruction of
Amenemope* to the verses in Proverbs? Although ERMAN declared
himself unequivocally in favour of the priority of the Egyptian
work,[64] BUDGE who first published the text suggested the possibility
of Semitic influence on *Amenemope*.[65] This view was soon taken up by
SIMPSON [66] and especially OESTERLEY [67] who argued for an earlier
Hebrew source common to both *Amenemope* and the section in Proverbs. Nevertheless, the view of ERMAN continued to hold the field,

[62] G. POSENER, "Quatre tablettes scolaires de basse époque (Aménémopé et
Hardjédef)", *RdÉ* XVIII (1966), pp. 45-65.
[63] B. J. PETERSON, "A New Fragment of *The Wisdom of Amenemope*", *JEA*
LII (1966), pp. 120-128.
[64] A. ERMAN, "Eine ägyptische Quelle der 'Sprüche Salomos'," *SPAW* XV
(1924), pp. 86-93.
[65] E. A. W. BUDGE, *The Teaching of Amen-em-Apt, Son of Kanekht* (London,
1924), p. 103.
[66] D. C. SIMPSON, *JEA* XII (1926), p. 232.
[67] W. O. E. OESTERLEY, "The 'Teaching of Amen-em-ope' and the Old Testament", *ZAW* XLV (1927), pp. 9-24.

despite an ill-advised attempt by KEVIN to prove the dependence of *Amenemope* on Proverbs.[68] Beginning in 1957, however, DRIOTON revived in a series of articles the earlier belief of OESTERLEY that both works were based on a common Semitic source, and put forth the view that the latter was produced during the Persian period.[69] Apart from the late date he would assign to the source which we have seen to be no longer tenable, the linguistic arguments which he advanced were soon refuted.[70]

In 1972 a new theory was advanced by GRUMACH in which she postulated a common Egyptian source for both Proverbs and *Amenemope*.[71] Taking as her point of departure the literary analysis of *Amenemope* by ALT,[72] she attempted to reconstruct this hypothetical source, assuming that it followed the order of the passage in Proverbs. I fail to see any cogent reason for this assumption, since that part of the Hebrew collection which shows an affinity with *Amenemope* also contains sayings which are certainly Israelite (Prov. xxii 23, xxiii 11) and *Aḥiqar* is clearly the source of Prov. xxiii 13f. The Hebrew compiler seems rather to have made brief excerpts from *Amenemope*, very probably quoting from memory.

In addition, GRUMACH showed that the Egyptian author incorporated material from earlier instructions such as those of Ptaḥḥotpe and Any into his own composition. It can be accepted with some degree of assurance that Amenemope did utilize some materials from his predecessors, but the existence of the source that GRUMACH has called the *Alte Lehre* remains highly problematical. If, however, her sugges-

---

[68] R. O. KEVIN, "The Wisdom of Amen-em-Apt and its Possible Dependence upon the Hebrew Book of Proverbs", *JSOR* XIV (1930), pp. 115-157.

[69] É. DRIOTON, "Sur la Sagesse d'Aménémopé", in H. CAZELLES (ed.), *Mélanges bibliques rédigés en l'honneur de André Robert* (Paris, 1957), pp. 254-280; "Le Livre des Proverbes et la Sagesse d'Aménémopé", in J. COPPENS et al. (eds.), *Sacra Pagina: Miscellanea biblica congressus internationalis Catholici de re biblica*, Vol. I (Paris, 1959), pp. 229-241; "Un livre hébreu sous couverture égyptienne", *La Table Ronde* CLIV (1960), pp. 81-91; "Une colonie israélite en Moyenne Égypte à la fin du VIIe siècle av. J.-C.," in *À la rencontre de Dieu: Mémorial Albert Gelin* (Le Puy, 1961), pp. 181-191.

[70] R. J. WILLIAMS, "The Alleged Semitic Original of the *Wisdom of Amenemope*", *JEA* XLVII (1961), pp. 100-106; B. COUROYER, "L'origine égyptienne de la Sagesse d'Amenemopé", *RB* LXX (1963), pp. 208-224.

[71] I. GRUMACH, *Untersuchungen zur Lebenslehre des Amenope*, MÄS XXIII (Munich /Berlin, 1972).

[72] A. ALT, "Zur literarischen Analyse der Weisheit des Amenemope", in M. NOTH and D. W. THOMAS (eds.), *Wisdom in Israel and in the Ancient Near East*, VTSup III (Leiden, 1955), pp. 16-25.

tion should prove correct, the material which was included in Proverbs would be still earlier in date than *Amenemope*.

The remaining collections in the Book of Proverbs (apart from the miscellany in xxx-xxxi, some of which is of foreign origin) are i-ix, x-xxii 16 and xxv-xxix. The first of these, long regarded as post-exilic and the latest portion of the book, has been shown by ALBRIGHT to have close affinities with Ugaritic and Phoenician texts,[73] and therefore to contain early material. More recently it has been sub-jected to a re-examination in the light of Egyptian literature by WHYBRAY.[74] KAYATZ has also carefully documented the remarkable parallelism between the syntactic forms of both Egyptian and Hebrew instructions.[75] It is clear, for instance, that the view advanced by RICHTER [76] that clauses expressing motive or purpose are later additions to imperative statements is not supported by the much earlier evidence from Egyptian instructions. The result of such studies has been to strengthen the growing conviction that even these chapters are in large part pre-exilic.

The two other collections to which we referred consist mainly of aphorisms and precepts, with a few true proverbs interpersed. In his commentary McKANE makes a painstaking syntactic analysis of this gnomic wisdom in comparison with the Egyptian sapiential literature.[77] There is surely no valid reason today for doubting that they were originally compiled during the period of the early monarchy.

The work of these scholars has been particularly valuable in correcting misconceptions about the nature of Hebrew Wisdom literature. The commonly held view that the single-line saying is the more primitive in the Old Testament, developing into the saying consisting of two or more lines, and finally into the longer Wisdom poem, attractive as it may seem to the form critic, is difficult to main-tain in face of the tradition of millennia in Egypt where from earliest times we find the longer units.[78] Even if such a development could

[73] W. F. ALBRIGHT, "Some Canaanite-Phoenician Sources of Hebrew Wisdom", VTSup III (Leiden, 1955), pp. 1-15.

[74] R. N. WHYBRAY, *Wisdom in Proverbs: The Concept of Wisdom in Proverbs 1-9*, SBT XLV (London, 1965).

[75] C. KAYATZ, *Studien zu Proverbien 1-9*, WMzANT XXII (Neukirchen-Vluyn, 1966).

[76] W. RICHTER, *Recht und Ethos: Versuch einer Ortung des weisheitlichen Mahn-spruches* (Munich, 1966), p. 116.

[77] W. McKANE, *Proverbs: A New Approach* (London, 1970).

[78] W. BAUMGARTNER, *Israelitische und altorientalische Weisheit* (Tübingen, 1933), pp. 7f.

be traced in ancient Egypt, it had reached completion long before the production of the Hebrew Wisdom literature. Now that this fact has been realized by biblical scholars,[79] the earlier excesses of form criticism may be avoided.

Another belief which prevailed for a long time in scholarship has likewise had to be modified. This is the thesis that Wisdom literature gradually evolved from a secular to a religious viewpoint throughout the ancient Near East. BREASTED was the outstanding champion of this position.[80] A perceptive article by DE BUCK was responsible for the change in attitude on the part of Egyptologists,[81] and this has had an effect on Old Testament studies. There can be no doubt that Egyptian didactic literature always had a deeply rooted religious basis, although of course this does not mean that there was no development in religious ideas.[82] The all-pervasive concept of *M3't*, the divinely established world-order, has its counterpart in the Hebrew belief in a similar order established by Yahweh.[83]

It is important to bear in mind that, apart from the fact that but few proverbs in the strict sense of the word are to be found in the Book of Proverbs, the form of the individual aphorisms it contains suggests that they were intended for teaching and were not merely folk-sayings collected together for the enjoyment of readers.[84] We have already alluded to the close affinity between part of this material and *Amenemope*, and other striking parallels have been drawn with individual verses elsewhere in Proverbs,[85] where direct influence

---

[79] Cf. C. KAYATZ, *op. cit.*, p. 4.

[80] J. H. BREASTED, *Development of Religion and Thought in Ancient Egypt* (New York, 1912), and *The Dawn of Conscience* (New York, 1933).

[81] A. DE BUCK, "Het religieus karakter der oudste egyptische wijsheid", *NTT* XXI (1932), pp. 322-349.

[82] For an admirable exposition of the gradual development within Egyptian Wisdom literature see H. H. SCHMID, *Wesen und Geschichte der Weisheit: eine Untersuchung zur altorientalischen und israelitischen Weisheitsliteratur*, BZAW CI (Berlin, 1966), pp. 8-84.

[83] H. GESE, *Lehre und Wirklichkeit in der alten Weisheit: Studien zu den Sprüchen Salomos und zu dem Buche Hiob* (Tübingen, 1958), pp. 33-38; U. SKLADNY, *Die ältesten Spruchsammlungen in Israel* (Göttingen, 1962), pp. 89-92.

[84] R. B. Y. SCOTT, *Proverbs-Ecclesiastes*, AB XVIII (Garden City, 1965), p. 20; R. N. WHYBRAY, *op. cit.*, p. 15.

[85] E.g. Prov. iii 16, cf. KAYATZ, *op. cit.*, p. 105; xvi 2 (cf. xxi 2, xxiv 12), cf. GRESSMANN, *op. cit.*, pp. 43f.; xvi 9 (cf. xix 21, xx 24), cf. K. H. SETHE, " 'Der Mensch denkt, Gott lenkt' bei den alten Ägyptern", *NGWG* 1925, pp. 141-147; xvii 27, cf. L. GROLLENBERG, "À propos de Prov. VIII, 6 et XVII, 27", *RB* LIX (1952), pp. 42f.; xxv 22, cf. S. MORENZ, "Feurige Kohlen auf dem Haupt", *TLZ* LXXVIII (1953), cols. 187-192; xxv 23, cf. MORENZ, *ibid.*, col.

is indicated rather than an independent and comparable development.

The *Satire on the Trades*, which was popular as a school-text in Egypt at least until the New Kingdom, as more than a hundred copies bear witness, and which survived in many later imitations, has left no trace in the Old Testament. However, it was clearly the inspiration for a passage in what we may regard as the lecture notes of the Hebrew teacher Jesus ben Sira (Sir. xxxviii 24-xxxix 11). [86] It is hard to believe that this work was not known in Israel long before the beginning of the second century B.C.

As we noted earlier, the Egyptian prescribed texts also included works of political propaganda, one of which, the *Tale of Sinuhe*, took the form of a short story. A Hebrew composition which is without political motivation, but which is also in narrative form, is that of Joseph (Gen. xxxvii, xxxix-l). It has been argued by von RAD that this is a product of the Wisdom movement and portrays Joseph as the ideal sage.[87] It would, he believed, be an appropriate text for the instruction of pupils. REDFORD has taken issue with this thesis, questioning the suitability of the work for the purpose suggested.[88] Although VERGOTE, in his earlier study of these chapters,[89] saw no difficulty in dating them as early as the Mosaic period, REDFORD's more critical treatment insists on a date between 650 and 425 B.C. He arrives at this conclusion from a study of the anachronistic details of the purported Egyptian background, including the Egyptian names, the vocabulary of the passage and the complete lack of evidence for an earlier substratum which might make the theory of a later redaction plausible.

A second document found in the Old Testament, however, is more suitable as a basis for the inculcation of proper ethical attitudes in the minds of pupils. This, as WHYBRAY has so excellently dem-

---

190; xxvii 1, cf. J. G. GRIFFITHS, "Wisdom about Tomorrow", *HTR* LIII (1960), pp. 219-221.

[86] B. VAN DE WALLE, "Le thème de la satire des métiers dans la littérature égyptienne", *CdÉ* XXII (1947), pp. 55-72.

[87] G. VON RAD, "Josephsgeschichte und ältere Chokma", VTSup I (Leiden, 1953), pp. 120-127, repr. in *Gesammelte Studien* (Munich, 1958), pp. 272-280; Eng. trans. in *Problem of the Hexateuch* (Edinburgh/London, 1966), pp. 292-300.

[88] D. B. REDFORD, *A Study of the Biblical Story of Joseph* (*Genesis 37-50*), VTSup XX (Leiden, 1970), pp. 100-105; so also J. L. CRENSHAW, "Method in Determining Wisdom Influence upon 'Historical' Literature", *JBL* LXXXVIII (1969), pp. 129-142.

[89] J. VERGOTE, *Joseph en Égypte*: *Genèse chap. 37-50 à la lumière des études égyptologiques récentes*, Orientalia et Biblica Lovaniensia III (Louvain, 1959).

onstrated,[90] is the Succession Narrative preserved in II Sam. ix-xx and I Kings i-ii. And like the corresponding Egyptian texts, this does have a political motivation. That it was composed during the reign of Solomon is highly probable.

At this point we should draw attention to the fact that a closely related group of texts was produced during the same period and inspired by a peculiarly Egyptian genre of literature which has been called the *Königsnovelle* or royal romance.[91] The theme in Egypt is the myth of the divine, all-conquering ruler which is reflected in so much of the iconography which portrays the king as single-handedly destroying his enemies. In this literary type the sovereign declares his intention, often arrived at as the result of a divine command sometimes mediated through a dream, to engage in battle or to build an edifice for the gods. The proposal is then presented to his advisers who raise doubts about the feasibility of the project. In spite of this, the pharaoh carries his plans through to a successful conclusion, thus demonstrating his surpassing wisdom and might.

We encounter the Hebrew adaptation of this literary form in the story of David's determination to construct a temple for Yahweh in II Sam. vii and the account of Solomon's dream in I Kings iii 4-15. The description of Solomon's building of his temple in I Kings v-viii also betrays features of this genre. It is worth noting that in the first passage the promise to "make a great name" (II Sam. vii 9), as we saw earlier (p. 5), is identical with the Egyptian expression for the proclamation of the royal titulary. In the second passage two more Egyptianisms have been recognized: Solomon's reference to himself as an innocent little child (I Kings iii 7),[92] and his request for a "hearing heart" (I Kings iii 9).[93] The Solomonic Narrative (I Kings iii-xi), in the opinion of NOTH,[94] is a contemporary document. SCOTT, on the other hand, argued for a date in the postexilic period,[95] but PORTEN later gave persuasive reasons for

---

[90] R. N. WHYBRAY, *The Succession Narrative: A Study of II Sam. 9-20 and I Kings 1 and 2*, SBT, 2nd Ser. IX (London, 1968).

[91] A. HERMANN, *Die ägyptische Königsnovelle*, LÄS X (Leipzig, 1938); S. HERRMANN, "Die Königsnovelle in Ägypten und in Israel", *Wiss. Zs. d. Karl-Marx-Univ. Leipzig* III (1953/4), pp. 51-62.

[92] S. HERRMANN, *op. cit.*, pp. 54f.

[93] H. BRUNNER, "Das hörende Herz", *TLZ* LXXIX (1954), cols. 697-700.

[94] M. NOTH, "Die Bewährung von Salomos 'Göttlicher Weisheit'," VTSup III (Leiden, 1955), pp. 225-237.

[95] R. B. Y. SCOTT, "Solomon and the Beginnings of Wisdom in Israel", ibid., pp. 262-279.

a date soon after the disruption of the monarchy at the latest.[96]

A type of literature which was included in the miscellanies of the New Kingdom curriculum was the hymn. Whether Hebrew pupils were also given examples of hymnic style to study we cannot say, but Egyptian influence has been noted in some of the biblical hymns [97] and royal psalms.[98] The outstanding instance of this is Ps. civ which has long been thought to be in some way related to the Egyptian *Hymn to Aten*.[99] Any direct dependence seems to be excluded by the strenuous efforts which were made to eradicate all traces of the hated Atenist heresy after the death of Akhenaten in the middle of the fourteenth century B.C. Only one copy inscribed on the wall of a tomb at Tell el-Amarna has survived. Yet, despite these efforts, the art and literature of subsequent ages in Egypt inherited many features of the Atenist movement. Expressions and ideas from Amarna hymns were incorporated into later religious texts at least down to the end of the fourth century B.C. and became part of the stock phraseology of solar hymns. Indeed, a line from another text in the same Amarna tomb appears to have been reproduced in Ps. xxxiv 12 (Heb. 13),[100] and a simile in Isa. xl 12 is remarkably similar to yet another passage found in this tomb.[101]

The Egyptian schoolboy, as we have observed, also copied out the text known as the *Scribal Controversy*, and made use of the extensive lists which we call "onomastica". It has been proposed by VON RAD that the sarcastic interrogation of Job by Yahweh is in the style of the former, and that the cataloguing of natural phenomena in Job xxxviii-xxxix finds its model in the latter.[102] Other scholars have

---

[96] B. PORTEN, "The Structure and Theme of the Solomon Narrative (I Kings 3-11)", *HUCA* XXXVIII (1967), pp. 93-128; see also J. LIVER, "The Book of the Acts of Solomon", *Biblica* XLVIII (1967), pp. 75-101.

[97] A. BARUCQ, *L'Expression de la louange divine et de la prière dans la Bible et en Égypte*, Bibl. d'Étude XXXIII (Cairo, 1962).

[98] J. DE SAVIGNAC, "Essai d'interprétation du Psaume CX à l'aide de la littérature égyptienne", *OTS* IX (1951), pp. 107-135, and "Théologie pharaonique et messianisme d'Israël", *VT* VII (1957), pp. 82-90.

[99] Cf. G. NAGEL, "À propos des rapports du Psaume 104 avec les textes égyptiens", in W. BAUMGARTNER et al. (eds.), *Festschrift für Alfred Bertholet* (Tübingen, 1950), pp. 395-403, and H. KRUSE, "Archetypus Psalmi 104 (103)", *Verb. Dom.* XXIX (1951), pp. 31-43; for an annotated translation see D. W. THOMAS (ed.), *Documents from Old Testament Times* (London, 1958), pp. 142-150.

[100] B. COUROYER, "Idéal sapientiel en Égypte et en Israël (à propos du Psaume xxxiv, verset 13)", *RB* LVII (1950), pp. 174-179.

[101] B. COUROYER, "Isaïe, XL, 12", *RB* LXXIII (1966), pp. 186-196.

[102] G. VON RAD, "Hiob xxxviii und die altägyptische Weisheit", VTSup III (Leiden, 1955), pp. 293-301, repr. in *Ges. Stud.*, pp. 262-271; Eng. trans. in *Problem of the Hexateuch*, pp. 281-291.

suggested that the onomastica lie behind other biblical passages, *viz.* I Kings iv 33 (Heb. v 13) and the numerical sayings in Prov. xxx 15f., 18-20, 24-31,[103] Gen. i [104] and probably also Pss. civ and cxlviii. The important point to note here is that, although the Mesopotamian scribes also employed similar lexicographical lists, the arrangement is not the same as that of the Egyptian onomastica. The biblical passages to which reference has been made all follow the Egyptian order. This fact alone implies an acquaintance with the Egyptian type of list.

It goes without saying that a full curriculum would require other materials for instruction in such subjects as mathematics, geography, the composition of letters and business documents, and the study of foreign languages. Such texts would not be preserved in biblical literature, nor would they leave their mark on it. Yet we have now been able to discover some evidence for instructional aids similar to those known from ancient Egypt. Certain of these have been preserved in the Bible, but others can only be inferred from the traces they have left there.

Before we leave the subject of schools in Israel, two matters should be mentioned. First, the misconception seems to be still prevalent among Old Testament scholars that schools in the ancient Near East were always associated with temples.[105] In actual fact, the earliest schools in Egypt were connected with the palace, and only much later do we find some attached to temples.[106] Even in Mesopotamia, except in the earliest period, schools were not usually located in the temples.[107]

Secondly, it is maintained by NIELSEN that in Egypt scribes "were recruited from the highest class of the population,"[108] and that in the ancient Near East there was developed "a special guild of writers".[109] The fact is that Egyptian pupils were not always drawn from

---

[103] A. ALT, "Die Weisheit Salomos", *TLZ* LXXVI (1951), cols. 139-144, repr. in *Kleine Schriften*, Vol. II, pp. 90-99.

[104] S. HERRMANN, "Die Naturlehre des Schöpfungsberichtes", *TLZ* LXXXVI (1961), cols. 413-424.

[105] E.g. W. McKANE, *Prophets and Wise Men*, SBT XLIV (London, 1965), p. 36.

[106] R. J. WILLIAMS, *JAOS* XCII (1972), pp. 215f.

[107] J. J. A. VAN DIJK, *La sagesse suméro-accadienne* (Leiden, 1953), p. 22; H. W. F. SAGGS, *The Greatness that was Babylon* (London, 1962), p. 189.

[108] E. NIELSEN, *Oral Tradition: A Modern Problem in Old Testament Introduction*, SBT XI (London, 1954), p. 25.

[109] Ibid., p. 28.

the upper classes of the population.[110] As far as the existence of an exclusive guild is concerned, in studying the correspondence of Ḥeqanakhte, an Egyptian farmer and landowner, and his sons Siḥathor and Merisu, BAER has argued that they themselves, and not public letter-writers, wrote the letters ca. 2000 B.C.[111]

We come now to the question of the method by which these Egyptian influences were transmitted to the Hebrews. Two possibilities offer themselves for the process of borrowing: the influences may have come directly from the Egyptian sources, or indirectly through the mediation of others. These two ways, of course, are not mutually exclusive, and the probabilities favour a combination of both. The presence of Egyptians on the soil of Palestine for so many centuries must have resulted in a lively exchange of cultural features.

The many Egyptian motifs displayed on Phoenician ivories bear witness in a striking fashion to the extensive artistic influence which was exerted by the Nile valley on Syria.[112] It is naturally more difficult to trace literary influences. Yet the oft-quoted and rather arrogant words of the ruler of Byblus recorded in the eleventh century B.C. *Tale of Wenamun* reveal that Syria was beholden to Egypt for both technical and intellectual contributions:

> It was all the lands that Amun established, and it was after he had first established the land of Egypt from which you came that he established them. Craftsmanship came forth from it for the purpose of reaching the place where I am, and learning came forth from it in order to reach the place where I am. (2, 19-22)

Educated Egyptians, such as physicians and scribes, were frequently resident in foreign courts.[113] The Amarna tablets reveal that a scribe of the Tyrian ruler Abimilki was an Egyptian, for ALBRIGHT has shown that his letters include an Akkadian rendering of two Egyptian solar hymns.[114] There is also evidence that female musicians and singers were despatched from Egypt to Phoenicia, and they would certainly have introduced a repertoire of songs and hymns.[115] The

---

[110] H. BRUNNER, *Erziehung*, pp. 40-42.

[111] K. BAER, *JAOS* LXXXIII (1963), p. 19.

[112] W. HELCK, *Beziehungen*, pp. 576-581.

[113] Ibid., pp. 432-434.

[114] W. F. ALBRIGHT, "The Egyptian Correspondence of Abimilki, Prince of Tyre", *JEA* XXIII (1937), pp. 190-203.

[115] H. HICKMANN, *Le métier de musicien au temps des pharaons*, Cahiers d'Histoire égyptienne VI, 5/6, 2nd ed. (Cairo, 1954), pp. 286f.

role of the Phoenicians in transmitting much of the literary heritage of Egypt to Israel has been stressed by BARUCQ and ALBRIGHT.[116]

We must also remember that many Semites were temporarily or permanently settled in Egypt as captives of war, slaves, labourers, craftsmen or merchants.[117] Some of these, as we have already seen, even held high positions at the court. We have alluded to the Jewish colonies that were established throughout Egypt during the seventh and sixth centuries B.C. They must have been in constant communication with their compatriots and relatives in the homeland.

Another factor to be taken into account is the practice of the earlier New Kingdom pharaohs of taking the young sons and brothers of the rulers of the city-states in Canaan as hostages to Egypt, at the same time providing them with an Egyptian education. Thutmose III refers to the custom in the annals of his sixth campaign.[118] One purpose of this was to imbue the young men with an appreciation of the Egyptian cultural heritage, so that when they were sent back home to replace a ruler on his demise they would prove to be loyal and enthusiastic spokesmen on behalf of Egypt. They would certainly return with a first-hand knowledge of the language and literature of their temporary home.

The conclusion that we may draw from all this is that, long before the establishment of the Hebrew kingdom, the inhabitants of Syria-Palestine must have been familiar with many of the masterpieces of Egyptian literature. But for the fact that papyrus was fated to perish in the soil of Western Asia, the excavations would probably have yielded tangible proof of this long ago. How widespread the diffusion of literary works actually was in the ancient world has been revealed by the discovery of more durable clay tablets. Fragments of the Akkadian *Gilgamesh Epic* have been unearthed at Ugarit, Megiddo and, in Hittite and Hurrian versions, at Boğazköy. An Ugaritic translation of a Hurrian hymn to the goddess Nikkal was also found at Ugarit.

Turning to Egypt, we note the discovery among the Amarna tablets of copies of the Akkadian myths of Adapa and of Nergal and Ereshkigal, together with a Hittite recension of the epic known as *King of Battle*. A magical spell contained in a hieratic papyrus of the thirteenth

---

[116] A. BARUCQ, *op. cit.*, pp. 507-511; W. F. ALBRIGHT, *Yahweh and the Gods of Canaan* (London, 1968), pp. 223f.

[117] W. HELCK, *op. cit.*, pp. 342-369.

[118] *Urk.* IV, 690, 2-10, trans. in *ANET*, p. 239.

century B.C. incorporates an account of the rape of 'Anat by Seth (whom the Egyptians identified with the Semitic god Baal), an episode which is patently of Canaanite provenance. From the fifth century B.C. comes the Aramaic version of the Assyrian *Sayings of Aḥiqar* found at Elephantine. There is even a demotic fragment of papyrus from the Roman period which mentions this sage.

When we enquire as to the time when Israel was especially receptive to cultural influences from Egypt, we find that there were two periods during which the relations between both states were particularly close. The first, of course, was the age of David and Solomon, a time when the emerging kingdom required models for the novel institutions of kingship, government administration and a system of education. It is explicitly stated that Solomon sought material assistance from Phoenicia (I Kings v 1-12 [Heb. 15-26]), continuing the contacts with Tyre established by David, and there can be little doubt that he turned also to Egypt for other than material aid.

The second period was that of Hezekiah at the turn of the seventh century B.C. He was the first sole ruler in Israel since Solomon, and strove to emulate the latter (cf. II Chr. xxx 26). As we learn from the writings of Isaiah, this was a time when political and military assistance was sought from Egypt, a course which the prophet vehemently denounced (Isa. xx 5f., xxx 1-5, 7, xxxi 1-3, xxxvi 6, 9). It is clear that the "wise men" in Israel were an influential party at the court and pro-Egyptian. Just about this time we see the beginnings of a literary renaissance, with a fresh appreciation of the cultural achievements of the past, taking place in Egypt and Mesopotamia and probably in Phoenicia as well.[119] It is thus appropriate that the editorial work of the "men of Hezekiah" (Prov. xxv 1) should have been undertaken during this reign. Although these were the periods when Egypt and Israel were most closely associated, the contact was never entirely severed, but continued down into the Graeco-Roman period.

We have now completed our survey of some of the more important areas in which the Egyptian civilization contributed to that of Israel. Due caution must always be observed in assessing claims of direct influence, but the evidence is overwhelming that Israel drank deeply at the wells of Egypt. In a very real sense the Hebrews were "a people come out of Egypt" (Num. xxii 5, 11).

---

[119] W. F. ALBRIGHT, *From the Stone Age to Christianity* (Baltimore, 1940), pp. 241-244.

BEITRÄGE ZUR GESCHICHTE GROSS-JUDAS IN FRÜH- UND VORDAVIDISCHER ZEIT

VON

HANS-JÜRGEN ZOBEL

Greifswald

In der gegenwärtigen alttestamentlichen Forschung ist die Darstellung der frühen Geschichte Israels und damit auch Judas kontrovers. Während J. BRIGHT [1] und A. MALAMAT [2] — natürlich mit mancherlei Unterschieden im Einzelnen — davon ausgehen, daß der eigentliche Beginn der Geschichte Israels in der Zeit des Exodus- und Sinai-Geschehens durch die Volk- oder Nationwerdung Israels charakterisiert sei, mithin also die sog. Richter-Zeit als eine Epoche der Auflösung und Infragestellung dieser schon längst zuvor gewonnenen Einheit verstanden wird, rechnet M. NOTH mit einer nach Beendigung des Landnahmeprozesses entstandenen israelitischen Zwölfstämmeamphiktyonie und zugleich mit einer auf das judäische Gebirge und den Negeb begrenzten Sechsstämmeamphiktyonie, zu der er außer den Judäern noch die Kalebiter, Othnieliter, Keniter, Jerachmeeliter und Simeoniten zählt. Dieser Verband habe als "Sondergruppe innerhalb und neben dem großen israelitischen Zwölfstämmeverband" existiert, habe ein "Eigenleben" geführt und eine "Sonderstellung" eingenommen,[3] die durch die Königserhebung Davids in Hebron bestätigt und doch zugleich auch, jedenfalls in gewissem Grade, aufgehoben wird. Wie bei dieser Gegenüberstellung die grundsätzliche Frage danach, ob die Einheit Israels am Anfang seiner Geschichte steht oder ob diese Einheit erst das Ergebnis eines langen geschichtlichen Prozesses ist, gestellt wird, so ist damit zugleich die Problematik Judas aufs engste verknüpft. Denn wenn Juda von vornherein zum Ganzen Israels gehörte, erübrigt sich die Herausarbeitung seiner eigenständigen Geschichte; wird jedoch ein dauerhafter Zusammenschluß Judas mit den mittel-

---

[1] *Geschichte Israels*, 1966, S. 126. 183-184 u.ö.

[2] "Syrien und Palästina in der zweiten Hälfte des 2. Jahrtausends" in: *Fischer Weltgeschichte*, Bd. III, 1966, S. 177-221, S. 208-210. 215 u.ö.; DERS., *History of the Jewish People*, Bd. I, 1969, Teil 1.

[3] *Geschichte Israels*[6], 1966, S. 167.

und nordpalästinischen Stämmen erst z.Zt. Davids angenommen, dann setzt das die Sondergeschichte Judas zwingend voraus. Aber auch unter denen, die den zuletzt skizzierten Standpunkt vertreten, besteht darüber ein Dissens, ob Juda, wie es M. Noth [4] und A. Alt [5] vertraten, schon vor David als eine eigenständige, mehrere Glieder umfassende Größe bestand oder ob erst David die Integrierung der anderen auf dem südjudäischen Gebirge und im Negeb lebenden Stämmegruppe in den Stamm Juda bewirkte und somit die Heraus- bildung der Größe "Juda" inaugurierte, wie es zuletzt S. Mowinckel[6] und R. de Vaux [7] annahmen. Angesichts der weitreichenden Konse- quenzen, die mit dieser Frage verbunden sind, erscheint es nicht nur gerechtfertigt, sondern auch geboten, der Geschichte Judas in früh- und vordavidischer Zeit einmal gesondert nachzugehen. Dabei soll die Königserhebung Davids in Hebron den Ausgangspunkt für unsere Untersuchung bilden, weil wir mit der Überlieferung darüber einigermaßen festen Boden unter den Füßen haben.

I.

Von der Erhebung Davids zum König über Juda berichtet 2 Sam. ii 1-4a ganz knapp: Nachdem David auf die Frage an Jahwe, ob er von Ziklag aus "in eine der Städte Judas" ziehen solle, eine be- jahende Antwort erhalten und sodann Hebron genannt bekommen hat, bricht er mit seinen beiden Frauen und seinen "Männern" samt deren Familien auf und läßt sich "in den Städten Hebrons" nieder. Daraufhin kamen "die Männer Judas" und salbten David zum König über "das Haus Juda". Dabei ist zu bedenken, daß David vor seiner Wahl "auf die Seite des internationalen Berufskriegertums" gehörte.[8] Die Zahl seiner Söldner wird in 1 Sam. xxii 2 mit 400, in 1 Sam. xxiii 13; xxv 13; xxvii 2; xxx 9 aber mit 600 angegeben, woraus zumindest soviel erhellt, daß dieses Berufsheer einen die folgenden Vorgänge wesentlich mitbestimmenden Machtfaktor dar- stellt. David handelte entschlossen und zielstrebig, löste damit die Aktion der Männer Judas aus und lenkte sie in ihm genehme Bahnen. Hierbei werden wir genauso wie in 2 Sam. v 3 einen Vertrag

---

[4] *Das System der zwölf Stämme Israels*, 1930, 1966, S. 107-108.
[5] *Die Staatenbildung der Israeliten in Palästina*, 1930, in: *Kl. Schr.* II, ²1953, S. 1-65, S. 41.
[6] " 'Rahelstämme' und 'Leastämme' " in: *Von Ugarit nach Qumran (BZAW LXXVII)*, 1958, 1961, S. 129-150, S. 137-138.
[7] *Histoire Ancienne d'Israël*, 1971, S. 508-510. 616.
[8] A. Alt, a.a.O. (Anm. 5), S. 37.

(בְּרִית)[9] anzunehmen haben, wie denn A. ALT mit Recht darauf verweist: "der Initiative des einen entspricht die Initiative der anderen, und beide zusammen ergeben die gegenseitige Bindung, auf der das Staatswesen beruht" und sogleich fortfährt: "Dagegen fehlt hier jene Initiative Jahwes vor allem Handeln von Menschen, die uns in der Urgestalt des Reiches Israel als grundlegender ideeller Faktor so kräftig entgegentrat".[10] David wird selbst in der Tradition noch "die Priorität der politischen Idee" [11] belassen. Die Königswahl Davids ist im Gegensatz zu der Sauls "ein rein politischer Vorgang".[12] Auch die dynastische Bindung der Thronfolge markiert diesen Unterschied, und der Tatbestand, daß die "Männer Judas" stets nachdrücklich daran festhalten und sie gegen andersartige Bestrebungen hartnäckig verteidigt haben,[13] deutet auf die tiefe Verwurzelung dieser Tradition in Juda hin. Und schließlich ist festzuhalten, daß die ideelle Begründung des judäischen Königtums ein der Wahl erst später nachfolgender Akt ist und in den sog. Letzten Worten Davids (2 Sam. xxiii 1-7)[14] in den Begriff einer בְּרִית עוֹלָם gefaßt wird, die Jahwe mit David geschlossen hat. Den gleichen Sachverhalt finden wir in der Nathanweissagung (2 Sam. vii), die durch die auffällige Häufung des Wortes עוֹלָם (v. 13, 16 bis!, 24-26, 29bis!) auch begrifflich 2 Sam. xxiii recht nahe steht. Wie damit einerseits auf die Bedeutung der Berit-Vorstellung in der judäischen Tradition aufmerksam gemacht wird, so ist anderseits die Präponderanz des politischen Vorgangs vor dem religiösen Akt zu beachten.

Für unsere Fragestellung ist zunächst die Tatsache von Belang, daß bei der Königserhebung Davids Juda als eine politische Größe fungiert, also kein geographischer Terminus ist. Könnte man an letztes noch bei der Bezeichnung "Städte Judas" oder auch "Männer Judas" denken, so wird ein solches Verständnis durch den Begriff "Haus Juda" als unzutreffend erwiesen. Da בֵּית יְהוּדָה stets mit dem Plur. des Verbs konstruiert wird,[15] ist damit eine Vielzahl von Menschen gemeint. Weiter macht 1 Kg. xii 21: "Als Rehabeam

---

[9] Vgl. dazu ALT, a.a.O. (Anm. 5), S. 41.
[10] a.a.O. (Anm. 5), S. 41.
[11] a.a.O. (Anm. 5), S. 41-42.
[12] M. NOTH, a.a.O. (Anm. 3), S. 168; ebenso über 2 Sam. v 1-3 auf S. 172.
[13] Vgl. 2 Kg. xi; xiv 19-21; xxi 23-24; xxiii 30.
[14] Vgl. H. NEIL RICHARDSON, "The Last Words of David: Some Notes on II Samuel 23:1-7" in: JBL XC, 1971, S. 257-266.
[15] Vgl. z. B. 2 Sam. ii 7, 10; Jer. iii 18; xxxvi 3.

nach Jerusalem kam, versammelte er das ganze Haus Juda und den Stamm Benjamin, 180 000 auserlesene Krieger, um mit dem Haus Israel Krieg zu führen" deutlich, daß der Begriff "Haus Juda" offenbar von Hause aus eine zusammenfassende Bezeichnung für die Vollbürger, also die wehrfähigen Männer der fest umgrenzten politischen Einheit Juda ist. Folglich ist zumindest prinzipiell der Begriff "Haus Juda" mit der Bezeichnung "Männer Judas" identisch, woraus sich ergibt, daß Juda in allen diesen Wendungen stets die gleiche Größe meint. Da nun das kalebitische Hebron zu den Städten Judas gezählt wird, ist der Umfang der politischen Einheit Juda viel weiter als nur der des nördlich von Hebron ansässigen Stammes Juda. Die Tatsache, das David im Zuge des Aufbaus und der Abrundung seines Königtums Jerusalem erobern, sodann mit den Philistern kämpfen und sich u.a. der Amalekiter und Edomiter erwehren mußte, macht deutlich, daß das Territorium Judas vom jebusitischen Jerusalem im Norden bis zum Negeb bzw. zur Wüste im Süden, von der philistäischen Pentapolis im Westen bis zum Toten Meer im Osten reichte. Es handelt sich demnach um einen geographisch fest umgrenzten Raum, dessen Zentrum Hebron bildete. Davids Königtum war also von Anfang an ein Territorialkönigtum. Die Tatsache, daß David nach Hebron zieht und somit die Männer Judas zur Anerkennung seiner Person als Königs über Juda bewegt, läßt erkennen, daß dieses geographische Gebiet bereits eine politische Einheit darstellte, daß Hebron die Funktion einer Metropole inne hatte und daß die "Männer Judas" die politischen Entscheidungen zu treffen hatten und somit die politische Macht repräsentierten. Aus alledem ergibt sich die Schlußfolgerung, daß das "Haus Juda" zum Zeitpunkt der Königswahl Davids in Hebron ein politisches Gemeinwesen war, in dessen Geschichte David bestimmend und verändernd eintrat. Mit M. NOTH [16] wollen wir dieses Gemeinwesen "Groß-Juda" nennen.

II.

Ein wertvolles Zeugnis für dieses Groß-Juda in der Zeit vor der Königserhebung Davids in Hebron stellt die Aufzählung der von David mit Beuteanteilen aus einem Kampf gegen die Amalekiter beschenkten "Ältesten Judas" in 1 Sam. xxx 27-31 dar. Daß es sich um eine Liste handelt, die "eine Größe eigener Art ist", hat zuletzt

---

[16] a.a.O. (Anm. 4), S. 107.

H. J. Stoebe [17] betont; denn *v.* 26 und 31b haben die Funktion von
Klammern, um die von Haus aus eigenständige Liste in den er-
zählenden Kontext einzufügen. Daß dabei eine gewisse Spannung
zwischen *v.* 31b und der Liste selbst entsteht, vermag das Gesagte
ausreichend zu begründen. Denn die Absicht von *v.* 31b, die zuvor
genannten Ortsnamen als Stationen des Flüchtlingslebens Davids
zu deuten, findet in der Liste insofern keinen Rückhalt, als, worauf
H. J. Stoebe [18] hinwies, die "Stätten, an denen die Davidüber-
lieferung in besonderem Maße haftete, nicht genannt werden, ja
daß sie alle etwas außerhalb seines Wirkungsbereiches als Flüchtling
liegen". Auf der anderen Seite aber ist, wenn auch kein ursprünglich
literarischer, so doch ein sachlich-inhaltlicher Bezug zwischen dem
Terminus "Älteste Judas" in der Überleitung zur Liste (*v.* 26) und
der Liste selbst insofern anzunehmen, als das durchgängige לַאֲשֶׁר בְּ
der Liste eine solche Wendung wie Älteste oder Männer Judas
voraussetzt. Und schließlich ist H. J. Stoebe auch darin zuzustimmen,
daß die Liste nicht aus nachdavidischer Zeit stammt, weil *v.* 31b sie
bereits voraussetzt und sie nicht etwa umgekehrt den *v.* 31b erläutert.
Das heißt, daß man mit guten Gründen diese listenhafte Aufzählung
der Zeit zuweisen darf, der sie dem erzählerischen Zusammenhang
gemäß angehören will, nämlich der Frühzeit Davids.[19]

Ehe wir uns der Auswertung der Liste selbst zuwenden, ist noch
eine weitere Vorfrage zu beantworten. Welche Absicht verfolgte
David mit der Verteilung von Beutegeschenken der Amalekiter
an judäische Älteste? Der Gedanke, den H. J. Stoebe [20] in Weiter-
führung einer Bemerkung B. Stades [21] äußerte, daß "diese Geschenke
und Aufwendungen eine Rolle bei der Anerkennung des Königtums
Davids in Hebron gespielt haben, etwa in der Form von Gaben, die
die Verhandlungen begleiteten", ist dahingehend zu präzisieren,
daß David damit wohl Zweierlei im Auge hatte. Die Bezeichnung
der Amalekiter als "Feinde Jahwes" innerhalb der Übergabeformel
der Geschenke: "Seht! Da habt ihr eine Gabe aus der Beute der
Feinde Jahwes" (*v.* 26) läßt David als Rächer Jahwes erscheinen, verteidigt ihn also gegen den möglichen Vorwurf, er stehe als Vasall
der Philister auf Seiten des Gegners und vertrete nicht die Inter-

---

[17] *Kommentar*, z. St., S. 518.
[18] *Kommentar*, z. St., S. 519.
[19] So auch zuletzt H. J. Stoebe, ebenda.
[20] *Kommentar*, z. St., S. 519.
[21] *Geschichte des Volkes Israel*, Bd. I, 1887, S. 260.

essen und Belange Judas. Obendrein ist zu bedenken, daß die Beute eigentlich denen gehört, die den Krieg geführt und seine Lasten getragen haben.[22] Indem David die Amalekiterbeute nicht für sich und seine Söldner verwendet, sondern an judäische Älteste verteilen läßt, drückt er aus, daß er den Kampf als in deren Auftrag und zu deren Gunsten geführt betrachtet. David gibt sich damit als echten Judäer aus, anerkennt die Führungsposition der Ältesten und weist sie auf seine ihnen zugute kommende militärische Potenz hin. Er wirbt um die Gunst der Ältesten und stellt sich als ein Heerführer vor, der bei den Ältesten, mithin bei den Judäern selbst zu großen Erwartungen berechtigt. Gewiß war es Davids Absicht, damit seine Königswahl aufs Nachhaltigste vorzubereiten;[23] die Wahl selbst aber war wohl noch nicht im Gespräch. Das besagt, daß wir die hier vorausgesetzten Ereignisse in die Frühzeit Davids zu datieren und von den Vorgängen in und um Hebron zeitlich abzurücken haben.

Treffen diese Überlegungen zu, dann liegt die Schlußfolgerung auf der Hand: 1 Sam. xxx 26-31 bezeugt die Existenz der politischen Einheit Groß-Juda.[24] Die in neuerer Zeit mehrfach wiederholte Meinung,[25] die in 1 Sam. xxx genannten Maßnahmen Davids hätten der Vorbereitung des eigentlich erst mit seiner Königserhebung in Hebron zustande gekommenen Zusammenschlusses der Stämme des Südens gedient, die Bezeichnung "Älteste Judas" sei also "eine zusammenfassende Vorwegnahme des Ergebnisses"[26], hat einmal den Text gegen sich, der von "Ältesten" spricht,[27] und zum anderen den Umstand, daß nur dann, wenn die Ältesten die Gewalt in Händen halten und wirklich "die Machthaber"[28] sind, Davids Geschenkaktion den an sie geknüpften Erwartungen gerecht werden und er darauf hoffen kann, aus ihrer Hand die politische Gewalt übertragen zu bekommen. Nicht zuletzt aber sei darauf hingewiesen, daß Juda in dem gleichen weitausgreifenden, nämlich

---

[22] Vgl. H. Peucker, "Beute" in: *BHH* I, 1962, Sp. 236.

[23] So mit Recht H. Gressmann, *SAT* II, 1, ²1921, S. 111, und H. W. Hertzberg, *ATD* X, ³1965, S. 184.

[24] M. Noth, a.a.O. (Anm. 4), S. 107.

[25] Zuletzt H. J. Stoebe, *Kommentar*, z. St., S. 518.

[26] So Stoebe, ebenda.

[27] In seiner Art ist es konsequent, wenn R. de Vaux, a.a.O. (Anm. 7), S. 510, Anm. 82 diese Wendung als "une glose évidente" bezeichnet, weil er mit LXX den Plur. "seine Freunde" statt MT Sing. רֵעֵהוּ liest. In dieser Frage richtig H. J. Stoebe, *Kommentar*, S. 509: "ein nachträglich erläuternder Zusatz zu זִקְנֵי יְהוּדָה".

[28] So H. Gressmann, a.a.O. (Anm. 23), S. 111.

Hebron (*v.* 31a) und den Negeb (*v.* 27a: Ramoth-Negeb) samt Jerachmeelitern und Kenitern (*v.* 29) mit umfassenden Sinn gebraucht ist, wie wir es in dem Bericht von 2 Sam. II beobachteten.

Mit diesen Feststellungen haben wir die Möglichkeit gewonnen, der Liste von 1 Sam. xxx präzisere Informationen über den Umfang Groß-Judas und über die Zahl der zu ihm gehörenden Glieder zu entnehmen. Von den 13 völlig gleichartig gestalteten, mit בַּ לַאֲשֶׁר "denen in" eingeleiteten Elementen der Liste werden zwei mit עָרֵי "Städte" + Stammesnamen, die übrigen elf geweils mit einem Ortsnamen gebildet. Die folgenden Ortschaften werden aufgezählt:

1. *Beth-El*: Es ist nicht an das bekannte ephraimitische Bethel zu denken, sondern an eine Örtlichkeit des Negeb, die Jos. xv 30 (LXX[B]) Βαιθηλ, Jos. xix 4 (MT) בְּתוּל und 1 Chr. iv 30 בְּתוּאֵל heißt.[29] H. W. HERTZBERG [30] und H. J. STOEBE [31] lesen nach Jos. xix 4 בְּתוּל. Dieser Ort wird zum Besitz Simeons inmitten Judas gerechnet,[32] gehört zum 1. Gau Josias und wird durchweg auf der heutigen *chirbet el-ḳarjetēn*, ca. 8 km nördlich von *tell 'arād*, etwa 30 km nordöstlich von Beerseba angesetzt.[33]

2. *Ramoth-Negeb*: Die LXX hat Ραμα νότου, was mit dem Ramath-Negeb von Jos. XIX 8 identisch ist. Wahrscheinlich handelt es sich hier um denselben Ort.[34] Er wird ebenfalls zu Simeon gezählt. Eine Lokalisierung steht noch aus.

3. *Jattir*: Es gehört nach Jos. xv 48 zum 6. Gau Josias und nach Jos. XXI 14 zu den Levitenstädten, die in Juda und Simeon lagen. Es wird auf der *chirbet 'attīr*, ca. 20 km südsüdwestlich von Hebron, etwa 25 km nordöstlich von Beerseba angesetzt.[35]

4. *Aroer*: Die LXX weist neben Αροηρ als korrigierenden Zusatz noch Αμμαδι, ohne das bei ihr sonst übliche ἐν, auf. Das zeigt, daß die LXX hinter עֲרֹעֵר noch einen weiteren Buchstaben vorfand.[36] Das bestätigt Jos. xv 22, wo der Ort Ararah heißt. Er gehört zum 1.

---

[29] O. THENIUS-M. LÖHR, *Die Bücher Samuels* (KeH IV), ³1898, S. 118.

[30] *ATD* X, S. 184.

[31] *Kommentar*, z. St., S. 509.

[32] Vgl. M. NOTH, *Das Buch Josua* ², 1953, S. 113-114.141.

[33] So F.-M. ABEL, *Géographie*, II, S. 283; A. ALT, *ZDPV* LXIX, 1953, S. 85ff.; J. SIMONS, *Texts*, § 321.

[34] H. W. HERTZBERG, *ATD* X, S. 184, Anm. 4; H. J. STOEBE, *Komm.*, S. 509.

[35] A. ALT, *PJB* XXVIII, 1932, S. 15f.; F.-M. ABEL, *Géographie*, II, S. 356; J. SIMONS, *Texts*, § 722; vgl. auch H. J. STOEBE, *Komm.*, S. 509.

[36] So schon J. WELLHAUSEN, *Der Text der Bücher Samuelis*, 1871, S. 145.

Gau Josias und wird lokalisiert auf einer *chirbe* am *bīr ʿarʿāra* im *wādi ʿarʿāra*,[37] 21 km südöstlich von Beerseba.

5. *Siphmoth*: Es findet sich nur hier im AT. Eine Lokalisierung steht aus.

6. *Estemoah*: Es ist identisch mit dem gleichnamigen Ort von Jos. xv 50; xxi 14 (1 Chr. iv 17, 19), gehört wiederum zum 6. Gau und ist Levitenstadt. Es ist das heutige *es-semūʿa*, ca. 7 km nordöstlich von Jattir, 15 km südlich von Hebron.[38]

7. *Rakal*: Mit LXX ist der MT zu verbessern zu כַּרְמֶל.[39] Jos. xv 55 zählt es zum 8. Gau. Der Ortsname findet sich noch in 1 Sam. xv 12; xxv 2ff. Es ist das heutige *el-kirmil*, ca. 6 km ostnordöstlich von *es-semūʿa*.

8. *Horma*:[40] Nach Jos. xii 14 ist es eine kanaanäische Königsstadt gewesen;[41] nach Jos. xv 30 gehört es zum 1. Gau; nach Jos. xix 4 (1 Chr. iv 30) wird es Simeon zugerechnet, was offenbar mit M. NOTH [42] darauf beruht, daß es nach Jdc. I 17 von Simeon erobert wurde. Als Kanaanäerstadt mit vormaligem Namen Zephat ist sie noch Num. xiv 45; xxi 3; Deut. i 44 erwähnt. Mit A. ALT [43] suchen wir die Stadt auf dem *tell el-mšāš*, 5 km östlich von Beerseba.[44]

9. *Bor-Aschan*: Nach M. NOTH [45] ist es identisch mit Aschan von Jos. xv 42; xix 7. Es wird dem 4. Gau zugewiesen und zählt zu Simeon (so auch Jos. xxi 16cj.). Es wird lokalisiert auf der *chirbet ʿasan*, ca. 2 km nördlich von Beerseba.[46]

10. *Atak*: In Jos. xv 42; xix 7 ist der Name verschrieben zu Eter (Jos. xv 42 LXX: 'Ιθαχ). Nach Jos. xv 42 gehört es zum 4. Gau und nach Jos. xix 7 zu Simeon. M. NOTH [47] sucht es "in derselben Gegend".

---

[37] Vgl. A. ALT, *JPOS* XII, 1932, S. 133; DERS., *PJB* XXX, 1934, S. 19; F.-M. ABEL, *Géographie*, II, S. 250; J. SIMONS, *Texts*, § 723; auch H. J. STOEBE, *Komm.*, S. 509.

[38] So zuletzt H. J. STOEBE, *Komm.*, S. 509.

[39] So schon J. WELLHAUSEN, a.a.O. (Anm. 36), S. 146; zuletzt R. DE VAUX, a.a.O. (Anm. 7); dagegen hält H. J. STOEBE, *Komm.*, S. 509 am MT fest.

[40] Vgl. K.-H. BERNHARDT, "Horma" in: *BHH* II, 1964, Sp. 749.

[41] Dazu vgl. M. NOTH, a.a.O. (Anm. 32), S. 71f.

[42] a.a.O. (Anm. 32), S. 113.

[43] *JPOS* XV, 1935, S. 322f.

[44] So auch F. M. ABEL, *Géographie*, II, S. 350; J. SIMONS, *Texts*, § 727. Anders jüngst F. CRÜSEMANN, *ZDPV* LXXXIX, 1973, S. 211-224.

[45] a.a.O. (Anm. 32), S. 113.

[46] A. MUSIL, *Arabia Petraea*, II, 2, 1908, S. 66. 245; zuletzt H. J. STOEBE, *Komm.*, S. 509.

[47] a.a.O. (Anm. 32), S. 113.

11. *Hebron*:[48] Es ist eine kanaanäische Königsstadt, die nach Jos. xi 21 von Josua, nach Jdc. i 10 von Juda, aber nach Jdc. i 20 in Wirklichkeit von Kaleb eingenommen wurde, der die Enakiter aus der damals Kirjat-Arba heißenden Stadt verdrängte (vgl. Jos. xiv 6-15). Es ist der heutige *tell er-rumēde*, westlich der arabischen Stadt *el-chalīl*.

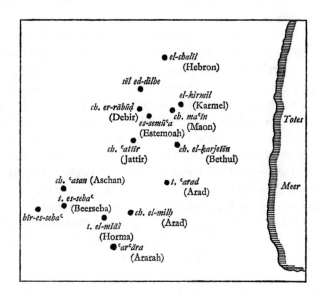

Aus dieser Übersicht erhellt, daß es sich bei den Orten ausschließlich um solche handelt, die südlich von Hebron liegen und die über das südliche oder südöstliche Gebirge Juda und den angrenzenden Negeb bis zum Rande des Kulturlandes jenseits von Beerseba fast gleichmäßig verteilt sind. Damit wird offenbar, daß die Liste ein im Osten, Westen und Süden fest umgrenztes Territorium zum Gegenstand hat.

Wie die alttestamentliche Überlieferung zu erkennen gibt, gehört Hebron den Kalebitern. Auch Karmel ist ein kalebitischer Ort, denn dort befand sich nach 1 Sam. xxv 2 das Anwesen Nabals, der selbst in Maon (= *chirbet ma'īn*), ca. 15 km südlich von Hebron, wohnte und nach *v.* 3 ein Kalebiter war. Demnach erstreckte sich das Gebiet Kalebs von Hebron aus nach Südosten hin.[49]

---

[48] K. ELLIGER, "Hebron" in: *BHH* II, 1964, Sp. 669-670.

[49] Vgl. R. DE VAUX, a.a.O. (Anm. 7), S. 496-497.

Daneben deutet die Überlieferung bezüglich der Stadt Horma an, daß sie zum Besitztum Simeons gehörte. Nun werden im Josua-Buch von unseren Städten noch Bethul, Ramath-Negeb, Bor-Aschan und Atak zu Simeon gezählt. Daß es sich hierbei um eine späte Konstruktion handelt, ist nicht auszuschließen. Indes liegen alle diese Orte im Bereich von Horma und kennzeichnen somit ein bestimmtes Gebiet, das südwestlich an das von Kaleb anschließt und wohl doch simeonitisch war.

Von den bisher lokalisierten Orten sind übrig Estemoah und Jattir südlich von Hebron sowie Ararah südöstlich von Horma. Daß diese Städte den Kalebitern oder den Simeoniten gehörten, ist möglich, aber nicht zwingend. Denn einige alte Überlieferungen führen die Eroberung der vormals kanaanäischen Stadt Debir und die Nutzung zweier nahebei gelegener Wasserbecken auf die mit den Kalebitern nahe verwandten Othnieliter zurück (Jos. xv 13-19; Jdc. i 11-15; iii 9; 1 Chr. iv 13). Die Lage der genannten Becken und der Stadt Debir sind umstritten. Was die Becken angeht, so hat die größte Wahrscheinlichkeit ihre von F.-M. ABEL [50] und M. NOTH [51] vertretene Ansetzung im *sēl ed-dilbe*, ca. 9 km südwestlich von Hebron, für sich.[52] Deshalb wird man Debir auf dem *tell ṭarrāme*, unmittelbar südwestlich von diesen Becken [53] oder auf der 5 km weiter südlich gelegenen *chirbet er-rābūḍ* [54] suchen dürfen. Wie A. KUSCHKE mitteilt,[55] hat die Identifizierung von Debir auf der zuletzt genannten *chirbe* "durch Sondierungen des israelischen Survey Bestätigung gefunden". Damit liegt das othnielitische Debir südlich von Hebron. In jener Gegend finden sich auch die beiden Ortschaften unserer Liste, Estemoah und Jattir. Die Schlußfolgerung, daß sie zum Gebiet der Othnieliter gehören, liegt auf der Hand.

Als letzter der lokalisierten Orte ist noch Ararah übrig. Etwa 21 km nordöstlich von ihm liegt Arad. Die Überlieferung von Jdc. i 16 verbindet den Negeb von Arad mit den Kenitern. Von daher wäre es denkbar, Ararah auch den Kenitern zuzuweisen. Auf Grund der Erwähnung einer Stadt "Arad vom Beth Jerachmeels" in der Scheschonk-Liste, identifiziert mit dem *tell el-milḥ*, knapp 10 km

---

[50] *Géographie*, I, S. 454.
[51] *JPOS* XV, 1935, S. 48f.
[52] So auch R. DE VAUX, a.a.O. (Anm. 7), S. 498.
[53] So M. NOTH, a.a.O. (Anm. 51), S. 49f.
[54] So K. GALLING, *ZDPV* LXX, 1954, S. 135-141.
[55] *ZDPV* LXXXVII, 1971, S. 218.

nordöstlich von Ararah,[56] wäre jedoch eine Zuordnung unserer
Stadt an die Jerachmeeliter ebensogut möglich. Gegen beide Zuwei-
sungen spricht indes, daß unsere Liste ausdrücklich "Städte der
Jerachmeeliter" und "Städte der Keniter" aufführt. Daraus ergibt
sich mit hoher Wahrscheinlichkeit, daß Ararah weder den Jerachmeelitern noch den Kenitern zugehört hat. Die Tatsache, daß die
Lokalisierung auf der *chirbet 'ar'āra* diese Stadt weit in den Süden
verlegt, ja zum südlichsten Ort unserer Liste überhaupt macht,
läßt Zweifel an der vorgeschlagenen Ansetzung aufkommen. Diese
werden noch dadurch verstärkt, daß die Gaueinteilung Josias, wie
sie das Josua-Buch widerspiegelt, das auch von uns erarbeitete
Zueinander der jeweiligen Orte im großen und ganzen bestätigt,
werden doch Jattir und Estemoah zum 6., Karmel und Hebron zum 8.
und 7., Horma und Bethul zum 1. und Bor-Aschan und Atak zum 4.
Gau gezählt. Daß Hebron als eigener Gau vom einstmals kale-
bitischen Gebiet losgetrennt wurde, läßt sich ohne weiteres verstehen. Indes fällt Ararah bei seiner Zuweisung zum 1. Gau völlig
aus der Reihe. Denn trotz mancher Unsicherheiten scheint die
Aufzählung der Orte in der Liste bei Bethul beginnend etwa nach
Westen oder Nordwesten und Norden über den wie Bethul ebenfalls simeonitischen Ort Ramoth-Negeb nach Jattir gelaufen zu sein.
Da die nächsten uns bekannten Orte Estemoah und Karmel von
Jattir aus nördlich und dann weiter nordöstlich liegen, müßte man
erwarten, daß sowohl Ararah als auch das sonst unbekannte Siphmoth in der Gegend zwischen Jattir und Estemoah zu suchen sind.
Weiter zählt die Liste summarisch die Städte von Jerachmeel und
Kain, offenbar in der Folge von Ost nach West, auf, um mit den
ebenfalls beieinander liegenden Orten Horma, Bor-Aschan und
dem von M. NOTH zurecht in der gleichen Gegend gesuchten Atak [57]
zu schließen. Daß dann Hebron folgt, ist aus seiner Funktion als
Hauptstadt heraus verständlich. Damit sind die Zweifel gegen die
bisher vorgeschlagene Ansetzung unseres Aroer-Ararah zur Genüge
begründet.

Wie man sich auch in dieser Frage entscheiden mag, fest steht,
daß in der Liste Ortschaften der Simeoniten, Kalebiter und Othnieliter sowie der Jerachmeeliter und Keniter genannt werden. Nur
der Bereich des eigentlichen Stammes Juda fehlt. Aber das erklärt
sich ohne Schwierigkeit aus der erzählerischen Absicht, der die Liste

---

[56] Vgl. R. DE VAUX, a.a.O. (Anm. 7), S. 499.
[57] S. Anm. 47.

dienstbar gemacht wurde. David ist gebürtiger Judäer. Mithin
erschien es dem Erzähler unangebracht, daß David erst durch
Geschenke seinen eigenen Stamm hätte gewinnen müssen. Deshalb
blieb der Raum nördlich von Hebron unberücksichtigt. Das besagt aber für unsere Fragestellung, daß wir Juda zum ermittelten
Stämmekreis hinzuzählen müssen, auch deshalb, weil diese Ältesten
als Älteste Judas bezeichnet werden und Hebron dadurch, daß es
als letzter Ort der Liste genannt wird, den Rang einer zentralen
Stadt inne hat. Demnach können wir als weiteres Ergebnis festhalten,
daß auch in frühdavidischer Zeit das Gemeinwesen Groß-Juda
existierte und daß ihm die Stämme oder Stämmegruppen Juda,
Kaleb, Othniel, Simeon, Jerachmeel und Kain zugehörten.

<h2 style="text-align:center">III.</h2>

Wenn wir die innere Struktur dieses politischen Gemeinwesens
zu erfassen versuchen wollen, so bietet sich wiederum die Liste
aus 1 Sam. xxx als wertvolle Quelle an. Das sie bestimmende
Prinzip ist das der Gliederung nach Städten. Selbst bei den Stämme-
bezeichnungen wird ausdrücklich von "Städten der Jerachmeeliter"
und "Städten der Keniter" gesprochen. Mit aller nur wünschenswer-
ten Deutlichkeit ist damit ein territoriales Gliederungsprinzip
ausgedrückt. Demnach zerfällt das Gebiet Groß-Judas in einzelne
Distrikte, deren jeweilige Zentren die Städte waren. Dieses territoriale Prinzip galt offenbar nicht nur auf der unteren Ebene, den
Distrikten oder Bezirken, sondern auch auf der höheren Ebene
insofern, als das zentral gelegene Hebron nun seinerseits die Hauptstadt für ganz Groß-Juda war.

Voraussetzung für eine solche straffe, das gesamte Territorium
erfassende Gliederung ist sein uneingeschränkter Besitz. Immerhin
erfahren wir noch darüber soviel, daß die Städte Hebron, Debir und
Horma von Kalebitern, Othnielitern und Simeoniten erobert wurden.
Und die Annahme, daß die Judäer sich der Stadt Bethlehem mit Gewalt bemächtigten, ist deshalb nicht unwahrscheinlich, weil sie noch
in einem Amarna-Brief (290, 15f.) als "eine Stadt des Landes Jerusalem" erscheint. Obendrein begegnet uns in der alttestamentlichen
Überlieferung nicht der geringste Anhalt für eine Art Abgrenzung
zwischen Judäern und Kanaanäern; im Gegenteil wird ein selbstver-
ständliches Miteinander von judäischen und kanaanäischen Bevölke-
rungsgruppen bezeugt, was darauf schließen läßt, daß die Kanaanäer
sich zu arrangieren wußten und den Judäern keine besonderen

Schwierigkeiten bereiteten.[58] Somit ist nichts Ernstliches gegen eine Territorialordnung für Groß-Juda einzuwenden.

Nun würde jede derartige Gliederung eines Gemeinwesens ein lebensfremdes, hemmendes Prinzip bleiben, wenn nicht die wirtschaftlichen Gegebenheiten des Landes für ein solches staatliches Ordnungsschema sprechen würden. Hinsichtlich Groß-Judas hat A. ALT[59] in einem wenig beachteten Anmerkungssatz darauf aufmerksam gemacht. Das Land geht nach Süden, aber auch nach Osten hin in weite, dünn oder gar nicht besiedelte Steppengebiete über. Das bedingt eine ganz spezifische Wirtschaftsstruktur und anderseits eine dementsprechende Aufteilung des dafür verfügbaren Landes. Seine Nutzung durch die in der Regel weit entfernt wohnende Bevölkerung mußte so geordnet sein, daß Reibungen und Auseinandersetzungen innerhalb des Gemeinwesens weitestgehend ausgeschaltet und der Zusammenhalt nicht gefährdet oder in Frage gestellt wurde.

Daß wir mit diesen Erwägungen auf dem richtigen Wege sind, zeigen einige verstreute Notizen des AT. Was über die Erwerbsform in Groß-Juda zu erkennen ist, läßt sich schnell zusammentragen. In 1 Sam. xxiv 4 werden Kleinviehhürden in der Midbar von En-Gedi (v. 2) erwähnt. In der schon oben herangezogenen Erzählung über die Zuweisung von Debir an Othniel ist von Wasserstellen die Rede, auf die jede Kleinviehhaltung im Negeb angewiesen ist (Jos. xv 19; Jdc. i 15). In 1 Sam. xxvii 9 werden Klein- und Großvieh, Esel und Kamele als Beutestücke aus Groß-Juda aufgezählt. Desgleichen werden Schafe und Rinder genannt (1 Sam. xxx 20). Und nicht zuletzt entwirft die Erzählung über Nabal (1 Sam. xxv) ein gewiß zu verallgemeinerndes Bild von der Wirtschaftsstruktur in jenem Gebiet. Nabal wird als überaus begüterter Mann (v. 2) geschildert; er hält ein Gelage wie ein König (v. 36), besitzt 3000 Schafe und 1000 Ziegen (v. 2), die von seinen Lohnhirten (v. 7) in der Midbar (v. 21) geweidet werden. Insgesamt bekommt man den Eindruck des Vorherrschens einer Kleinviehwirtschaft, neben der auch Ackerbau betrieben wurde.

Die Kleinviehwirtschaft ist auf die Steppengebiete angewiesen. So mußten die Nutzungsrechte an ihnen genau festgelegt werden. Daß das geschehen ist, läßt die alttestamentliche Überlieferung noch

---

[58] Vgl. vor allem Gen. xxxviii; zuletzt dazu R. DE VAUX, a.a.O. (Anm. 7), S. 503-505.

[59] a.a.O. (Anm. 5), S. 41, Anm. 2.

deutlich erkennen. Jedes der zu Groß-Juda gehörenden Glieder besaß ein Stück Negeb, das demnach "Negeb der Judäer" (1 Sam. xxvii 10; vgl. auch 1 Sam. xxx 14), "Negeb der Jerachmeeliter" (1 Sam. xxvii 10), "Negeb der Keniter" (1 Sam. xxvii 10; vgl. Jdc. i 16: Negeb bei Arad sowie Num. xxi 1; xxxiii 40), "Negeb der Kalebiter" (1 Sam. xxx 14) und — so ist aus Jos. xv 19; Jdc. i 15 zu schließen — "Negeb der Othnieliter" hieß. Lediglich die Bezeichnung "Negeb der Simeoniten" fehlt im AT. Daneben begegnet der Ausdruck "Negeb der Kreti" für den Anteil der Philister (1 Sam. xxx 14; vgl. 1 Sam. xxx 1). Die zusammenfassende, ganz Juda meinende Wendung lautet "Negeb Judas" (2 Sam. xxiv 7). Daß die einzelnen Gebiete Teile Groß-Judas waren, bezeugt 1 Sam. xxx 16 insofern, als die verschiedenen Negeb-Stücke dann als "Land der Philister" und "Land Judas" zusammengefaßt werden.

Gerade dieser Sachverhalt, daß man unter sich den Besitz am Negeb genau aufgeteilt und sich zugleich gegenüber den Philistern abgegrenzt hatte, setzt ein hohes Maß von innerem Zusammenhalt dieses Gemeinwesens voraus und zeigt obendrein, daß Groß-Juda als eine einheitliche geschlossene politische Größe den Philistern gegenüberzutreten vermochte. Die Frage nach der Verfassungsstruktur ist folglich legitim, wenn sie auch schwer zu beantworten ist. In der Einführung unserer Liste wird von "Ältesten" Groß-Judas gesprochen. Das läßt an eine Stammesverfassung denken. Ihr widerspricht jedoch die durchgängige territoriale Gliederung. Denn die Ältesten vertreten nicht eine genealogische, sondern eine territorial umgrenzte Wohngemeinschaft, also nicht einen Stamm oder eine Sippe, sondern eine Stadt oder einen bestimmten Distrikt. Die Bezeichnung "Älteste" ist demnach ein Rudiment aus der nomadisch-halbnomadischen Vergangenheit der zu Groß-Juda verbundenen Gruppen. Darauf führt auch die Beobachtung, daß in den Büchern Richter, Samuel und Könige insgesamt zwar 15mal die Wendung "Älteste Israels", aber mit unserer Stelle nur 3mal die Verbindung "Älteste Judas" gebraucht wird. Die Bezeichnung "Älteste" ist also für Juda nicht typisch, eher für Israel. Für Juda indes ist die Bezeichnung עַם הָאָרֶץ bezeugt. 14mal kommt die Wendung in den genannten Quellen vor und bezeichnet ausschließlich die politisch handelnden einflußreichen Kreise Judas, nie Israels. Dabei spielt der territoriale Aspekt, der in dieser Wendung enthalten ist, eine wichtige Rolle, worauf E. WÜRTHWEIN [60] mit Recht hinwies. Weiter

---

[60] *Der ʿamm haʾareẓ im AT* (*BWANT* LXIX), 1936, S. 14.

machte er darauf aufmerksam, daß die Bezeichnung "Männer Judas" mit dem Ausdruck "Volk des Landes" identisch ist und das Gleiche meint.[61] Folglich ist mit beiden Bezeichnungen der gleiche Männerkreis angesprochen, der in 1 Sam. xxx "Älteste Judas" heißt.

Damit ist die Annahme einer Stammesverfassung für Groß-Juda unwahrscheinlich geworden. Von der Territorialstruktur her könnte man an die kanaanäische Stadtstaatverfassung denken. Aber schon A. ALT hat diese Möglichkeit nach gründlicher Erwägung mit dem Hinweis darauf zurückgewiesen, daß "das Reich Juda offenbar von Anfang an etwas anderes war und sein wollte als ein kanaanäischer Stadtstaat oder eine Vereinigung mehrerer solcher Gebilde".[62] Wegen der vor allem hinsichtlich des Territorialprinzips, aber auch bezüglich der Funktion der "Männer" zwischen dem frühen Königtum Davids und dem groß-judäischen Gemeinwesen bestehenden Kontinuität gilt diese Feststellung A. ALTS im großen und ganzen auch für das vordavidische Groß-Juda. Da die "Männer" bzw. die "Ältesten" bzw. "das Volk des Landes" die tragende politische Kraft darstellten, wird man von einer demokratischen Verfassung sprechen können,[63] wobei demokratisch meint: Die auf einem umgrenzten Territorium lebenden, durch verwandtschaftliche Bande miteinander verknüpften Gruppen bilden eine völkisch-nationale Einheit, die durch den in der gemeinsamen Hauptstadt agierenden Männerrat vertreten wird. Dieser trifft alle, die gesamte Gemeinschaft berührenden Entscheidungen.

Im Anschluß daran sei noch eine letzte Vermutung geäußert. Sie wird veranlaßt durch die offenbar zentral geregelte Weidenutzung untereinander und gegenüber den philistäischen Nachbarn sowie durch die Frage nach der Art des Zusammenschlusses. Die Verflechtung beider Fragen miteinander weist auf eine für beide Fragen in gleicher Weise gültige Antwort hin. Das schließt schon jetzt die Möglichkeit einer kultisch-sakralen Form des Zusammenschlusses etwa in der Art einer Amphiktyonie aus, weil damit nicht die wirtschaftlichen und politischen Gegebenheiten hinreichend erklärt werden können. Vielmehr scheint die oben gemachte Beobachtung, daß sowohl bei der Einrichtung des judäischen Königtums

---

[61] a.a.O. (Anm. 60), S. 15.

[62] "Das Königtum in den Reichen Israel und Juda" in: *Kl. Schr.* II, ²1953, S. 116-134, S. 128.

[63] E. WÜRTHWEIN, a.a.O. (Anm. 60), S. 19 betont mit Recht, daß bei Davids Königserhebung in Hebron "ein starkes demokratisches Element lebendig" war.

als auch bei seiner ideellen Begründung die Berit eine Rolle spielt, in unsere Erwägungen eingefügt werden zu müssen. Die Tatsache, daß wir im Zusammenhang der Erzväter-Erzählungen der Genesis von einer Berit Gottes mit Abraham (Gen. xv; xvii) sowie von einer Berit Abrahams bzw. Isaaks mit dem Philisterkönig Abimelech (Gen. xxi 27; xxvi 28), außerdem von vertragsähnlichen Abmachungen Abrahams und Lots über Weiderechte (Gen. xiii) hören, läßt darauf schließen, daß diese Art der Berit-Vorstellung in der Geschichte Groß-Judas verankert ist, zumal die Abrahams- und Isaaks-Erzählungen um Hebron, Beerseba und Beer-lahaj-roi kreisen. Dann aber erscheint es naheliegend, den die Besitzrechte und die wirtschaftlichen Notwendigkeiten zugleich festlegenden politischen Zusammenschluß der südpalästinischen Stämme und Stämmegruppen auf eine Berit, einen Vertrag, zurückzuführen.

IV.

Durch eine letzte Beobachtung kann das Bild, das wir von Groß-Juda als einem demokratisch verfaßten Staatswesen entworfen haben, abgerundet werden. Dazu verhilft eine allgemeinere, grundsätzliche Erwägung.

Bei jeder größeren, weitere Kreise umfassenden menschlichen Gemeinschaft ist zu beobachten, daß sie ihren Stellenwert im Gegenüber zu anderen menschlichen Gemeinschaften ihres näheren geschichtlichen Umkreises und in Abgrenzung von ihnen zu bestimmen versucht. Das ist insofern ein überall und zu allen Zeiten notwendiger Prozeß, als er den Zusammenhalt der jeweiligen Gemeinschaft durch die Herausbildung eines Gemeinsinns zu fördern und ein allen Gruppen und Gliedern dieser Gemeinschaft einheitliches Bewußtsein ihres Selbst zu geben und damit die Gemeinschaft nach innen zu stärken vermag. Damit ist die letzte Frage gestellt: Wenn Groß-Juda ein solches verfaßtes Gemeinwesen war, muß es auch ein Selbstverständnis und Selbstbewußtsein gehabt haben.

Wir sind in der glücklichen Lage, diese Frage durch Selbstzeugnisse aus groß-judäischer Quelle beantworten zu können. Es handelt sich dabei um eine Reihe von Sprüchen, die von den ältesten pentateuchischen Erzählungswerken überliefert werden und die durch dieselbe Form und Thematik ausgezeichnet sind und deshalb eine eigenständige Spruchgattung bilden. Es handelt sich um die Sprüche über Kanaan, Sem und Japhet, d.h. den Noah-Segen (Gen. ix 25-27), um den Ismael-Spruch (Gen. xvi 12), die Sprüche über Jakob und Esau in Gen. xxv 23 und im Isaak-Segen (Gen. xxvii 27-29, 39-40) und um die Bileam-Lieder, vorab das vierte Lied über Moab mit seinen Anhängen über Edom, Amalek und Kain (Num. xxiv 15-17, 18-22). Weil die in diesen Sprüchen vorkommenden Eigennamen Bezeichnungen für Völker oder zumindest Völkerschaften sind, wollen wir die Sprüche "Völkersprüche" nennen. Diese Sprüche widerspiegeln Geschehnisse zwischen etwa 1200 und 1000 v. Chr. [64]

Die Berechtigung dafür, die Völkersprüche als Selbstzeugnisse Groß-Judas zu werten, entnehmen wir der Tatsache, daß die Sprüche von Auseinandersetzungen mit den Ismaeliten und Philistern, mit den Amalekitern, Kenitern, Kanaanäern, Edomitern und schließlich auch mit den Moabitern reden. Das verlegt ihre Entstehung in den geographischen Bereich Palästinas, in dem nachbarschaftliche Berührungen mit jenen Völkern und Völkerschaften überhaupt nur möglich waren. Das ist eindeutig der groß-judäische Raum. Demnach stellen die Völkersprüche eine groß-judäische Tradition dar.[65] Dazu paßt auch das Wort gegen Moab, weil es nicht nur der Frühzeit Davids zugehört, sondern weil unsere Quellen noch gewisse Verbindungen der judäischen Sippe Davids mit den Moabitern erkennen lassen. Denn David bringt seine Eltern zum Schutz vor Saul zum Moabiter-König (1 Sam. xxii 3f.; später 2 Sam. viii 2), und im Büchlein Ruth (iv 17) wird eine moabitische Urgroßmutter Davids genannt. Vielleicht stehen hinter diesen vereinzelten Nachrichten noch Erinnerungen an Kontakte zwischen Juda und Moab.

Die Tatsache, daß diese Sprüche die Machtstellung Groß-Judas zu den Nachbarn etwa nach dem Schema "Knecht — Herr" oder auch unter dem Gesichtspunkt "Wer ist der Erstling der Völker" abhandeln, erlaubt keinen anderen Schluß, als daß sich Groß-Juda selbst als ein den anderen ebenbürtiger Partner und als eine ihnen vergleichbare politische Größe verstand. Damit ist das Selbstverständnis Groß-Judas als eines festgefügten und deshalb auch politisch handlungsfähigen Ganzen erwiesen. Zugleich zeigen die Sprüche mit ihrem Inhalt noch den weiteren Vorgang auf, daß die als eine solche gewachsene Einheit sich verstehende Gemeinschaft sich ihres Eigenwertes bewußt wird, sich also dessen bewußt wird, "eine von allen anderen Menschengruppen spezifisch geschiedene

---

[64] Vgl. dazu H.-J. ZOBEL, *Israel und die Völker* (Habil.-Schrift, Halle 1967).
[65] Vgl. dazu vornehmlich M. NOTH, *Überlieferungsgeschichte*², 1960, S. 209-210.

Einheit" zu sein und sich als solche nun zu betätigen.[66] Das be-
zeugen unsere Sprüche insofern, als sie von der stolzen Freude
über die bereits erzielte Unterwerfung anderer Völker wie der
Kanaanäer und gewisser Gruppen der Edomiter und dem daraus
resultierenden Zuwachs an Macht und Ansehen erfüllt oder von dem
Wunsch nach baldiger Überwindung etwa der Amalekiter und
Ismaeliter oder der Philister und Moabiter beseelt sind. Wenn das
nationale Selbstbewußtsein eines Volkes infolge "Aufsummierung
von Erlebtem" [67] zu entstehen und zu erstarken pflegt, dann können
wir bei Groß-Juda mit Recht von einem solchen Bewußtsein seiner
Nationalität sprechen.[68]

Schließlich fällt auf, daß die Völkersprüche das — hier einmal
ganz weit verstandene — völkisch-nationale Moment stark be-
tonen. Von Jahwe ist in ihnen lediglich ein einziges Mal am Rande
die Rede (Gen. ix 26). Das will nicht so verstanden werden, als
sei in Groß-Juda vormals die Jahwe-Verehrung unbekannt gewesen.
Dagegen spricht Gen. ix 26 insofern, als hier Jahwe dafür gepriesen
wird, daß Kanaan der Knecht Sems wurde. Jahwe wurde also,
was man auch ohne diese Stelle auf Grund der Zugehörigkeit der
Keniter zum groß-judäischen Bund [69] sowie wegen des Aufgehens
zumindest eines Teils der Lewiten in Juda [70] mit Sicherheit an-
nehmen kann, in Groß-Juda verehrt. Aber — und das muß mit aller
Deutlichkeit gesehen werden — der Stellenwert dieser Jahwe-
Verehrung war ein geringerer als im Hause Joseph. Darauf wurden
wir bereits beim Vergleich der Königtümer von Israel und Juda
aufmerksam. Dazu paßt, daß wir nichts von judäischen Propheten
aus der Zeit vor dem 8. Jh. v. Chr. hören und auch keinen Richter
aus Juda kennen. Denn selbst wenn das Bethlehem des Ibzan (Jdc.
xii 8-10) nicht der naphthalitische, sondern der judäische Ort
ist, fehlen bei ihm alle Merkmale für eine charismatische Bega-
bung.[71] Und Othniel ben-Kenas (Jdc. iii 7-11) ist, abgesehen von
der Schwierigkeit der Deutung des Aramäer- oder vielleicht Edomi-
ter-Königs Kusan-Risatajim, wie K.-D. SCHUNCK richtig feststellte,[72]

---

[66] E. MEYER, *Geschichte des Altertums*, I, 1, ⁵1925, S. 79.

[67] J. BURCKHARDT, *Weltgeschichtliche Betrachtungen* (Kröner-Ausgabe), 1935, S. 25.

[68] Vgl. dazu auch den Juda-Spruch aus dem Jakob-Segen (Gen. XLIX 8-12).

[69] Dazu zuletzt H. HEYDE, *Kain, der erste Jahwe-Verehrer*, 1965.

[70] Vgl. dazu zuletzt R. DE VAUX, a.a.O. (Anm. 7), S. 490-496.

[71] Vgl. dazu H.-J. ZOBEL, *Stammesspruch und Geschichte* (*BZAW* XCV), 1965, S. 78.

[72] "Die Richter Israels und ihr Amt" in: *SVT* XV, 1965, S. 252-262, S. 257.

nur eine "Füllfigur in der Richterliste". Denn diese Notiz verdankt
ihre Aufnahme in das Richter-Buch lediglich dem Bestreben, Gesamt-Israel als einheitliche Größe auch in der sog. Richter-Zeit
zu belegen und das bis zur Zeit Davids von Nordisrael getrennt
lebende und deshalb auch im Debora-Lied (Jdc. v) nicht erwähnte
Groß-Juda [73] schon in der Richter-Zeit zu Gesamt-Israel zu zählen.
Und schließlich sei mit bedacht, daß die Auseinandersetzung mit
der kanaanäischen Religion nicht im Raum Judas geführt wurde.[74]
Das alles war also kein Zufall, sondern bestätigt erneut unsere
Feststellung, daß Groß-Judas Selbstverständnis und Selbstbewußtsein
völkisch-nationaler und nicht vorherrschend religiöser Natur waren.

V.

Hatten wir bisher die Existenz eines eigenständigen, staatlich
verfaßten Gemeinwesens Groß-Juda zu erweisen verfolgt, so wollen
wir uns nun einigen Momenten seiner Geschichte zuwenden. Daß
Groß-Juda in der 2. Hälfte des 11. Jh. v. Chr. zum Einflußbereich
der Philister gehörte, ist ebenso wahrscheinlich wie der Umstand,
daß seine Geschichte auf weite Strecken durch die Philister bestimmt
wurde. Auffällig ist jedoch, daß uns im Unterschied zum Gebirge
Ephraim kein Philisterposten des Bereichs Groß-Juda bezeugt ist.
Das könnte Zufall sein. Indes hat B. GEMSER [75] aufgezeigt, daß
im Unterschied zu den alttestamentlichen Geschichtsbüchern in den
Patriarchen-Erzählungen der Genesis "nichts von einer Antithese
gegen die 'unbeschnittenen Philister' " zu finden, also eine gewisse
Loyalität im Verhältnis zu ihnen zu beobachten sei. Diese Beobachtung ist noch dahingehend zu präzisieren, daß uns Kontakte mit
den Philistern nur in den an Orten Südjudas haftenden Abrahams-
und Isaaks-Erzählungen, nicht aber in den mittelpalästinischen
Jakobs-Erzählungen bezeugt sind. Damit stimmt auch die Notiz
in 1 Sam. xxx 14 vom Negeb der Philister als einem gegenüber
den groß-judäischen Negeb-Anteilen abgegrenzten Gebiet insofern
überein, als sie ein loyales und geregeltes Nebeneinander von Philistern und ihren judäischen Nachbarn zu erkennen gibt. Man möchte
an einen Vertrag oder doch an ein vertragsähnliches Übereinkommen
zwischen der philistäischen Pentapolis und Groß-Juda zur Regelung

---

[73] Anders zuletzt R. SMEND, "Gehörte Juda zum vorstaatlichen Israel?" in:
Fourth World Congress of Jewish Studies, Papers, I, 1967, S. 57-62.
[74] Diesen Hinweis verdanke ich Herrn Kollegen H. P. MÜLLER.
[75] "God in Genesis" in: *Ou. Stud.* XII, 1958, S. 1-21, S. 3.

dieser Gebietsfrage denken. C. A. Simpson [76] sieht in der Erzählung vom Bundesschluß Isaaks mit dem Philisterkönig Abimelech von Gerar (Gen. xxvi 26-33) diese in die Patriarchenzeit zurückdatierte Abmachung. Dazu paßt der ¡geographische Bereich von Gen. xxvi 12-23 zwischen Beerseba und Gerar. Dafür spricht aber auch die Tatsache, daß es um das Besitzrecht an Brunnen geht, die für Weidewirtschaft von grundlegender Bedeutung sind. Nicht zuletzt aber zeigt der Hergang in Gen. xxvi 12-23, daß eigentlich die Philister die Sieger sind, weil sie die Brunnen Esek und Sitna ihren Kollegen abnehmen, sich dann aber damit einverstanden erklären, daß diese den Brunnen Rechobot ihr eigen nennen. Am Schluß dieses Streits, der zwar den philistäischen Einflußbereich erweitert, steht doch eine wie auch immer geartete Abmachung zwischen beiden Parteien.

In die gleiche Richtung weist der merkwürdige Japhet-Spruch (Gen. ix 26): "Gott schaffe dem Japhet weiten Raum, daß er in den Zelten Sems wohne! Und Kanaan sei sein Knecht!" Wie hier Kanaan die Kanaanäer meint, so Japhet die Philister und Sem die Israeliten oder doch einen Teil von ihnen, nämlich, wie wir auf Grund der Herleitung Abrahams von Sem (Gen. xi 10-26) vermuten möchten, die Angehörigen Groß-Judas. Abgesehen davon, daß die Philister die Kanaanäer verknechten konnten, setzt dieses vaticinium ex eventu eine Einigung zwischen Philistern und Judäern in einer territorialen Streitfrage voraus. Der auffällige Tatbestand, daß im Japhet-Spruch wie im Hirtenwort von Gen. xxvi 22 von der Beschaffung weiten Raums die Rede ist, legt den Bezug des Spruchs auf diese Genesis-Erzählung nahe und weist damit ebenfalls auf eine vertragliche Vereinbarung zwischen Philistern und Groß-Juda hin.

Eine letzte indirekte Bezeugung einer solchen Übereinkunft entnehmen wir der sonst unbegreiflichen Tatsache, daß David die Philister viel freundlicher behandelt hat als alle anderen von ihm besiegten gegnerischen Völker. Denn als David nach der Einnahme Jerusalems zum Entscheidungskampf gegen die Philister antrat und sie besiegte, löste er damit zwar für Groß-Juda die Bindungen an die Philister und befreite auch die von ihnen annektierten israelitischen Gebiete, beließ ihnen jedoch innerhalb ihres ureigenen Territoriums ihre volle Selbständigkeit und respektierte sie.[77] Offenbar wirkte

---

[76] *The Early Traditions of Israel*, 1948, S. 461.

[77] So zuletzt O. Eissfeldt, "Israelitisch-philistäische Grenzverschiebungen von David bis auf die Assyrerzeit" in: *Kl. Schr.* II, 1963, S. 453-463, S. 453-456, und M. Noth, a.a.O. (Anm. 3), S. 168-169.

darin der einstige Vertrag nach. Auch die unterschiedliche Haltung der Philister zu Juda und Israel mag darin ihren Grund haben.

Diese durch die Oberheit der Philister über Groß-Juda bestimmte Phase, die etwa von 1100 v. Chr. bis zu David gereicht hat, wird gewiß mancherlei Kämpfe mit anderen Gegnern, etwa mit den Edomitern, Ismaelitern und vorab den Amalekitern gesehen haben. Denn erst Saul und David gelang es, die von ihnen ausgehende akute Gefahr weithin zu bannen. Für unser Vorhaben, die Geschichte Groß-Judas zu skizzieren und die Entstehungszeit dieses Zusammenschlusses zu eruieren, darf als Ergebnis der bisherigen Überlegungen festgehalten werden, daß Groß-Juda offenbar schon an der Wende vom 12. zum 11. Jh. v. Chr. als ein geordnetes Gemeinwesen bestand, das als solches den expandierenden Philistern entgegentrat.

Seine noch weiter zurückreichende Geschichte ist nur schwer zu erhellen. Ein gewisses Licht fällt auf sie von dem Spruch über die Amalekiter (Num. xxiv 20). Ihr Gebiet liegt südlich von dem Groß-Judas. Kann die Erwähnung von Kamelen in den Tagen Sauls und der Richter (1 Sam. xxx 17; Jdc. vi 3, 5; vii 12) den Eindruck erwecken, als seien die Amalekiter Vollnomaden gewesen, so weist die Nennung von Rindern und Schafen in 1 Sam. xv 3, 9, 14-15; xxvii 9 viel eher auf eine bäuerlich-ansässige oder doch halbnomadische Lebensweise hin. Außerdem werden in Num. xvi 25, 43, 45 Amalekiter zusammen mit Kanaanäern des südjudäischen Kulturlandes genannt und somit als den Kulturlandbewohnern vergleichbar erachtet. Hinzu kommt noch, daß wir aus 1 Sam. xv 8, 9, 20, 32, 33 und aus Num. xxiv 7 einen König der Amalekiter, nämlich Agag, kennen und von einem Königtum hören. Schließlich bezeugt 1 Sam. xv 5 eine Hauptstadt im Lande der Amalekiter, die nach Auskunft von Gen. xiv 7 keine andere als die Oasenstätte Kades gewesen sein kann.[78] Alle diese Nachrichten machen es wahrscheinlich, daß die Amalekiter oder doch ein gewisser Teil von ihnen schon als Halbnomaden lebte und sich anschickte, seßhaft zu werden.

Das macht einerseits die Machtstellung der Amalekiter im Süden Palästinas deutlich, wie sie aus dem Wort Num. xxiv 20: "Der Erstling der Völker ist Amalek" spricht, und anderseits wirft es

---

[78] Vgl. dazu A. T. OLMSTEAD, *History of Palestine and Syria*, 1931, 1965, S. 254; J. H. GRØNBAEK, "Juda und Amalek" in: *Stud. Theol.* XVIII, 1964, S. 26-45, S. 35; O. EISSFELDT, "Achronische, anachronische und synchronische Elemente in der Genesis" in: *Kl. Schr.* IV, 1968, S. 153-169, S. 167.

ein helles Licht auf die erhebliche Bedrohung, die von ihnen für
das Volk Groß-Judas ausging und die den uns schon in einem
frühen Stück des Pentateuch, in Ex. xvii 16 (vgl. Deut. xxv 17-19)
ihnen entgegentretenden abgrundtiefen Haß und den in Num. xxiv
20 enthaltenden Wunsch nach Vernichtung dieses bedrohlichen
Gegners erklärt.

Wenn es auch nicht mit letzter Sicherheit auszumachen ist, so
deuten doch alle diese Nachrichten darauf hin, daß die größte Ge-
fährdung für Juda in der Zeit vor 1100 v. Chr., also vor der Expansion der Philister, von den Amalekitern ausging. Die Tatsache,
daß die Amalekiter bereits ein festgefügtes, גוי "Nation" [79] genanntes
Gemeinwesen mit monarchischer Spitze und einer Hauptstadt
bildeten und daß sie offenbar die Ansiedlung anstrebten, läßt ermessen, daß es in der Auseinandersetzung mit Amalek für die im
südpalästinischen Kulturland samt seinen Randgebieten seßhaft
gewordenen oder noch in der Landnahme befindlichen Stämme [80]
um Sein oder Nichtsein, um Leben oder Tod ging. Diese äußerste
Bedrohung ihrer Existenz von außen wird, wie das in der Geschichte
immer wieder der Fall ist, im Verlauf des 12. Jh. v. Chr. zur inneren
Einigung, zum Zusammenschluß aller dort lebenden Stämme geführt haben. Denn nur durch eine Zusammenfassung und Konzen-
tration ihrer Kräfte konnten sie hoffen, sich mit einigem Erfolg der
aus der Wüste nachdrängenden Scharen zu erwehren und ihren
Besitzstand zu behaupten. Das wird, wie wir meinen, die Geburts-
stunde Groß-Judas gewesen sein.

VI.

Überblicken wir noch einmal die Ergebnisse unserer Untersuchung, so ist die gewiß wertvollste Erkenntnis die Existenz eines
Zusammenschlusses der im Bereich des Gebirges Juda und des
Negeb ansässigen Stämme zu Groß-Juda. Durch die sich in der
alttestamentlichen Überlieferung von einer Eroberung der bedeu-
tenden Kanaanäerstädte Horma, Debir und Hebron sowie Bethlehem
ausdrückende Unterwerfung der vormaligen Herren dieses Bereichs
verfügten die dort seßhaft gewordenen Stämme über ein von ihnen
allein beherrschtes und kontrolliertes Gebiet, daß durch natürliche

---

[79] Vgl. dazu L. Rost, "Die Bezeichnungen für Land und Volk im AT" in:
Das kleine Credo, 1965, S. 76-101, S. 86-89.
[80] Darauf könnte die summarische Bezeichnung "Städte der Jerachmeeliter
bzw. Keniter" in 1 Sam. xxx 30 zurückgehen.

Gegebenheiten im Osten und durch politische Konstellationen im Norden und Westen eindeutig abgegrenzt war. Lediglich im Süden war die Grenze offen. Wohl unter dem Druck nachdrängender und gewiß ebenfalls landsuchender nomadischer oder halbnomadischer Stämme und Stämmegruppen wie der Amalekiter, wohl auch der Ismaeliter und Edomiter, verbanden sich diese dort lebenden Stämme zu einem größeren politischen Gemeinwesen, das wir der alttestamentlichen Überlieferung entsprechend "Haus Juda" oder Groß-Juda nennen. Auf Grund der noch in späterer Zeit nachwirkenden Traditionen und Institutionen ist anzunehmen, daß dieser Zusammenschluß ein weltlich-politischer und kein sakraler Akt war, basierte er doch auf einer Berit, einem Vertrag zwischen den einzelnen Gliedern. Das gesamte Gebiet war nach territorialen Gesichtspunkten aufgeteilt. Die zentrale Stadt war Hebron. Die öffentliche Gewalt lag in der Hand der "Männer" oder "Ältesten Judas" oder "des Volkes des Landes". Sie waren die über Grundbesitz verfügenden wehrfähigen Männer, die die politischen, wirtschaftlich-sozialen und militärischen Angelegenheiten des Gemeinwesens gemeinsam regelten. Demnach war Groß-Juda demokratisch verfaßt.

Die weitere Geschichte Judas zeigt, daß das mit dem Zusammenschluß der einzelnen Glieder angestrebte Ziel einer Abwehr nachdrängender Gruppen erreicht werden konnte. Groß-Juda vermochte sich in mancherlei Auseinandersetzungen zu behaupten. "Es verteidigte seinen Wohlstand, der ihm aus den natürlichen Gegebenheiten des Landes zugefallen war, mit Energie und strebte schließlich nach einer seine eigenen Grenzen übersteigenden Macht" [81].

Von dem Erstarken der Philister an der westlichen Grenze blieb auch Groß-Juda nicht unberührt. Immerhin scheint seine Eingliederung in das philistäische Machtgefüge doch nur eine recht lose gewesen zu sein, derzufolge Groß-Juda zwar auf eine eigene "Außenpolitik" verzichten mußte, innenpolititisch aber selbständig blieb. Offenbar verstanden sich die Philister als Nachfolger der Pharaonen in Palästina und handelten so, wie einst die Ägypter mit ihnen verfahren waren. Mit der Wahl Davids als Königs über Groß-Juda in Hebron und dem Vertragsabschluß zwischen ihm und den Männern Groß-Judas erfährt die Verfassung eine dem monarchischen Prinzip Rechnung tragende Umgestaltung. Indes bleibt die Funktion des Männerrates als einer zweiten, das demokratische Element vertre-

---

[81] S. HERRMANN, "Autonome Entwicklungen in den Königreichen Israel und Juda" in: *SVT* XVII, 1969, S. 139-158, S. 142 im Blick auf den Stamm Juda.

tenden Kraft im Staate erhalten.[82] Mit der der Einnahme Jerusalems folgenden und für David siegreichen Auseinandersetzung mit den Philistern werden zwar für Groß-Juda die Bindungen an diese gelöst, aber es wird nun der Stadt Jerusalem und damit der Davidischen Dynastie zugeordnet. Das bedeutet faktisch das Ende der groß-judäischen Geschichte.

Die Folgerungen, die sich aus diesen Bemerkungen ergeben, sind vielfältig. Was die historischen Konsequenzen angeht, so läßt sich das Königtum Davids über Juda und die Stellung Judas im Gesamtgefüge seines Reiches von hier aus weit besser verstehen. Und da sich die Geschichte Groß-Judas offenbar seit Anbeginn getrennt von der der anderen israelitischen Stämme vollzog, erklärt das sowohl die Sonderstellung Judas im Reiche Davids und Salomos als auch die Reichstrennung nach Salomos Tode.

Bedeutsamer indes sind die sich daraus ergebenden theologischen Konsequenzen. Von einem Vorrang religiöser Fragestellungen haben wir in der Geschichte Groß-Judas nichts wahrgenommen. Wie seine Staatsbildung, so war auch die Umwandlung zu einer Art konstitutioneller Monarchie ein rein weltlich-politischer Vorgang. Charismatische Gestalten kennen wir aus Groß-Juda nicht. Statt dessen begegnen uns Zeugnisse eines kräftigen, stolzen Selbstbewußtseins, das ausschließlich weltlich-nationale und keine religiösen Züge aufweist. Schon die Tatsache, daß uns Völkersprüche aus der vormonarchischen Epoche Judas, nicht aber aus der Israels überliefert worden sind, macht uns darauf aufmerksam, daß mancherlei Traditionsgut aus Groß-Juda in die gesamtisraelitische Überlieferung eingeflossen ist. Denn so unbestreitbar groß auch der Beitrag Israels ist, so muß man sich doch vor einer einseitigen Überschätzung jenes Beitrages hüten. S. HERRMANN hat mit Recht festgestellt,[83] daß der Grundgedanke eines theologischen Gesamtverständnisses Israels zwar aus dem Nordreich stammt, der Grundgedanke der ethnischen Einheit Israels aber von dem Südreich zum gemeinsamen Selbstverständnis beigesteuert wurde. Das wird durch unsere Untersuchung insofern bestätigt, als der Zusammenschluß des groß-judäischen Bundes die Vereinigung aller israelitischen Stämme und die Herausbildung des dementsprechenden und doch ideellen, weil nicht der damaligen Wirklichkeit gemäßen Zwölfstämmeschemas beförderte und vorbereitete. Dem ist noch hinzuzufügen,

---

[82] Vgl. dazu E. WÜRTHWEIN, a.a.O. (Anm. 60), S. 19.
[83] a.a.O. (Anm. 81), S. 157.

daß das uns in allen Quellen über die Zeit Davids und Salomos begegnende national-religiöse Empfinden Israels offenbar in erheblichem Grade aus judäischer Quelle gespeist worden ist. Denn das hervorstechende nationale Moment steuerte Juda bei, und das religiöse Element ist die Mitgift Israels. Aus beiden erwuchs das Gesamtverständnis Israels, das je nach der Betonung dieser oder jener Seite ein national-religiöses oder ein religiös-nationales Selbstverständnis war.